Reclaiming Mission as Constructive Theology

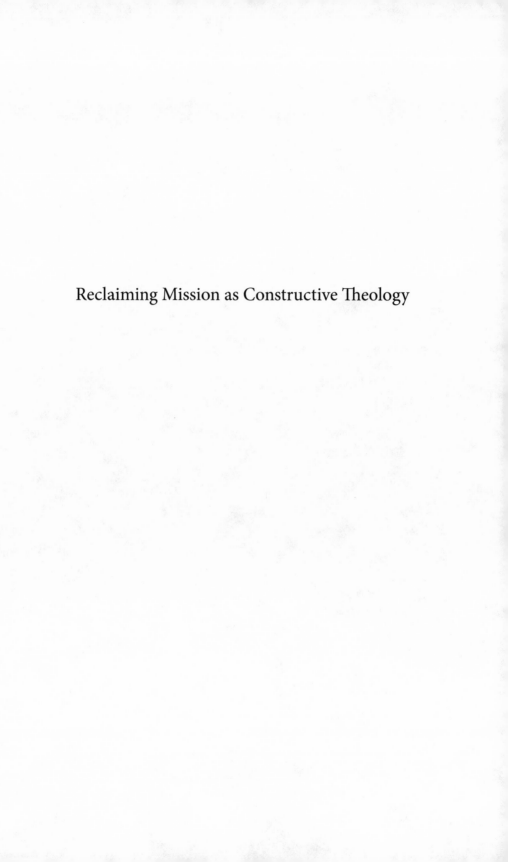

Reclaiming Mission as Constructive Theology

Missional Church and World Christianity

by
PAUL S. CHUNG

Foreword by
Richard Bliese

CASCADE *Books* • Eugene, Oregon

RECLAIMING MISSION AS CONSTRUCTIVE THEOLOGY
Missional Church and World Christianity

Cascade Books
An Imprint of Wipf and Stock Publishers
199 W. 8th Ave., Suite 3
Eugene, OR 97401

www.wipfandstock.com

ISBN 13: 978-1-61097-227-7

Cataloging-in-Publication data:

Chung, Paul S., 1958–

   Reclaiming mission as constructive theology : missional church and world Christianity / Paul S. Chung.

   XIV + 316 p. ; 23 cm. — Includes bibliographical references and index.

   ISBN 13: 978-1-61097-227-7

   1. Missions — Theory. 2. Missions — Theory — History of doctrines. 3. Christianity and other religions. I. Bliese, Richard. II. Title.

BV2063 .C549 2012

Manufactured in the U.S.A.

Contents

Foreword

We live in exhilarating yet challenging times. This intensity is evident everywhere in the world. Change has come! And it is dramatic in terms of scope, speed, and complexity. Monumental shifts in economy, culture, politics, religious commitments, technology, and media affect every neighborhood. To keep current on the events swirling around us is hard enough, but interpreting these developments seems even more daunting, especially when one moves from local to global realities. It is in this world of "raplexity" (rapid and complex change) that the church of Jesus Christ is challenged to bring its witness.

In regard to bearing witness in a world of raplexity, the missional church conversation continues to make a vital contribution to considering how Christian communities can engage challenging contexts, both global and local. This conversation is now in its second decade, with roots that can be traced back primarily to the work of missiologist Lesslie Newbigin. The present work from Paul Chung, *Reclaiming Mission as Constructive Theology*, takes seriously the missional church conversation, especially as it has developed at Luther Seminary within the Center for Congregational Mission and Leadership. In developing his constructive theology, he lifts up Christian witness as it addresses issues of American society, civil religion, multiculturalism, and the postmodern condition. For Chung, a theology of mission and the *Missio Dei* needs to be actualized in light of Christ's *diakonia* within local congregations as they serve the world.

But Paul Chung's essays take the conversation one step further, projecting these issues onto the larger framework of World Christianity. His goal is to reconstruct an understanding of mission in a strongly hermeneutical, postcolonial, and cross-cultural framework. Thus, a theology of God's mission and *diakonia* must begin with a self-critical reflection of the unhappy alliance between Christian mission and co-lonialism. To do this, Chung draws heavily from numerous sources including church history (e.g., Bartolomé de Las Casas and Matteo Ricci). He cites both positive examples of prophetic witness and those testifying to "human confusion." Reclaiming mission as constructive theology, and doing so in a way that is publicly relevant, demands a strong hermeneutical circle for Chung that is both self-critical and self-renewing as it dialogues with multiple disciplines and contexts. This is no easy task. These essays testify to Chung's range of expertise as he draws a remarkable array of scholarship and contexts together to reconstruct an understanding of God's mission as "word-event" (building on his recent book, *God's Mission as Word-Event in an Age of World Christianity*).

Ever since Gustav Warneck's (the father of modern missiology) stinging critique of Martin Luther, the prevailing view has been that Lutheran theology provides no real resources for a contemporary, rel-evant Christian missiology. The late David Bosch, in his monumental text on contemporary missiology, *Transforming Mission*, agreed with the main thrust of Warneck's critique. Paul Chung knows these critics. And he disagrees with them. Chung's call to generate a constructive missiology builds solidly on the Reformation tradition, drawing par-ticularly heavily from Luther and Barth. This present work, therefore, should be judged in the light of past critiques, and read as a rebuff to both Warneck's and Bosch's criticisms. If Lutheran theology has a future at all, it is linked to the gospel's own future. It is this tradition of the Reformation, and its genius for focusing in on the gospel, that informs the heart of Chung's pro-missio (*promissio*) theology.

It has been said that any adequate theology—and this would in-clude any missiology—has to be "self-involving," "world-involving," and "God-involving" (David Ford). Ultimately, God should be the agent and author of theology; the whole of nature, history, and culture should form the horizon of study; and the subject matter should in fact transform the person involved. If these standards are true, then the present work of Paul Chung is more than adequate, and uniquely suited to the task of leading a missional church and World Christianity in reclaiming mission as a constructive theological task.

A primary issue that confronts Christians in our day—in the midst of shifting global realities and raplexity—is the need to reexamine and reenvision what it means to be church in the world. This present work contributes significantly to furthering that cause, and inspiring that adventure.

Richard Bliese
President, Luther Seminary

Acknowledgments

The volume *Reclaiming Mission as Constructive Theology* consists of my essays on public mission in regard to God's mission and *diakonia* in a post-Western era. After my study of *God's Mission as Word-Event in an Age of World Christianity* (2010), I began to feel a need to improve the classic concept of *missio Dei* in a twofold way: first, a theology of God's mission needs to be actualized in light of Christ's *diakonia* by relating this dimension to missional church, congregational life, and stewardship in the American context. The missional church conversation and Center for Congregational Mission and Leadership at Luther Seminary, St. Paul, has played a decisive role in inspiring me to pursue mission as constructive theology in an analysis of American society concerning American civil religion, multiculturalism, and the postmodern condition.

Secondly, a theology of God's mission and *diakonia* begins with self-critical reflection on the link between Christian mission and colonialism. In the logic of God's providence and human confusion in an unfortunate chapter of the history of Christian mission, it is essential to reconstruct God's mission in hermeneutical, postcolonial, and cross-cultural frameworks. This project of reconstruction aims at rendering mission as constructive, public theology more amenable and accountable to a lifeworld that is threatened with colonization in a civilization of globalization. An important anthropological missiologist, Paul Hiebert, demonstrated his anthropological-theological study of epistemological shifts for missiological implications by affirming truth in a modern/postmodern world. Sharing his concern about epistemological shifts, I am more interested in redefining a constructive mission of word-event discursively and anthropologically in regard to the public sphere as well as the globe. The hermeneutical reclaiming of mission as constructive theology takes seriously the challenge heard from World Christianity, postcolonial (or postmodern) critique, and intercultural theology.

In this volume, missiology, missional church, and congregational study come together in a holistic manner in light of God's mission as word-event as we engage with the *missio Dei* in Christ's *diakonia* of reconciliation to the world. Thus a study of mission and missional ecclesiology is basic and central, redefined and refurbished in hermeneutical, anthropological deliberation of the living voice of God (*viva vox Evangelii*) in the public and multicultural arena. The Reformer's hermeneutics of the gospel of Jesus Christ as living voice of God penetrates this project of constructive, public mission related to God's narrative in the grace of justification and reconciliation. It is further contextualized, even audaciously renewed, in cross-cultural fertilization in dialogue with the wisdom of non-Christian religion, in particular Confucianism.

My life journey as a mission developer began in the multicultural congregation of Holy Shepherd Lutheran Church, Orinda, California (1995–2005). That journey and my current teaching at Luther Seminary underlie my hermeneutical, anthropological fulcrum in the study of mission in regard to the *missio Dei*, missional church, and World Christianity in a post-Western era.

Special thanks are extended to my colleagues and friends at Luther Seminary and also Ph.D. students with international backgrounds. I appreciate President and Professor Richard Bliese who wrote a foreword by encouraging my confessional-hermeneutical study of mission as constructive theology. I am grateful to Rolland Martinson whose support and friendship enables me to academically develop an integration between congregational mission and global mission through my hermeneutics of confessional mission. I am indebted to Professor Gary Simpson, Director of Congregational Mission and Leadership at Luther Seminary, for his insights into public theology and missional church. Professor Steven Paulson helped me sharpen my confessional hermeneutical mission through a lively discussion with me and valuable comments on the manuscript.

I extend my personal thanks to Professor Craig Van Gelder and Professor Dwight Zscheile at Luther Seminary, who took the trouble to read the manuscript and to give valuable comments. Developing mission as constructive theology in a biblical, hermeneutical, eschatological manner, I am also privileged to understand the missional meaning of the Word of God and eschatology in regard to *parrhēsia* and *paranesis*. My biblical, hermeneutical learning comes from the works of great biblical scholars at Luther Seminary. My special thanks extend to Terence E. Fretheim, Arland J. Hultgren, and Craig R. Koester, who helped me develop constructive mission of *viva vox evangelii* in this direction. I also thank Professor Darrell L. Guder at Princeton Theological Seminary, who invited me as the guest lecturer at the conference on "The Church Is as Such a Missionary Church: Karl Barth as a Missional Theologian" in the Center for Barth Studies to stimulate the project of the *missio Dei* and missional church. My gratitude also extends to my assistant Dana Scopatz, who proofread the whole of the manuscript.

Finally, I want to acknowledge Charlie Collier for accepting my project and bringing it to completion as a Cascade Book. Acknowledgment is given to the New Revised Standard Version Bible (NRSV), copyright 1989, Division of Christian Education of the National Council of the Churches of Christ in the United States of America. I also appreciate Brill publishers and the editor of Studies of Interreligious Dialogue for allowing me to revise my previous paper "Matteo Rici and His Legacy for Christian-Confucian Renewal" in *Constructing Irregular Theology*.

Paul S. Chung
St. Paul, Minnesota
New Year, 2011

Abbreviations

BC *The Book of Concord: The Confessions of the Evangelical Lutheran Church*. Edited by Robert Kolb and Timothy J. Wengert. Minneapolis: Fortress, 2000.

CD Karl Barth, *Church Dogmatics*. 13 vols. Translated and edited by G. W. Bromiley and T. F. Torrance. First paper edition. London and New York: T. & T. Clark, 2004.

WA *D. Martin Luthers Werke: Kritische Gesamtausgabe*. 61 vols. Weimar: Hermann Böhlaus Nachfolger, 1912–1921.

LW Helmut T. Lehmann, editor. *Luther's Works*. Vols. 31–55. Philadelphia: Fortress, 1955–1986; Jaroslav Pelikan, editor. *Luther's Works*. Vols. 1–30. St. Louis: Concordia, 1955–1967.

Introduction

*World Christianity, Missional Church,
and Public Theology*

Multicultural Reality in North American Society

Through the process of globalization, the lifeworld of North Americans has become multiculturalized and pluralized. The mainline churches face challenges from the non- or post-denominational churches. Traditional worship is in decline, and postmodern emerging ministry has come to the fore, along with various eruptions of electronic church and televangelism. A new wave in the resurgence of Christian religion is anchored in the Southern Hemisphere, and the relationship of gospel and culture has become a central motif in the congregational mission of North America as well as in World Christianity.

It is clear that civil religion as a form of political culture is widespread. In newspapers and magazines, the term "civil religion" is used to refer to ritual expressions of patriotism as practiced in all countries. This public religious dimension, which is expressed in a set of political beliefs, religious symbols, and ceremonial rituals in the United States, has been referred to as the American civil religion.[1]

We cannot sidestep the fact that the emergence of Asian religions in North America is quite remarkable despite the fact that American civil religion remains powerful. This trend means that phrases like "American Buddhist" or "Boston Confucian" are no longer contradictory terms.[2] Multiculturalism and globalization increasingly characterize the

1. Bellah, *Beyond Belief*, 171.
2. Neville, *Boston Confucianism*.

1

socio-political and religious reality of U.S. society. The *missio Dei* and the missional church movement in the U.S. try to articulate contextual components like spirituality, national identity, and multiple cultures in the midst of a postmodern lifestyle.

A missional interpretation of Scripture and the church's catholicity call attention to both cultural diversity and the particularity of the local community. The church is essentially of multicultural character in the New Testament context: Jerusalem, Samaria, Antioch, Philippi, Ephesus, and Rome. This multicultural character of the early Christian communities demonstrates that the gospel is translatable.[3]

In addition to multicultural configurations of culture, we are also experiencing the "clash of civilizations" in the process of the remaking of a world order.[4] In this cultural and political course, an encounter between different cultures and civilizations is vulnerable to clashes and conflicts between different religious and cultural communities. Though there has been a "marbling of civilization and peoples,"[5] there is still a likelihood of continued "clashes of civilizations." This complex reality emphasizes that the fact of multiculturalism requires an effective strategy of communication within the public sphere. *E Pluribus Unum* (From Many, One); our *unum* is expressed in the midst of plurality.[6]

It is important to notice that the World Council of Churches endeavors to cope with the unevenness of neo-liberal capitalist globalization that is generating impoverishment and misery for millions of people, as well as ecological devastation.[7] In today's reality of economic globalization or Empire,[8] the vast majority of humanity is enthralled in a form of neo-serfdom or outright slavery as a result of the rise of the multinational, mega-corporation. This results in an increase in the disparity of wealth between the rich and the poor and simultaneously destroys ecological life and the environment. Against the trend of economic globalization, we observe that postcolonial theologians are challenging the reality of Empire and critiquing the vestige of neo-colonialism and expansionism in Christian missionary practice. This challenge and

3. Sanneh, *Translating the Message*, 1–8.

4. Huntington, *Clash of Civilizations*.

5. Eck, *New Religious America*, 4.

6. Ibid., 9.

7. Duchrow, *Colloquium 2000*, 5.

8. Hardt and Negri, *Empire*.

crisis offers an opportunity for those engaged in the congregational life of the faith community to explore new possibilities for making the faith community and its missional vocation more amenable to people in a post-Western context.

The Voice from World Christianity

At the turn of the third millennium, we observe the rise of a new Christianity in Africa, Asia, and Latin America. This is characterized by the postcolonial project of emancipation and inculturation. The proponents of World Christianity argue that indigenizing the faith calls for the decolonization of Western Christendom and theology. For the indigenous discovery of the gospel, priority is given to indigenous response and local appropriation by critically uncovering the implanted missionary gospel of the colonial past. God's mission in one context may not be imposed in the same form in another context. The proponents of World Christianity argue that there must be sufficient mutual appreciation of the different embedded assumptions and cultural constructs in each context for effective communication between the Global North and Global South.

Translation becomes a key concept in reconceptualization of God's mission, bringing a hermeneutics of suspicion and refusal to the painful histories of colonial conquest and imperialism. Only through this refusal can a genuine hermeneutics of reconstruction and appreciation become possible. The translatability of the biblical narrative is the source of the success of the Christian religion across cultures. According to the model of God's mission as translation, the gospel is equally at home in all languages and cultures and also among all races and social conditions.[9] The translatability of Scripture into different languages and the indigenous naming of God becomes a watershed for the indigenous contribution to World Christianity.[10]

A critical, even provocative voice from World Christianity makes it crucial for missologists to take into account ethnographical research, and utilize its anthropological perspective on culture. Ethnography is the process of discovering and describing a culture in engagement with indigenous informants. The cultural, anthropological research method

9. Sanneh, *Translating the Message*, 51.

10. Sanneh, *Whose Religion Is Christianity?* 10.

is discovery-oriented, distancing itself from naïve realism and Euro- (or Western-) centrism.[11] Culture is acquired and learned through language. Its knowledge is socially shared knowledge, generating patterns of behavior. Culture is the framework that interprets human experience. Culture fluctuates with new and different peoples and groups.[12]

The reality of World Christianity challenges us to engage the reigning "plausibility structure." According to this structure, patterns of belief and practice are accepted within a given society and are diversely expressed in a different time and place.[13] Transforming mission, according to David Bosch, challenges an instrumental way of thinking in favor of a communicative way of thinking with others in the public sphere. He argues that "Togetherness, interdependence, and symbiosis" are integrated to promote an "epistemology of participation" in God's mission in accompaniment with the other.[14]

Postcolonial Resistance and Decolonization

In contrast to transforming mission, postcolonial theologians argue that it is important to critically analyze missional discourse about the representation of non-Western people and culture. They utilize a postmodern critique of the modernist assumption of metanarrative and the logic of Orientalism (Edward Said). Lyotard concisely defines postmodernity as an "incredulity toward metanarratives."[15] Postmodern resistance wages war on totality, universality, and the metaphysical story of grand sameness told by modernity. In the Western Christian tradition, the other has been labeled in diverse ways: the heathen from the sixteenth century through the period of colonialism; the unenlightened and irrational in the age of Reason; "the other" in the twentieth century. In Western civilization over the last century women, native and indigenous peoples, and homosexuals have been marginalized. This marginalization of otherness was successfully accomplished by the prevalence of what Lyotard calls "metanarratives." Postmodernists insist that the power of the metanarrative totalizes and reduces the specific, different, and unique narratives

11. Ibid., 11.
12. Spradley and McCurdy, *Cultural Experience*, 6–7.
13. Newbigin, *Gospel in a Pluralist Society*, 8.
14. Bosch, *Transforming Mission*, 362.
15. Lyotard, *Postmodern Condition*, xxiv.

of non-Western people into a metaphysic of sameness. Thus the voice of the other and the different is unheard, unnoticed, and suppressed in the modernist assumption of representing and transforming the other.

Driven by the postmodern denunciation of the metanarrative, postcolonial theologians argue that colonial annexation and subjugation expatriated native and indigenous cultures and languages under Christendom. In the church in China today we notice that an ongoing effort is being undertaken to overcome an unfortunate chapter in the history of mission associated with the opium war. In the current development of the church in China, we observe that a postcolonial or post-denominational orientation, grounded in self-propagation, self-governance, self-support, and self-theologizing, is beginning to come to the fore, although the legacy of colonialism is still present.

Postcolonial theologians attempt to transcend the aftermath of colonialism by moving beyond the neocolonial forms of global domination of Western Christendom. A postcolonial hermeneutic interrogates the ideology of colonization embedded in the Christian practice of mission. It also argues that the Bible is imbued with an oppressive and hierarchical-patriarchal structure. A postcolonial ethos undergirds a third-world perspective, claiming justice, hybridity, and liberation for the sake of the subaltern. It also holds that liberation becomes a potent symbol for those whose rights are circumvented, marginalized, and put in abeyance.[16] It articulates counter hegemony, identity in formation, and a reading posture which emerges among former victims of colonialism. Postcolonial strategy is also connected to minority voices in the first world such as socialists, radicals, feminists, and racial minorities. It affirms a hybridized identity as a consequence of colonialism, and forges a wider and more complex web of cultural negotiation and interaction. It incorporates and redeploys both the local and the imported elements for the sake of intercivilizational alliance.[17] This aspect undergirds a global-critical epistemology concerning the relationship between the colonizer and the colonized.

---

16. Sugirtharajah, *Asian Hermeneutics and Postcolonialism*, 15.

17. Ibid., 16–17.

Mission: Prophetic Justice and Recognition of the Other

A crucial part of this investigation involves exploring the postcolonial aspect of God's mission in the midst of World Christianity. To do so, we begin by examining the important examples of Bartholomé de Las Casas in the New Indies and Matteo Ricci in China as historical examples of the church's mission. Las Casas marks a paradigm shift in the age of discovery (1492–1773) by breaking away from the European model of mission and colonialism. The Catholic missionary movement since Christopher Columbus' discovery in 1492 was unfortunately associated with colonial expansion and economic pursuit of gold. This imperial mission of the *conquistador* undergirded the *tabula rasa* (in modern terms, "blank slate") approach. The *tabula rasa* approach argued that the religious-cultural beliefs and practices of the indigenous people must be destroyed before they converted to the Christian church. Against this trend, Las Casas becomes a symbolic, prophetic figure of mission by promoting the full humanity of indigenous peoples.[18]

In contrast to the *tabula rasa* approach, we read that the Jesuit missionaries in the Asian context promoted a model of *il modo soave* (the sweet or gentle way) by breaking away from the *conquistador* mentality espoused by missionaries to South America. Matteo Ricci shared some theological assumptions with Las Casas, because both of them were influenced by the renewed Catholicism initiated by the school of Salamanca, in Spain, which was influential in Italy.

Ricci's mission in China marks an important example of inculturation in encounter between Western Christianity and Chinese religious culture, especially Confucian philosophy.

Unlike Ricci's mission in China, however, mission in Japan around the same time experienced serious trials and persecution. According to Endo, Christian mission in Japan began with the arrival of Francis Xavier in the year 1549. The Christian religious community was flourishing; however, in 1614 the edict of expulsion was promulgated. This was the deathblow to Western missionaries and Japanese Christians. During this period of persecution Christians apostatized after long and terrible tortures which complied with the order to trample on the sacred image of Jesus Christ.[19] Endo's literary insight into God's *Silence* sharpens a

18. Bevans and Schroeder, *Constants in Context*, 176–77.

19. Endo, *Silence*, vii–xxiv.

theology of the cross in Japanese context concerning apostasy. This God stands in solidarity with human failure and even apostasy during the period of persecution. In the end, even the Catholic priest trampled on the ugly face of Christ who has been trampled on by so many feet. Endo writes: "The Christ in bronze speaks to the priest: 'Trample! Trample! I more than anyone know of the pain in your foot. Trample! It was to be trampled on by men that I was born into this world. It was to share men's pain that I carried my cross.'"[20] Endo poses a new perspective on God's compassion in connection with the ones who were forced to trample on the cross.[21]

According to Robert Bellah, the persecution of Christianity in the period of Tokugawa (1600–1867) needs to be understood as religious persecution rather than exclusively political. Christianity threatened the core of the traditional value system with its religious base, becoming fatal to loyalty and filial piety. This basic structure of Japanese society ordered and permeated their cultural and social life.[22]

However, in contrast to the missionary situation in Japan, Ricci became successful in China, and was hailed as "the wise man from the West." Ricci's model of accommodation to Chinese cultural practices and belief systems led him to a profound learning of language, culture, and Confucianism, appreciating indigenous rites concerning ancestors. However, Ricci's affirmation of Chinese belief systems continued to be a field of controversy in the subsequent development of missiology. In regard to the Catholic model of constants in context, Bevans and Schroeder characterize interreligous dialogue, inculturation, and reconciliation in light of mission as prophetic dialogue.[23]

Evangelization and Inculturation in Congregational Life

A prophetic dialogue is not merely an issue in foreign mission, but also in multicultural ministry in American society. Evangelization and inculturation do not merely belong to the narrative of Ricci's mission in the past; they became arduous issues during my pastoral life in multicultural ministry in the Evangelical Lutheran Church in America, Orinda,

---

20. Ibid., 259.
21. Ibid., xix.
22. Bellah, *Beyond Belief*, 124.
23. Bevans and Schroeder, *Constants in Context*, 187, 192–95, 378–95.

California. My ministry was undertaken with people from East Asian cultures living in the United States. The parish environment became more and more filled with people of East Asian religious backgrounds after the transfer of sovereignty over Hong Kong from the United Kingdom to the People's Republic of China (on July 1, 1997). Engagement with psychological pain, cultural gaps, pessimism, and socio-economic disturbance shaped my pastoral directive, involving it in a struggle of love against the culture of despair. It is central to the community of the different, innocent, and *dukkha* (in Sanskrit: suffering).[24]

Jenifer was an intellectual layperson, a graduate of the business school at the University of California, Berkeley. She became a "born-again" Christian through the ministry of Campus Crusade for Christ. But her mother-in-law, Ms. Mercy (not her real name), grew up with little education with a strong background of Mahayana Buddhism, especially the Pure Land Buddhism which emphasizes the infinite compassion of Amida Buddha. Family tension became an emotional and cultural reality between an evangelical Christian and a committed Buddhist. With Jenifer's urging of her mother-in-law to attend the multicultural parish, Ms. Mercy reluctantly joined the congregation. Her first question sounded quite weird to the pastor. "[Zen] Master, is there any difference between born again Christianity and the reincarnation of Buddhism?" The term "born again Christian" sounded to her like the doctrine of reincarnation in Buddhism.

In meeting with Ms. Mercy and Jenifer, I enjoyed sharing my understanding of Buddhist compassion in regard to the unfailing and unflinching grace of God in Jesus Christ for all. Surprisingly enough, in the course of dialogue Ms. Mercy deeply appreciated my openness in welcoming the stranger, saying that "Master, I do not know even the genuine meaning of *Namu Amidabutsu* [Amen, Amida-Buddha] you are now talking about, although I attended the Buddhist temple over thirty years." Ms. Mercy learned the meaning of Buddhist salvation from a local Lutheran pastor (or master)! This dialogue in welcoming the stranger led Ms. Mercy to become a part of the multicultural faith community.

I believe that her conversion came through the mysterious power of the Holy Spirit. Through Bible study, her understanding of Jesus' self-identification with the way, truth, and the life was colored by her sense of

24. Chung, *Martin Luther and Buddhism*, xix.

the Buddhist Way of compassion which does not exclude other ways, but embraces them. It was a marvelous experience for me to read the biblical narrative in conversation with a lay person with a former Buddhist background. Congregational mission and leadership were shaped and enriched by the strangers who joined the congregation through hospitality, dialogue, and *diakonia*. Justice comes along with the recognition of others in today's pastoral setting located within the multicultural public sphere. Human life is characterized by existence on the way—striving, waiting, and hoping in a quest for the truth. Along the historical line of prophetic justice and recognition of others, I will undertake a constructive, public mission in regard to World Christianity and postcolonial challenge (Part I).

Mission and Theological Disciplines

Discussing mission in the context of theological discipline, I distinguish the term missiological in a more academic sense from missional in a general sense. In this definition "missional" can be used as an adjective for any subject related to or characterized by mission. However, "missiological" and "missiology" refer to the study of mission: the science of biblical narrative and mission in an academic setting, including biblical, theological, historical, hermeneutical, and practical reflection and research about evangelization and missionary work and structure in non-Christian contexts. We can refer generally to a missional reading of the biblical narrative (for instance, the Exodus, the cross and resurrection of Jesus Christ), exploring its significance in God's mission for Israel and the church, and its relevance for Christian mission today. We may also speak of a missiological reading of biblical narrative, while it is more appropriate to speak of a missional role of Israel and the church.[25]

For conceptual clarity of missiology in a hermeneutical and practical framework, it is necessary to mention two different academic traditions. In the German context, Schleiermacher placed the field of missiology into practical theology in his organization of theological curriculum. Schleiermacher implies a significant element of hermeneutics in terms of language and life connection.[26] Schleiermacher understood

25. For the distinction between "missional" and "missiological" see Wright, *Mission of God*, 24–25.

26. For the hermeneutic in Schleiermacher, see Palmer, *Hermeneutics*, 96.

practical theology to be the goal and crown of theology. He envisioned it primarily as theological reflection on the tasks of the ordained minister or the leadership of the church. The fourfold pattern—the discipline of Bible (text), church history (history), systematic theology (truth), and practical theology (application)—became established under the influence of Schleiermacher. He viewed missions as a cultural responsibility in missional situations where Western culture penetrates non-Western cultural areas. Here we observe a cultural-Protestant ethos, because the missionaries must carry the laws and customs of their nation to bring the higher and better things of life to an indigenous context.[27]

Some shortcomings of Schleiermacher are also noticed in his concept of theory and practice. His view is critiqued as running in the direction of a theory-to-practice structure.[28] Nevertheless, his language-centered shift in his hermeneutical development in connection to life-setting can bring the relation between theory and practice to complementarity. Unlike Schleiermacher, however, scholars in the United States of the late nineteenth century contended that the major methodologies that characterized the development of missiology were history and the social sciences, in particular, ethnography.

Missiology and Cultural Anthropology

Anthropology grew out of the Society for the Abolition of Slavery and was further developed by the successors involved in the removal of racial injustice and cultural discrimination. Anthropologists have accused missionaries of disregarding the good in other cultures through Eurocentrism and its oppressive knowledge system of the other. They have offered an important understanding of human life through the study of diverse socio-cultural contexts. In a missional context, an indigenous church, based on the idea of self-supporting, self-governing, and self-propagating Christianity, was given a greater voice in administrative affairs and decision-making.[29]

In recent years, anthropologists have become aware of the importance of human beliefs and their relationship to the social realm through cultural analysis which is seen in symbolic and cognitive

27. Verkuyl, *Contemporary Missiology*, 7.

28. For this critique, see Browning, *Fundamental Practical Theology*, 43.

29. Verkuyl, *Contemporary Missiology*, 65.

anthropology (Clifford Geertz, Mary Douglas, Victor Turner, and Paul Hiebert). Anthropology helps us understand and appreciate people of other societies rooted in their own cultural settings, making the biblical message more relevant to them. Anthropology is of particular importance for missiology, because missiology is based on the embodied narrative of God in Jesus Christ, that is, on the theology of the incarnation. Anthropology helps missionaries counter their ethnocentrism in relation to the indigenous culture. It can also help missionaries understand the process of contextualizating the biblical message; thereby, the gospel and the church can become meaningful to people in the missionary's building of relationships and communication across cultural boundaries and barriers.[30]

In the diverse schools of anthropology, from classic thinkers such as Franz Boas, Bronislaw Malinowski, and A. R. Radcliffe-Brown via Ruth Benedict, to the structural anthropology of Claude Lévi-Strauss, to the interpretive anthropology of Geertz, we learn how anthropologists contributed to a culture-specific analysis of indigenous cultures and life systems without falling into the trap of Western ethnocentrism and racial prejudices. Theologically, H. Richard Niebuhr did groundbreaking work in articulating the different ways churches understand the relationship between Christ and culture in a typological configuration. He defines culture as social and value-oriented in regard to human life in society and a world of value (according to Malinowski). Also culture is regarded to be a human achievement in the diverse relationship of individual to society, thus it has characteristics of diversity and pluralism (according to Benedict).[31] However, Niebuhr's engagement addresses only the different postures of the Christian church in regard to its surrounding culture, neglecting the variation of different cultures' reception and expression of the biblical narrative.

I learn from practical theology (also in hermeneutical tradition) and cultural anthropology, while critically appreciating Niebhur's contribution to Christ and culture set within the framework of Western Christendom.[32] I further attempt to refine our understanding of mission as a hermeneutical, constructive reflection on the word of God in

30. Hiebert, *Cultural Anthropology*, xvi–xxi.

31. Niebuhr, *Christ and Culture*, 32–33.

32. For the critique of Niebuhr's typology of Christ and culture, see Yoder, "How Niebuhr Reasoned," 31–89; Carter, *Rethinking Christ and Culture*.

connection to the church's practice for the world. Mission as constructive theology is not isolated from other theological disciplines, but entails an interdisciplinary implication for theology in engagement with cultural anthropology, comparative study of religion, and cultural theory of interpretation. I argue that we must reclaim mission as constructive, public theology in a hermeneutical-practical manner for the sake of embarking on innovative initiatives in missional theology. In other words, missiology as a hermeneutical-practical discipline provides an academic locus for the interdisciplinary investigation of God's mission, the church, congregational study, and culture. It employs the methodologies of theology, hermeneutics, anthropology, history, intercultural relations, and communications. It seeks effective mission in addressing the biblical narrative at places the gospel encounters unbelief (evangelization) and provides the church's discipleship and *diakonia* in light of God's reconciliation with the world.

According to missiology as a complementary science (J. Verkuyl), the study of evangelization belongs to the practical disciplines, and it complements the other theological studies by bringing the perspective of the other to exegesis, hermeneutics, church history, and systematic theology. Biblical studies (especially exegesis and hermeneutics) are crucial for developing a methodology of communicating the biblical narrative in a missional context. It considers the horizon of the indigenous life which is involved in translation of the biblical narrative. Thus missiology acts as a complement to biblical exegesis and hermeneutics. In dealing with the Christian relationship with non-Christian religions, missiology adds a more complementary side to the systematic teaching of the Trinity, Christology, the Holy Spirit, ecclesiology, and eschatology. Learning from church history, missiology renews and improves on the limitations and setbacks of mission in the past tainted with colonialism and Eurocentrism. Here the ethical issue becomes central to missiology in interaction with the culture and life of indigenous people. Nontheological disciplines (cultural anthropology, world-economy, and comparative study of religions) are significant for missiology in understanding the context of the younger churches.[33]

Paul Hiebert made groundbreaking work for incorporating anthropology missiology. In the study of people's social and cultural contexts, he argues that the fundamental differences among cultures have posed a

33. Verkuyl, *Contemporary Missiology*, 9–11.

number of questions about cross-cultural communication, the church's ministry, contextualization, and the relationship between theology and socio-cultural contexts. In this regard Hiebert proposes a trialogue in missions in which systematic theology, biblical exegesis, and anthropology interact with each other. Complementing one another, we learn how to view and comprehend a reality from different perspectives. This interdisciplinary standpoint is necessary because of the limitations of human understanding. Furthermore, this interdisciplinary trialogue leads missiology to a constructive, hermeneutical study of people with whom we communicate and serve. The anthropological study of other people, their cultural and religious belief systems, and histories teach us that we are creatures in historical and socio-cultural life settings and that these contexts shape our way of looking at things.

This anthropological study helps us also recognize missionary biases and the limitations conditioned by Western cultural and philosophical assumptions. One major contribution that anthropology has made is the recognition that all people have their own views of themselves and reality in an equal manner. We must understand other people not only from our own standpoint (etic analysis) but also as they understand themselves (emic analysis). The final step taken in this form of missiology is to evaluate the people through the encountering of different analyses and horizons, in light of the Kingdom of God. [34] Through these steps Hiebert concurs with David Bosch's definition of God's mission: "God . . . has personally intervened in human history and has done so supremely through the person and ministry of Jesus of Nazareth who is the Lord of history, Savior and Liberator. In this Jesus, incarnate, crucified and risen, the reign of God has been inaugurated."[35] The study of missions is not only the way to communicate the gospel more effectively to people of other cultures; it is also helpful for us to understand ourselves, our contexts, and the gospel more fully in dialogue with anthropological reflections.[36] This calls for a reframing of missiology in a hermeneutical-constructive manner.

---

34. Hiebert, *Anthropological Reflections*, 10–13.
35. Bosch, *Transforming Mission*, 412.
36. Hiebert, *Anthropological Reflections*, 15.

Missiology as Hermeneutical, Constructive Theology

I undertake missiology as a complementary science to other theological disciplines. An integration of anthropology becomes foundational for us to advance the character of missiology in a direction of hermeneutical-constructive theology. Browning grounds a fundamental practical theology upon a revised correlational model. A critical correlational practical theology (Tracy) determines the conditions for the possibility of the theological enterprise. It tends to sidestep the priority of God's narrative in connection with a locus of confessional language of the faith community. A fundamental practical theology is not adequate to hermeneutically and exegetically ground the subject-matter of the biblical narrative in regard to missiology.[37]

As for theological discipline, missiology engages in the biblical narrative of God's salvific drama, beginning with the covenant with Israel and Noah and reaching its culmination in the ministry and mission of Jesus Christ in the presence of the Holy Spirit. It invites the world to prepare for the kingdom of God through eschatological expectation. Biblical exegesis and hermeneutical reflection on God's salvific drama play a pivotal role in shaping research methods and interpretation of missiology as constructive, public theology. In light of the cultural communication of the biblical narrative, missiology can also provide insight to the academic discipline of biblical exegesis. Missiology can complement systematic theology, for example, in teaching the Trinity, Christology, and salvation in dialogue with Judaism, Islam, and others. Thus, missiology has a different perspective in dealing with the Trinitarian dimension of God's mission. Missiology elaborates on what God has done in Christ through the Holy Spirit (the grace of justification and reconciliation) and continues to do in Word and Spirit (God's ongoing creation). This underlines God's activity for embracing the church and the world.

Thus missiology takes on multi-disciplinary and intercultural-hermeneutical bearings in all aspects of the announcement of the biblical narrative, emphasizing God's grace of justification and reconciliation for the world. From an intercultural-hermeneutical perspective, missiology shapes research methodology and interpretation, making interdisciplinary connections with cultural anthropology, comparative study of religions, and cultural theories of interpretation. A hermeneutical,

37. Browning, *Fundamental Practical Theology*, 47.

cross-cultural perspective on missiology recognizes the fact that different persons in different cultures understand the biblical narrative differently. Culture is a context, something within which social events, behaviors, institutions, or processes can be intelligibly, i.e., "thickly" described.[38]

Anthropologists utilize emic categories and participant observation, examining how their own assumptions color their interpretation of the data. They utilize emic (for generating statements which the people accept as real, meaningful, and appropriate) and etic (related to the anthropologists' own view of things) analyses in order to develop complementary ways of seeing and describing reality in a fresh way. This comparison calls for a reconstruction of etic-emic metacultural epistemology which explores the deep cognitive and social structures underlying all human systems.[39]

From the theological-interdisciplinary perspective, missiology advanced in a hermeneutical, cultural-anthropological reframing develops and reshapes Christian discourse on the *missio Dei* and missional church conversation in an interdisciplinary and cross-cultural manner. A semantic of missiology elaborated in a hermeneutical circle is self-critical and self-renewing in dialogue with varying contexts. It is shaped and driven in a socio-critical interplay in terms of the dialogical step: the appropriation of meaning from the past and critical distance from the limitations of Christian mission (tied to colonialism), and reconstruction of missional self in dialogue with the other. Reclaiming mission as constructive theology enables theoretical theology (for instance, systematic theology, biblical exegesis, church history) to become publicly relevant in missional contexts. This aspect reinforces our discussion of God's mission and missional church conversation.

Missio Dei and Missional Church

The term *missio Dei* is widely used in the missiological study of the activity of the triune God in the world. The Chinese Communist government expelled all of Western missionaries in the 1940s, calling them representatives of Western imperialism and culture. This political incident became a watershed for church leaders and theologians to take seriously

38. Geertz, *Interpretation of Cultures*, 12, 14.

39. Hiebert, *Missiological Implications*, 96.

a shift from ecclesiocentric mission to God's mission. This is because God's mission is basically shaped in a postcolonial trend.

We see this shift in the final report of the 1952 Willingen conference, which states that the missionary movement has its source in the triune God. Karl Hartenstein (1894–1952) was one of Germany's most prominent missiologists in the prewar era. Working as the director of the Basel Mission until 1939, he was also influenced by Karl Barth. After the Willingen conference, George Vicedom wrote his influential book *Missio Dei*.[40] God is the acting subject in mission, because God the Father sent the Son and the Son is both the Sent One and the Sender. Together with the Father the Son sends the Holy Spirit who in turn sends the church, congregations, apostles, and servants.

In the theological debate over the *missio Dei*, we observe that there is one trend in the usage of the term implying that the world sets the agenda for the church. Putting aside the church, God is seen as active in the secular political and social realms (as strongly seen in J. C. Hoekendijk's Dutch school of mission). Against this trend, Vicedom's notion of God as the acting subject in mission, while embracing the church's role of participation in God's mission, created a larger space for an ecumenical approach. Vicedom defines *missio Dei* in the special revelation of Jesus Christ and also in light of God's universal reign. According to Richard Bliese, Lutheran missiology is charged to refine and improve the missionary thrust of the Reformer's theology in a paradigm shift from reactive reform to innovative initiatives in mission theology. It should assist congregations and mission agencies to reframe their work theologically and hermeneutically within a comprehensive missiological perspective.[41]

In the discussion of God's mission and the missional church conversation, Lesslie Newbigin remains a central figure in discerning the future course of *missio Dei* theology and missional ecclesiology. In contrast to Hoekendijk's approach, Newbigin refines studies of mission within the framework of a Trinitarian ecclesiology. In the Gospel of John 20:21–22, we see a continuity between the Father's mission, Jesus' mission, and the ongoing mission of the Holy Spirit in the life and witness of the church.[42] In re-envisioning a theology of the *missio Dei* within

40. Vicedom, *Mission of God*.

41. Bliese, "Lutheran Missiology," 25, 19.

42. Newbigin, *Open Secret*, 29.

this Trinitarian-ecclesial model, Newbigin describes the church as a sign, agent, and foretaste of the kingdom of God. The gift of the Holy Spirit, the *arrabōn*, which is a true measure of the justice and peace of the kingdom, makes the church a witness to the gospel. His theology of the Holy Spirit widens the horizon of the missional church, because he articulates the work of the Spirit by exploring the prevenient grace of the Spirit in the world.

Newbigin's missional-theological legacy is succeeded and developed in terms of the missional church conversation in a movement entitled "The Gospel and Our Culture Network." This movement has worked to offer a theological, congregational, and spiritual response to the decline of Christianity in North America. Addressing the individualistic and private form of American religious behavior, the missional church movement proposes missional ecclesiology and congregational leadership by emphasizing what it means for the church to be a part of the *missio Dei* in the world.[43]

In Barth's model of sending, I sense that God's word-event in the context of daily life seems to be left behind for the sake of a model of revelation from above. This is because Barth emphasizes God's eternal decree of predestination in the inner-Trinitarian life.[44] Mission is based in election. Overcoming limitations in Barth's conception of *missio Dei*, it is important to construct a public mission by taking into account the particularities of human life affirmed by God's embodiment in Jesus Christ. This can be done through a hermeneutical conversation with people of other cultures and also sharpened in social engagement with the multi-cultural American society. Here mission springs from God's Word as event.

For this task, our theological perspective on God's mission begins by reflecting on God's word-event as *pro-missio* in Israel, reaching its climax in the incarnation of Jesus Christ. It also actualizes the reality of the coming of God here and now in an eschatological dynamism. A theology of Trinitarian mission can be seen through the hermeneutical perspective on God's living word-event by deepening and refurbishing a classic concept of the *missio Dei* while emphasizing the corresponding concept of the *diakonia Dei* in Christ and articulating an ecclesiology

---

43. Guder, *Missional Church*. For further discussion of missional theology from a Lutheran perspective, see Bliese and Van Gelder, *Evangelizing Church*.

44. Bosch, *Transforming Mission*, 389–93.

for the pluralized life of the world. This implies a constructive, public missiology which centers on God as the One speaking in the church and the world. This perspective can be developed by incorporating a Reformation theology of grace into ministerial and missional practices, as we engage with Israel, the church. It promotes the full humanity of innocent victims (including the sustainability of ecological life) and religious others. The Reformation teaching on justification and its theological hermeneutics establish a constructive framework for deliberation in the public sphere and the realm of creation. The hermeneutic of word-event in public missiology enters into conversation with local congregations, and attends to the emerging postmodern context.[45] This missiological aspect turns "a past-oriented hermeneutic of inquiry"[46] toward a future-oriented hermeneutic of God's *pro-missio* (in Part II). This delves into the Trinitarian sense of divine freedom in relation to the human experience of God's grace.

Divine Freedom and Human Experience

Catherine LaCugna develops a Trinitarian ontology by defining *perichoresis* (indwelling) in terms of the mystery of the one communion of all persons, divine as well as human. She utilizes the etymology of the word closely related to the word "to dance" (i.e., *perichoreo*, signifying "cyclical movement or reoccurrence"). I maintain that *perichroesis* should be translated as circulation and that LaCugna has confused it with a similar word meaning dance or choreography. For LaCugna, the divine dance of *perichoresis* becomes an image of persons in communion, so that creatures take part in the life of *perichoresis*. LaCugna interprets God's election from all eternity (Eph 1:3–14) to support her argument that humanity has been made a partner in the divine dance. The one *perichoresis* includes God and humanity as beloved partners in the dance.[47] Her chiastic model of Trinity is built on Neo-Platonic dialectics of *exitus* (emanation) and *reditus* (return), and it affirms that there is only the economic Trinity as the concrete realization of the immanent Trinity. This model is the one dynamic movement grounded in *a Patre ad Patrem*. It emphasizes the economic Trinity as the comprehensive plan of God

45. Van Gelder, ed., *Missional Church*, 27.

46. Bliese, "Lutheran Missiology," 12.

47. LaCugna, *God for Us*, 274.

reaching from creation to consummation. An immanent Trinitarian theology is nothing but a theology of the economy of salvation.[48]

LaCugna tends to eliminate the freedom of God in self against God for us and she argues that the life of God is not something belonging to God alone. Rather Trinitarian life is also our life, so that Trinity is a teaching about God's life with us and our life with each other. This aspect could possibly cause an impression that God's life depends on our life.[49] The *perichoresis* or divine dance is radicalized as the mutual interdependence of God and all, in our present time. It is unfortunate that such a perspective contradicts St. Paul's theology of eschatological reservation, in which the Son is subject to God the Father (1 Cor 15:28).

God's triune identity—eternally Father, Son, and Holy Spirit—is not something belonging to our life, but it becomes manifest in God's self-introduction in the historical life of Jesus Christ in the presence of the Holy Spirit. The mission and ministry of Jesus is embedded within the kingdom of God which is clearly shown in Jesus' commanding of baptism in the name of the Trinity. So, Trinitarian mission is grounded in the narrative of the gospel, which shapes and characterizes the directive and content of God's mission. Jesus Christ himself acknowledges the freedom and sovereignty of the God of Israel by praying the Shema Israel. Jesus never stood in competition with the God of Israel. Thus, St. Paul affirms that the freedom and covenant of God with Israel embraces the Jewish "No" to Jesus Christ as the Messiah.[50] As Paul states, "O the depth of the riches and wisdom and knowledge of God! How unsearchable are his judgments and how inscrutable his ways! 'For who has known the mind of the Lord? Or who has been his counselor?'" (Rom 11:33–34).

For a biblically grounded Trinity, I undertake a hermeneutical deliberation of public mission in terms of the Word of God revealed, written, proclaimed, while also including the living word-event in the sense of *creatio continua*. In such a hermeneutical-missional configuration human experience and the knowledge of God is renewed, deepened, contextualized, and guided by the triune God who as the living and emancipating God is the source of our theological knowledge and missional direction. Thus God's mission as God's *pro-missio* is grounded in God's word-event in covenant and reconciliation to which proclamation

48. Ibid., 223–24.
49. Ibid., 228.
50. Marquardt, "Enemies for Our Sake," 3–30.

corresponds and witnesses. In the mission of the *viva vox evangelii* (gospel as the living voice of God) Jesus Christ as the eternal Word of God comes together with God's universal reign in covenant and creation.

The triune God is the One who speaks in creation and Torah, and reaches a climax in Jesus Christ as the eternal, incarnate Word of God and the eschatological Lamb of God. Thus, the theological subject matter of the living God in the Trinitarian sense becomes the ground for us to develop our ability to listen to God's word in the church as well as God's ongoing work in the reconciled world. A Trinitarian theology of mission insists: no Word of God, no mission! Mission is our participation in God's grace of justification and reconciliation which in turn shapes missional theology as a theology of vocation. Missional theology as a theology of vocation recognizes diverse formations of Christianity in different contexts, by acknowledging the wisdom and experience of religious others.

God's Narrative in Service to the World

In constructing mission through God's narrative, missiology is a critical-hermeneutical science of the grace of justification in light of God's universal reign. It becomes a discipline in service to the Christian faith and the proclamation of the living Word of God. Missiology is based on the Word of God and ecclesial life, bringing the universal message of the gospel and a special life of communion, fellowship, and *diakonia* together in the public sphere. It is grounded in the biblical narrative of God's gracious justification, reconciliation, and vocation, and takes on public concerns in light of the eschatological reality of God's coming.[51]

Here it is important to incorporate *diakonia* into the essence of the life of Jesus Christ. In the Acts of the Apostles, the community is introduced and characterized in light of communion, fellowship, and *diakonia* (Acts 2:42–47). Paul's Christological concept of *diakonia* reaches its climax in his hymn of Christ's self-humiliation (Phil 2:6–11). It engages with God's narrative in Christ's *diakonia* of reconciliation and it sharpens a model of the Trinity in solidarity with the public sinners and tax collectors (*ochlos-minjung*). It challenges an American version of the *missio Dei* which tends to become a Trojan horse, undermining

---

51. For this insight, see Bonhoeffer, *Ethics*, 282.

postcolonial theology and World Christianity. [52] In this light this book proposes a new understanding of the *missio Dei* and missional ecclesiology in a diaconal, Trinitarian, and eschatological framework, especially concerning North American society and the culture of premillenarism that persists in evangelicalism. This perspective re-envisions the missional church and public faith in American society. This examines public theology and faith in the American way of life (Part III).

Public Theology and the American Way of Life

Thus far, we have dealt with the missional theology in the diaconal, Trinitarian, hermeneutical, and inclusive dimensions. This book also frames God's mission in dialogue with public theology concerning the socially engaged dimension of interpretation, emancipation, and recognition of the religious outsiders.

The term "public theology" derives from Martin Marty's modification of the term "public religion," originally used in 1749 by Benjamin Franklin. Marty favored it over and against Robert Bellah's retrieval of Rousseau's term "civil religion" during the era of the Vietnam War. Public theology assumes a prophetic character in contrast to American civil religion. In American civil religion, America is God's country, and American power in the world is identical with morality and God's will. Such notions have not died, and they are still powerful in today's American society. These ideas have formed an important tradition of interpretation in North American literature and religion. The best antidote to this tendency toward archaic regression is the critical tradition "which has been expressed in what Martin Marty called a public theology and what Walter Lippmann called a public philosophy."

> A strong public theology opposed our more unjust wars, especially the Mexican-American, Spanish-American, and Vietnamese wars, demanded racial and social justice, and insisted on the fulfillment of our democratic promise in our economic as well as our political life.[53]

In our study of public mission it is important to engage the tradition of American civil religion and its apocalyptic view of millenarianism. Then we will attempt to provide a theological corrective to the

---

52. Bosch, *Transforming Mission*, 392.
53. Bellah and Hammond, *Varieties of Civil Religion*, xiii.

tendency of American civil religion and its divine mission of manifest destiny which results in archaic regression into White American nationalism. A renewed public theology in the current debate challenges the ecclesial narrowness of a Christian mission that is easily led into ecclesial-cultural imperialism. Here, a sociological concept of communicative rationality and civil society can become the crucial idea guiding theological discourse.[54] Taking issue with colonization of the lifeworld, a public theology involved in dialogue with socio-critical science attempts to retrieve and invigorate the prophetic vocation of missional congregations as genuine public servants.[55]

Word-Event and Evangelization

According to Wright, a missional hermeneutic sees the whole of Scripture as a missional phenomenon in the sense that it witnesses to the self-giving movement of God toward creation. A missional hermeneutic of the Bible is based on the assumption that the whole Bible renders to us the story of God's mission through God's people in their engagement with God's work for the sake of the whole of God's creation.[56]

If God's salvific drama is missional, consisting of a series of historical entrances and liberations in the life of Israel and the incarnation, crucifixion and resurrection in the life of Jesus Christ and in the coming of the Holy Spirit (Pentecost), a missiological hermeneutics takes seriously the dynamic interaction of the biblical narrative with the life horizons of people in different times and places. Instead of the term "missional hermeneutics," I prefer to use the term "missiological hermeneutics" for the cultural-linguistic fusion of horizon in this regard.

I am interested in reframing God's mission as word-event by emphasizing a dynamic character of the living voice of God which can be heard in the church as well as in the world of creation. The gospel refers essentially to the language of faith in communication with the reality of the world in the sense of *creatio continua* through which God continues to speak.

I bring biblical exegesis and cultural hermeneutics into engagement with the life of the public sphere by reclaiming a public mission as

54. Valentin, *Mapping Public Theology*, 83.

55. Simpson, *Critical Social Theory*, 141–45.

56. Wright, *Mission of God*, 48, 51.

constructive theology grounded in the linguistic-creational role of God's narrative in Christ's service to the world. This perspective undergirds our joyful participation in the *viva vox evangelii* in the spirit of *parrhēsia* (speaking the truth of the gospel with boldness and audacity) in the public world in effective engagement with challenges from liberation theology, postcolonial theology, and World Christianity.

Every relationship is influenced by history and is in flux regarding cultural and social economic life engagement. In regard to the missional implications of epistemological shifts (Hiebert), I put forward a hermeneutical, anthropological discussion of God's word-event which embraces the ecclesial sphere, while also emphasizing God's unexpected voice through the face of the other. God's word-event in this perspective offers a form of ethical resistance, challenging a totalizing, universalistic metanarrative of Western mission. My strategy comes into full swing with fuller interpretation integrating issues of ethnic race, postcolonial critique, cultural identity, economic reality of empire, and the devastation of ecology into hermeneutical circulation.

An experience of God's grace (first naiveté or naïve literalism) is first of all asserted in terms of the literal identification between the Scripture and God. The first naiveté is characterized by immediacy of belief in the Word of God in which one understands oneself within the horizon of scriptural signification. This scriptural understanding is a hermeneutical principle. The word of God poses the problem of understanding, opening up and mediating a new understanding other than that of the first naiveté. The word as event brings something to a new configuration of understanding the biblical narrative, renewing and deepening the act of the first naiveté. Letting the word perform its own hermeneutical work, a missiological hermeneutic implies a deeper penetration into the linguistic realm of faith and public discipleship. It understands the biblical narrative in a different context by means of language, discourse, and the verbal activity of evangelization.

The *verbum Dei* as the living word of God seeks to be interpreted in different times and places through the universal activity of the Holy Spirit; it continues to be undertaken as a word-event in all sorts of human discourse and communication. Therefore, a hermeneutic has to do with the word-event in the internal testimony of the Holy Spirit and with a discursive practice of evangelization. We must understand in order to believe, while we must believe in order to understand. This is a hermeneutical interaction between faith and understanding, seeking new meaning in the biblical narrative by exploring different perspectives.

Faith comes to expression and understanding in our daily communication. The language of faith is the language of communication in the experience of the world. Exegesis is the process of exposition itself while hermeneutics is the theory of exposition[57] related to the word-event taking place in the public world. In the interaction of faith and understanding we come into the hermeneutical process of engaging the biblical narrative and Christian symbols in our own social and cultural lifeworld. Human understanding and interpretation take place through language and discourse. The triune God comes to us as word-event, or language-event. By a linguistic featuring of the Trinity we invoke the Creator (Father), the Redeemer (Son), and the Sanctifier (Holy Spirit) in their Trinitarian relationship.

The meaning of faith in the first act of naiveté is shared, practically mediated, and reacquired in the discursive act of evangelization in conversation with the other. Evangelization implies a hermeneutical conversation with the other. I characterize this process of faith, understanding, and acquired meaning in terms of a semantic of mission. In the semantic of mission. God's *pro-missio* and evangelization are inseparably connected with our dialogue with the other and praxis of *parrhēsia*. Such a discourse practice implies a critique of structures of social injustice and violence which continue to generate mechanisms of victimization and scapegoating.[58]

The word of God as event seeks to be orally announced and discursively practiced in solidarity with the world. This hermeneutical-discursive perspective shapes and sharpens a theology of God's mission as word-event in a prophetic, diaconal profile. Interpretation is an important dimension of the Christian narrative of the gospel (*kerygma*). Without Philip's interpretation of the Word of God, the Ethiopian eunuch would not have been capable of accepting the gospel (Acts 8:26–38). Christian mission as the interpretation of the Word of God takes shape in concrete social life settings. It contextualizes a bodily dimension of the Christian narrative, projecting its prophetic resistance to the reality of violence and injustice. A Trinitarian mission in a hermeneutical focus underpins

57. Ebeling, "Word of God and Hermeneutic," in Robinson and Cobb, eds., *New Hermeneutic*, 89.

58. Girad, *Things Hidden*.

an interculturation, which implies an exchange of theologies between the Western church and the third-world church. It serves liberation of the church from the Babylonian captivity of the imperial culture.[59]

A Thematization of Mission as Constructive Theology

Developing God's mission as constructive theology, I describe diverse models of God's mission in each part. This may be useful in understanding how God's mission is conceptualized in historical and contemporary context.

First, Part I deals with an interactive model of missional theology, dealing with the historical examples of Bartholomé de Las Casas and Matteo Ricci. This model can be seen in terms of the Catholic approach based on constants of God's grace in the context as described by Bevan and Schroeder. The interactive model finds its inspiration and becomes sharpened in the context of World Christianity which emphasizes mission as translation. This model supports a postcolonial approach to mission as re-presentation of those on the margin. In a critical dialogue with postcolonial theology, I shall propose mission as constructive theology as I emphasize the concept of word-event in linguistic, cross-cultural, and comparative study of religion. This perspective appreciates Confucian insights into ethics and interpretation to overcome a shortcoming of postcolonial theology, which tends to undermine an interpretive engagement with other religions and their literature.

Part II is a discussion of the *missio Dei* and the missional church conversation. Here a hermeneutical model of missional theology is proposed and refurbished in light of the living voice of God (*viva vox evangelii*) which is foundational for a model of the *missio Dei* which takes seriously Christ's *diakonia* of reconciliation. Constructing an innovative missiology within the context of North American and World Christianity, this hermeneutical model aims at contextualizing confessional issues (such as justification by grace through faith, promise and faith, word and sacraments, law and gospel, the priesthood of all believers, the two kingdoms, and economic justice, among others) in conversation with the *missio Dei* theology and the missional church. (This missional model is inspired hermeneutically and socio-critically

59. Bosch, *Transforming Mission*, 456.

by the prophetic legacy of the Confessing Church in Germany, especially Dietrich Bonhoeffer and Georg Vicedom.)

Part III is a study of the hermeneutics of word-event with an emphasis on its public expression. Luther's hermeneutics of word-event based on the law-gospel-relation is explored in its multifaceted dimensions, notably in dialogue with Karl Barth. A public mission is constructed and developed especially in dealing with American civil religion, millennialism, and its multicultural configuration. A public mission is refined in terms of socially engaged interpretation and embodied narrative. An ethical dimension of mission can be refined in dialogue with theological-political deliberation of God as the Place of the world. This aspect undertakes the discursive dimension of *paranesis* and *parrhēsia*.

Through the interdisciplinary-intercivilizational study of mission, mission is reclaimed as constructive theology and takes up the challenge of doing theology with a vision for God's mission and church as God's people within the American context and the globe. In my study of mission I undertake a practical-hermeneutical reframing of God's mission and the missional church in order to clarify the place of mission in theological disciplines and congregational study in dialogue with postcolonial theology and World Christianity.

PART I

Embodying World Christianity in the Mission of God

Within Catholic perspectives, a theology of grace and nature comes into sharp focus for grounding Christian mission. God's grace fulfills and completes nature rather than excluding and supplanting it. Bevans and Schroeder outline six constants, doctrinal themes which are important for the church in mission. They are Christology, ecclesiology, eschatology, salvation, anthropology, and culture. In the various missional contexts God's elements of grace work through the world of creation culminating in Christ and finally in Christ's eschaton. The importance of methodology in the analysis of these constants in context can be seen in their interaction and articulation—Christology, ecclesiology, eschatology, salvation, anthropology, and culture.[1] The church's missionary practices are shaped and implemented in the various times and places of its history, situated within various cultural, political, social, religious, and institutional contexts.

In the "Age of Discovery" Christian mission demonstrates the painful history of its collaboration with colonialism and ecclesial triumphalism. "Compel them to come in" (Luke 14:23) and just-war theory became the dominant model in the imperial missional theology. This imperial missional position was justified by the axiom: "Outside the church there is no salvation."

Bevans and Schroeder have written a typology of Catholic missionary models which identified three types. Their third type is mission as commitment to liberation and transformation, which they call type C.

---

1. Bevans and Schroeder, *Constants in Context*, 2.

In 1968, at the Second General Assembly of the Latin America Bishops' Conference at Medellín, Colombia, the type C perspectives of Vatican II were further developed, which laid the foundation for liberation theology. Liberation theologians in Latin America sought to understand Jesus Christ contextually as one who sided with the poor and marginalized of his day. For Gutiérrez, the church as the sacrament of liberation is a community in witnessing to God's liberating work in history. Liberation theologians share both the high regard for the human and the strong sense of the power of sin. Calling humanity to full consciousness of its possibilities (*conscientization*) is related to denouncing the greed and selfishness enslaving humanity in the structures of institutionalized violence.[2] It is important to examine the legacy of Las Casas in this regard.

In their second model (type B), Bevans and Schroeder understand mission as a discovery of the truth. Within the contemporary discussion of religious pluralism, the type B perspective (in contrast to type A which is exclusivism) embraces the inclusivist position and the pluralist position. Central to type B anthropology is confidence and trust in human reason or experience to find the truth. What is truly human is good and it becomes the door to the holy. Mission built on this anthropology sees itself as helping to give birth to what is already there. Grace builds on and perfects nature. Type B theology sees mission as engaged affirmatively in the cultural life. This perspective is related to the "three self formula" (self-supporting, self-governing, and self-propagating) that Henry Venn (1796–1873) and Rufus Anderson (1796–1880) formulated. This principle undergirds a fourth: self-theologizing. In this regard we will examine Matteo Ricci's concept of mission as inculturation in China.

In moving to Asia, the Jesuits practiced a different type of mission informed by Italian humanism and Ignatian mystical-activist spirituality. The missionary should enter the world of the religious outsiders with gentleness (*il modo soave*). This missional attitude furthers an attitude of accommodating the Christian message to the culture of those who receive it. The Catholic paradigm of liberation and inculturation can be best exemplified in the missional works of Las Casas and Matteo Ricci. Evangelization necessitates a profound dialogue with the host culture, language, and scholarship and leads to respect for religious freedom and human dignity. In such dynamic interaction between grace and nature,

2. Ibid., 66, 70.

grace (constant) brings the world (context) to God's intended fulfillment. Christian mission becomes possible and meaningful to the extent
that the grace of God recognizes, embraces, and completes the others in
the world of nature. This perspective continues to be influential in studies of World Christianity and in postcolonial theology.

1

Bartolomé de Las Casas

Mission as Prophetic Justice

The Journey toward Gold and Mission

Prior to the conquest and colonizing of Latin America, there existed two major civilizations: the Inca in Peru and the Mayan-Aztec in Mexico, as well as other native cultures, for example, the Chibchas in Colombia.[1] At the time of the arrival of the European conquistadores and colonialists, these indigenous cultures had their own forms of cultural development. The Hispanic people were the descendents of the Caucasoid tribes who originally inhabited the Iberian Peninsula.

The Iberian "discoverers" of the "New World" forcefully imposed their culture and dominion upon the native peoples. The conquistadores had a twofold objective: the conversion of the indigenous peoples and the acquisition of their wealth. The history of this period is marked by the genocide of native peoples, slavery, and dependence upon the European metropolis. The white people colonized the rest of the world in order to spread civilization, religion, knowledge, and development. The church was an accomplice in this sordid history, the religious rationale of Christian mission for the colonization process in which the

---

1. Dussel, *History and Theology of Liberation*, 42.

31

Catholic faith was imposed upon the native people as an indistinguishable dimension of Spanish rule.[2]

Capitalism unfolded in two stages: the first was marked by the conquest and pillage of America (sixteenth century), the second by the rise and affirmation of the bourgeoisies (seventeenth and eighteenth centuries). What Western history calls "the great discoveries" drove both of these stages. In 1486 Bartholomeu Diaz rounded the Cape of Good Hope and in 1492 Christopher Columbus discovered America. In 1498 Vasco da Gama arrived in India after a nine-month voyage around Africa. A great hunt after wealth—trade and pillage—began.

Reflecting on the conquests, Adam Smith wrote, "The pious purpose of converting inhabitants to Christianity sanctified the injustice of the project. But the hope of finding treasures of gold there, was the sole motive which promoted them to undertake it . . . . All the other enterprises of the Spaniards in the new world, subsequent to those of Columbus, seem to have been promoted by the same motive. It was the sacred thirst of gold . . ."[3]

Columbus stood out as a very staunch Catholic whose voyage mission was to convert the heathen to Catholicism. However, the heathens he did find were killed or enslaved rather than converted. In a passage from Hans Konig's *Columbus: His Enterprise* we read: "We are now in February 1495 . . . . Of the five hundred slaves, three hundred arrived alive in Spain, where they were put up for sale in Seville by Don Juan de Fonseca, the archdeacon of the town. 'As naked as the day they were born,' the report of this excellent churchman says, 'but with no more embarrassment than animals . . .'" The slave trade immediately turned out to be "unprofitable, for the slaves mostly died." Columbus decided to concentrate on gold, although he writes, "Let us in the name of the Holy Trinity go on sending all the slaves that can be sold."[4]

Hernán Cortés began the conquest of Mexico from Cuba in 1519, and he confessed: "We Spanish suffer from a sickness of the heart for which gold is the only cure."[5] In 1519 the pillage of the treasure of the Aztecs in Mexico began; in 1534 the pillage of the Incas in Peru followed. According to Columbus, "one who has gold does as he wills in the

2. Dussel, *History of the Church*, 38, 41.

3. Smith, *Wealth of Nations*, 711.

4. Konig, *Columbus*, 82.

5. Ibid.

world, and it even sends souls to Paradise."[6] In 1524 twelve Franciscan missionaries had arrived and the evangelization of Mexico began; the Indians were subdued by force of arms.

Due to Rome's weakness, the king of Spain had right to nominate bishops and deal with the Archbishop in order to enact his own plan. The king of Spain chose all the bishops during the colonial period. The expansion of Christendom in Latin America from 1492 to 1808 was one of the successes of the colonial style of mission.[7] The Spanish adventures saw the natives of the Antilles as inferior and subhuman. As these civilizations were discovered and conquered, the Indians were viewed as idolaters.

Las Casas, Mission, and the Colonial Economic System

However, Bartolomé de Las Casas (1484–1566) saw the New World as it truly was. He was a famous and influential name as the defender of the Indians during the Spanish conquest. His writings had a political implication as well as a religious one. He watched the rapid decimation of Cuba at the start of the colonial gold rush. His intensive experiences from 1512 to 1514 convinced Las Casas that he was called by God to plead for the Indians. He advocated the dignity and liberty of the Indians and peaceful conversion. Who was Bartolomé de Las Casas? He was born in Seville in 1484. His father, Pedro de Las Casas, like all of Seville, was caught up in the fever of the Discovery and along with Bartolomé's uncle and other relatives sailed across the ocean with Columbus. Bartolomé first saw Columbus and his captive Indians in his hometown in the Palm Sunday procession, March 1493. Las Casas' father and uncle joined the second voyage to the New World.

Becoming lavishly wealthy with the money made in the New World, his merchant father decided to send Las Casas to Salamanca to become a priest. The boy continued his studies there in classic and canon law. At the age of eighteen in 1502, Bartolomé de Las Casas sailed across the ocean to help his father on the island of Hispaniola. While Las Casas' father and uncle were loyal to Columbus, Las Casas came to view Columbus severely as one who was blinded to the truth of Indian freedom in seeking to gain wealth for the kings of Spain. What Christopher

6. Ibid., 19.

7. Dussel, *History and Theology of Liberation*, 89.

Columbus had done to the Indians of the New World became a destructive pattern that the Spaniards followed. He seized sovereign territory without warrant, subjugated indigenous people, enslaved many of them, and forced the rest to pay tribute to the Spaniards.[8] During his first five years on Hispaniola, Las Casas came to realize the predicament and sufferings of Indian life.

On April 17, 1492, King Ferdinand and Queen Isabella signed a contract with Christopher Columbus, appointing him as viceroy and governor of all the newly discovered lands and granting him one-tenth of all precious stones, gold, silver, or other articles of trade by purchase, barter, or conquest, including commercial privilege.[9] In 1496—when not one grain of the gold was left—the Spaniards cut out estates for themselves in which the Indians were still living. The Indians became their property.

The church and state were intertwined with the Spanish king on top. Conquest, destruction, and genocide beyond our imagination were an accepted fact all over the New World followed by gold and slavery. The Spaniards used a system known as *encomienda* instead of slave plantations. The *encomienda* in Hispanic America was a direct creation of the crown. The Spanish crown had sent Nicolás Ovando to reestablish royal authority. Ovando ensured the proper operation of the *repartimiento*, that is, an allocation of Indians to individuals known as *encomenderos*. The *encomendero* was given trusteeship of a number of Indians and was charged with instructing them in Spanish language and culture and the Catholic faith. In return they could extract tribute in labor or goods. The *encomienda* worked between 1501 and 1509, and led to the eradication of Indian society.

Intellectual Background, Conversion, and Prophetic Witness

In 1506, Las Casas returned to Seville to resume his studies and sought ordination to the priesthood. He finished his studies in the degree of bachelor of canon law at Salamanca. The School of Salamanca was surrounded by the renaissance of thought in diverse intellectual areas influenced by the intellectual and pedagogical work of Francisco de Vitoria (c. 1492–1546).

8. Las Casas, *Indian Freedom*, 17.
9. Parish, *Bartolomé de Las Casas*, 9.

From the beginning of the sixteenth century, the traditional Catholic conception of human beings and of their relation to God had been assaulted by the rise of humanism, by the Protestant Reformation, and by the new geographical discoveries and their consequences. These new problems were addressed by the School of Salamanca. Leading scholars such as de Vitoria, Domingo de Soto, and Francisco Suarez founded the school and sought to reconcile the teachings of Thomas Aquinas with the new political and economic order. The School of Salamanca (called the Salmanticenses) began with de Vitoria, and reached its high point with Domingo de Soto (1494–1560).

Another form of the same school (called the Conimbricenses) was developed by the Jesuits, who at the end of the sixteenth century took over the intellectual leadership of the Catholic Church from the Dominicans. Francisco Suárez (1548–1617) continued the tradition of Jesuit Thomism in Italy. The School of Salamanca reformulated the concept of natural law, arguing that all that exists in the natural order shares in this law. Given that all humans share the same nature, they also share the same rights to life and liberty. De Vitoria worked to limit the type of power the Spanish empire imposed on the Native Peoples. Such views constituted a novelty and went counter to those predominant in Spain and Europe upholding the view that indigenous people in the Americas had no such rights.

On March 3, 1507, Las Casas was ordained a priest in Rome. After ordination, Las Casas studied cannon law in Spain for two years, then sailed back to the New World in 1509. There he took up his task as Indian catechist. During this time he continued to remain a holder of Indians and property.

In the history of the church in Latin America, the Dominican Antonio de Montesinos was the first great figure; he began to publicly condemn all Spaniards who held assigned Indians in *encomienda*. He advocated that the natives be freed, otherwise their holders had no hope of salvation. On the third Sunday of Advent in 1511, he quoted the prophetic texts of Isaiah and John the Baptist to initiate an attack on the Spaniards privileged in the *encomiendas*. A prophetic interpretation of the biblical texts amounted to prophetic action and solidarity with people in the Hispanic culture. "You are all in mortal sin! You live in it and die in it! Why? Because of the cruelty and tyranny you use with these innocent people."[10] There was an uproar against Montesinos who denounced the Spanish islanders for their tyranny. However, the Superior Pedro de Córdoba along with the brothers of the monastery of Hispaniola supported Montesinos.[11]

Las Casas went to a Dominican for confession, but he was refused absolution. He still regarded himself as a good and kind *encomendero*. His Dominican confessor was willing to absolve him only on the condition that he changed his pattern of life by freeing the Indians he held. Dominicans, who had come in 1510, judged that Spain's actions in the New World were mortal sin. Las Casas had accepted an invitation to work in Cuba as part of a pacifying expedition for his old friend Diego Velásquez, governor of that island. Knowing how good Las Casas was with the Indians, Velásquez assigned Father Las Casas as chaplain to his commander-in-chief. He ordered that they should rule the rest of the island by peaceful means if possible, by force if necessary. Las Casas in his new role as the white priest and healer was successful in protecting the Indians from Spanish misconduct and ruthless violence.

In the process of pacification, Las Casas observed a horrible massacre that happened one day at Caonao. The description of the Caonao massacre on the island of Cuba in 1513 comes from Las Casas' recollection of the event, which he observed on the spot. "Right before my eyes, they put to the sword without provocation or cause more than three thousand souls who sat in front of us, men, women, children. I saw there cruelty on a scale no living being has ever seen or expects to see."[12] Despite Las Casas' effort to stop the slaughter, the captain in charge was heartless and cruel. The Caonao massacre stamped him with an indelible scar, leading him to recognize the presence of Jesus Christ "in the tortured, scourged natives of the Indies."[13]

In 1514, Las Casas underwent a major conversion. He was preacher to the Indians and itinerant chaplain for the Spaniards. His sermon text on Pentecost Sunday, *Ecclesiasticus* 34:18, triggered a profound spiritual crisis. "Unclean is the offering sacrificed by an oppressor. . . . The Lord is pleased only by those who keep to the way of truth and justice. The Most High does not accept the gifts of unjust people . . . . The one

---

10. Cited in Bevans and Schroeder, *Constants in Context*, 176.
11. Dussel, *History and Theology of Liberation*, 83.
12. Las Casas, *Indian Freedom*, 146.
13. Gutiérrez, *Las Casas*, 45.

whose sacrifice comes from the goods of the poor is like one who kills his neighbor."[14]

Las Casas saw that everything the Spaniards had done was completely wrong. The whole *encomienda* system was damnable on grounds of racial and social justice. On the Feast of the Assumption, Las Casas made his decision public and told a congregation that damnation awaited those who held Indians. He continued to preach against the *encomienda*. He challenged the method by which conversion was imposed upon the Indians. This method consisted of declaring to the Indians the rights that the Spaniards had over them in the newly imposed social and religious structure. Further religious instruction was neglected. The Pope had granted such rights of just war to Spain if the Indians did not accept the faith and submit to Spanish rule. The consequence of Las Casas' awakening is the church doctrine of Indian liberty that is enshrined in the Papal Bull, *Submis Deus* (1537) and Spain's new laws for the protection of the Indians (1542). In them we read articles of prohibition of the enslavement, abuse, allotment, and brutal *encomienda* of Indians and special protection for island Indians.[15]

Massacre, Slavery, and Just War

The Devastation of the Indies: A Brief Account,[16] which concerns the mistreatment of Native Americans in colonial times, was written by Las Casas in 1542 (published in 1552) and was sent to King Philip II of Spain. Las Casas depicts a firsthand account of Europe's earliest colonization of the Americas in terms of the cruelty and sadism of many Spanish seamen and colonists. One of the stated purposes for writing the account is his fear for Spain, which would come under divine punishment, and also his concern for the souls of the Native Americans. The account is one of the first attempts by a Spanish writer of the colonial era to depict the unfair treatment that the indigenous people endured during the Spanish conquest of the greater Antilles, particularly the island of La Hispaniola. This was a violent and tragic place of the indigenous victim. Spain violated every divine and natural law that protected innocent people and lands because of the blindness and greed for power

14. Parish, *Bartolomé de Las Casas*, 20.

15. Las Casas, *Indian Freedom*, 249–52.

16. Las Casas, *Devastation of the Indies*.

and wealth. Spaniards behaved like ravening wild beasts, "killing, terrorizing, afflicting, torturing, and destroying the native peoples . . . never seen or heard before."[17] The island of Hispaniola whose population was estimated at more than three million was left with a population of nearly two hundred persons.

Las Casas reports that between 1495 and 1503 more than 3 million people disappeared from the islands of the New World. Spanish conquistadors killed millions of Indians through enslavement, demographic catastrophe, and outright murder. They were slain in war, sent to Castile as slaves, or worked to death in the mines and other labors. The production of sugarcane, for rum, molasses, and sugar, the trade in black slaves, and the extraction of precious metals established considerable sources of wealth for Spain throughout the sixteenth century. The "New Spain" (Mexico) was discovered in 1517. The massacres lasted from April 1518 until 1530. The devastations, the blood-drenched hands and swords of the Spaniards, worked in the four hundred and fifty leagues that comprised the city of Mexico and its environs. One of the massacres took place in a large city called Cholula, which had more than thirty thousand people. The Spaniards decided to perform a massacre—a chastisement in their language—only to make themselves feared.[18]

The capitalist era began in the sixteenth century with the flow of precious metals to Europe as a result of the conquest, pillage, and extermination in the colonies. The pattern established by Spain in the conquest of the Americas would later repeat in Britain's occupation of India and the French empire in Indochina. Hence, it is important that we do not put exclusive emphasis on the availability of proletarian labor in explaining the rise of capitalism.

It is also instructive to mention Las Casas' confrontation with Juan Ginés de Sepúlveda (1489–1573), one of Spain's leading humanists. Sepúlveda was a Spanish humanist, philosopher, and theologian. He was an adversary of Las Casas in the Valladolid Controversy in 1550 concerning the justification of the Spanish Conquest of the Indies. Sepúlveda was the defender of the Spanish Empire's right of conquest, colonization, and conversion-evangelism in the so-called New World. He developed the position about natural law that is different from the position of the School of Salamanca, as represented famously by Francisco de Vitoria.

17. Ibid., 29.

18. Las Casas, *Indian Freedom*, 226–27.

The Valladolid Controversy was organized by Charles V (grandson of Ferdinand and Isabella) to give an answer to the question whether the Native Americans were capable of self-governance. The issue of the confrontation was related to the Christian doctrine of just war and the Aristotelian logic of slavery.

According to the argument of Sepúlveda, wars against Indians were justified because Indians had committed grave sin by idolatry and sins against nature. The Indians' natural rudeness and inferiority concurred with the Aristotelian notion that some people were born natural slaves. Military conquest formed the most efficacious method of converting Indians to Christianity. Finally, conquering Indians made it possible to protect the weak among them.[19] Las Casas' anti-slavery tract was a sharp attack on the just-war moral license for Indian enslavement used since Columbus' time.

In 1522, he realized that the Portuguese, with Papal blessings, had used Europe's defensive war against Islam to cloak trade in innocent blacks captured on the African Guinea coast. It is unfortunate to see Las Casas' support of African slavery in the early stage. However, he immediately repented of his blindness to the reality of Africa. As compared to his early view on black slaves, Las Casas' later attitude changed radically, and he denounced the African slave trade by the Portuguese. Around 1547, he, as the bishop of Chiapa, stopped in Lisbon on the way back from the Indies. Here he received certain information about the inhuman situation to which the Africans as slaves are subject. Given this fact, it is a specious argument to accuse Las Casas of starting the black African slave trade.[20]

Extended to Mexico and South America, the system of *encomienda* was undertaken in return for the use of native labor. The Crown instructed *encomenderos* to take adequate care of the Indians and instruct them in civilized behavior. However, this system soon degenerated into virtual slavery. In 1515 no more than ten thousand Indians were left alive. Twenty-five years later, the entire nation had disappeared from the earth. None of the Indians had ever converted to what Columbus called "our Holy Faith," but experienced genocide.

Its ideological justification was Christianization. Civilization gave birth to barbarism in the name of conversion and gold. Economic

19. Ibid., 289–97.
20. Ibid., 159. Gutierrez, *Las Casas,* 325.

development of the colonizing country and underdevelopment of the colonized country are inseparable as the two sides of holy mission and colonialism.[21] The Indian on the *encomienda* was more poorly treated than the slave, largely because of the insecure social situation of the *encomendero*. The expansion of the sixteenth century is not only a geographical expansion, but an economic expansion that increased the first industrial revolution. In the sixteenth century (1450–1640) there came to be a European capitalist world economy in vast but weak form drawing upon colonial exploitation.[22] In the new laws (1542–43) Las Casas introduces radical change into the regime of the *encomienda* through favoring the freedom of the Indians. An article declares that the *encomienda* is incapable of being handed on as an inheritance. According to Las Casas, the Spanish Crown had the responsibility of protecting native laws and customs that were just. The Crown should have helped them overcome the defects and injustice in the indigenous system of governing.[23]

Evangelization and the Humanity of the Indians

Spain brought together the sword and the cross in its economic search for gold and silver. Moving from the Caribbean areas to New Spain (Mexico) and later the Peruvian region, the Spanish encountered the societies of the Aztecs and the Incas. The Incas of the Peruvian area were at the time united as a theocratic empire with strong economic, political, and religious foundations. A devastating consequence of this encounter was social disintegration and deculturation in which many indigenous people died as a result of malnutrition, dietary changes, new illness, armed conflict, and enforced labor.[24]

For Las Casas, evangelization must include respect for the humanity of the Indians. In light of the free gift of God's grace in Jesus Christ, Las Casas contends that God's chosen should be called from every race, every tribe, and every language. No race in the entire globe should be left untouched by the divine grace. This is true of Indian nations. The Indians as human beings received their mind from the will of God. God

21. Frank, *Capitalism and Underdevelopment*, 9.

22. Wallerstein, *Modern World System*, 102, 68.

23. Traboulay, *Columbus and Las Casas*, 168.

24. Bevans and Schroeder, *Constants in Context*, 175.

gave them the conditions of the places to live in.[25] Las Casas wrote that the natives were very clean in their persons, having intelligent minds and that they were docile and open to receive Christian teaching of faith. They are endowed with virtuous customs and behave in a godly fashion. When they begin to hear the message of the gospel, they are eager to know more and participate in the sacraments of the church.[26]

Among Indians there exist extraordinary kingdoms and large groups of human beings living in accordance with a political and a social order. Their republics are properly established, and work according to a fine body of law. There are religions and institutions. Indians cultivate friendship by living in life-giving ways and managing their affairs with goodness and equity, in peace as well as war. They manage the government according to laws, often surpassing the English, the French, and some groups in Spain. "Their society is the equal of many nations in the world renowned for being politically astute."[27] Equal to the Greeks and Romans, the Indians outdo in many maintaining good customs. Although there some certain corrupt customs in the Indians, these are to be cured with human effort or better with the preaching of the gospel.[28]

The Indians are endowed by force of nature and then by force of personal achievement and experience with what is known as the three self rule: 1) personal knowledge by which to rule oneself, 2) domestic knowledge by which one knows how to rule a household, and 3) political knowledge by which to set up and rule a city.[29] So the Indians are God's chosen, and elected to the faith of Christ, invited into the Christian way of life. All natures flow from the goodness of God, so every creature has a capacity to want goodness based on the imprint of the creator upon it.

With respect for the humanity, cultural achievements, and civilization of Indians, Las Casas argues for true evangelization to be undertaken in such a way that divine providence leads the human to fulfill its natural purpose in a gentle, coaxing, and gracious way. This leads to a living faith under the universal command of Jesus Christ (Matt 28:19–20). Paul in his letter to the Romans (10:17)—"faith comes from

25. Parish, *Bartolomé de Las Casas*, 63.

26. Las Casas, *Devastation of the Indies*, 29.

27. Parish, *Bartolomé de Las Casas*, 65.

28. Ibid., 66.

29. Ibid., 65.

hearing, hearing from the word of Christ"—points to the Christian way of teaching people in a gentle, coaxing, and gracious way.[30]

What is interesting in Las Casas' view of mission is how it is framed in Trinitarian perspective. Christ, the Son of God, is the Wisdom of his Father, is true God, one God with his Father and Holy Spirit. The activity of the Son is connected with that of the Father and the Spirit. The actions of the Trinity reach outward together. Drawing people to a living faith must be implemented by what Christ himself fashioned and prescribed for his apostles: meekness and humbleness of heart (Matt 11:29–30). In the teaching of Jesus, the kingdom of God is at the center: Christ himself was the kingdom of God (Matt 12:28), the bringer of the kingdom. The kingdom of heaven was what Christ commanded the apostles to announce (5:20). The kingdom of heaven was the gospel (Matt 13:52).[31]

Evangelization as Announcement of the Gospel of Peace

Las Casas emphasizes the gospel of peace by relating missionaries as the lovers of peace and messengers of peace. "How beautiful upon the mountains are the feet of him who brings the good tidings of peace" (Isa 52:7; Col 1:20). The apostles were poor, humble, and kind, and so they were not after riches, not even asking for a meal if people were not willing to provide it.[32] The norm and fashion Jesus Christ taught and established has little to do with power to punish the unwilling by using any force, pressure or harshness, or inflicting earthly punishment on those who refuse the faith.[33] The Spirit of Christ is a gentle Spirit (Luke 9:55–56; Isa 61:1). The Spirit has anointed Jesus to bring good tidings, to announce the good news of peace to the afflicted, to bind up the broken hearted, to proclaim liberty to the captives, sight to the blind, and a year of the Lord's favor.

Christ wanted the disciples to possess this Spirit—"He will not break the half-broken reed, nor snuff out the dimly burning wick" (Isa 42:3)—to be good disciples in likeness and imitation of Jesus Christ.[34] A triple duty the Lord laid on the apostles, when they were sent to preach

30. Ibid., 68.
31. Ibid., 71–72.
32. Ibid., 75.
33. Ibid., 77–78.
34. Ibid., 79.

to the world: 1) to preach the faith; 2) to nourish believers with sacraments; and 3) to teach believers nourished by sacraments to keep the commandments of God and live a good life.[35] The apostles were given the model of humanity to imitate. "They drew people to the truth of salvation by patience, by humility, by faith, by justice. And by a gentle exposure of the truth. And by a gentle persuasion. And by a blameless life . . . Using no force, causing no harm, but giving gifts gratis."[36] Christ wanted to teach humility and compassion; which filled Christ and overflowed from him. The way of humility, peace, and rejection of worldliness draws people to moral life better than force of arms.[37]

Christ the Evangelizer championed a peaceful proclamation in humility, poverty, persuasion, and dialogue. Divine providence must have been granted in the nations of the Indians, naturally endowing them with a capacity for doctrine and grace and graciously furnishing them with the time of their calling and conversion. God's salvific assistance is denied to no one. Las Casas implies that there is a possibility of the salvation of the Indians despite their spiritual status as heathen. Experiencing the cruelties and injustices committed under the hands of greedy Christians, God has not forgotten the Indians. The number of heathen saved may be greater than that of the faithful. The final judgment described in Matt 25:31–46 is central in the theology of Las Casas in the acknowledgment of the dignified place of the religious outsiders.[38]

In light of the ideal missionary, Las Casas draws the guidelines of how to preach the gospel in accordance with the mind and mandate of Christ: 1) the preachers who announce the gospel to non-Christians want no power over them as a result of the preaching, not by using the language of seduction nor deceit; 2) the preachers do not look after wealth; 3) the preachers should address with modesty and respect, creating a climate of kindness, calm, and graciousness; 4) the preachers present the faith in the love called charity; and 5) the preachers must

35. Ibid., 82.

36. Ibid., 93.

37. Ibid., 96.

38. Gutiérrez, *Las Casas*, 259, 271. In this regard Gutiérrez quotes the passage from Pope John Paul II: "Rigorous respect for religious freedom and for its corresponding right is the principle and foundation of peaceful coexistence. . . . finally, I exhort the heads of nations and leaders of the international community always to demonstrate the *greatest respect for the religious conscience of every human being*, and for the valuable contribution of religion to the progress of civilization and the development of peoples."

witness to the gospel respectfully, carefully, honestly, and blamelessly. This is prescribed for the preaching of Christ's gospel as a living example. This is a virtuous life that harms no one, that is a life blameless from any quarter.[39]

In this principle of evangelization, Las Casas denounces wars for conversion as mindless and unjust. People who are not evangelized can yet be invited to faith and salvation "not by war but by peace, by good will, kindness, generosity, credibility, by charity from the heart."[40] Throughout his life, Las Casas witnessed to the rights of the Indian people and advocated non-violent evangelization.[41] The poor and the other are preferred by God. The Indies are the place of a painful encounter with a scourged Christ who experienced untimely, innocent, and unjust death.[42]

In addition to the work of Bartolomé de Las Casas, other early voices of protest against the injustices of colonial power recur in the writings of the theology of liberation.[43] The witness of Las Casas serves as a symbol of the spirit of liberation theology early in the colonial period. We read the meaning of Las Casas' whole life in his last Will and Testament written a few years before his death (July 18, 1566): "I testify that it was God in his goodness and mercy who chose me as his minister . . . on behalf of all those people out in what God calls the Indies. . . . For almost fifty years I have done this work, back and forth between the Indies and Castile . . . . All that the Spaniards perpetrated against those [Indian] peoples . . . was in violation of the holy and spotless law of Jesus Christ . . . such devastation, such genocide of populations, have been sins, monumental injustice!"[44]

Mission and Liberating Evangelization

Life and culture did not begin in Latin America when Columbus discovered America 1492. There were already many long-established cultures in the Andes and along the Amazon before so-called Western civilization

39. Ibid., 103–9.

40. Ibid., 163.

41. Dussel, *History and Theology of Liberation*, 84.

42. Gutiérrez, *Las Casas*, 95.

43. Eagleson and Scharper, *Puebla and Beyond*, 124, 128.

44. Las Casas, *Indian Freedom*, 9.

first appeared. Later the Spaniards and Portuguese had to decimate an indigenous population in order to gain gold and possession of the land. The sixteenth-century Spanish conquistadores were merely conquerors. To them, the Amerindians were treated as subhuman, to be used for labor and killed if recalcitrant.

Latin American liberation theology lives in a vital connection to the history in which it developed. Its rise has been accompanied by a surge of interest in the colonial history of Latin America. One contribution of liberation theology is a new method of understanding and implementing Christian faith in the sense of orthopraxis. Segundo proposed the hermeneutic circle as a way of developing the method of liberation theology. Two preconditions are claimed for such a circle: 1) profound and enriching questions and suspicions about our real situation (a critical mythological analysis of society); 2) a new interpretation of Scripture (a critical biblical exegesis).

In these two preconditions, four decisive factors are important in understanding the hermeneutic circle. First, our way of experiencing reality leads to ideological suspicion. Second, an ideological suspicion is applied to the whole ideological superstructure in general and to theology in particular. Third, a new way of experiencing theological reality leads to exegetical suspicion in the prevailing interpretation of the Scripture. Fourth, a new hermeneutic of liberation is a way of interpreting the fountainhead of our faith in terms of the social, political element.[45]

A hermeneutic of liberation is deepened by linking social-analytical mediation to hermeneutic-theological mediation for the sake of clarification of the dialectic between theory and praxis. Such a hermeneutic attempts to see the oppression/liberation process in the light of faith or the word of God. The whole of Scripture is examined from the viewpoint of the oppressed, which is central in a hermeneutic of liberation. The hermeneutic of liberation stresses liberation as the most relevant to the poor in their situation of oppression, and relate it to the theological themes of conversion, grace, and resurrection. A theological exegesis of the word of God is undertaken "in fidelity" or "in openness to God's ever new and always surprising revelation."[46] A hermeneutic circle is emphasized in the mutual relationship between the word of God and the poor.

45. Segundo, *Liberation of Theology*, 9.
46. Boff, *Introducing Liberation Theology*, 33.

The following five elements are important in the method and interpretation of liberation theology: 1) a living encounter with social-political reality in Latin America; 2) engagement in and commitment to the project of working for liberation; 3) social-critical analysis of political, economic, and ideological spheres as well as the social context of the biblical narrative; 4) theological-hermeneutical reflection on the word of God in this perspective and reformulation; and 5) liberative hermeneutics in activation of the transforming energy of biblical texts toward conversion and revolution in its messianic and eschatological character.[47]

This critical method and hermeneutic of liberation theology and praxis undergirds active participation in liberating humankind from what dehumanizes and prevents it from living in accordance with the will of God. "The salvation of Christ is a radical liberation from all misery, all despoliation, all alienation."[48] Liberation theology is critical reflection on praxis in the light of the Word of God among the suffering innocent. Poverty is given a hermeneutical priority. Material poverty which generates a subhuman condition must be opposed as evil. Spiritual poverty "in the sense of a readiness to do God's will"[49] leads to non-attachment to the goods of the world. In a biblical understanding of poverty, material poverty is seen as "a subhuman situation," that is "a scandalous condition inimical to human dignity and therefore to the will of God."[50] There is a biblical denouncement of the rich's exploitation of the poor.

On the other hand, Scripture understands poverty as spiritual childhood synonymous with faith and trust in God. The poor are blessed because the coming of the kingdom of God will put an end to their material poverty by creating a world of fellowship and companionship.[51] This is the third meaning of poverty as a commitment to "solidarity with the poor, along with protest against the conditions under which they suffer."[52]

---

47. This is my modification of Nessan's proposal. See Nessan, *Orthopraxis or Heresy*, 64.

48. Gutiérrez, *Theology of Liberation*, 104.

49. Ibid., xxv.

50. Ibid., 164, 165.

51. Ibid., 171.

52. Ibid., xvx; 171–73.

Christian poverty is an expression of love, solidarity with the poor, and a protest against poverty in light of Christ' kenosis (Phil 2:6–11);[53] it has nothing to do with the romanticization of material poverty. Spiritual poverty opens up humankind and history to the future promised by God. In this way the church can fulfill its prophetic function of denouncing every human injustice and preach the word of genuine fellowship. This witness is a sign of the authenticity of the church's mission.[54] What makes us understand God's preferential option for the poor is gratuitous love, which is the key to authentic divine justice. "To know God is to do justice."[55] God loves the poor because they are poor, not because they are good.

In this light, liberation theology seeks to interpret history from the point of view of the poor and the victims of history as engaged in the current structure of political oppression (political colonialism and economic injustice). Given the colonial history of mission and Western capital expansion, the theology of liberation interprets the history of Latin America as one of dependency. The sixteenth and seventeenth centuries were marked by a continuation of the evangelization process of the Indians by the church and by the development of an extensive organizational system.

The notion that the church must adopt a preferential option for the poor and the emergence of the base communities are central in the church's witness to social justice and liberation. A mission serving evangelization must convert to a preferential option for the poor which mean, opting for the kingdom of God Jesus proclaimed. Jesus is the example of this poverty associated with the message of the kingdom of God. Jesus Christ is precisely God who became poor. Service to the poor is a central message in Jesus' teaching about the coming kingdom of God. The poor evangelize the church, challenging and summoning it to conversion and repentance. Finally, evangelical poverty summons Christians to combine the trust in God with praxis by implementing the giving and sharing of material and spiritual gifts.[56]

In contrast to the dominant forces of colonial Christendom, the figure of Bartolomé de Las Casas stands in sharp contrast as the first

53. Ibid., 172.
54. Ibid., 173.
55. Ibid., 110.
56. Brown, *Gustavo Gutiérrez*, 59.

liberation theologian. Las Casas was the most well-known name of those who, from the point of view of the gospel and of the poor, denounced the conquest and the colonization of the Indians. Las Casas protested against the use of force as a means of provoking conversion and demanded that justice be included in the policy of the church toward the Indians. Having direct experience of the terrible poverty and decimation of Amerindians, Las Casas said, "God has the freshest and keenest memory of the least and most forgotten."[57]

In 1992, the five-hundred-year anniversary of the arrival of Christopher Columbus in the Americas gave occasion for addressing the decimation of the native peoples by the European conquest. Theologians were able to offer analysis of the failure of the church to defend the rights of the indigenous peoples from the perspective of liberation. Now mission becomes denunciation of institutionalized injustice, the announcement of God's justice centered around the gospel of the kingdom of God which holds a preferential option for those at the margins.

Gustavo Gutiérrez authored a major work on Las Casas as a significant contribution to the historical memory of this event regarding mission, colonialism, and economic injustice.[58] In the investigation of the forgotten legacy of Las Casas, Gutiérrez is convinced that there was a close link in Las Casas' thought regarding salvation and social justice. The Spaniards exploited the Amerindians, to the extent that their salvation was jeopardized. The Spaniards felt justified in murdering Amerindians because they regarded them as infidels. However, Las Casas saw in the Indians a fully human other who differed from Western culture. His respect of people of another culture and religion separates evangelization from a way of subjugating the Indian nations. A genuine understanding of the gospel includes respecting the human condition of others as bearers of the presence of God. This is foundational for the inculturation of faith. The only way to evangelization lies in persuasion and dialogue.[59]

Las Casas saw in the Indian the poor one of the gospel, Christ himself; this aspect is at the heart of Las Casas' spirituality and theology. The poor occupy a central place in the biblical narrative of the gospel. The right to life and freedom, the right to be different, and the perspective

57. Gutiérrez, *Theology of Liberation*, xxvii.

58. Gutiérrez, *Las Casas*.

59. Ibid., 456.

of the poor are inextricably connected in the experience of God in Jesus Christ, which promotes the liberation of the Indian. According to the guidelines of the Medellin Conference in our times Gutiérrez affirms the defense of the rights of the poor and oppressed.

Theology must be judged by its fruits. Theology which leads to murder, enslavement, and sanction of structures of injustice invalidates itself in its service and witness to the gospel. Las Casas' theological method and interpretation began with the specific and concrete situation of exploited Amerindians as composed to the abstract principles and logics of Sepúlveda. Las Casas practiced theology as a participant in the struggle between conquistadores and the Amerindians rather than as an outside spectator. Las Casas saw his time as the time of vocation, the time when God decided to open the treasures of the divine mercy to Indian nations while greed and arrogance distorted such time of divine mercy into a time of tribulation, affliction, and dissipation. Las Casas' life and work is thus a witness to the God who is rich in mercy (Eph 2:4).[60]

The various Indian nations and cultures in the sixteenth century have become visible in the intricate process of later centuries, characterized by the situation of injustice and dispossession with the arrival of new races and cultures. In this situation, the poor of today find themselves. A project of a new evangelization undertaken by Medellin and John Paul II must be heralded by the poor: the members of the races, cultures, and social classes on the margins in the society. The foundation for a new evangelization is based on the impulse for a preferential option for the poor.[61]

In the midst of the Amerindian predicament and suffering, Las Casas saw the face of Jesus Christ: "In the Indies I left behind Jesus Christ, our God, suffering affliction, scourging, and crucifixion, not once but a million times over." According to Las Casas, "in and through the 'scouraged Christ of the Indies,' Jesus is denouncing exploitation, denying the Christianity of the exploiters, and calling people to understand and heed his gospel message."[62] A new evangelization is "to be carried on in solidarity with all, beginning with the poorest and least important in our

---

60. Ibid., 457.

61. Ibid., 458.

62. Brown, *Gustavo Gutiérrez*, 3; see further Gutiérrez, *Las Casas*, 45–66.

midst."[63] The signs of the times call for interpretation and commitment to others that will make us friends of Jesus Christ. The Indians mourned will be the ones who will receive the tender consolation by the Lord. "The Lord God will wipe away the tears from all faces; the reproach of his people he will remove from the whole earth" (Isa 25:8).

Mission, Colonialism, and Beyond

Mission in the colonial period was driven by economic motives and the identification of mission and gold. Noblemen and soldiers as well as colonizers represented the interests of the Crown and of the *Patronato* in the New World. The church was accountable for the work of evangelization and acculturation of the indigenous peoples. The *Patronato* system held that the Spanish State and government officials had charge of the church and its mission.

The slave trade in the time of conquest marks a sordid chapter in the development of Western Christendom. Along with the demand of the Muslim Ottomanns for slaves, Spain and Portugal looked around the Mediterranean and North African worlds for the sake of labor on sugar cane plantations. In the middle of the fifteenth century, sub-Saharan African people were enslaved by Spaniards and then by the Portuguese. This African slave trade under Portuguese control after 1493 began to replace the indigenous peoples of the Caribbean and the Americas.[64]

Mercantilism helped create trade patterns such as the triangular trade in the North Atlantic, in which raw materials were imported to the mother country and then processed and redistributed to other colonies: rum (and goods) to Africa / slaves to the Americas/ sugar to New England. Triangular trade, or triangle trade, is a historical term indicating trade among three ports or regions. Triangular trade thus provided a mechanism for rectifying trade imbalances. Christian mission was spread through such triangular trade.[65]

In this setting, Christian mission was undertaken in terms of a profitable slaving mission. Christian missionary propaganda was spread through the forces of imperial expansion. During the stage of the 1870s and 1880s missionaries from overseas accompanied colonial

---

63. Gutiérrez, *Theology of Liberation*, xlvi.

64. Bevans and Schroeder, *Constants in Context*, 172.

65. Frank, *Dependent Accumulation and Underdevelopment*, 14–17.

ships. The policy of Europe regarding colonies did nothing for their prosperity; rather than working toward sustainable colonies, the European policy chased after gold and silver mines, which turned out to be a chimerical project.[66]

By the late eighteenth century, Dutch and English colonies stretched from India to South Africa, to Indonesia and across North America. The triangular trade gave a triple stimulus to British industry; the maintenance of the slaves and their owners on the plantations supplied another market for British industry. The accumulation of capital in this process of triangular trade (African slaves, Caribbean sugar and New England rum) finally financed the Industrial Revolution.[67] Mission work in the colonial period appealed to the white man's consciousness of burden and responsibility of taking the civilization to the rest of the world. There were underlying economic motives in Christian mission. Missionaries became agents of the Western imperialistic enterprise. Christianity, commerce, and civilization became intertwined.[68]

Running counter to imperial mission, we read in the story of Las Casas that evangelization in a genuine sense comes from a prophetic awareness of the signs of the times and reading of the gospel in terms of denouncing the reality of political and economic injustice. A liberating evangelization becomes possible and meaningful when the church follows in conformity to the life and mission of Jesus Christ in his preferential option for those on the margins. In this light, Las Casas remains a prophetic voice for God's mission, which entails emancipation and solidarity in the context of World Christianity.

66. Smith, *Wealth of Nations*, 747.
67. Williams, *Capitalism and Slavery*, 51–52.
68. Bevans and Schroeder, *Constants in Context*, 207.

2

Matteo Ricci

Mission as Inculturation

Unlike Las Casas' mission of prophetic denouncement of the actions of Western Christendom in the New World, Matteo Ricci's mission in China opens a new chapter of inculturation and interreligious dialogue. From the beginning, the Jesuit missionaries came to Asia with appreciation of and respect for non-Western cultures and religions. The legacy of Ricci's mission is still appreciated and valued in China today. The study of Ricci's mission and Confucianism has practical relevance and value for today's discussion of God's mission in a post-Western Christian era.

In current studies of mission in ecumenical and global contexts, a paradigm shift toward transformative mission emphasizes inculturation as an indispensable issue. This involves the recognition of the other while at the same time transforming one's own position. A prophetic dialogue with other faith communities becomes effective in a hermeneutical-anthropological endeavor of translating and interpreting the biblical narrative in the context of World Christianity. This endeavor engages anthropological study of culture in a non-ethnocentric manner. Thus inculturation becomes a central locus in characterizing missional perspective on the prophetic dialogue. Matteo Ricci's mission in sixteenth century China deserves attention in regard to undertaking this task today. This chapter presents a historical and theological analysis of Ricci's interaction with the Confucian religious beliefs and ethics. It also includes a critical evaluation of Ricci's attitude toward Buddhism and Daoism.

Our interpretive methodology lies in critically examining Ricci's engagement as expounded in his masterpiece, *The True Meaning of the Lord of Heaven*. It is essential to explore his hermeneutical strategy of transliterating and accommodating the Chinese indigenous terms *Shang-di* and *Tian* into the Western name of God. Based on this historical, interpretive approach, this chapter explores Zhu Xi's implications for Christian-Confucian dialogue while reviewing the limitations of Ricci's critique of Zhu Xi. Finally we will discuss the repercussions of Ricci's acceptance of ancestral rites in the subsequent historical development of the church in China and Korea and appreciate his legacy in the study of mission as interreligious dialogue.

Background of Ricci and External Accommodation

Matteo Ricci, an Italian Jesuit missionary, is a central figure in discussion of gospel and culture for the study of mission.[1] Ricci arrived in China in 1583 and remained there until his death in 1610. Europe had experienced the High Renaissance. The Counter-Reformation had been initiated and energized by the Society of Jesus, established in 1534 by the Spaniard, Ignatius of Loyola. It was given formal recognition by Pope Paul III in 1540. It proclaimed that "We are to be obliged by a special vow to carry out . . . the progress of souls and the propagation of the faith" and also "to go . . . to whatsoever provinces they [the popes] may choose to send us—whether they are pleased to send us among the Turks or any other infidels, even those who live in the region called the Indies . . ."[2] The Society of Jesus was eager to spread Roman Catholicism to both India and China. Aided by Portuguese travelers and traders who were already in Japan in 1543, Francis Xavier (1506–1552), the father of the Jesuit Oriental mission, preached in India and Japan without really even knowing the native languages.

Matteo Ricci was born in the hill town of Macerata, Italy, on 16 October, 1552. His father sent him to Rome to study law at the age of seventeen. However, feeling called to a religious vocation, Ricci entered the Order of the Feast of the Assumption and became a novice in the

1. Bosch, *Transforming Mission*, 447–57.
2. Cited in Spence, *Memory Palace*, 99.

Jesuit order in Rome on August 15, 1571. Ricci was trained in the institutional influence of the Jesuit curricula and pedagogical directive of the late sixteenth century, especially those of *Collegio Romano* (a Roman Jesuit's school), under Renaissance humanism and Jesuit Thomism.

As already discussed, Thomism was introduced to Italy by Jesuits who studied at the University of Salamanca, in Spain. Interest in Aristotle and Aquinas continued during the Renaissance in Italy. Scholars such as Francesco de Vitoria (1485/6–1546) paved the way for Spanish Thomism, proposing a new style of understanding Aquinas's work, *Summa theologiae*. His work on natural law in universal sense was related to indigenous people in Latin America. The Salamanca school of thought also influenced Las Casas.

Ricci had studied at the Jesuit College in Rome and was probably influenced by Suarez. His book the *De Arte Rhetorica* was required reading for Jesuit students in the 1570s.[3] Christopher Clavius was an influential figure for Ricci's studies of sciences at the college through his analysis of and reworking of Euclid's *Elements of Geometry*. Ricci remained in affectionate relationship with Clavius.[4] Emphasizing mathematical skills, the Jesuits stood at the frontiers of modern knowledge and had inherited the legacy of late Renaissance Italian humanism.[5] Ricci was happy to use Erasmus in the *Friendship* who had been severely criticized by Ignatius of Loyola.[6] The late sixteenth-century Jesuit Thomism became foundational for Ricci's missionary approach to accommodation of local "pagan" cultures.

After extensive training in theology, humanities, and science, he became interested in the foreign mission of the Society. Ricci was given the opportunity to spend a five-year apprenticeship in India and Macao. Ricci arrived in Goa on September 13, 1578, and worked in India for four years. He entered China in 1583, continuing his mission work. In 1595 he took up residence in Nanchang, the eastern province of Jiangxi and became fluent in the Chinese language.[7]

Alessandro Valignano, Xavier's successor, had an immense effect on Matteo Ricci. Valignano was born in 1539 in the town of Chieti in the

3. Ibid., 5.
4. Ibid., 142–44.
5. Ibid., 145.
6. Ibid., 150.
7. Ibid., 3.

southern Italian Abruzzi. By 1566 he had entered the Jesuit order and become a student in the Roman College where he studied mathematics, physics, philosophy, and theology under Clavius. By 1571 he was appointed master of novices and administered first-year examinations to the young Matteo Ricci. Valignano's mission, which had been infused with spiritual ardor,[8] became successful in breaking free from the conquistador mission system. His model of mission was based on *il modo soave* (the sweet or gentle way), which later became the guideline for Jesuit missionaries' profound study of language, culture, and politics in India, Japan, and China. This intercultural study became instrumental in defending their missions against the *conquistador* and *tabula rasa* (blank slate) mentalities of the time.[9]

Ricci arrived in the southern Chinese town of Zhoaquing in 1583. In 1591, with the help of Chinese friends, he began to translate the four classical books of Confucianism (*The Confucian Analects, The Book of Mencius, The Great Learning,* and *The Doctrine of the Mean*) into Latin and transliterated the Chinese name Kong Fuzi as Confucius.[10] Ricci arrived in the capital of China in 1601. He served as a clock repairman and entered the emperor's palace at least four times each year. Placing himself in the role of a barbarian, Li Ma-tou (the Chinese name for Matteo Ricci) presented himself very humbly to the imperial court.

Ricci is referred to by some Chinese historians as "the wise man from the West." Ricci's scientific knowledge of astronomy, mathematics, and geometry gave him authority as well as opportunity for his evangelism. With integrity, humility, and respect, his missionary goal was to link Confucian culture with Roman Catholicism. He developed an intensive knowledge of Chinese culture and recognized its positive value for Christianity.

Ricci's First Step toward External Accommodation

As we have already said, Ricci arrived in the southern Chinese town of Zhaoqing in 1583 and began to draw a map of the world, inserting the names of the countries in Chinese phonetic equivalents. Between 1584 and 1602 he worked on improving it into a fuller and more ac-

8. Ibid., 40.

9. Bevans and Schroeder, *Constants in Context,* 186. See further Ricci, *True Meaning of the Lord of Heaven,* 4–5.

10. Cronin, *Wise Man,* 103, 107.

curate version. According to his observation, everyone in China held to the religion of the Lord of Heaven, and no superstitions were allowed. The highest class was occupied with religion, the people of the second rank were involved in judging temporal affairs, and the lowest rank was devoted to arms. They all believed in the five relationships (father-son, ruler-subject, husband-wife, elder-younger siblings, and friends) and studied astronomy and philosophy.

Ricci believed that dressing in the robes of a Buddhist monk would be deemed as holy. He saw a parallel between Christianity and Buddhism: the priestly robes, the chanting in their service, the espousal of celibacy and poverty, the temples, statues, and even some of the painted images. Ricci changed his soutanes into the cloak of Buddhist bonze and shaved off his hair and beard. In a letter to his friend Fuligatti (November 24, 1585) he wrote, "Would that you could see me as I am now: I have become a Chinaman. In our clothing, in our looks, in our manners and in everything external we have made ourselves Chinese."[11] This letter shows Ricci's first step toward external accommodation. Ricci's companion, Michele Ruggieri, also wrote in a letter to his friend (February 17, 1583) "so, before long, we became Chinese to win China for Christ."[12]

Based on the experience of the Jesuit missionaries in Japan, they had hoped to be accepted as honored Buddhist clergy in China with due social respect. Several years later, however, Ricci and his fellows came to realize that in China, unlike Japan, Buddhist clergy belonged to a low social class. Around this time Ricci was surprised to find pockets of Christians in Nanjing and elsewhere in central China. The only trace of Christianity among them seemed to be some knowledge of the Psalter and how to make the sign of the cross. But Ricci failed in his endeavor to ascertain a major link between the early church and China. In his letter to General Acquaviva in July 1605, we read: "for lack of the few *scudi* we need for the journey we have not been able to send anyone to find how many there are and whence they came."[13] The discovery of these Christians as Nestorians was left to Ricci's Jesuit successors.

Local Chinese scholars, who knew that the "Nestorian" Christians grew their hair long, persuaded Ricci to abandon his shaved head according to the style of a Buddhist monk. In the summer of 1595 Ricci

11. Spence, *Memory Palace*, 114.

12. Chung, *Syncretism*, 59.

13. Spence, *Memory Palace*, 120.

made a final break with Buddhist dress, replacing it with the style of dress worn by the Confucian literati. He became opposed to Buddhist robes, and also to the Buddhists themselves. Ricci acknowledged that there were three religions of major significance in China: Confucianism, Buddhism, and Daoism. In his study of the *Analects*, Ricci became convinced that Confucius had taught about a reverence for Heaven that had little to do with idolatry. In light of reverencing Heaven, Confucius also put an emphasis on human ethical morality, which was inherently good. Confucian teaching also instructed that reason alone was not enough for people to know the nature of God or the reality of life after death.[14]

Ricci's Mission and Multireligious Context in the Ming Dynasty

It was the Ming dynasty (1368–1644), and these three religions co-existed, fusing with each other. This led to the growth of religious syncretism. As Ricci states, "[t]he commonest opinion held here among those who consider themselves the most wise is to say that all three of these sects come together as one, and that you can hold them all at once."[15]

The term Neo-Confucianism is a Western coinage, referring to the later development of Confucianism as metaphysical thought (literally the learning of Principle). One of the most important representatives of early Neo-Confucianism was Zhu Xi (1130–1200). The basic Neo-Confucian quest was oriented toward self-transcendence in the achievement of sagehood. Finding the world of metaphysics in the Four Books and the *Book of Changes*, Neo-Confucianists made an effort to transform Confucian doctrines by integrating an evolutionary cosmology, humanistic ethics, and a rationalistic epistemology into the Confucian metaphysics.

This development of Neo-Confucianism was stimulated and energized by Buddhism and Daoism.[16] Nevertheless, Neo-Confucianism did not succumb to the worldview of Buddhism or Daoism. Rather it articulated the value of family and communal ethics, and it stressed public life in this world, in contradiction to the Buddhist doctrine of impermanence or the Daoist lifestyle of non-action.[17] During Ricci's

14. Cronin, *Wise Man,* 56.

15. Ibid.

16. Chang, *Development of Neo-Confucian Thought,* 43.

17. Yao, *Introduction to Confucianism,* 96–97. See further Ching, *Chinese Religions,* 157–58.

missional activity, Neo-Confucianism prevailed in the Ming Dynasty of China. Having a good command of the Chinese language, Ricci knew a great deal about Chinese customs and etiquette. Ricci observed that the Chinese greatly appreciated the principle of filial piety. They faithfully followed natural law and did not simply worship idols. In Ricci's observation, "Chinese books on morals are full of instructions relative to the respect that children should pay to parents and elders. Certainly if we look to an external display of filial piety, there are no people in the whole world who can compare with the Chinese."[18]

In China, worship of Heaven and Nature was also moral, and hence reasonable. Immersed into Chinese culture and language, Ricci began to regard Confucianism as natural law instead of religion. It is certain that the literati recognized one supreme deity, but they did not erect special places or temples for worship. There were no public or private prayers or hymns in honor of a supreme deity.[19] As a Catholic, Ricci did not sidestep idolatry but weighed in on the side of opposing idolatry and advocating morality. In contrast to his appreciation of Confucianism, he strongly countered the elements of idolatry that he observed in Buddhism and Daoism.[20]

Ricci's Intercultural Dialogue with Confucian Philosophy

Ricci's strategy of intercultural dialogue becomes clear when engaging with Confucian moral teaching in light of the Catholic theology of virtue. In connecting Christianity with Confucianism, Ricci's process of interpretation can be summed up in the following way: He utilizes Catholic doctrines as a complement to Confucianism. In some respects, he elevates the Catholic doctrines over and against Confucian teaching by transcending and transforming the Confucian one. But he does not hesitate to undertake some revisions of the Catholic teaching in seeking concordance with Confucian instruction. His dialogical principle is based on a critical complement to Confucian instruction and the self-renewal of Catholic teaching in harmonious co-existence with Confucian philosophy so that mutual respect and harmonious life are underscored.

18. Ricci, *China in Sixteenth Century*, 72.

19. Ibid., 95.

20. Ibid., 99–105.

During the years of 1601–1610, Ricci witnessed the conversion of Xu Guangqi (Paul) (1562–1633) who held the office of Grand Secretary of the government, Li Zhizao (Leo) (1565–1630), Ricci's collaborator in several publications on religion and science, and Yang Tingyun (Michael) (1557–1627). These three men were called the three pillars of the early church in China. In November 1594, after he completed his translation of the Four Books, Ricci continued to study the Six Classics and in 1596 Ricci completed his first draft of *The True Meaning of the Lord of Heaven*.

This book is Ricci's masterpiece and is composed of a dialogue between Matteo Ricci, his friends, and Chinese scholars. The edition of *The True Meaning of The Lord of Heaven* produced during the Ming dynasty often used the titles God (*Shang-di*) and Heaven (*Tian*) for the Lord of Heaven. However, in 1704 Pope Clement XI banned the use of the terms *Tian* (Heaven) or *Shang-di* (Sovereign on High) to designate God. Hence, in the present English edition "the Lord of Heaven" (*Tian-ju*) is used simply to replace the Confucian traditional terms.[21]

In the introduction to *The True Meaning of The Lord of Heaven*, Ricci grounds the Confucian principles of the Five Human Relationships (between king and minister, father and son, husband and wife, among brothers, and among friends) and the three Bonds (between king and minister, father and son, husband and wife) in terms of the Supremely Honored One who is not only worshiped but also conceptualized as the first Father and Creator of all.[22]

As humanity is created with the five basic virtues (humaneness, righteousness, propriety, wisdom, and trustworthiness), Ricci argues that his teaching of the universal Lord of Heaven refers to the Lord of Heaven as the final and active cause, as well as the cause of our moral and virtuous life. Ricci's hermeneutical strategy is to discover the early theism of ancient Chinese writings in the personal concept of *Shang-di* or Lord on High.[23]

To explicate the Lord of Heaven as the most universal and the most supreme cause, Ricci introduces the famous story of a Western Catholic sage, St. Augustine. St. Augustine met a child on the beach making a

21. Ricci, *True Meaning of the Lord of Heaven*, 20. See translators' Introduction, 33–35.

22. Ibid., 63.

23. Ibid., 85.

small pool in the ground. The child wanted to use a shell to scoop all the water from the sea to fill the pool. The sage questioned the silly child, but the child illuminated him, saying in response that the truth of the Lord of Heaven is likened to the great ocean, which cannot be drawn with a shell and a small pool cannot contain it.[24]

The Lord of Heaven transcends all categories that refer to the material universe, as conceptualized in the *via negativa* (that is, the apophatic way of speaking about God). The human being, as a small and lowly vessel, cannot contain nor investigate fully or adequately the great truth and mystery of the Lord of Heaven. The Lord is the transcendent, unmoved One, the active cause of all movements, supreme source of all phenomena, and source of goodness in creation. God the Creator is the God of providence who was revealed through the ancient Chinese canonical writings.[25]

The Confucian teaching of the Great Ultimate instructs that human existence becomes the basic principle of all things, including sincerity (i.e., the subject of self-cultivation). The Confucian teaching of the Great Ultimate can be regarded as being close to the Catholic teaching of the Lord of Heaven.[26] Observing that Confucianism refuted the void-ness or nothingness in Buddhism and Daoism, Ricci attempted to avoid any misunderstanding: The Lord of Heaven, the source of all, should not be identified with nothingness in Buddhism or Daoism. Ricci learned that the Confucian term for the Great Ultimate or reverence of the Sovereign on High in ancient Chinese times was grounded on the interplay of yin and yang in the *Book of Changes* (*Yi jing*).

Given the Neo-Confucian connection with the metaphysical-evolutionary cosmology of the *Book of Changes*, Ricci was reluctant to harmonize the Neo-Confucian concept of the Supreme (or Great) Ultimate (*Tai-ji*) with the truth of the Lord of Heaven. The Great Ultimate, which is the first Principle, is found in the appendices to the *Book of Changes*. All things emerge and are differentiated from the Great Ultimate. For instance, Zhou Dunyi (1017–1073), an important representative of Neo-Confucianism, attempted to integrate into his idea of Supreme reality the Taoist concept of non-being and the Buddhist idea of emptiness. He further combined these Daoist-Buddhist elements with his theory of

24. Ibid., 92–93.

25. Ibid., 97.

26. Ibid., 99.

Wu-xing, which says that the universe consists of five elements (metal, wood, water, fire, and earth). In his Neo-Confucian framework, the Great Ultimate becomes ultimate-less or empty. Ultimate-less became the Neo-Confucian term of integrating Daoist non-being and Buddhist emptiness into Neo-Confucian metaphysics. In the statement of the Great Ultimate as the Ultimateless, Ricci argued that Neo-Confucianism was not so very different from the teaching of Buddhism and Daoism.[27]

Cultural-Ethical Entry Point: The Lord of Heaven and the Ethical Self

It is certain that Confucius invoked Heaven in his time of distress. The notion of a deity in a personal sense began to be transformed into the essence of an ethical self in subsequent Confucian development. Ricci's concern was for retrieving Confucius' own idea of a personal deity as visible in the Doctrine of the Mean and several classics. Ricci contends that the Lord of Heaven is the Sovereign on High (*Shang-di*) as mentioned in the ancient Chinese writings. The Sovereign on High in Confucianism and the Lord of Heaven in Catholicism are the same, different only in name in Ricci's view.[28]

Given the commonality in difference of the name of God, Ricci boldly utilizes the ancient term *Shang-di* to claim an identity between the God of Christianity and Confucianism. Ricci's interpretive strategy in *The True Meaning of the Lord of Heaven* is to draw the Confucian teaching of Heaven and ethical self-cultivation close to the Catholic teaching of God and human virtue, while at the same time repudiating the teachings of Buddhism, Daoism, and Neo-Confucianism about nothingness or the ultimateless. This cultural-ethical approach works as a springboard for expounding the Confucian idea of self-cultivation positively from the Catholic perspective.

In the *Analects,* Confucius uses an important term *Tian-ming* (mandate of Heaven) along with reverence and affirms heaven in a personified sense. His successor Mencius argued for the goodness of human nature. Mencius taught that Heaven is present within human nature, identified with the heart-mind. Thus Heaven becomes the source and principle of ethical laws and values in human personal and social life.

27. Ibid., 113.
28. Ibid., 125.

Ricci observed that Confucianism recognized sincerity as the foundation for the rectification of one's name. This teaching of sincerity was embedded with ethical self-cultivation, the regulation of the family, the ordering of the state, and the bringing of peace to the world. Developing the teaching of sincerity with reverence in its own historical and cultural context, representatives of Neo-Confucianism accentuated the teaching that humanity, righteousness, decorum, and wisdom are essential characteristics of human nature, which comes from Heaven (Principle).

In siding with Mencius, Ricci argued that if the essence of human nature and feeling is produced by the Lord of Heaven and if reason is the master of it, then human beings are essentially good.[29] Ricci arranges humanity, righteousness, decorum, and wisdom as subsequent to the capacity to reason. However, reason is not identified with the Principle in Neo-Confucianism. The Absolute (*Li* Principle), more than human reason, is called *xing* (nature) in a human self and *ming* (order, destiny, mandate of Heaven) in Heaven.

Mencius and Zhu Xi in Ricci's Confucianized Christianity

Ricci contends that Augustine understood evil as "a lack of goodness" in the sense of "speaking of a lack of life," thus this teaching is helpful in his aim of harmonization with a Confucian ethic.[30] Since the Lord of Heaven bestowed this innate nature on human beings, one is capable of doing both good and evil. The true merit of virtue, when added to goodness, expresses this. It is salient for Ricci to distinguish between two kinds of goodness, that is, "innate goodness" and "acquired goodness." The former refers to the goodness of human nature while the latter refers to the goodness of virtue.[31] Merit is confined to acquired goodness, which humanity accumulates through its own efforts.

According to Mencius, humanness (equated with humanity) is closely related to righteousness, which is taken up to the level of a cardinal virtue. Humanness and righteousness are essential ingredients of true humanity in that the former is the mind/heart of a human and the latter is its path. Therefore, humanness is rooted in the human mind/heart. Humans are by nature good. Evil comes from the formation of

29. Ibid., 351.
30. Ibid., 353.
31. Ibid., 357.

bad habits. Based on the teaching of the four beginnings (dispositions) in the human heart, Mencius instructs that people are born with a good disposition. When they are cultivated like a shoot, they "would grow up to be a beautiful blossoming tree" which is "full of expressed virtues."[32]

Ricci values Mencius' theory of the four beginnings as it manifests innate goodness, maintaining that the Catholic category of meritorious virtue is granted to a person who does what is right. Subsequently Ricci sees that the Catholic teachings of human nature and meritorious virtue complement the Confucian teaching of superior person and self-cultivation. A human virtue is "the precious adornment of the spirit" or the genuine treasure of the human inner spirit.[33] A person who cultivates virtue becomes more beautiful and sanctified like a blossoming tree. Ricci uses the illustration of memory, intellect, and affection to clarify the virtue of the superior person, namely, humanity and righteousness. The intellect clarifies what is right, while affection is based on humanity. For Ricci, "humanity is the essence of righteousness" or "the noblest of virtues."[34]

A person who is enriched and mature in humanity cultivates intellect through education or self-cultivation. Thus Ricci underscores the Catholic teaching of sanctification or perfection in accordance with the will of the Lord of Heaven. This teaching means a return to the origin of God.[35] Here the Confucian core teaching of humanity and righteousness is renewed and elaborated in terms of loving the Lord of Heaven as well as the neighbor. The Lord of Heaven has engraved sage learning into the human heart-mind. In Confucian teaching virtue is clouded by human selfish defilement and thus engulfed in darkness. People who learn to do good have to prepare themselves to cultivate and learn in all of life's journey. The Jesuit's way of spiritual discipline and moral virtue appreciates Confucian self-cultivation to increase virtue by concern for God and the neighbor.

In the journey of the ethical self, a person eventually attains the highest level of perfection as he or she habitually has the Lord of Heaven in mind. This happens in the following way: feeling genuine and profound remorse over evil thoughts (contrition), purifying them from the

---

32. Yao, *Introduction to Confucianism*, 74–75.
33. Ricci, *True Meaning of the Lord of Heaven*, 357, 359.
34. Ibid., 367.
35. Ibid., 369.

mind, entering into harmony with the will of the Lord of Heaven, and, finally, being in union with the Lord of Heaven.[36]

Ricci explicates the commonality between Catholic spiritual discipline and Confucian self-cultivation by learning from the *Book of Changes*. Here the great and originating Principle in the human being is called the first and chief quality of goodness.[37] Ricci proposes his definition of humanity by using biblical statements: love the Lord of Heaven and others as you love yourself on behalf of the Lord of Heaven (Matt 22:34–40; Mark 12:28–34; Luke 10:25–38).[38] Ricci utilizes these biblical statements to support the importance of human charitable love that accordingly makes a meritorious work acceptable to the Lord of Heaven. In this respect, Augustine's dictum serves as a good example: "Love the Lord of Heaven and do as you wish."[39]

Equating Christian love with Confucian humanity, Ricci fully undergirds the Confucian way of a virtuous life and self-cultivation in light of the Catholic teaching of perfection. The Lord of Heaven makes use of rites and ceremonies as a means of worship, bestowing grace, instructing people, strengthening faith. Ritual is a way of adoration and praising of the grace of the Sovereign on High.[40]

Ricci further emphasizes the place of the Catholic God in Confucian teaching; thus he critiques Zhu Xi's explanation of the Great Ultimate in terms of *Li* (Principle) of heaven and earth. Zhu Xi (1130–1200) remains a stumbling block for Ricci's harmonious relationship with Confucianism. Ricci argues that Zhu Xi obscured the personal character of the Sovereign on High, because Zhu Xi's metaphysical concept of *Wu-ji erh Tai-ji* (The Ultimate is the Ultimateless) has a materialistic tendency.

The Significance of Zhu Xi for Christian–Confucian Dialogue

Contrary to Ricci's evaluation noted above, Zhu Xi's notion does not in fact reduce the supreme deity merely to a materialistic manifestation. According to Julia Ching, Zhu Xi's concept of the Great One (*Li*) implies

36. Ibid., 375, 389.
37. Ibid., 375.
38. Ibid.
39. Ibid., 383.
40. Ibid., 389.

a supreme deity that is closer to a personal God in a panentheistic sense. This is different from the personal God of classical theism.[41] In my view Ching's evaluation seems to lose the freedom and transcendence of *Li* in Zhu Xi's metaphysics. Furthermore, Zhu Xi's theory of investigation also offers an important insight, according to which the Truth in one's nature is likened to a pearl shining in pure and clear water. The truth manifests itself in the sense of *aletheia*. "There will be thorough comprehension of all the multitude of things, external or internal, fine or coarse, and every exercise of the mind will be marked by complete enlightenment."[42]

In the religious thought of Zhu Xi, Zhou Dunyi's *Diagram of the Great Ultimate* plays an important role. This diagram incorporates speculations of the appendices to the *Book of Changes* (dated to the Han dynasty, 206 BCE–220 CE) into itself. Further, the diagram integrates the yin-yang and Five Phases theories, as well as Buddhist and Taoist ideas and practices into the diagram metaphysics.

The term "Great Ultimate" is derived from the *Great Commentary* which is one of *Ten Wings of the Book of Changes*. The authorship of the *Great Commentary* is ascribed to the historical Confucius. Zhu Xi attempted to reinterpret the *Book of Changes* for cultivating virtue and establishing the balance between the internal and the external through seriousness. Seriousness to straighten the internal life and righteousness to square the external life help one obtain a sense of equilibrium and harmony. Thus one can "face the Lord on High," overcome all evil desires, and preserve sincerity.[43] Underlying Neo-Confucianism is the basic concept of The Principle (*Li*; the Great Ultimate). The Principle is the basis for bringing things into existence through the interaction between *yin* (the cosmic force of tranquility) and *yang* (the cosmic force of activity).

Zhu Xi insists that Zhou's concept of the Great Ultimate in the diagram represents what Confucius and Mencius instructed. This is a symbolic expression of cosmology that articulates the interconnection between the world and humans in terms of macrocosm and microcosm. Interpreting the Great Ultimate with the concept of *Li* (the Principle),

41. Ching, *Religious Thought of Chu Hsi*, 251–52. According to Zhu Xi, *Li* as the principle makes all things what they are, with their being and goodness. The one *Li* between Heaven and earth has multiple manifestations.

42. Fung, *History of Chinese Philosophy*, 2, 562.

43. *Reflections on Things at Hand*, compiled by Zhu Xi and Lú Tsu-Ch'ien, 110–11.

Zhu Xi states that *Li* belongs to the realm above external and material shapes. This is the Form or essence in interaction with *qi* (matter-energy). *Qi* is pervasive in the universe, giving rise to all things endowed with life and energy. *Qi* belongs to the realm within shape.

The Great Ultimate is more *Li* than *qi*, but it also retains its immanence in *qi*, without being fully absorbed into *qi*. The rider does not depend on the horse. This perspective keeps *Li*'s transcendence from being manifested immanently. Zhu Xi interprets Zhou Dunyi's concept *Wu-ji erh Tai-ji* in light of the relationship between *Li* and *qi*. For Zhu Xi, *Wu-ji* refers to the infinite and limitless beyond concepts or language, understanding the Great Ultimate as embracing both being and non-being. The transcendence of *Li* is present even in the immanence of its manifestation, *qi*. *Wu-ji* (the ultimateless) safeguards the transcendence of *Li* in the midst of immanence. This is because the ultimateless is ultimate (*Wu-ji erh Tai-ji*). As Zhu Xi states, "This is like having only one moon in the sky but when its light is scattered over rivers and lakes, it can be seen everywhere."[44] For Zhu Xi, *Wu-ji erh Tai-ji* denotes the Heavenly Principle (*T'ian-li*), which is transcendence in immanence within the universe and every individual human and thing. *Wu-ji* literally means the Infinite and Limitless—that which is beyond concept and language. This other face of the Great Ultimate keeps the Heavenly principle from falling into pan[en]theism.

This perspective has some potential for Christian theology. If God is generally and universally revealed in all creaturely life through God's universal covenant with Noah or human conscience, Ricci should have paid attention to the Neo-Confucian idea that the Great Ultimate is the Ultimateless. This Neo-Confucian perspective is more relevant to a Christian theology of divine action with the world in a more dynamic and relational way.

At its base, Zhu Xi's notion of self-cultivation stands in the orthodox tradition of Mencius. *Li* is the source of goodness and the criterion used to judge what is right or wrong. Nature or essence (*xing*) is identified with *Li* making human beings what they are. The human self exists through a combination of *Li* and *qi*. Human nature is essentially good and sincere. Insofar as one follows it, one's task is to investigate *Li* to the utmost. When human nature is cultivated to the fullest, one's nature will be in accord with the *Li*. On the other hand, there is *xin*

44. Ching, *Religious Thought of Chu Hsi*, 98.

usually translated as mind or mind-and-heart. Nature (*xing*) is full of *Li* while the mind (*xin*) is full of *qi*. Human nature transcends mind, yet not in separation from it. For Zhu Xi, humanity (*ren*) belongs to human nature (*xing*), while compassion and emotion are manifest in mind. The human mind is marvelous and fascinating for its dynamism. The manifestation of *Li*, remaining latent, is to be actualized through ethical self-cultivation. Thus, Zhu Xi proposes an attitude of reverence toward one's own nature and its capacity for doing good. This moral attitude can be deepened in terms of the investigation of *Li* in external things and extension of knowledge according to ethical investigation.

Mencius constructed the doctrine of four beginnings, which denotes the possibility of attaining the ideal of sagehood and virtue. Developing this Confucian tradition, Zhu Xi insists that there is *Li* of morality in human nature: humanity, righteousness, order, and wisdom. Preserving the Heavenly *Li* and purifying human impure and selfish desire is the goal of moral self-cultivation. Zhu Xi integrates Confucius' notion of *ren,* which means subduing oneself (self-conquest) and returning to the virtue of propriety (*Analects* 12:1).

Self-cultivation requires seriousness and reverence. The pursuit of learning depends on the extension of moral knowledge.[45] Moral knowledge is discovered through the practice of seriousness and reverence. In this process of moral journey, truth itself reveals itself and becomes radiant to the mind. The teaching of the extension of knowledge and the investigation of principles are interconnected with the doctrine of *ren*: self-conquest and return to propriety. In the lifelong search for sagehood, perfect virtue (*ren*), which is universal impartiality and the foundation of goodness, becomes the crowning achievement.[46]

Ricci's Accommodation of Confucian Teaching

Ricci's limited knowledge of the Neo-Confucianism of Zhu Xi can be traced in Ricci's understanding of *Li* as human reason. However, *Li* is more than reason. In the Neo-Confucian sense *Li* may be identified with the Catholic concept of God. If Ricci had paid attention to the transcendental aspect of *Li*, he could have had a fruitful dialogue with Neo-Confucian philosophy. Because of his excessive emphasis on the

45. *Reflections on Things at Hand*, xxiv.
46. Ibid., 13.

place of the Catholic God within Confucian ethical life, Ricci did not manage to take into account Zhu Xi's notion of moral self-cultivation in connection with the revelation of the Tao-truth. Against the current of Neo-Confucianism, Ricci argues that Confucianism in Ming China must return to its Confucian-Mencian roots, which teach that there is inner transcendence connected with the theism of outer transcendence. The Confucian virtue of humanity is in this regard to be seen in light of Confucian love for the Sovereign on High.

The Confucian teaching of the Five Cardinal Relationships is taken up and refurbished in Ricci's strategy to promote the Love of the Lord of Heaven and the neighbor. In Confucian instruction, one has little need of divine help and can reach the path of sagehood through one's own moral cultivation. But Ricci contends that one can hardly reach this culmination of sagehood through one's own moral cultivation. One must be helped by God's grace from the outside. It is necessary to believe in and worship God to obtain moral self-cultivation and the perfection of sagehood.

Ricci found it necessary to make some revisions of the Catholic belief system to accommodate the Confucian idea of sagehood and reach concordance with the Confucian belief system regarding Heaven. Ricci also made some revisions to the idea of sin in order to more closely approach the idea of virtue in the Confucian tradition. The person and work of Jesus Christ remains left behind for the sake of a theocentric-ethical approach in cooperation with Confucian philosophy. The Confucian idea of sin does not sidestep the fact that human nature may be considered virtuous. Human nature is essentially good and cannot be destroyed in spite of moral corruption. People who are determined to do good turn from evil. Sin and evil have to do with moral negligence and lack of cultivation of the good. People have only to change their minds by exercising human will. In Ricci's view, the Lord of Heaven is sure to reward them through protection and support.[47]

Ricci expounds his theology of human motives and morality,[48] adding the medieval scholastic ideas of merit and reward to Confucian moral philosophy. Ricci expounded his scholastic theology of human motives and morality in three points: 1) doing good to reach Heaven and to avoid Hell; 2) doing good to repay the Lord of Heaven; and 3) doing

47. Ricci, *True Meaning of the Lord of Heaven*, 447.
48. Ibid., 313.

good to harmonize with the will of the Lord of Heaven.[49] The medieval scholastic theology of merit and reward contradicts the non-attachment to one's achievements found in ancient Chinese wisdom, based on the idea of living with the freedom of a stream. Confucian self-cultivation, which basically has nothing to do with reward and merit, is modified and transformed by Ricci into a theology of God the heavenly banker who rewards according to human deeds, ultimately in terms of Heaven and Hell.[50] The method of accommodation taken by Ricci and his Chinese missionary group had already become an issue of controversy both at home and abroad. The most controversial issue was the accommodation of ancestral rites and terms about God.

The Rites and Terms in Historical Controversy

Ricci's sensitivity to people of other cultures becomes overt in his recognition of ancestral rites and acknowledgment of the indigenous term of Heaven as God. When food is offered to the dead, for example, it is seen as the way the Chinese present affection and gratitude in the same way that Europeans lay flowers at a grave. Both cultures fully acknowledge that the dead have no power to smell or taste. Ricci's option for inculturation and his evangelism through friendship were influential in the development of Christianity in China. Even the Emperor Kang Xi (1662–1723) in the subsequent Qing dynasty (1644–1911) studied Ricci's writings for six months and then issued an edict of toleration in March, 1692. The seventeenth-century Sino-Western relationship was mutually respectful and friendly, unlike later Western incursions.

However, other Catholic orders (such as the Dominicans and the Franciscans) began to speak out against such compromise or accommodation. They walked through the streets holding up crucifixes, not hesitant to proclaim that all Chinese emperors were burning in hell. Denouncing the Jesuit method of adaptation as protective mimicry, they complained to Rome. The result was that the veneration of Confucius and dead ancestors was declared to be superstitious.[51]

Nicola Longobardi, Ricci's successor, opposed the mission policy of acculturation. The so-called "Rites Controversy" involved eight popes

49. Ibid.
50. Ibid., 297, 303, 313.
51. Cronin, *Wise Man*, 267–69.

and the leading European universities for seventy years. Those who were more tolerant of Chinese rites favored greater cultural adaptation, declaring the rites to be non-religious. Others who opposed such inculturation denounced these rites as a practice of superstitious paganism.

Ricci's approval of the Chinese rites manifests in his way of incorporating Confucian respect for ancestors into the Christian narrative of respect for parents, contextualizing Catholic liturgy and catechesis in an intercultural exchange. Concerning the veneration of figures like Confucius, Ricci takes an accommodating approach in which he thinks of the ancestral rite as a way of strengthening filial piety in an ethical way, having little to do with idol worship.

Unfortunately, the Rites and Terms Controversies remained a stumbling block, greatly hindering the growth and survival of Christianity in China. Behind this controversy we need to mention the painful experience of Francis Xavier. Xavier was a missionary who reached India in 1542 and by 1549 had arrived in Japan. He saw the Japanese mission as a springboard for the conversion of China to Roman Catholicism. The Jesuits in Japan were good and skillful at accommodating their Christian faith and ritual practices to the indigenous culture and belief system in Japan.

Xavier preached the *Dainichi* upon his arrival to Japan. He learned this term from a Yajiro (or Nanjiro), a Japanese escapee to India, with little education. It was unfortunate that Xavier was misinformed that *Dainichi* would be equivalent to the Christian idea of *Deus*. However, this term in the Japanese language and religious culture signifies one of the local deities or even the human sex organs! After scandalizing people by proclaiming faith in *Dainichi*, Xavier returned to the places where he had previously preached, shouting, "Do not pray to *Dainichi*." Xavier's mistake of translating *Deus* as *Dainichi* was controversial and instrumental in creating tension between the accommodation approach of the Jesuits and the *tabula rasa* approach of other missionary orders.[52]

Given Xavier's historically fatal translation mistake, a safer path between Ricci's associates and conservative missionaries was taken in using the term *Tian ju* (The Lord of Heaven) to signify the Christian God. Although this term has roots in Taoism and Buddhism, *Tian ju* (literally meaning Master of Heaven), as compared with *Tian* and *Shang-di*, was preferred as the equivalent to the Christian term for God. For the more

52. Chung, *Syncretism*, 102.

fundamentalist-minded, *Deusu* (a transliteration of Latin *Deus*) was preferred in Japan. However, *Deusu* sounded like *dai-uso* in Japanese, which means "big lie."[53]

There are many signs in Ricci's books of the Catholic stance against idolatry; the criticism of Buddhist idolatry is particularly strong.[54] However, he never criticized Confucian offerings to the sage, nor did he criticize Chinese offerings to their ancestors. Ricci did not challenge the veneration of the historical figure of Confucius in a grand Confucian temple or the literati's offering sacrifices to him four times every year. These rites were not regarded as idolatrous acts. In Ricci's view, Chinese rites were first of all instituted for the benefit of the living rather than for the dead. The practice of placing food on the graves of the dead has little to do with any superstition and transcends any charge of sacrilege. Ricci's recommendation is that Christian converts should view the money necessary for these rituals as "alms for the poor and for the salvation of souls."[55]

Ricci and His Three Pillars: Contribution and Setback

After Ricci died in 1610 there were still about two thousand, five hundred believers in China. During the years of 1601–1610 Ricci witnessed the conversion of three important Confucian scholars: Xu Guangqi (Paul) (1562–1633) from Shanghai, and Li Zhizao (Leo) (1565–1630), and Yang Tingyun (Michael) (1557–1627), both of whom were from Hangzhou. All three came from upper-class backgrounds and were distinguished in government service and intellectual studies. They were called the three great pillars of Chinese Catholicism because of their enormous influence in the building up of Chinese Catholicism. Through their efforts, Hangzhou and Shanghai became the center of missionary activity in late Ming China.

Paul Xu held the office of Grand Secretary, a position of rank described as "second only to the emperor."[56] He helped Ricci translate several classic Western texts into Chinese as well as several Confucian texts into Latin. After Ricci passed away, Paul Xu became

---

53. Ching, *Chinese Religions*, 193.

54. Ricci, *China in Sixteenth Century,* 99.

55. Ibid., 96.

56. Moffett, *History of Christianity*, 2, 112.

the acknowledged leader of the Chinese Christian community and protector of the missionaries.

Leo Li became Ricci's collaborator in several publications on religion and science. Leo Li was acquainted with Ricci when he was seriously ill in Beijing in 1610. On the verge of his death Ricci took care of him. After coming back to health, Li was baptized. He donated a large amount of gold to Ricci for the purpose of building a church in Beijing. Li was also the first scholar to, in 1625, receive a copy of a recently discovered inscription on a monument of a "Nestorian Church" near Xian. Michael Yang (1562–1627), a relative of Leo Li, assumed an important position in government. Being impressed by the teaching of the Jesuit missionary Lazzaro Cattaneo at the home of Leo Li, he converted and was baptized. Leo Li and Michael Yang made the provincial capital of Zhejiang the most successful Christian Community in China.

In 1700 there were around two hundred thousand Catholics in China.[57] The propaganda office of the Vatican in 1659 supported the Jesuit mission: "What could be more absurd than to transport France, Spain, Italy or some other European country to China? Do not introduce all that to them but only the faith. It is the nature of men to love and treasure above everything else their own country and that which belongs to it. In consequence, there is no stronger cause for alienation and hate than an attack on local customs, especially when these go back to a venerable antiquity."[58]

In 1692 when Christians learned of an edict of toleration from the Emperor Kang Xi, it was a sign of great hope, recalling the conversion of the Roman Empire to Christianity. Luo Wenzao became the first Catholic bishop of Chinese origin, consecrated in 1685. However, in a 1704 decree Pope Clement XI banned the use of the terms *Tian* and *Shang-di* as designations for God. He gave orders that Chinese Catholics should not follow traditional Chinese rites, because these rites did not conform to Western Christianity. Confucius himself was denounced as a public idolater and a private atheist.[59] In 1742 Pope Benedict XIV in his decree *Ex quo singulari* condemned Chinese rites and opposed the Jesuits' mission of inculturation. In a response against such imperialistic Catholicism, in 1724 an Imperial edict banned Christianity from

57. Treadgold, *West in Russian and China*, chs. 1–2.

58. Cited in Jenkins, *Next Christendom*, 32.

59. Ching, *Chinese Religions*, 193–94.

China. In 1939, almost two centuries after *Ex quo singulari*, Pope Pius XII reversed the decision of 1742, authorizing Chinese rites for Chinese Christians.

A Historical Episode: The Legacy of Ricci in the Beginning of Korean Christianity

In addition to the legacy of Ricci in China, it is instructive to view his influence in the Chosun dynasty of Korea. The Spanish Jesuit Diego de Pantoja (1571–1618) arrived in Macao in 1599, and was sent to join Matteo Ricci. In 1600 they set out together to reach the emperor in the Forbidden City in Beijing. On the way they were briefly arrested, but released upon the condition that they send some Western-style clocks and oil paintings to the emperor. They gained permission to reside in Beijing in January of 1601 and were well received, although they never met the emperor in person. The emperor ordered the Jesuit missionaries to be ensconced in Beijing, and the reputation of the Society of Jesus in China was increased. Ricci's masterpiece. *The True Meaning of the Lord of Heaven,* was published in Beijing in 1603. This masterpiece produced unexpected results in Chosun Korea. Catholicism (known then as Western Learning) came to Korea through Korean Confucians' contact with Jesuit missionaries residing in Ming China.

There was a historical, cultural, and diplomatic relationship between China and Korea over a long period of years. The Korean government annually sent tributary emissaries to Beijing to present compliments and gifts to the emperor of China. There is no doubt that some of these Korean delegates came into contact with Ricci and his fellow Jesuit missionaries. In 1601 Matteo Ricci himself met with Koreans at the "Castle of Foreigners" in the Imperial city of Beijing. Ricci and Pantoja were detained by Chinese officials in the "Castle" where all foreign visitors took their lodging including Vietnamese, Burmese, and Arabians, as well as Koreans.[60]

Yi Sugwang (1563–1628) played an important role in the development of the Korean Confucian *Sirhak* movement. Sirhak (known as Practical Learning) in the Chosun Dynasty can be traced back to seventeenth-century China where Jesuit missionaries introduced natural sciences and European civilization. Yi Sugwang was one of the diplomatic

---

60. Chung, *Syncretism*, 5. See endnote 10.

envoys of the Chosun Dynasty to China. As a Confucian scholar, he met Italian Jesuit missionaries in China and brought back important books. Among them was *The True Meaning of the Lord of Heaven*. Yi promoted an open attitude to economics and trade that later became important themes of *Sirhak*. His appreciation of Catholicism was also significant for several representatives of *Sirhak* such as Yi Ik and Chung Yakyong.

In 1644 a Chosun prince, Sohyun, who had been a political detainee in China, returned to his home country. During his stay in China, a Jesuit missionary Johannes Adam Schall von Bell of Germany approached him with the intention of evangelizing him. Adam Schall presented the prince with many kinds of books in translation: books on astronomy, mathematics, and the truth of Catholicism. A globe and a portrait of Jesus Christ were included among the gifts.

Matteo Ricci was well known as a scientist in Korea through his first and second revised editions of the world map with Chinese nomenclature. His books on astronomy, mathematics, and geometry were well received and studied in Korea. It is certain that Zhu Xi was still respected among several *Sirhak* scholars. For instance, An Chungbok was a staunch defender of the doctrine of Zhu Xi, while following Yi Ik who is associated with the *Sirhak* movement.[61] Although mainly following Ricci's critical approach, *Sirhak* thinkers nonetheless appreciated some aspects of Neo-Confucianism. They looked at it critically and modified it to suit their purposes. They showed great interest in the practical application and the methodology of research based on scientific, empirical facts.

Yi Ik (Songho; 1681–1763) was one of the great Confucian scholars, and read Ricci's masterpiece with his follower An Jungbok (1712–1791). Impressed by the teaching of Ricci, they were convinced to accept faith in a personal God as a source of life through the book of Ricci. They did not find any difficulty in identifying the Lord of Heaven in Western Christianity with the Lord on High (*Shang-di*) in the Confucian belief system. These two scholars were converted to Western Christianity through *The True Meaning of the Lord of Heaven*.

In his book *Summary of the Holy Teaching*, Yi Ik deals with the commonalities between Confucian filial piety and Christian respect for parents. In commenting on *The True Meaning of the Lord of Heaven*, Yi Ik contends that "in their doctrine, the *T'ien-chu*, Lord of Heaven is

---

61. Setton, *Chong Yagyong*, 16.

their supreme deity. The Lord of Heaven 'is' no other than the *Shang-di* of Confucianism though the way of reverence and worship is rather similar to that of the religion of Shyaka [Buddha]. They use our familiar concepts of the Paradise and Hell for the purpose of exhortation and premonition. The universal master and savior is Jesus. Jesus is the Western name for the Savior of the World."[62]

Yi Byuk (1754–1786) was also intrigued by Jesuit teaching and discussed this teaching with several Confucian scholars such as Chung Yakchung (1760–1801) and Chung Yakyoung (Tasan, 1762–1836). In 1784 Yi Byuk wrote the Korean Christian book Essentials of the Holy Teaching. Another particularly significant event occurred in 1784 when Yi Sunghun (1756–1801) accompanied his father in a diplomatic entourage to China. His father was appointed the third-ranking ambassador in the embassy. The Chung brothers and Yi Byuk had encouraged Yi Sung-hun to contact the Catholic priests in Beijing and bring back more information about the teaching of Western Christianity. Later Chung Yakchong wrote *Principles of the Christian Faith* (*Chugyo joji*), which is the first Korean Christian book written in the indigenous Korean language (*Hangul*).[63]

Tasan, eulogized as a synthesizer of the *Sirhak* movement, was nationally famous, serving as an advisor to the king. He retrieved the message of Confucius and Mencius. In his early life he sought points of resonance between Confucianism and Catholicism. Although friendly to Catholics, he never formally joined the church. His elder brothers Chung Yak-chon and Chung Yakchong were deeply involved in the founding of the early church, and later became martyrs during the persecution.[64]

Yi Sunghun went to Beijing in 1783 with the annual envoy, visited the Jesuit priests, and received their instruction about Western Christianity. During his forty-day stay in Beijing, he frequently visited the North Catholic Church and eventually asked the Western priests there to baptize him. Father Jean-Joseph de Grammont, a French ex-Jesuit missionary, decided that Yi was well qualified for baptism. He baptized Yi Sunghun in February of 1784 and gave him the name of Peter. This incident marks the beginning of the Catholic Church, made

62. Cited in Chung, *Syncretism*, 67.

63. Moffett, *History of Christianity in Asia*, 314.

64. Setton, *Chong Yagyong*, ch. 2.

up entirely of lay people, in Korea. After returning to Korea in the spring of 1784 Yi baptized three friends, one of whom was Yi Byok. Through their evangelical activity, they led many of their friends and relatives to convert to Western Christianity. Yi Sunghun became the first lay leader to organize a Catholic faith community in Korea in 1785. The Church of Korea offers a unique example in the history of Christian mission, organized in a rather independent and spontaneous manner. However, as the movement spread, it generated persecution. The major issue was ancestral rites that had already been prohibited in a papal bull in 1742.

Alexandre de Gouvea, the bishop of Beijing at the time, was chiefly responsible for the cultivation of the new born Church in Korea. He praised evangelical activity in the face of persecution and recognized their baptisms as valid lay baptisms. He sent a missionary to Korea, James Chou Wen-mo, a forty-two-year-old Chinese priest, who arrived in Seoul on the verge of the first great persecution in 1795. He, as the first Chinese missionary to Korea, became martyred.

A letter which De Gouvea had written to Saint-Martin, the bishop of Sichuan, on August 15, 1798, was later published under the title *De Statu christianismi in Regnum Coreae Mirabiliter Ingressi* (*On the Status of Christianity Miraculously Entered into the Kingdom of Korea*). This letter describes the miraculous introduction of Christianity into Korea as well as the extraordinary growth of the Christian community.[65] The organization of the first Korean Church was done with little foreign missionary activity. In the beginning of the Korean Catholic Church and Confucian *Sirhak* movement, it is noticeable that the legacy of Ricci remained alive. Jesuit work in China became the leaven that brought cultural, intellectual, and religious renewal and transformation to Korean Confucian society.

Appreciating the Legacy of Matteo Ricci

Ricci was successful in opening the doors of China to Christianity. But his legacy is viewed with ambiguity today. Evangelicals accuse Ricci of diluting the meaning of the gospel and even charge him with responsibility for Christian-Confucian syncretism. Progressively minded intellectuals view the Jesuit mission in China as trickery, deception, and

---

65. Chung, *Syncretism*, 4.

expedience.[66] Although Ricci took a positive stance on ancestral rites, his hostile position against Buddhism and Daoism remains a problem. His accommodation principle remained paralyzed when it came to tolerating other religions such as Buddhism and Daoism. He played classical Confucianism against Neo-Confucianism, and thereby misunderstood the Neo-Confucian understanding of the Great Ultimate and human nature. Ricci's interpretation of Neo-Confucianism as a materialistic deviation from orthodox Confucianism seems unfortunate. Zhu Xi's notion of the Great Ultimate functions like the Form of the Good in Platonism. Zhu Xi's concept of the Great Ultimate, called the Heavenly principle, does possess a personal character as "creator and organizer of the universe."[67]

Ricci's understanding of Daoist Non-Being, Buddhist emptiness, and Neo-Confucian ultimate principle were limited. His attempt at accommodation centers only on a theistic-ethical framework in the Christian-Confucian relationship, undermining the place of Jesus Christ. This is a shortcoming in his missional approach.[68] His accommodationist approach assumes that there is no dichotomy between the natural theology of China and the revealed theology of Europe.

Ricci's accommodationist method goes back to Ignatius Loyola himself. The greater glory of God was his motto. For the glorification of God and the salvation of souls, the principle of *tantum quantum* applies to all that exists such as tools, means, and ways. Following in the footsteps of Ignatius Loyola, Ricci became a Chinese man, Li Ma-tou, adopting a pure Chinese three-syllable name. He accommodated to Chinese language, literature, morality, and social customs successfully in his Catholic consciousness and teaching. For him, idealized Confucianism is none other than orientalized Christianity. His masterpiece, *The True Meaning of the Lord of Heaven,* utilizes the literary style of dialogue used in Chinese literature rather than a Catechism. Such dialogue is undertaken in the manner of a soul-searching conversation with mutual understanding and respect between a Confucian scholar and a Jesuit missionary.[69]

66. Levenson, *Confucian China and Its Modern Fate,* 121.

67. Ching, *Religious Thought of Chu Hsi,* 70.

68. Ricci, *True Meaning of the Lord of Heaven,* 449–53.

69. Chung, *Syncretism,* 61.

In the Catholic tradition, faith and reason were conceptualized in mutual dependence: knowledge of God is found in creation and can be acquired naturally. God can be known through demonstrative arguments in terms of a relation of cause and effect. In China, Ricci contextualized Thomas Aquinas' dictum: *gratia naturam non tollit, sed supponit et perfecit* (grace does not destroy nature, but supports and perfects it). Pope John Paul II appreciated Ricci's legacy in his commemoration of the four hundredth anniversary of Ricci's arrival in China (at the international Ricci Studies Congress held at the University of Macerata and the Pontifical Gregorian University on October 25, 1982). Ricci promoted the concept that faith in Christ would not bring any harm to Chinese culture. Rather, Christian faith could enrich and perfect it, just as the church fathers had been convinced of the same thing with regard to Greek culture.

In the midst of his contribution and limitations, Ricci's legacy for the mission of inculturation remains intact, inspiring his followers to devote themselves to creatively developing the translatability of the Christian narrative in an age of World Christianity. Ricci remains an example for making inroads with Christian thought into Chinese culture.

The Gospel is the internal basis for inculturation, as inculturation is the existential-hermeneutical basis for a dialogue between living people and the Gospel. Inculturation refers to a Christian witness to *viva vox Dei* that injects the meaning of the gospel into a culture. All the while, the task of inculturation prophetically renews and transforms that culture and spiritually recognizes its uniqueness as it serves the universality of the Gospel in the world of non-Christian religions. The Gospel becomes enriched and deepened when more East Asians are able to embrace it truly and bring a Confucian, Hindu, Buddhist, or Daoist lens to the reading of it.

Summary of the Catholic Model of Justice and Inculturation

The Catholic integrative model of grace in context led to prophetic action in the case of Las Casas and respect for the religion of outsiders in the case of Matteo Ricci. If Las Casas promotes a peaceful proclamation on the basis of persuasion and dialogue, Ricci's inculturation paradigm severed the colonial link between Christian faith and European power. Ricci engaged in conversing between equals in studying Confucian classics, identifying himself within the cultural-religious world of

Confucian China. This perspective creates a space for contextualizing Christian faith and church in dynamic interaction with the wisdom and spirituality of the indigenous people.[70] Embarking on a program of re-conceptualizing God's narrative in the Chinese world, Ricci contributed to a hermeneutic of appreciation (analogous to early Greek and Latin church fathers) which is relevant to today's missional study of inculturation. Translation of the biblical message in a form of adaptation or indigenization transcends the colonial mission of Christendom which is currently an emerging model of World Christianity.

According to Niebuhr, a Thomistic view of Christ above culture refers to the synthesis model of Christ and culture. Aside from some radical, dualistic, or exclusivist believers, all Christians are in agreement with the synthesists' affirmation of the civil virtues and social institutions. What is now presented comes from God, because God is to rule now and has ruled. God's rule is established in the nature of things. The theological principle—the Creator and the Redeemer are one—becomes a corrective to the excessive concentration on the future kingdom of God which neglects the present reality of God's reign. Salvation does not mean the destruction of the created. The synthesist model provides us with intelligent cooperation of Christians with non-believers in performing the work of the world, while maintaining the distinctiveness of Christian faith. Nevertheless, the gospel promises and requires more than the rational knowledge of God's plan for creation. In the synthesist model there is a tendency to absolutize what is relative; it reduces the infinite to a finite form, materializing the dynamic. It easily runs into institutionalization of Christ and the gospel. In the synthesis effort socio-historical understanding of the relationship between the gospel and culture is left behind. Human reason is involved with cultural life and its social context, which is in the continual movement of history.[71]

Nevertheless, Niebuhr fails to acknowledge the reality of nature and culture in light of Christ's grace of reconciliation as visible in the synthesis model. Christ is not only transformer, but also recognizer of the culture. All human achievement is changing, dynamic, and open-ended. The gospel as the living voice of God challenges a synthetic attempt at institutionalizing or reducing its living reality into

70. Bevans and Schroeder, *Constants in Context*, 202; further see Burrows, "A Seventh Paradigm?" in Saayman and Kritzinger, *Mission in Bold Humility*.

71. Niebuhr, *Christ and Culture*, 142–46.

ecclesiastical and rationalistic systems. God as the creator works in the world of culture constantly and eschatologically. If all creatures are masks of God, God definitely speaks to us through the people, their wisdom and spirituality of other religions and cultures. Theology of the cross which is the basis for God's universal reign renders God's mission more explicit, calling attention to limitations and backwardness in cultural life. The Word of God in *diakonia* (service) of Christ's justification and reconciliation becomes the hermeneutical filter and criteria of spiritual discernment in analyzing the cultural lifeworld in terms of critique, recognition, and emancipation.

In East Asia particularly, cultures have been multiculturally formed and fused in interaction with diverse religions: Confucianism, Buddhism, Daoism, and Shamanism. Any dialogue with culture in East Asia entails a need for a profound study of religious outsiders in recognition of and respect for their dignity, uniqueness, and distinctiveness. In this hermeneutical exploration the meaning from religious others can be appropriated while maintaining a critical distance from their limitations and weaknesses. This will better facilitate the church's mission and evangelization in different locations, while enriching the cultural connection by interpreting the gospel through a Confucian, Hindu, Buddhist, or Taoist lens in light of God's universal reign in creation.

As God's on-going activity directs and transforms cultural expressions of the gospel toward the eschatological promise of God, each culture is changing, creative, and dynamic. Cultures are also in need of self-renewal, since they become analogical witnesses to God's mission in the world. Inculturation finds its locus dynamically in the relation of the grace of justification to eschatological coming ("already and not yet"). The task of inculturation never becomes an accomplished fact. Western theologies also are culturally conditioned in their understanding of the gospel. They also are in need of the exchange of comparative study and a multilateral relationship with non-Western theologies. Such encounters and exchanges facilitate and precipitate Western theologies' freedom from their Babylonian captivity of the past.[72] Thus, a mission of inculturation paves the way for serving the gospel with a creative interpretation, that aims to keep the living voice of God from exclusive parochialism and contextual relativism.

72. Bosch, *Transforming Mission*, 456.

3

Shaping Public Missiology

World Christianity and Postcolonial Voice

The interactive model is inspired and sharpened by the model of the *missio Dei* as translation, a welcome change in the postcolonial setting. Being "transcultural" means indigenous discovery of the biblical narrative and vernacular interpretation of it. Non-Western Christians' understanding of the biblical story and their articulation of Christian identity is influenced by different narratives and worldviews. A missiological study of World Christianity and postcolonial theology is also of special significance for the North American congregation embedded in the multicultural, postmodern, and post-Christian world.

A Land of Many Religions and Cultures

In addition to the juxtaposition of postmodern culture and the national ethos of American civil religion, we see the emergence of Asian religions in the United States. The Federation of Zoroastrians or the Jain Associations in North America are no longer strange. We do not doubt that American society is being shaped and is in flux along with a multitude of native-born American Buddhists, Confucians, Hindus, Muslims, or Sikhs, and so on. A multilocal formation has shaped and characterized complex national identities within the United States. We are diverse in geography, in culture, in religion, in ethnicity, and in philosophies.

While earlier Parliaments of World Religions were gatherings of international religious leaders, the 1993 parliament demonstrated for the first time America's own religious plurality. There is no peace among the nations without peace among the religions. There is no peace among religions without dialogue between the religions. There is no dialogue between the religions without investigation of the foundations of the religions. A new paradigm of international relations is being pursued on the basis of global ethical standards.[1] Multiculturalism has become a term that expresses the sociopolitical and religious reality of North American society;—i.e., a land of many religions and cultures.

Fundamentalism and Translatability: Global Christianity and World Christianity

World Christianity breaks radically from the Enlightenment framework that has been and is still influential in Western Christianity. In the context of World Christianity, theology of *missio Dei* is reconceptualized as the translation of biblical narrative that emphasizes the human experience of God's Word in one's own linguistic-cultural life setting. Human experience of God's Word is linguistically mediated and social-existentially understood in a polyvalent, multiple-meaningful, and open-ended direction. Thus, indigenizing the faith calls for the decolonization of Western Christianity and theology. The Christian religion is culturally translatable into varying and different contexts. In this translation, traditional and popular religious concerns and belief systems resurge and persist with strength.

According to Philip Jenkins, the newer churches in the Global South retain deep personal faith and communal orthodoxy, mysticism, and Puritanism, characterized as "traditionalist, orthodox, and supernatural."[2] They all are founded on clear scriptural authority. Their message is charismatic, visionary, and apocalyptic. Here, prophecy is an everyday reality; faith-healing, exorcism, and dream-visions are all basic components of religious sensibility. Intentionally, Jenkins characterizes the coming of global Christianity by using the term *the next Christendom*, which is a primary form of cultural reference. Along with

1. Küng, *Global Responsibility*.
2. Jenkins, *Next Christendom*, 8.

the process of globalization, he argues that its early consequence was a growing sense of identity among Global South Christians.[3]

Jenkins examines the faith in Biblical inerrancy in global Christianity in light of supernatural aspects including dreams and prophecy. A return to scriptural roots remains in force in his generalization of the phenomenon of the new Christendom in Africa, Asia, and Latin America. His distance from the theologies he is studying is shown in his quotation from a liberal-minded Korean theologian: "Christianity in Korea has been and is thoroughly indigenized into the Korean religious cultures. The hierarchical structure of the Korean churches is more Confucian than Christian . . . The literary Biblical fundamentalism of many Korean Christians is in fact deeply rooted in the old ethos of neo-Confucian literalism rather than in influences from outside sources."[4]

If Christianity in Korea is thoroughly indigenized into the Korean religious culture, why is Korean Protestant church vandalism against the Korean high religions (for instance, Confucianism and Buddhism) becoming a social issue? In contrast to the Protestant attitude toward indigenous religion, the Catholic Church in Korea incorporated Matteo Ricci's *The True Meaning of the Lord of Heaven*, thus the Neo-Confucian literati played an important role in the initial stage of the Korean Church. In contrast to the Catholic Church, the Korean Protestant Church under the colonial influence of Protestant missionaries was by and large negative towards inculturation and social justice. If the biblical fundamentalism of many Korean Christians is deeply rooted in the old ethos of neo-Confucian literalism, does it mean that many Korean Christians have such a literati-privileged background? Most of the early Protestant Christians in Korea were women and people with low social status and little education. They received biblical instruction from the Korean pastors who were under the control and dominion of Western missionaries who promoted biblical inerrancy and Puritan-styled moral standards. Contrary to Jenkins' speculation, literary biblical fundamentalism had more to do with influences from outside sources and was then spurred by the status quo of neo-Confucian culture in Korean society at that time.

The current rapid growth of the Catholic Church in South Korea can be found to be partly due to its openness to cultural issues (for instance, ancestral rites) and engagement with interreligious dialogue and

3. Ibid., 10, 12.

4. Jenkins, *New Faces of Christianity*, 21.

cooperation with other faith communities, and partly due to its commitment to the human rights of the poor. Traditional methods of conversion (based on Western Protestant missionary strategy and disrespect of indigenous culture), a gospel of prosperity, overemotionalism, and apocalyptic premillennialism have been distracting the public and hindering growth. Especially the younger generations in South Korea are turning away from the Protestant Church. Jenkins' biblicist and wrongheaded assumptions concerning Global South Christianity do not fit the reality of Korean Christianity, at all.

In contrast to Jenkins, proponents of World Christianity such as Lamin Sanneh challenge the term "global Christianity," because it is the faithful replication of Christian forms and patterns developed in Europe. Sanneh argues that the term "global Christianity," which parallels economic globalization, carries vestiges of imperialism. Global Christianity, which is interchangeable with Christendom, is anachronistic.[5] Proponents of World Christianity argue that the biblical narrative must be interpreted through a plurality of models of inculturation, acknowledging various local idioms and practices. The metaphor of "taking off one's shoes" when approaching the cultural-religious place of the other because it is a holy place shows a new appreciation of others.[6] Insofar as the biblical narrative is culturally and linguistically translatable into varying and different contexts, the task of translation includes a serious hermeneutical exegesis and project about the subject matter of the biblical narrative. In this hermeneutical process of fusion of horizons between biblical narrative and indigenous cultural-religious lifeworlds, traditional and popular religious concerns and belief systems can be redefined and refurbished for the sake of God's mission in Christ's service to the world.

The churches in the New Testament context brought Jew and Gentile, male and female, slave and slave owner into a new relationship in light of Christ's atonement, peace, and reconciliation. Crossing cultural and ethnic boundaries, the churches strove to bear ongoing witness to God's narrative of glad tidings in Christ though hospitality, administration, generosity, encouragement, material support (Acts 6) and the various ministries of the Word. The impoverished church in Jerusalem was supported by the apostolic collection throughout Asia Minor.

5. Sanneh, *Whose Religion Is Christianity?* 23.

6. Bevans and Schroeder, *Constants in Context*, 259.

In the Council of Jerusalem in Acts 15, we read that the gospel is to be translated for the sake of the mission to the Gentiles. The apostolic community creates missional communities in new cultural contexts. In the process of translation and interpretation the faith community forms itself for the continuing witness ranging from the Palestinian church to the diverse churches in the Hellenistic world.[7] Insofar as the church is essentially multicultural from the beginning in the New Testament, the reality of World Christianity must be understood from within this biblical perspective.

In order to discover the gospel indigenously, scholars of World Christianity also contend that priority must be given to the response to the gospel and the local appropriation of it by critically uncovering the missionary-colonial residue implanted in a previous era. At issue here is how to articulate the indigenous discovery of the Christian religion rather than the Western missionary discovery of indigenous societies. The translatability of Scripture into different languages and the indigenous naming of God in different religious contexts becomes a watershed for recognizing and promoting the indigenous contribution to God's mission in an age of post-Western Christianity.

Classically, Alopen's mission in Tang China, Francis Xavier in Japan, Robert de Nobili in India, and Matteo Ricci in sixteenth-century China offer important lessons for present-day theological debate and participation in God's mission through inculturation. The Jesuit missionary Alexandre de Rohdes' (1593–1660) mission in Vietnam is appreciated as one that finds the vernacular expression of the Bible and the catechism to be indispensable for constructing a Christian theology of mission.[8] It is also important to critically examine the limitations of accommodationist mission from the historical examples of Francis Xavier in Japan and Matteo Ricci in China. It is polemical to talk of the existence of Christianity without biblical exegesis or confessional expressions, and hermeneutically refined interpretation and biblical symbols.[9]

7. Sanneh, *Translating the Message*, 9–85.

8. Bevans and Schroeder, *Constants in Context*, 105, 184, 187, 189. See further Phan, *In Our Own Tongues*, 161.

9. Sanneh, *Whose Religion Is Christianity?* 35.

Difficulty in Translation and the Biblical Subject Matter

From a hermeneutical perspective, we cannot fully translate the subject matter of the living God into any language. The interpretive principle of Scripture and confessional expression are not replaced by the principle of indigenization. The subject matter of the living God guides and sharpens the dynamic power of the gospel and the eschatological and open-ended character of the community of faith. In this regard, it is pivotal to consider the translation of the God-name in assorted contexts. In the translation of the name of God (YHWH) into indigenous cultural life settings, it calls for an exquisite and refined task to undertake the translation of God's name as predicates (appellations) witnessing to the God of Israel in the Trinitarian economy of salvation (John 3:16).

Hermeneutical experience in the translation of biblical narrative and God's name uphold that the incarnation is connected to the problem of the word. The sending of the Son, the mystery of the incarnation is described in the word. That which emerges and externalizes itself in utterance is always and already a word. There is a correspondence—although it is imperfect—to the divine relationship of the Trinity in the human relationship between thought and speech.[10] "Being an event is a characteristic belonging to the meaning itself."[11] In the character of language as event, the process of concept formation and translation must be grounded in God's redemptive act in Jesus Christ through the Holy Spirit.

In terms of Trinitarian mission in the context of World Christianity, Christian mission is connected with and defined by Jesus' mission mandate (Matt 28:19). In fact, the doctrine of the Trinity can become the interpretation of the name of the God of Israel who is fully revealed in Jesus Christ. To avoid Trinitarian supercessionism (or anti-Semitism) in Jewish-Christian-Islamic dialogue, it is important to take seriously the Hebrew Bible and Israel's faith-experience as well as God's blessing on Abraham-Ishmael-Hagar. For instance, "Allah" as the translation of "Elohim" which is used by Christians in Pakistan, Malaysia, and Indonesia, is connected with God's name in the Hebrew Bible. This usage has little to do with the understanding of Allah as attested in the Quran.[12]

10. Gadamer, *Truth and Method*, 420–21.

11. Ibid., 427.

12. Teuffel, *Mission als Namenszeugnis*, 184.

The distinction between God and the Word in the prologue to the Gospel of John preserves the freedom of God (YHWH). In the Greek, *ho logos* ēn *pros ton theon, kai theos* ēn *ho logos.* (The Logos was with *ho theos* [God] and the Logos was *theos* [divine]). Or we might translate: "the Word was in God's presence and the Word was God."[13] In the translation of God's presence, the article (*ho*) is used with *theos.* The Logos is translated as *theos* in the sense of predicate. It does not identify the Logos as *ho theos.* When it comes to Elohim or Adonai in the Hebrew Bible in connection with YHWH, appellation occupies a central meaning, for instance, Adonai YHWH or YHWH Elohim. Elohim or Adonai is representative for the name YHWH rather than an alternative name of God. Because of the holiness of God's name (Exod 20:7; Lev 24:16), the Tetragram (YHWH) was read as Adonai. In the Greek Septuagint, Adonai is translated as *Kyrios* while Elohim as *ho theos.* God's self-introduction (Exod 20:2ff.) keeps God's name intact, although we recognize cultural translations of it.

Although there was marked development in regard to the Prologue's "the Word as God" and the later church's confession of Jesus Christ as "true God of true God," we also perceive that in the Nicene Creed Jesus Christ is conceptualized as the Son of God based on the relations of origin. A theological principle—*distinctio et non-separatio*—keeps Trinitarian theology from running into modalism, while defending the freedom of YHWH from social-doctrinal projection of human experience into the Trinitarian life. This Trinitarian perspective underlies a mission centered on God's revelation as word-event, practiced in a form of non-colonialist engagement with emerging theology and the cultural experience of World Christianity. However, it should also be kept in mind that God is not captive to the world or translation.

Postcolonial Challenge to Western Mission and Empire

In a post-Christian era, some pundits view Christian mission as cultural imperialism and religious bigotry. In China, for instance, while there is a national resurgence of the Christian religion, there is also an ambivalent attitude toward Western Christianity and civilization. China

13. Brown, *Gospel according to John*, 3–5. "The Word was God" is more convincing than "the Word was divine," because an adjective for divine (*theos*) in Greek is not used in the Johannine prologue. In John 20:28: "Thomas answered him, 'My Lord and my God!'"

has endured painful humiliation at the hands of Western imperialists (Japan) from the times of the Opium War (1839–1842, 1856–1860) until the founding of Communist China in 1949. During the Opium War, Western Christianity was used by imperial government, as a tool for aggression against China, and a number of Western missionaries played a part in this war.

Robert Morrison (1782–1834), the first Protestant missionary of the London Missionary Society (an interdenominational body founded in 1795), arrived in Canton in 1807. George Staunton, President of the Select Committee of the East India Company, befriended him and secured for him the post of translator to the Company. Morrison worked as translator for the East India Company from 1809 to 1815, and participated in dumping opium into China. Morrison's double position made it difficult for the Chinese to differentiate between his missionary aims and business for merchants in the Company. Morrison accompanied Lord Amherst's embassy to Beijing in 1816 as an interpreter. After twenty-seven years of service, Morrison and his colleagues baptized only ten Chinese—most of whom were either students in Christian schools or missionary employees.[14]

Morrison was joined by other missionaries, notably by Karl F. A. Gützlaff (1803–1851), a Prussian missionary. Gützlaff was accused of working as a translator and a negotiator for the British commander-in-chief. He was denounced as one involved in "the communication of reports from the invaders' Chinese spies." Drawing up plans for a victorious advance on Nanjing, he saw a British victory as "a decisive opening for the Christianizing of China."[15]

On the other hand, China has desired to learn from Western modernization with its technological advancement and achievements. Mr. Den Xiao Ping's Open Door Policy was inaugurated in 1978, and it is well expressed in his often quoted remark: "Who cares whether the cat is black or white as long as it catches mice!" Following China's Open Door Policy, the phenomenal growth of the Chinese Christian population has made China "the largest Christian community in Asia."[16]

In the context of liberation-oriented theologies, we are aware that the project of emancipation is brought together with the people's

14. Hughes, *Invasion of China*, 61.

15. Moffett, *History of Christianity*, 297.

16. Kim, *Christian Theology*, 97.

religious and spiritual life.[17] Liberation theology's contribution is that it identifies our social and public location in terms of revealing power and dominion relations. By sharing an interest in liberation, postcolonial theologians attempt to transcend the aftermath of colonialism by moving beyond the colonial or neocolonial forms of global domination. Postcolonial theology shares the following critical concerns of liberation theology: 1) a critique of the oppressive powers of state; 2) a critique of the relationship between church and state; and 3) a critique of the way institutionalized structures internalize and colonize the poor and oppressed.[18] In this light, postcolonial theologians attempt to transcend the aftermath of colonialism by moving beyond the colonial or neocolonial forms of global domination. A critique is undertaken of the way institutionalized structures internalize and colonize the indigenous people and the culturally voiceless. Thus, postcolonial theology retains a discourse of resistance, calling into question cultural and discursive domination.

The term "postcolonial" has little to do with the prefix "post" in the temporal sense or period. Colonialism has been replaced by neocolonialism in phase of late capitalism. "Post" denotes having gone through, however,"after" in a temporal, linear sense must be understood as referring to the events in contrast flux and in consideration of devastation left behind. The political dimension of the postcolonial critique in the temporal sense and its discursive and critical aspects come together without eradicating their tension since the colonization process is conceptualized at both the social and political levels as well as the cultural and discursive levels.[19]

Postcolonial theology gives credit to Michael Hardt and Antonio Negri, proponents of Empire theory. They argue that the emerging Empire is building a globalized and decentralized network of international financial institutions, globalized mass media, and communication systems. This enables multinational corporations with flexible labor and capital across geographical and ethnic boundaries. Empire eliminates geographical boundaries and cross-cultural difference by integrating them into the hands of the new globalized powers, namely one single market metanarrative.[20]

17. Boff, *Ecology and Liberation*.
18. Keller et al., *Postcolonial Theologies*, 8.
19. Kwok, *Postcolonial Imagination*, 2.
20. Hardt and Negri, *Empire*, 166–67, 142.

In the post-socialist era, the nation-state retreats and in its place the international economic system (codified by the IMF and the World Bank that are associated with institutions such as the Trilateral Commission and the G-8 or G-20 countries, among others) appears to be in command and control. Empire, according to Joerg Rieger, has to do with massive concentrations of power permeating all aspects of life over which the empire seeks to extend its control. This control and dominion are based on top-down systems established on the back of those who are burdened by the political-economic reality of Empire. This political-economic reality is tied to the growth of global capitalism that exerts power through cultural, ideological, and intellectual webs.[21] A reality of the power of Empire in this regard is manifested as "biopower," that is, a power of regulation of social life from its interior side, putting together economic, political, and cultural forces.[22]

Utilizing the model of Empire, postcolonial scholars advocate a reading strategy of critique to unmask and debunk colonial assumptions. This interpretive theory attempts to unravel the Eurocentric logic of theology and philosophy and questions stereotypical cultural generalizations and representations. Postcolonial theologians see the Bible as a political text that is written, collected, and redacted by male colonial elites under the shadow of the empires. The Bible is to be interrogated with respect to the deployment of gender in the story of identity, revealing the power structure between the colonizers and the colonized in the world of the Bible. It critically analyzes the reinforcement of patriarchal dominion that is imbued with an oppressive and hierarchical-patriarchal structure in the biblical narratives.

The British civilizing mission is denounced as a Western colonial strategy to spread Western civilization. Likewise, the North American mission is unmasked as an attempt to spread American ideas and values of individualism, democracy, and materialism. Such mission by Empire amounts to the colonizer's dominion and expansion. Postcolonial theologians, along with theologians of Third World, take issue with colonialism or imperialism embedded within present-day globalization, which in turn generates postcolonial hybridity. After the collapse of European colonial empires in the mid-twentieth century, Third World

21. Rieger, *Christ and Empire*, 2–3.

22. Hardt and Negri, *Empire*, 23. For the concept of "biopower" see Foucault, *Discipline and Punish*, 195–228.

theologians began to dismiss the missionary project as wrongheaded colonialism. Native American novelist Leslie Marmon Silko writes that "the Europeans . . . had gone through the motions with their priests, holy water, and churches built with Indian slave labor. But their God had not accompanied them. The white man had sprinkled holy water and had prayed for almost five hundred years in the Americas, and still the Christian God was absent."[23]

Critique of Ideology, Recognition, and Translation

In the history of Christian mission, cultural imperialism has been enmeshed with the propaganda of evangelism. Indigenous cultures have been humiliated, suppressed, and destroyed as alien, ominous, even devilish things and contrary to the (Western) gospel. A radical hermeneutic of suspicion and refusal emerges in the colonized experience in the context of World Christianity. For a public theology of mission, we need to consider a hermeneutic of suspicion that aims at debunking the linking between mission and impure motives.[24] When properly understood, all reflection about the Christian narrative is shaped by social-existential questioning about its relation to the cultural world. Thus, it is also essential to note that socio-critical or postcolonial method is itself shaped and influenced by social practices of liberating discourse and its own epistemological framework. It does not occupy a transcendental, ideal place of rationality as if it is privileged to exist outside historical contingency or social interplay between knowledge and power—as though it could exercise an almighty critique.

In the New Testament we read that "God spoke to our ancestors in many and various ways by the prophets" (Heb 1:1). God's self-communication in Jesus Christ for all cannot be properly understood apart from the appearances of God's word-event throughout all the ages in their plural horizons. The coming of God in Jesus Christ means that the God of Israel is enfleshed in the human being, Jesus of Nazareth. The Word of God (*Dabar*) is God's Word in action, incarnated and embodied in the life, death, and resurrection of Jesus Christ. God's Word is happening so that it is an illuminating word in an ongoing way, involving human

---

23. Cited in Jenkins, *Next Christendom*, 40–41.

24. Newbigin, *Gospel in a Pluralist Society*, 171–83; Bevans and Schroeder, *Constants in Context*, 378–85.

social existence. Insofar as the Word of God is not conveyed as any special and supernatural language, the word-event opens up existence in promise and transformative recognition of the multiple meanings of biblical narrative in worldly affairs. In this light, the true nature of word, and language in general, can be transculturally translated and fulfilled in the gospel story as the *pro-missio Dei*—the living embodiment of God in Jesus Christ embracing the lifeworld of religious outsiders.

In this theological hermeneutic, the gospel narrative can be more precisely understood by examining Jesus' use of parable language for the kingdom of God. The gospel is understood as analogous speech about God. The analogy of God's kingdom is an approximation of the truth of God's eschatological coming. God is a speaking God, to whom human beings, in responding to the Word of God, express their own experience of God in an analogical-cultural language. The missional aspect of the word-event involves a surplus of meaning, undertaking a thick description of biblical narrative.

The Word of God is action, which is "speaking," discursive action. The priority of saying over the said can be seen in the Hebrew understanding of *dabar* (Ps 33:9). Driven by God's word-event, this theological hermeneutic strives to find its subject matter in the Scriptures and in the way the living voice of God speaks in the world through the face of the other. This perspective undergirds recognition of religious outsiders. Based on similarity-in-difference (analogical language), a hermeneutic of the word-event articulates the significant place of the dissimilar and different discourses in the text and also of those vulnerable and voiceless in the world.

For instance, the universality of God's word-event is compared to the Chinese chess game (*Xiangqi*—a two-player Chinese board game) that operates like guerrilla warfare. In this game every particular chess piece has its unique and different role, representing distinctive features in a battle between two enemies. No one in this battle game is marginalized and excluded, but each contributes an important and representational role to the game. Each unique role is compared to our experience of sitting in a train looking at the landscape outside. Sitting in the train, we see and experience each unique landscape in passing, but we do not reduce diverse, different, and unique landscapes into our cognitive consciousness by totalizing them into the same landscape. The transversal dimension of each chess piece corresponds to the different landscapes seen outside a train window.

The irregular, transversal side of God's narrative can be heard in the world of non-Christian communities and does not necessarily contradict the regular, confessional side of God's Word in the form of physicality and incarnation. Rather, this irregular side promotes the prophetic, diaconal horizon of God's narrative in the life of Jesus Christ, who stands in fellowship and solidarity with those in the margins and in other cultures. This irregular perspective holds God's mission ahead of us, acknowledging a transversal and localized uniqueness of people's narratives in different public locations.

One concept of translation suggest that vernacular translation of the Scripture brings the gospel into terms of familiarity. "Familiarity breeds faith."[25] Vernacular translation stimulates indigenous religious and cultural renewal and reception so that language may serve an instrumental function and be contextual in character. This vernacular perspective has encouraged the role of recipient cultures as arbiters in appropriating the biblical narrative, entailing the anti-elitist popular impulse of ordinary usage. Taking into account vernacular primacy in translation, mission is fundamentally congruent with indigenous cultural integrity when it comes to God's mission as word-event. Here, all languages and cultures are equal in expressing the word of God.[26]

A linguistic interaction between biblical narrative and vernacular translation invests an indigenous culture with an ethical, qualitative power. As translation, mission generates faith and obedience to God. God's narrative in the humility and humanity of Christ are to be conveyed in multiple linguistic cultural systems against the exclusive model of mission coupled with colonialism. Mission must not be understood as a destructive arbiter of indigenous distinctiveness and originality.

To what extent does the vernacular Scripture stand in interaction with biblical exegesis, the hermeneutic of word-event, and promote Christian discourse in ethical, cultural engagement with non-Christian religious belief systems and worldviews? The living power of the Gospel (as *viva vox evangelii*) is not merely reduced into a vernacular fixed translation. If human experience of the Word of God can be a

25. Sanneh, *Translating the Message*, ch. 7.
26. Ibid., 250–51.

reading of meaning, an exegesis, a hermeneutic,[27] it is essential to develop a theological hermeneutic of word-event assuming analogical-discursive direction, expressing a "not yet" completed dimension of translation. Faith seeks understanding while the word-event contextualizes and deepens faith.

For the sake of conceptual clarity, I insist that translatability entails commensurability. In the process of translation there is a factor of equivalence. Here convergence is usually the case. This equivalence could denote a contextual equivalence, with emphasis on the commonalities or similarities in the contexts of those corresponding beliefs. In early Christianity we see that contextual equivalences are sought for establishing points of encounter with the wisdom of non-Christian societies. It is worth noting that between different traditions there are also zones of untranslatability. "You cannot express some of Plato's key thoughts in the Hebrew of Jeremiah or even of the Wisdom literature, but you [also] cannot express them in Homeric Greek."[28] Not to mention: we cannot translate a kerygmatic thought in the Bible into the Totemic system of thought. Two distinct modes of translation are delineated: translation by same-saying and translation by linguistic innovation, by which to transmit the original tradition to other tradition. The task of translation requires "not only same-saying and paraphrase but also a possible extensive use of interpretive glosses and explanations"[29] which could make the difficulty of an exact or literal translation more plausible or amenable to the reader. The untranslatability of central expressions still remains.

Nevertheless, paraphrasing untranslatable meanings of expressions enables us to bring the original language world into our own language world. The experience of incommensurability of language worlds is fused into a broadened horizon of possible understanding. The un-equivalent or untranslatable portions and the equivalent or translatable elements are involved in different cultural configurations, encountering difficulty in communication. In spite of the obstacles, communication may occur as an adventure, creating open space for the dynamic movement of fusion between multiple horizons. It is certain that translation (as hermeneutical dialogue) prevents the subject matter from translation reductionism. The dynamism of the fusion of horizons between

27. Levinas, *Basic Philosophical Writings*, 38.

28. MacIntyre, *Whose Justice?* 375.

29. Ibid., 379.

two different linguistic worlds is undertaken as a confluence or convergence between "our" (etic) perspective and theirs (emic) guided by
mutual learning and respect in an open-ended manner; translation as
hermeneutical conversation has little to do with the ethnocentric self-
centeredness or dominion guided by assimilation and conversion. Good
translation conforms to the model of acquiring a second first language.
The linguistic meaning is revealed from the contexts in which it is used.
The linguistically structured lifeworld shapes and guides the process of
translation in terms of dialectical interplay between equivalent and non-
equivalent elements in an analogical-metaphorical manner.

Grounding Public Missiology: Evangelization and the Semantics of Mission

The signifying content of biblical narrative is a proclamation of the action of YHWH. It is constituted by a complex sequence of events. This is
a salvific drama that defines God's mission. The object of this history is
recieved by faith. The historicity of the living interpretation of Scriptures
constitutes a tradition implies the historicity of faith and hermeneutics.
The Christian faith confesses that God became a human being, the incarnation of the word of God in Jesus Christ. This implies that the actual
mystery of God is revealed in the identification of God with the man
Jesus, while this identification preserves the difference. Analogy, like a
pendulum, never arrives at a conclusion. This perspective overcomes an
anthropocentric principle: whatever is received is received according to
the condition of the recipient.

Talk about God which speaks of the death of Jesus Christ on the
cross is drawn into the event of which it speaks (1 Cor 1:18). What is
expressed in the word of the cross is in the full relation of language.
What is spoken of is described as a language event. In Jesus Christ every
one of God's promises is a "Yes," and we say the "Amen" to the glory of
God. Through the Word of God, God gives us the Holy Spirit in our
hearts as a first installment (2 Cor 1:18–21). Thus a missiology of word-
event based on a hermeneutic of analogy and discourse witnesses to the
gospel narrative with creative freedom and audacity of testimony under
the guidance of the Holy Spirit.

Philip interprets the prophet Isaiah to the Ethiopian eunuch who
was reading the text. He relates the metaphor of a slaughtered sheep
to the good news about Jesus, and in this creative act of interpretation

evangelization takes place. The speaker creatively formulates a metaphor or parable about the gospel message in freedom and testimony. The hearers involve themselves in the same creative freedom by permitting themselves to be addressed and gripped by what is said. Without interpretation, the Ethiopian eunuch would not be introduced to the life of the Word. Missiological hermeneutics bears witness to the embodied Word, the good news about Jesus. Interpretation and witness lead to the action of baptism in the encountering story between Philip and the Ethiopian eunuch. Interpretation connects people with the embodied Word, which became human flesh.

The risen Lord, accompanying the two disciples disappointed on the way to Emmaus, interpreted all of the biblical narrative that the prophets had declared in regard to the suffering Messiah. Beginning with Moses and all the prophets, Jesus Christ "interpreted" to the disciples the things about himself in all the Scriptures. Jesus Christ relates his interpretation to his promise of the Lord's Supper. The Eucharist exhibits itself as the place of a hermeneutic of word-event, accomplishing and completing its missional function. The disciples recounted the things that happened on the way and how the risen Lord was recognized by them in the Eucharist (24:34). When he was taking bread, blessing and breaking it, and giving it to them (24:30), the Word intervened in person, opening their eyes. The Eucharistic experience strengthens the recollection of the disciples to the risen Lord; when the risen Christ opened the Scriptures to the disciples, their hearts were burning within them (24:32). The Holy Spirit is the internal testimony of the word-event within the heart of the believers. By giving a new meaning to the expectation of Jesus as the one to redeem Israel, the risen Lord transforms the disappointed disciples into witnesses to Christ. Christ's interpretation of the Scripture denotes interpretation as the act of service, awakening the disappointed people to become witnesses to the gospel of Jesus Christ; interpretation theory in this regard has little to do with dominion. The risen Lord is self-authenticating in the interpretation of the Scripture as the living voice of God. So, translation must be an act of serving Jesus Christ. Missiology goes beyond the text to the living Word, interpreting the text from the standpoint of word-event.

The language of metaphors, discourse, and parables implies a language event of creative freedom embodied in social-cultural location. In a parable, language is so focused and embodied that the subject of the discourse becomes concrete in language itself. Thus it defines anew the people addressed in their own existence and life setting. Structural anthropology is built on anthropological semiotics. Language is treated as a conceptual model for other aspects of culture, that is, as systems of communication.[30] In the semiotics of structural anthropology there is no hermeneutic circle, nor historicity to the relations of understanding.[31] Studying customs, beliefs, or institutions, structural anthropology as the science of the concrete views savage and totemic logic in terms of the construction of a kaleidoscope. Savage logic works like a kaleidoscope whose chips fall into a variety of patterns. The basis of totemic thought functions like language in communications system.[32] Lévi-Strauss' anthropology as the science of the concrete builds models of reality.

In totemism people analogically arrange the unmistakable differences between kangaroos and ostriches, the seasonal advance and retreat of flood waters, the progress of the sun or the phases of the moon. It grasps the reality by means of *imagines mundi,* fashioning mental constructions that render the world intelligible. Thus, the analogy between eating and marrying, or between fasting and chastity constitutes a metaphorical relation. For instance, when the savage says that the members of his clan are descended from bears or members of the neighbors from eagles, this remark does not mean illiterate biology. The savage says in a concrete metaphorical way that there is an analogous relationship of the clan and the neighbors with the perceived relationship between species. An anthropological perception of communications systems in cultural context does not necessarily contradict a semantic of hermeneutics. Translation implies a transfer from the invisible to the visible. This is the semantic constitution of the similar-dissimilar relationship which is at the roots of symbols.[33]

Understanding the other in an analogical way helps us avoid modernist assumptions about history and interpretation that tend to sacrifice the singularity of the particulars, especially cultures, for the explanatory power of generalized conceptual systems (a metanarrative of rationality). An interpretation without the other is vulnerable to Western theological

30. Lévi-Strauss, *Structural Anthropology*, xii.

31. Ricoeur, *Conflict of Interpretations*, 33.

32. Ibid., 352, 354.

33. Ibid., 60.

ethnocentrism. What is worse, it leads to the illusions of universal sub-
jectivity without recognition of the others.[34]

According to Lévi-Strauss, totemic thought has an affinity to struc-
turalism. Nevertheless, in totemic thought we do not sidestep metaphorical discourse in an analogical relationship with the reality of the
world, thus reducing it to a synchronic linguistic system. The cultural-
linguistic discourse may instead become a tool through which God's
word-event works in the culture of the indigenous people. At this point,
I contend that diachrony (history of meaning) and synchrony (cultural-
linguistic communication system) come into encounter or confluence
through hermeneutical engagement with cultural, anthropological,
emic perspectives.

An interpretive shift in the postcolonial context marks an opportunity for the church to uphold and witness to the place of the God
of Israel and Jesus Christ in conversation with the religious and cultural dignity of those who receive the gospel in non-Western contexts.
Interpretation, as seen in light of a history of effect, inheres in human
life in the public sphere because of the use of language in daily communication. Being historical implies that one's knowledge can never be
complete, but remains always fragmentary, irregular, and open-ended. A
fusion or encounter of horizons between the past (history of meaning)
and the present (contemporary meaning in social-cultural location) is
dialectically structured and dynamically oriented in openness toward
the future. The dynamism of this fusion of horizons challenges narrowness in any given society and pushes for an expansion of new horizons.
The public sphere, the sociological setting in which we live, is not fixed;
rather it is malleable and in flux.

The public relevance of the biblical narrative is revealed in the act of
God's speech through life-giving and prophetic testimony, as witnessed
to in Scripture. In light of God's reconciliation, the church is primed for
and called to undertake public discipleship and service in conformity with
the living voice of Jesus Christ in the world: in dialogue with Israel and
religious outsiders, as well as in promoting a prophetic word of life, justice, forgiveness, and reconciliation in the public realm. This perspective
undergirds a hermeneutic of evangelization tied to the semantic of missiology in the context of World Christianity; it is through this hermeneutic
that we seek to meet the postcolonial challenges to Christian mission.

34. Geertz, *Interpretation of Cultures*, 353–54.

PART II

Contributing to the *Missio Dei* and Missional Church Conversation

4

New Directions

*From Edinburgh via Willingen to
the Missional Church Conversation*

In the study of the Protestant Reformation, some scholars contend that Reformation Protestantism, unlike Roman Catholicism, had no passion for foreign mission. They contend that the teaching of justification by faith alone and the concern to avoid works-righteousness could paralyze any missionary effort. However, I contend that the Reformation teaching of justification has an urgent motive for mission. Lutheran teaching on the priesthood of all believers articulates an idea of vocation and responsibility to serve God in the world. However, David Bosch argues that this idea of the priesthood was actually put into practice by the Anabaptists.[1] Through his evaluation, however, he tends to sidestep the historical legacy of ecclesial *diakonia* in the German Protestant context, especially initiated by John Wichern, Wilhelm Loehe, and Christoph Blumhardt.[2]

According to Bosch's evaluation, Calvin, unlike Luther, is to be appreciated as the reformer who takes responsibility in the world. Calvinism appears to keep alive a missionary spirit more than Lutheranism. Belief in predestination, which is central to the doctrine of the glory or sovereignty of God, included missionary expansion. Nonetheless, I contend

1. Bosch, *Transforming Mission*, 242.
2. Chung, *Christian Mission*, 83–132.

that Calvinist-Puritan mission had its own flaws, being associated with the idea of colonialism in the seventeenth and early eighteenth century. The Calvinist idea of theocracy finds its expression in the Puritan colonies in North America, which were taken to be a manifestation of the kingdom of God on earth. This theocratic direction emphasizes the universal lordship of Christ in society at large and became manifest in Calvinist missionary practice.[3] Calvinist integration of mission and millenarianism led to the firm conviction that England was divinely mandated to guide history to its eschatological end.[4] They believed that their culture was superior to non-Western culture. Divine mission was thus fused with the presumed superiority of Christian culture and undertaken by missionary agents who were in collaboration with the colonial or imperial motives of the state in the nineteenth century.

German Protestantism in the nineteenth century saw the rise of transconfessional, independent missionary societies in Basel, Barmen, Hamburg-Bremen, and Berlin, following Halle and Herrnhut (founded by Zinzendorf). After 1848, the Lutheran missionary societies (Dresden-Leipzig, Hermannsburg, Neuendettelsau, Beklum) attempted to transport the Lutheran confession into the foreign mission field. Gustav Warneck (1834–1910), a Lutheran missiologist, was an outstanding figure in the systematic development of *evangelische Missionslehre* (evangelical theory of mission).

According to him, Christianity alone possesses the fullness of truth and salvation while other religions may have hints of truth and intimations of salvation. Mission is the necessary consequence of the absolute character of Christianity and the biblical-theological basis for mission. Warneck paid special attention to the missional theology of St. Paul. For Warneck the church is the institution of salvation for all humanity. It must engage in mission because it exists for this purpose. Through the church and its missionary works, the Christianizing of all nations takes place.

Warneck was concerned with an ethnological world in which every human being must be regarded as inviolable on the basis of their distinctive personality. Erecting a bridge with ethnological culture helps in reaching the cultural and religious background of the indigenous people. At the center of Warneck's theory of mission is the Christianizing

3. Bosch, *Transforming Mission*, 261.

4. Ibid., 260.

of peoples and their nations. Missionaries bring their own national customs and attitudes and have a paternalistic relationship with those of the natives. His theory of mission connects biblical theology with national consciousness. Warneck's theory of mission remained in force in the German Protestant context until the discussion of *missio Dei* theology after the Second World War.[5]

Edinburgh Conference and Its Missional Direction

Protestant missional theology and activity at the beginning of the twentieth century can be summed up in the following catchphrase: mission as evangelization in one generation. The first World Missionary Conference was held in Edinburgh, Scotland, June 14–23, 1910. It is widely regarded as the most important Protestant missionary conference in the twentieth century. The Edinburgh conference can be seen as the culmination of nineteenth-century Protestant Christian mission as well as the initial stage of the modern Protestant ecumenical movement. The spirit of the Edinburgh Conference was driven by the publication of John Mott's (1865–1955) book *The Evangelization of the World in This Generation.*[6] John Mott became convinced that the entire world could be evangelized in one generation with better missional coordination and a strategic plan. Edinburgh is broadly regarded as the beginning of the ecumenical movement, established in 1948 and it also gave birth to the International Missionary Council (established in 1921).

In parallel with the Edinburgh conference, it is also important to discuss the legacy of the "three self formula" by Henry Venn (1796–1873) and Rufus Anderson (1796–1880) in connection with Roland Allen (1868–1947). In 1821, Henry Venn became an Anglican priest, then a member of the board of the Church Missionary Society. Appointed as its secretary in 1841 until resigning his post in 1872, he also served as editor of the *Christian Observer.* Venn is remembered as the father of the three-self formula along with his American colleague and contemporary Rufus Anderson, who also served as secretary of the American Board of Commissioners for Foreign Missions. Although Venn was an Episcopalian while Anderson came from a Congregationalist background, they were in agreement about the three-self formula. Their

5. Verkuyl, *Contemporary Missiology*, 27–28.
6. Mott, *Evangelization of the World.* See further Bosch, *Transforming Mission*, 336.

concern was about how young churches become independent. The three-self formula argued that the chief goal of Western missions must build churches that are self-supporting, self-governing, and self-propagating. Young churches, it was argued, needed to be given a greater independent voice in administrative affairs and decision making.

It was Roland Allen who genuinely embodied the indigenous church in a missional context. He was an Anglican missionary to China sent out by the Society for the Propagation of the Gospel. He experienced the Boxer Rebellion and saw his mission post devastated. The Chinese reaction to Christianity as a foreign entity led Allen to question the reigning mission policy. He underwent a revolution in his theological thinking, and in his book *Missionary Methods: St. Paul's or Ours?* (published in 1912), he called for a new approach. In this new approach to mission, St. Paul was held up as a crucial paradigm for the church. From the beginning, the earliest Christians were endowed with spiritual authority, and the building up of the churches became their responsibility and calling. Casting off paternalism and ecclesiastical colonialism, Allen argued that the churches must be built up by the new Christians who are led by the Holy Spirit. Rather than underscoring the foreign character of the gospel, the church must be indigenous. His view on the need for native churches to be independent, his call for ecumenical cooperation, and his appeal for responsible lay participation in building up the churches speak for his deep insight and prophetic courage over against the colonialism of his day.[7]

In the Edinburgh Conference, a wave of optimism was sparked in regard to fulfilling the Great Commission in that generation. Mott described the 1910 World Missionary Conference in Edinburgh as "the first attempt at a systematic and careful study of the missionary problems of the world."[8] The catchphrase aroused "the scintillating missionary optimism" of that period characterized as the general enthusiasm for conquering the world for Christian civilization. In this regard, David Bosch characterized the missionary atmosphere of the time as "pragmatic, purposeful, activist, impatient, self-confident, single-minded, and triumphalist."[9] Although fourteen hundred delegates joined, the vast majority of them were Western, British, or American.

7. Verkuyl, *Contemporary Missiology*, 53–54.

8. Walls, *Cross-Cultural Process*, 59.

9. Bosch, *Transforming Mission*, 336.

The Edinburgh Conference initiated a new structure and constituency through reflection on Christianity on the global scale. It worked as catalyst to begin a series of major worldwide conferences sponsored by the International Missionary Council, including Jerusalem (1928), Tambaram (near Chennai, India, 1938), and Accra, Ghana (1957–58). It also marked the genuine renaissance of mission studies.[10] The century of the First World Missionary Conference was characterized by extreme optimism until the advent of the two world wars.

Karl Barth and His Contributions to Missional Theology

After the First World War, Karl Barth began to challenge all theological-missional thought built on humanitarian optimism or theological liberalism through his dialectical theology of the crisis (the first edition of the Romans commentary approved in 1919; the thoroughly revised second edition of the Romans commentary in 1922). The legacy of Edinburgh was critically developed in his thought towards understanding mission as Trinitarian activity or *missio Dei*.

Karl Barth, in his pastoral period in Safenwill, already understood a significant dimension of the church's mission through his connection with the movement of the Blumhardts. Christoph Blumhardt (1842–1919) was a controversial figure in German Lutheran Pietism. His charismatic healing ministry in Bad Ball was connected with his social witness in the political sphere, driving him to become a member of Social Democratic Party. Richard Wilhelm (1873–1930) became the son-in-law of Blumhardt. In the years of 1899 to 1919, Wilhelm joined the service of the General Evangelical Protestant Mission Society (East Asian Mission). He was assigned to Tsingtau in the newly founded German colony of Kiachow, on China's Yellow Sea. During this period of missionary activity he had a significant amount of correspondence with Blumhardt. Shortly after Wilhelm arrived in China in 1899, the Boxer Rebellion erupted against European colonialism. Missionaries became special targets of hatred and attack. From 1900 to 1906, Blumhardt was active as a congressman for the Social Democratic Party in the parliament of Wurtemburg. In his lively letter exchange with Wilhelm, Blumhardt saw a parallel between his social witness to God's reign for the poor in Germany and Wilhelm's missionary activity for the colonized people in

10. Walls, *Cross-Cultural Process*, 61.

China. In his correspondence Blumhardt articulated an understanding of the church's mission quite different from Warneck, by recognizing the human rights and dignity of indigenous people.

Blumhardt contrasted the gospel of Jesus Christ with Western Christendom as a religion. Mission for him implies bringing together Christians and non-Christians under the Word of God, the gospel of Jesus Christ; it has little to do with "Christianizing," or "Westernizing" the indigenous people. Blumhardt argued that taking the gospel of Christ into the non-Christian world means doing justice against sin and promoting life against death rather than expanding the German form of Christendom as the absolute religion. God's kingdom turns itself toward those who became victims of Western colonialism. In light of the living reality of God's reign through Christ's reconciliation, Blumhardt recognized the dignity and value of Chinese culture and religion. Following the missional advice of Blumhardt, Wilhelm was committed to promoting God's love and reconciliation with the Chinese people through prophetic diaconal service in the foundation of a new provincial educational system. Wilhelm made cross-cultural contributions through the study and translation of Chinese philosophy and religion. In the cases of Allen, Blumhardt, and Wilhelm we see a Protestant parallel with Catholic mission as prophetic critique and solidarity with the victims in the examples of Las Casas and Ricci.

When Blumhardt died in 1919, the young Barth in Safenwil hailed Blumhardt as a theologian of hope for all humanity in his obituary (entitled *Vergangenheit und Zukunft*).[11] Blumhardt's theology of the eschatological hope considerably shaped and influenced Barth's theological thinking of mission. We find his influence on Barth even later in his doctrine of reconciliation in *Church Dogmatics*.[12]

Mission as Trinitarian Sending

Karl Barth articulated his understanding of mission as an activity of God in a paper at the Brandenburg Missionary Conference in 1932. In it he argued that the church can be authentically missional only in obedience to God's initiative in sending the Son and the Holy Spirit to the world.

11. Barth, "Past and Future," in *Beginnings of Dialectic Theology*, 1, 41–42.

12. For a detailed analysis of the relationship between Blumhardt and Barth see Chung, *Christian Mission*, 116–32. See Barth, *Church Dogmatics* IV.3.2 § 69.3 "Jesus is Victor."

Primarily, Barth's Trinitarian concept of mission accentuates that the church's mission follows what God has done for the earth, humanity, and living creatures. Barth's concept of Trinitarian sending accentuates God's act of sending the Son and the Spirit for the world. The church emerges where God is pleased to have it emerge in God's lordship and mercy. In his seminal paper "Die Theologie und die Mission in der Gegenwart" (1932),[13] Barth states that mission began with the divine sending of God's Son in the Holy Spirit. The church can be missional only in obedience to God. Mission and theology should receive the free grace of God. God, through divine omnipotence and mercy, desires a church, thus mission and theology are a matter of divine purpose and confirmation. Mission and theology are built upon the solid rock of God's election; God speaks God's word in God's time and God's Spirit blows wherever it wills. Mission and theology can only be considered in light of God's free and non-prejudiced grace.

Barth insists that the purpose and motive of mission must flow from the church's obedience to God's grace. The Lord of the church does not conform to any human system or points of view. According to Barth, the term *missio* is an expression of the doctrine of the Trinity. In other words, mission as God's initiative is an expression of the divine sending forth of the self, the sending of the Son and the Holy Spirit.[14] In this light, Barth defines mission as the church's act in confession of God's self-revelation in Jesus Christ as well as obedience to the calling of Jesus Christ. Jesus Christ is the content of the Word of God that the church serves. Thus the church's mission must be grounded in the activity of the triune God in service to the Word of God.[15]

The mission is the announcement of the gospel of Jesus Christ, so we cannot ground it on general ethics just as theology cannot be grounded on general concepts of science. Rather it is grounded on God's gracious election, which is the "sum of the gospel." At issue in mission is the service of the announcement of the gospel of the kingdom of God. The evidence, system, the point of contact, and the certainty should not be sought in human instances, but always in God as the ground of the

13. Barth, "Die Theologie und die Mission," in *Zwischen den Zeiten* 10:3 (1932), 189–215. Repr. Barth, *Theologische Fragen und Antworten*, 100–26.

14. Thomas, ed., *Classic Texts*, 105–6.

15. Barth, "Die Theologie und die Mission," 101.

church's mission. We must beg the action, will, and power of the mission always and only from God.[16]

However, according to Barth, theology cannot be fused with mission, because theological work has its own law and way.[17] Theology presupposes that the church attempts to become faithful in the service of proclamation. In this regard theology is related to the church by asking about the rightness of the church's missional action.[18] The church faces a theological critique which is based on Jesus Christ. Theology makes the church pay attention to the ground and objectives of its proclamation and mission. Hence the exegesis of Holy Scripture is the unique and central task of theology.[19] The Word of God and the Holy Spirit perform the actual and effective critique of the churchly and missionary act. This is the narrow gate that theological critique should serve.

Barth emphasizes that the mission motive should be clear. If the concept of mission is from the doctrine of the Trinity, and if it is the expression of the divine self-sending through the Son and the Holy Spirit to the world, mission motive must be grounded in God's free grace. The mission motive is inseparably connected with the right summons to the mission. This perspective opposes religious or civilizing propaganda or an economic political ideology or power play.[20] Barth's sharp critique of impure motives of Christian mission persists in his doctrine of the Church's ministry and mission within the framework of reconciliation in *Church Dogmatics*.[21] Jesus Christ as the living Word of God is the eternal subject of the gospel, which has little to do with "the aim to strengthen confessional positions," "to extend European or American culture and civilization," or "the desire to support colonial or general political interests and aspirations."[22] As the task of mission, announcement of the message of the kingdom of God is more than conversion of individuals.[23] The actual point of contact does not lie in the realm and

16. Ibid., 110–11.

17. Ibid., 111.

18. Ibid., 112.

19. Ibid.

20. Thomas, ed., *Classic Texts*, 104.

21. CD IV/3.2 §72 "The Holy Spirit and the Sending of the Christian Community."

22. CD IV/3.2:875.

23. Barth, "Die Theologie und die Mission," 120. See CD IV/3.2:876. "This [conversion] is the work of God alone."

power of human language, but God's grace—where and how always the language wants to connect itself—is proclaimed as God's miracle.[24]

The Trinitarian Aspect of Mission

It is unfortunate that Barth's concept of mission as Trinitarian initiative in his 1932 paper is not explored within his full theological reflection on the Trinity. In his exposition of the Trinity,[25] Barth insists that the root of the Trinity is expressed in a way that God revealed God's self as the Lord.[26] Barth's concept of God in the Jewish–Christian relationship is of special significance for his discussion of the Trinity and mission. "God's being is in becoming" (Eberhard Jüngel)[27] cannot be properly understood without consideration of the God of Israel. God's being shares itself in the history of God in the life of Israel.

Barth further defines God as the One who loves in freedom. If God reveals God's self as the Lord, loving the church, humanity, and the world in God's freedom, mission belongs to God's Trinitarian history characterized by lordship, love, transformation, and reconciliation. God's reconciliation in Jesus Christ who is the electing God as well as the elected man is the actual basis for God's mission to the world. More sharply, Barth articulates the love of the triune God in freedom as the one who changes everything (*alles in allem real verändernde Tatsache dass Gott ist*). As Barth provocatively elaborates, "the fact that not only sheds new light on, but materially changes, all things and everything in all things—the fact that God is."[28] In the light of Trinitarian mission and reconciliation, Barth's missional theology becomes more holistic, dynamic, and socially and critically engaged in the public sphere.

God's being is in the event of God's action; through the revelation of this action we have a share in God's life.[29] In this light, God's being as a personifying God is understood as "being in person" (incarnation). God as self-motivated person exists only on the basis of God's gracious

---

24. Barth, "Die Theologie und die Mission," 125.
25. CD I/1:295–489.
26. CD I/1:307.
27. Jüngel, *God's Being Is in Becoming.*
28. CD II/1:258.
29. CD II/1:263.

creation and providence. God underlines God's gracious reconciliation of the sinner with a view to God's future redemption.[30]

⟨God seeks and creates fellowship with us through the incarnation; this seeking and creating of fellowship is identical with the reconciliation of sinful people in the gospel of Jesus Christ.⟩This fellowship finds its crown and final confirmation in the eschatological future of God. ⟨God does not exist in solitude but in fellowship.⟩

In the mystery of God's loving, God communicates God's self to the one loved. A human being becomes a person on the basis of being loved by God and can thus love God in return. To be a person means to be what God is, that is the One who loves in God's way.[31] In this way God is the personifying person. Barth's concept of God's modes of being cannot be properly understood without connection to God-in-person as the personifying God. God's being in love means God's being in freedom. God's lordship must be understood in light of God's lordship in love and freedom standing in personal fellowship with us.[32]

At this point, Barth sees the world in the light of the primary creative freedom of God, which embraces God's true immanence as well as God's true transcendence.[33] Barth sharply rejects a mythology of partially identifying God with the world under the rubric of panentheism.[34] God is free to be immanent, so Barth advocates for God's freedom to transcend and to be immanent in light of God's identity as one who loves in freedom through seeking personal *koinonia* with creatures.

In the Trinitarian sending, the three modes of being are always together in a *perichoresis*. At this point, Barth recognizes the beauty of God in the Trinitarian communion so that the triunity of God is the foundation of God's beauty and mystery for us. The work of the Son reveals the beauty of God. We recognize the beauty of God in Jesus Christ.[35] Barth's theology of triunity is the secret of the beauty incarnated in Jesus Christ and it provides the church's mission with an aesthetical dimension.

30. CD II/1:272.
31. CD II/1:284.
32. CD II/1:301.
33. CD II/1:309.
34. CD II/1:312.
35. CD II/1:664.

Theology is the most beautiful of all the sciences, so mission reflects the beauty of God in sending the Son and the Holy Spirit.[36]

God lives eternally in a *perichoresis*, a mutual indwelling and interworking of the three forms of eternity (pre-temporal, supra [or co]-temporal, and post-temporal).[37] For Barth, the time of mission is grounded in the pre-temporality of the Father and the Son in the fellowship of the Holy Spirit, and it is actualized historically in God's supra-temporality in Jesus Christ in connection to God's post-temporality, God's Sabbath rest. The kingdom of God consists in the fact of God's final rest—God will be all in all.[38] God is the God of all hope. Our past is overcome and dissolved by God's future. This is Barth's attempt to conceptualize the theological concept of eternity by setting it free from "the Babylonian captivity of an abstract opposite to the concept of time."[39]

The triune God always stands unconditionally and passionately on the side of the threatened innocent, the oppressed poor, widows, orphans, and aliens against the lofty. God acts on behalf of the lowly against those who already enjoy rights and privileges and on behalf of those who are denied and deprived of them.[40] For Barth, the threefold aspect of the triune God can be characterized in terms of God's lordship, God's love in freedom, and God the Wholly Other as Wholly Changer. This perspective is fully integrated into his theology of the triunity (*Dreieinigkeit*) of God. Unity of Trinity and Trinity in unity rejects tritheism; Barth insists that biblical monotheism is precisely what is affirmed in the church's doctrine of the Trinity. The God of Israel is the basis and foundation for Christian understanding of God in Christ and through the Spirit.[41] Christian theology of the Trinity thus does not dethrone the God of Israel in a supercessionist sense.

The threeness is grounded in the one essence of the revealed God in Christ. God is God in a special way as Father, as Son, and as Spirit. The *perichoresis* implies that the Father, Son, and Spirit subsist in their relationship one with another.[42] Barth utilizes John of Damascus's

36. CD II/1:656.

37. CD II/1:640.

38. CD II/1:630.

39. CD II/1:611.

40. CD II/1:386.

41. CD I/1:351.

42. CD I/1:366.

notion of *perichoresis* which centers on the relations of origin, in contrast to the way the term *perichoresis* is used in social doctrines of the Trinity. However, God's works like the *missio Dei* are assigned to God's acts, not to God's essence as such. Here a concept of mission, a participation of divine *perichoresis* is not suggested,[43] because the *mysterium trinitatis* remains a mystery. Barth's missional theology should be understood as the church's participation in God's reconciling work in Christ with the world. This perspective endorses a spiritual formation grounded in Reformation theology of "happy exchange" (Luther) and union with Christ (Calvin). The Barthian sending model built on Trinitarian election includes the experiential aspect of our *koinonia* with the living Christ.[44] It marks theological progress in overcoming anthropocentric and ecclesiocentric notions of mission that are vulnerable to a charge of colonialism.

Missio Dei in Willingen and Beyond

Barth's theology of divine sending was the key idea in the 1952 meeting of the IMC in Willingen (1952), Germany. The defining phrase, *missio Dei* was originally coined by German missiologist and director of the Basel mission Karl Hartenstein in 1934. Hartenstein summarized the result of the World conference in Willingen: the commission of mission demonstrates that the church is not the final goal of the mission, but the kingdom that means the lordship of Christ over the world and the entire cosmos. The mission is not only the conversion of the individual, obedience to the word of the Lord, and the church's responsibility, but also participation in the sending of the Son, the *missio Dei*, with the comprehensive goal of the establishment of the lordship of Christ over the whole creation.[45]

However, I sense that Barth did not continue to develop his theology of *missio Dei* in a Trinitarian framework; rather after Bonhoeffer's critique of Barth's theology of predestination (which charged Barth with a positivism of revelation), Barth concentrated his approach to mission on God's reconciliation in Jesus Christ. In this new direction, Barth incorporated the Lutheran theology of *diakonia* represented by

43. CD I/1:371.

44. For Barth's positive evaluation of the Reformation theology of union with Christ in connection with divinization in christological and adopted sense, see CD I/1:239–40.

45 Freytag, ed., *Mission zwischen Gestern und Morgen*, 54.

John Wichern and the Blumhardts in his theology of God's reconciliation; Barth's theology of reconciliation cannot be properly understood without Bonhoeffer's insight into an ethics of reconciliation.

As a matter of fact, it was Georg Vicedom who reconceptualized the Trinitarian model of *missio Dei* theology in light of God's universal lordship, which is grounded in the Lutheran model of two kingdoms. Vicedom, a famous German missiologist, coming from the confessional tradition of Wilhelm Loehe in Neuendettelsau, must be truly regarded as the father of the theology of God's mission in the ecumenical context. In Vicedom's conception of the *missio Dei*, we perceive that God becomes not only the Sender but also the One who is sent. Catholic dogmatics since Augustine speaks of sending or the mission within the triune God. "Every sending of one Person results in the presence of the Other."[46] This perspective emphasizes God's embodiment in Jesus Christ. It is unfortunate that Bosch completely neglects the legacy of George Vicedom and Wihlem Loehe and their respective contributions to God's mission, missional church, and global mission.

Furthermore, God is not only the One sent but is the content of the sending, because "in every person of the deity God works in God's entirety."[47] Mission is grounded in the triune God: Sender, Sent, and Sending (John 17:18, cf. 16:5–16, 20:21–2). This perspective underlines the mutuality in sending or communion of Trinitarian life which characterizes mission as fellowship with God; thus the missional church exists as fellowship and communion, in continuity with the apostolic mission. "The apostles have the duty and assignment to establish the church and thereby they become the foundation of the building upon which all other work was to be based (1 Cor 3:9ff)."[48] Christ has given the church an office leading to missionary service and ministry of the divine Word. "Accordingly the pastoral office in the congregation in all its ramifications can have no other purpose than to lead the congregation to influence the world and to make her fit missionary service."[49]

Vicedom develops his conception of God's mission from God's intention in salvation in the historical sense. The church is defined as the outcome of the missional-salvific activity of the triune God.

46. Vicedom, *Mission of God*, 7.
47. Ibid., 8
48. Ibid., 64.
49. Ibid., 90. Cf. Stevens, *Other Six Days*, 194–96.

Thus Vicedom cites approvingly the concept of *missio Dei* from the Conference at Willingen: "[The mission] is participation in the sending of the Son, in the *missio Dei*, with the inclusive aim of establishing the lordship of Christ over the whole redeemed creation. The missionary movement of which we are a part has its source in the Triune God."[50] God's mission is to be seen in the mission of Jesus Christ, because "there is no participation in Christ without participation in His mission to the world.[51] The *missio Dei* which embraces the entire activity of the triune God is equated with God's universal lordship: in both a general and a special way. God identifies God's self with the promises to Israel for the sake of the One who is to come. Israel's mission is fulfilled in Jesus Christ, the Son of David—the Son of man.[52] The *missio Dei* begins with Jesus Christ, while in the incarnation and enthronement God made God's self the very content of the missional sending. Through the Spirit, the disciples become witness and co-workers with God.[53] The apostolate of the church is based on discipleship as the innermost fellowship with and service to the triune God.[54]

For Vicedom, God's mission is grounded in the death and resurrection of Jesus Christ, which is the foundation for the church as the body of Christ. The church's mission finds its expression in the fellowship with the gospel which was at the heart of Apostolic mission.[55] Mission as dialogue with people of other faiths can be seen in light of God's universal lordship. The world of other religions retains a positive meaning in light of God's ongoing creation. In configuration of God's mission as a hermeneutical dialogue, the gospel is a critique of and also a fulfillment of religions. Evangelization as dialogue remains central in interreligious dialogue.[56] The church's mission in pluralistic society becomes the church in diaspora as affirmed in Willingen Conference. The church in the diaspora becomes a fundamentally missional church. Missional church has only one means to help people: the Word of God. This is the love of Christ through effective work of the Holy Spirit. When the

50. Vicedom, *Mission of God*, 5.

51. Ibid., 6.

52. Ibid., 51.

53. Ibid., 80.

54. Ibid., 81.

55. Vicedom, *Mission im ökumenischen Zeitalter*, 16–7.

56. Ibid., 41–42.

missional church in the diaspora trusts in the triune God, the church's mission can be vibrant, following our vocation in witness to God's word and love.[57]

Sidestepping Vicedom's theology of *missio Dei*, Bosch outlines Willingen's message in terms of a Trinitarian model of sending and sent. Father, Son, and Holy Spirit send the church into the world. The church's mission is a participation in the sending mission of God.[58] Mission is seen as God's movement to the world in which the church becomes an instrument in witnessing to this divine mission. In the context of the *missio Dei* and the missional church conversation, Guder defines the *missio Dei* as the gospel, which expresses good news about God's goodness revealed in God's Word through Israel's experience. God's mission begins with calling Israel to be a blessing to the nations. It reached its climax and culmination in the incarnation of God's salvific work in the ministry, crucifixion, and resurrection of Jesus Christ. God's mission continues in the sending of the Holy Spirit to call forth and empower the church as the witness to God's good news in Jesus Christ, moving toward God's consummation in the eschaton. The missiological reorientation of theology under the mission of God, which is based on a sending or missionary God, redefines and refurbishes a theological understanding of the Trinity in a practical, dynamic, and relational way.[59]

In this framework it is stressed that God's mission continues to take shape in the apostolic community, the church. A movement entitled "The Gospel and Our Culture Network" makes an important contribution to missionary ecclesiology rooted in the Trinitarian *missio Dei* perspective. Here the nature and vocation of the church is articulated so as to emphasize a missional ecclesiology that is biblical, historical, contextual, eschatological, and practical.[60] In this project of the *missio Dei* and missional church, it is also important to notice that in the biblical definition of the church's mission the church is essentially multicultural. God's people are formed in distinctive and unique ways in each time and place in interaction with every culture in which the church is shaped and constituted as a community of witness.[61]

57. Ibid., 190, 194.

58. Thomas, ed., *Classic Texts*, 104–6.

59. Bosch, *Transforming Mission*, 390.

60. Guder, ed., *Missional Church*, 11.

61. Ibid., 233.

Barth's concept of the *missio Dei* influences David Bosch's *Transforming Mission* (reminiscent of Richard Niebuhr's typology of Christ and culture) and The Gospel and Our Culture Network within the Reformed and ecumenical framework. Bosch noticed that Karl Barth was the decisive Protestant missiologist in his generation. Under the rubric of soteriology, Barth develops his ecclesiology in three phases: the teaching of justification is followed by "The Holy Spirit and the Gathering of the Christian Community"; the teaching of sanctification leads to "The Holy Spirit and the Upbuilding of the Christian Community"; and the teaching of vocation is then followed by "The Holy Spirit and the Sending of the Christian Community."[62]

Beyond Barth, Bosch boldly defines the church-in-mission in terms of sacrament and sign. The church-in-mission is a sign in the sense of pointer, symbol, example, or model. Furthermore, it is a sacrament in the sense of mediation, representation, or anticipation. Mission is a foretaste or the sacrament of anticipation of God's reign in history.[63] If the church-in-mission is sacramentally understood, elevated to the status of a sacrament, this concept of *missio Dei* as a pledge of what is to come is to be developed within the framework of the theology of hope or eschatology.

Trinitarian Mission in New Direction

Developing the legacy of Karl Barth in the North American context, an attempt is undertaken to transform the church by serving and participating in the *missio Dei*, representing the reign of God. A transforming model of covenant and law[64] can be further developed in terms of the sending character of God (Augustine, Karl Barth, and Karl Rahner) as well as the social doctrine of the Trinity embedded with the intra-relationship of the three persons of the Godhead (*perichoresis*) (John Zizioulas and Jürgen Moltmann).[65] In their current writing project, Craig Van Gelder and Dwight Zscheile map and extend the missional church conversation and elaborate a *missio Dei* theology by integrating

---

62. Bosch, *Transforming Mission*, 373.

63. Ibid., 11.

64. Bliese, "Developing Evangelical Public Leadership," in Van Gelder, ed., *Missional Church*, 91.

65. Van Gelder, "Theological Education," in Van Gelder, ed., *Missional Church*, 43.

the divine sending with divine social communion. Here they attempt to undertake missional engagement with culture in a globalized world.[66]

Within the context of the missional literature, this literature has demonstrated a theological, congregational, and spiritual response to the decline of Christian religion in North America. Addressing the individualistic and private manner of American religious behavior, the missional church movement proposes missiological and congregational ecclesiology by emphasizing what it means for the church to be a part of the *missio Dei* in the world.

In the discussion of God's mission and the missional church, we need to mention the contribution of Lesslie Newbigin. As general secretary of the International Missions Council (1959–1965), Newbigin was a central figure during the post-Willingen period. As *missio Dei* theology was being used to separate God's mission from the church, Newbigin began to reemphasize the importance of developing missiology within the framework of Trinitarian ecclesiology.[67]

Against two extreme versions of mission, evangelistic church growth or practicing the gospel for the Kingdom of God, Newbigin reconceptualizes the theology of *missio Dei* in terms of a sign, agent, and foretaste of the kingdom of God. The gift of the Holy Spirit, the *arrabōn* which is a true measure of the justice and peace of the kingdom, makes the church a witness to the gospel.[68] A Trinitarian model of mission is found in the gospel of John 20:21–22. We see the continuity between the Father's mission and Jesus' mission and the ongoing mission of the Holy Spirit in the life and witness of the church. In his book *The Open Secret*, from the point of view of the Trinitarian faith, Newbigin elaborates missiology and ecclesiology by dealing with this threefold continuity as: 1) Proclaiming the Kingdom of the Father: Mission as Faith in Action; 2) Sharing the Life of the Son: Mission as Love in Action; 3) Bearing the Witness of the Spirit: Mission as Hope in Action.[69]

Recently, the Trinitarian perspective on the *missio Dei* has developed into a full-blown missionary ecclesiology with strong emphasis on the reign of God. This is the driving force for the church's missionary existence. Newbigin recovered the Trinitarian character of mission

66. Van Gelder and Zscheile, *Missional Church*, 146.

67. Newbigin, *Gospel in a Pluralist Society*, 118.

68. Ibid., 134–35.

69. Newbigin, *Open Secret*.

grounded in the person and work of Jesus Christ, and trust in the reality and power of the Holy Spirit. Here "God's fatherly rule in the events of secular history . . . [is] in the revolutionary changes which are everywhere taking place in the life of the world."[70] A Trinitarian discussion of the *missio Dei* within the perspective of missional ecclesiology and congregational mission makes an important contribution to our contemporary study of missional church.

In this context the term "missional theology" is *generalized* and missional hermeneutics in a generic sense is defined as cutting across the various disciplines within theological education, calling for an interdisciplinary approach. It sees the world as the larger horizon of God's work, focusing on congregational life in that broader context. Within the larger framework of God's mission in the world, it is stressed that the church's privileged participation in its formation, education, and vocation, along with various other foci, are integrated and incorporated in the study of God's mission. Contexts are attended to since missional theology recognizes the contextual character of all theology and cultivates missional imagination by relating it to the cultural and religious other. Scholars in the circle of the *missio Dei* and missional church conversation argue that missional theology privileges the development of practical theology and provides a larger framework within which all other disciplines (biblical exegesis, church history, systematic theology, and church practices) converse and work.[71]

Having considered this, if missional theology wants to privilege the development of practical theology and provides a larger framework for other theological disciplines, it is imperative for missional theology and missional church to professionally engage in biblical hermeneutics and exegesis. Notably in regard to Paul's theology of mission and Israel in Romans 9–11, missional theology must consider its significance for the church's relationship with Israel in biblical and post-biblical contexts. Furthermore, missional theology must avoid repeating itself as a Western-centric form of mission, by being open to the postcolonial reality of World Christianity. It should learn from the discipline of church history the painful history of mission tied to the Puritan notion of manifest destiny or colonialism in the past. When missional theology encounters systematic theology and church practices, it must be a form

70. Guder, ed., *Missional Church*, 82. Cf. Newbigin, *Trinitarian Faith*, 77.

71. Van Gelder, "Theological Education," in Van Gelder, ed., *Missional Church*, 44.

of constructive theology, seeking to reinterpret and refurbish the biblical narrative, the church's confessional language, and public practices in non-Christian, postcolonial contexts. In this light, missional theology cannot sidestep what public theology, World Christianity, and postcolonial proponents seek to do in challenging the missional church.

Theologically, a missional hermeneutics articulates the triune God (sending and *perichoresis*) as the creator and the redeemer for the sake of God's reconciliation, at the center of which remains the kingdom of God. The church exists now as a sign, foretaste, and instrument of the kingdom of God by debunking and challenging principalities and powers. It is a messianic and eschatological community.[72] The church militant and the church triumphant as a sign, foretaste, and instrument of God's reign stand in tension and conflict with the reality of lordless powers (power and principalities).

In the twentieth century, according to David Bosch, the church was perceived as a body of people sent on a mission. The guiding goal was to expand the church into new locales. After World War II the church as the sent people began to face a postcolonial challenge on the part of newly independent nations and young churches throughout the Third World. These dissenting voices attempted to dismantle the colonial worldviews of the European nations embedded within Western missionary agencies and institutions. In the wake of the colonial charge, there occurred a shift from an ecclesiocentric view of mission to a theocentric one, that is the view of *missio Dei* as translation.

In this context Newbigin's contribution to intercultural studies deserves attention. In addition to Trinitarian missiology, Newbigin made a substantial contribution to the relationship between the gospel and the plurality of human cultures. The question of the relation of gospel to culture is one of the most controversial and vigorously debated subjects in contemporary missiology. The gospel comes to human community in the words of a particular language because language is the primary vehicle of a culture. According to the pattern of dualism in regard to gospel and culture, gospel is defined as a disembodied message in contrast to culture as a historically conditioned pattern of social life. In this dualistic pattern, the gospel has been reduced to a matter of individual belief and conduct. In fact, this dichotomizing of gospel and culture reveals the dualism in deep-seated Western thinking: a purely individualistic

72. Van Gelder, *Ministry of Missional Church*, 110–11.

Christianity reflects the individualism of Western culture with the elevation of autonomous human reason as the judge of all things.[73] So, the gospel was colonized by the modern project of enlightenment.

In expressions of faith there are enormous cultural variations among Christians in Nigeria, India, Samoa, Europe, and the United States. In African churches, when devout and committed Christians were faced with a difficult decision, it was often the traditional African way of thinking which guided and determined the decision process. The "Church Growth" school of missiologists led by McGavran tend to absolutize culture and to minimize the cultural changes. In McGavran's words we read: "God accepts culture" (Lausanne Congress for World Evangelization, 1974).[74] They also agree that gospel challenges backward elements of culture such as cannibalism, the death penalty for petty offenses, or the ancient Indian custom of *sati* (the burning of a man's widow with his body on the funeral pyre).

According to Newbigin, the most fundamental element in culture is language. In the task of communicating the gospel narrative in a language, every translation involves a fresh interpretation. On the day of Pentecost the mighty works of God were communicated in their own languages. Pentecost is the biblical fulcrum affirming that God accepts language. Differing from the "Church Growth" school of missiology, Newbigin brings a dialectical stance about culture: a critical position regarding a total relativism concerning culture in which negative elements of human cultures must be rejected—such as cannibalism, *sati*, slavery, the inhuman treatment of the so-called "untouchable" under the traditional caste system, and tribal custom in Papua New Guinea.

In recognition of the falsity of the pattern of dichotomizing the gospel and culture, Newbigin also acknowledges the fact that there cannot be a gospel that is not culturally embodied. This refers to the historical nature of the gospel, which happened at a particular time and place in Palestine. As Christianity has developed and become established in Europe and the United States, the missionaries have brought a gospel expressed in their language and the life-style of a particular culture rather than "an ethereal something disinfected of all human cultural ingredients."[75] Later in deep study of the Bible in their own language, the

73. Newbigin, *Gospel in a Pluralist Society*, 188–89.

74. Ibid., 184.

75. Ibid., 189.

new Christians begin to look critically at the forms of Christianity that were received and implanted by the missionaries. Here, a hermeneutical filter of refining the biblical narrative occurs by distinguishing the gospel proper according to the Scriptures from the traditional culture of the missionaries.[76] Newbigin notices that the World Missionary Conference of Edinburgh is critiqued for its alleged confusion of confidence in the gospel with a great confidence in the expansive power of Western civilization. According to Newbigin, however, this charge is not entirely acceptable, because there were strong voices and critiques of the so-called Christian civilization in the Edinburgh Conference.

To overcome the conflation of Christianity and Western civilization, Newbigin argues that Western Christianity must learn to listen humbly to the voices of other cultures. Acknowledging that the gospel is always and everywhere culturally embodied and translatable, Newbigin proposes the basic ingredients of theological hermeneutics: the content of the revelation in Christ, defined by the double elements of cross and resurrection. The gospel is embodied as a living word-event in the mission of Jesus for the kingdom of God. This aspect can challenge culturally conditioned translations and interpretations of the biblical narrative confined within Western Christianity in light of the witness of those who read the Bible in different cultures. In listening to others, mutual correction is necessary and fruitful in light of the theological subject matter. The gospel endorses an immensely wide diversity among human cultures, while the theological subject matter of God's self-interpretation in Christ in the presence of the Holy Spirit transcends any total relativism undertaken in the name of cultural translation. The great diversity of cultures can be welcomed and cherished while the claim of any one culture to dominance can be resisted.[77] God's universal reign in the covenant with Noah and Christ's grace of justification (death) and reconciliation (resurrection) guides Newbigin's theology of culture and his missiology as intercultural study. "As long as the earth endures, seedtime and harvest, cold and heat, summer and winter, day and night, shall not cease" (Gen 8:22).

Having considered this, Newbigin paves a new horizon for undertaking a constructive missiology—with no Christendom hangover or colonialism vestige—in regard to recognition of culture, expansion

76. Ibid., 190.
77. Ibid., 197.

of God's grace, and critical distance from backwardness or individu-alistic dominance. Such perspective can be hermeneutically, cultural-anthropologically deepened and refurbished by reclaiming mission as constructive, public mission grounded in God's narrative in Christ's *diakonia* under the guidance of the Holy Spirit in engagement with the postcolonial challenge and the voice of World Christianity.

5

The Place of *Diakonia* in the Mission of God
Hermeneutical Construction

In continuity with the *missio Dei* and missional church conversation, this chapter is a hermeneutical-missiological endeavor to reframe God's mission and missional church through exploring Christ's *diakonia* of reconciliation and word-event understood in a Trinitarian sense. A hermeneutical focus brings an important perspective to the study of missions, because hermeneutics is by nature concerned with the encounter with something other. Hans Georg Gadamer used the term "fusion of horizons" to describe the process by which one perspective, with all its history, background, and presuppositions, encounters another perspective with its own history, background, and presuppositions. In a hermeneutical understanding it is acknowledged that one cannot see the other in a purely objective fashion—one's understanding will always be influenced by one's own horizon, what one brings to the table in dialogue with the other.

The concept of the fusion of horizons is illuminating for missiology in at least three ways. 1) It recognizes that every interpretation of Scripture is colored by the horizon of the interpreter. The missionary does not have a culture-neutral understanding of the Scripture, but one that is colored by his or her culture. The encounter of the missionary with the Word of God through Scripture (which has its own background and tradition) is one fusion. 2) It recognizes the horizon of the receiving culture. Non-Christian peoples are not a blank-slate on which the missionary can write. They have their own traditions, language, culture, laws, stories, etc. which influence how they hear and interpret what is said to them. The encounter of the missionary with the people to whom he or she is sent is another fusion. 3) It recognizes that the people of the receiving culture will have their own encounter with the texts and with the living voice of God, which may be different, and expressed in different ways, from that of the missionary's culture. This is yet another fusion. Gadamer's theory of the fusion of horizons also can be contextualized and deepened in encounter with cultural anthropological descriptions of the receiving culture.[1]

This hermeneutical perspective helps renew a model of Lutheran missiology, and it takes seriously a paradigm shift in the theology of mission in terms of a "move from 'reactive reform' to some kind of 'innovative initiative.'"[2] In this hermeneutical-missiological reenvisioning of God's mission as word-event, it is important to contextualize Luther's theological hermeneutics. Scripture is a witness to the Word of God, setting forth Christ ("what urges and promotes Christ"). Luther's hermeneutic of "canon within the canon" relates to the *viva vox evangelii* (gospel as living voice of God). A concept of *viva vox evangelii* implies a priority of the spoken word (God's Saying; *Dabar* in Hebrew) over the written word (the Scripture) while it is attested in accordance with the Scripture.[3]

God's Mission and a Theology of *Diakonia*

For missional and diaconal ecclesiology, a theological definition of *diakonia* is important and indispensable. A theology of *diakonia* can be understood as an interdisciplinary reflection on God's grace in the life of Jesus Christ (a grace of justification and reconciliation), as it engages in the Word of God through the hermeneutical principle of law and gospel and in its eschatological light. It also incorporates diverse methods and knowledge of the social and human sciences (such as sociology, psychology, economics, social pedagogy, ethics, and hermeneutics) into

1. I appreciate Dana Scopatz, my assistant, for this apt description of my hermeneutical thinking.

2. Bliese, "Lutheran Missiology," 222–25.

3. Ebeling, "Word of God and Hermeneutics," in Robinson and Cobb, eds., *New Hermeneutic*, 78–110.

the theological study of diaconal-missional institutions and implements them under systematic-hermeneutical guidance.[4]

Theologically, the church's *diakonia* can be defined as an ecclesial, congregational praxis in the life of public spheres as it is grounded in the grace of God's justification for and reconciliation with the world through the ecclesial mandate of public vocation and mission. Christian faith and missional vocation are acted out and carried on in terms of faith, love, and the eschatological hope of the coming of God's universal reign over the church and the world. Congregational mission is directed and inspired by the sacrament (gospel) and example (mission for the kingdom of God) of Jesus Christ and pursues its service to brothers and sisters on the margins of society. The service of the church assumes stewardship and responsibility for sustainable life for living creatures in the realm of creation, and contributes to human life through social and economic justice and peace among faith communities. The comprehensive and holistic understanding of mission can be defined by: witness, service, stewardship, and communion.

Communication of the gospel is at the center of the diaconal church and its practice, because the gospel is announced as the living voice of God in liturgical life and also articulated as its practical, socio-ethical consequence in the secular world. Seen in light of God's universal reign, a missional theology of *diakonia* is a critical, hermeneutical reflection of the biblical narrative grounded in God's covenant with Israel (including the universal Noahide covenant) and God's grace of justification and reconciliation in Jesus Christ for all. God's reign, characterized by forgiveness of sin, reconciliation, and peace among people in the world, mandates the church's engagement with people of other cultures and religions. In this way academic theology and a missional theology of *diakonia* come together in the project of diaconal ecclesiology and congregational mission. The study of God's mission and congregational service explores an ecclesiology as it relates to systematic-hermeneutical understanding of the word of God and the church in terms of communion, fellowship, vocation, and mission.

---

4. Ruddat and Schäfer, *Diakonisches Kompendium*, 91–121.

Missio and *Diakonia Dei* in Systematic-Hermeneutical Configuration

The God of Israel is the *diaconus*, revealed at Sinai as the deacon of the people, commanding a spirit of love toward the needy, debtors, orphans, widow, strangers, and prisoners (Isa 61:1; Luke 4:18). In the Hebrew Bible, a diaconal act, which is a basic dimension of the life of God's people, originates in God's special concern for the poor and the needy, as expressed in Exod 20:2: "I am the Lord your God, who brought you out of the land of Egypt, out of the house of slavery." This perspective penetrates the whole missional-diaconal dimension in the Hebrew Bible and becomes the backbone for the continuation of God's drama in the New Testament as it further unfolds God's missional story for the nations through Christ and the Spirit.

The call to service and merciful love toward the poor runs through Scripture like a golden thread until it is highlighted in the revelation of Jesus Christ. Christ's incarnation can be understood as the full revelation of God's *diakonia* because Jesus came to serve (Matt 20:28). Jesus Christ is the true *diaconus*, deacon of his people (Rom 15:8). Christ's diaconal mission invites and embraces the poor, the crippled, the lame, the blind, and the needy as it relates to the final judgment (Matt 25:40–45; 26:11; Mark 14:7; John 21:8).

A Christological unity between forgiveness and healing, redeeming words and helping deeds of love, becomes foundational for the internal unity of congregational life with worship, evangelization, and *diakonia*. *Christo Diakonos* and *Christo Doulos* shape and characterize Paul's Christology in Philippians 2. If Paul establishes Christian theology of service (in Phil 2:1–4) as the guideline for the life of Christians, Luther sharpens all our works to be done for the welfare of others. When our hearts are filled by the Holy Spirit with love, it "makes us free, joyful, almighty workers and conquerors over all tribulations, servants of our neighbors," while yet lords of all.[5] Christian life, which lives in Christ and in the neighbor, is called to participate in the servanthood of Jesus Christ.

God's lordship and *diakonia* in the life, death, and resurrection of Jesus Christ come together in the presence of the Holy Spirit for the church as well as the world. If the triune God is known to us through God's historical-missional activity, Jesus Christ as the embodiment of

---

5. Luther, "Freedom of a Christian," in *Luther's Basic Theological Writings*, 406.

diakonia Dei must be the lens for us to understand who God is and how to participate in and promote God's mission in the public realm. A Lutheran World Federation background paper (November 2002) on *diakonia* speaks to integration of *missio Dei* with *diakonia Dei*: "*Diakonia* belongs to the ecclesiastical substantial feature, which expresses the Church's essence. *Diakonia* is practiced in a specific time and a specific context." *Diakonia* as part of the life of the church shapes a prophetic direction to God's mission and the church's discipleship.

In this light, it is illuminating to construe God's mission through the *theologia crucis* in the context of Trinitarian eschatology. Christian mission understood eschatologically embraces both future-oriented and present-oriented perspectives.[6] Paul's theology of the word of the cross (1 Cor 1:18) becomes more obvious as we reframe his discussion of the *theologia crucis* in light of John's theology of life, *theologia vitae*, including the apocalyptic vision of a new heaven and a new earth (Revelation 21). The theology of the cross does not imply any theological moribund system in submission to the status quo, but undergirds the life-giving and life-enhancing mission of God and the ecclesial witness by vitalizing the congregational life in this direction. God lives and is known as the living God so that new life is the life coming out of God. Christ has set us free (John 8:36; Gal 5:1) for God's life in freedom and emancipation.

God's dynamic being in word-event can be read in the statement: I will be who I will be (Exod 3:14). The God of Israel works in the life of Abraham, Isaac, and Jacob and sends Moses. A Trinitarian discourse presupposes a Christian hermeneutic which articulates the relationship between God and Jesus Christ in the communion of the Holy Spirit regarding God's mission and *diakonia* in the church and the world.

Insofar as *God in self* before the creation becomes a presupposition for understanding *God for us* in the world as the creator, redeemer, and the sanctifier, the doctrine of appropriation can be a hermeneutical designation. A theological hermeneutic seeks to keep revelation as revelation and language as language at the place where revelation takes place, and where God comes to word-event. Appropriation as a hermeneutical process[7] brings God to word as creator, redeemer, and sanctifier, as we see the concept of Father and creation, Son and redemption, and Holy

---

6. Bosch, *Transforming Mission,* 507–8.

7. Jüngel, *God's Being Is in Becoming,* 49.

Spirit and sanctification in Luther's *Large Catechism*.[8] Insofar as God's being is explained and known only from God's historical activity and mission, God's "missional" being is in the act of God's "word-event." The historical form of the crucified Christ, central to understanding God's mission,[9] is to be refurbished for the sake of a hermeneutical mission of word-event.

The Trinitarian Aspect in Israel, Mission, and *Diakonia*

Seen in Trinitarian perspective, God's salvific activity *extra nos* is the basis for mission under the universal lordship of God.[10] Insofar as a concept of *homoousios* is seen in light of the relations of origin (be-getting-begotten) in a qualified sense (i.e., *distinctio et non-separatio*), it is difficult to accept the total identification between the immanent Trinity (God in self) and the economic Trinity (God for us).[11] In John 5:26 we read that "the Father has life in himself, so he has granted the Son to have life in himself." Articulating life in God's self, the tradi-tional idea of the immanent Trinity says that God is the living, sharing, and emancipating God. A classic notion of *perichoresis* refers to the reciprocal interiority or co-inherence in one another in the Trinitarian communal life without coalescence. It can also be elaborated as the lin-guistic expression of God's living freedom in love of, and communion with, the Son and the Spirit.

In this light, the teaching of "relations of origin" implies that God does not subsume God's creatures into God's perichoretic life, rather the Son and the Spirit are grounded and communicated to us from within God's life. The eternal Son of the Father is the Word who be-came flesh. Between the eternal Son, the Holy Spirit, and the eternal Father, there is a living and dynamic fellowship, each in communion with each other based on mutuality and interdependence (*perichore-sis*), in whose social-economic reality (God's missional activity for the world) we are discursively invited to participate, announcing Good News of the triune God.[12] This perichoretic life will be finally and fully

8. Luther, "Large Catechism," BC 440, 435.

9. Moltmann, *Crucified God*, 246.

10. Vicedom, *Mission of God*, 8, 13.

11. Rahner, *Trinity*, 22.

12. LaCugna, *God for Us*, 270–78. See further Volf, *After Our Likeness*, 208–13.

manifested in the eschatological consummation of the creation when God will be "all in all."

God becomes the personal object to be known to the Spirit who explores and searches the depths of God (1 Cor 2:10). The Spirit as the bond of agape is the Spirit of God's self-knowledge because the Spirit is from God (1 Cor 2:12). The Spirit who exists in the depths and the primordial ground of God is the God who questions, explores, and illuminates God. No one comprehends what is truly God's except the Spirit of God (1 Cor 2:11). If God is not communicated to us by the Word and the Spirit, God remains the unknown God (Acts 17:23). The Spirit who is deeply and mysteriously bound up with God is the Spirit of divine love and life in protest against death (Rom 8:13). Jesus embodied and fulfilled the Spirit of justice, hope, and emancipation against the culture of death and oppression. "I will put my Spirit upon him, and he will proclaim justice to the Gentiles . . . He will not break a bruised reed or quench a smoldering wick until he brings justice to victory. And in his name the Gentiles will hope" (Matt 12:18; Isa 42:1–3). Jesus' manifesto of God's mission under the anointing of the Holy Spirit (Luke 4:18–19) demonstrates how closely Jesus' prophetic *diakonia* is embedded within the evangelization of God's reign and the proclamation of the year of the Lord's favor.

A project of nonhierarchical but truly communal ecclesiology becomes meaningful and possible as it is based on Trinitarian theology in terms of biblical dialectics of divine lordship (freedom) and *diakonia* (*kenosis*) through the working of the Holy Spirit, the bond of agape. Thus I argue that *perichoresis* should be translated as circulation ("perichorein"), dwelling in one another (*circumincessio*). God's essence (*perichoresis* life) does not become a prisoner of human imagination or speculation. We are participants in God's grace in Jesus Christ, not in the intradivine *perichoresis* as a sort of mutual dancing partnership as is suggested by LaCugna.[13]

A revelation-based approach to Christian theology can thus become an icon for human thought and interpretation in the presence of the Spirit. Thus Trinitarian theology underlying God's self-interpretation as agape in Jesus Christ (the icon of the invisible God, Col 1:15) provides a hermeneutical climate for developing God's mission as word-event through the internal and external activity of the Spirit. Trinitarian

---

13. LaCugna, *God for Us*, 271–72.

theology based on God's self-revelation as agape emphasizes God's mission as word-event beyond "being" because God's "being" comes to us in and as a gift through Word and Spirit. "A voice came from heaven; I glorified you and I will glorify you" (John 12:28). In this voice the Spirit descends like a dove at the baptism (Matt 3:16) and transfigures Jesus and a voice comes in the name of the Father (transfiguration, Mark 9:7) who speaks the Son as the Beloved. The Word lets himself be said by the Father in the Spirit. The Word as the Son of the Father is the Said.[14] Trinitarian mission lets the Word speak through missional testimony and makes us witness of God's incarnation as *verbum Dei* in the presence of the Spirit. ". . . but you have received a spirit of adoption. When we cry, 'Abba! Father!' it is that very Spirit bearing witness with our spirit that we are children of God" (Rom 8:15–16).

If the divinity of the one God does not precede the divine persons, but exists as three persons (possibly in a fashion of "sitting around": *circuminsessio*) according to the social doctrine of the Trinity, such an argument emphasizes divine dance or cyclical movement (*perichoreo* or *perichorenein*) in which the classic notion of relations of origin tied to *distinctio et non-separatio* is suppressed. It tends to sidestep a biblical testimony to the God of Israel whose action is manifested and embodied in the death, life, and resurrection of Jesus Christ in the presence of the Holy Spirit. A social doctrine of the Trinity must find its validity in taking seriously God's self-interpretation or communication in the historical and missional context of Jesus Christ. When one talks about the co-existence of three persons in perichoretic communion as the starting point for Trinitarian relationship with us,[15] one undermines God's self-revelation in Jesus Christ coming to us in a this-worldly and linguistic fashion as a gift. Such an argument is not qualified in articulating an analogous and provisional relationship between the triune God and missional ecclesiology in light of the future of God.[16]

Furthermore, God's essence of *perichoresis* must not be literally applied to human life, including creaturely life in the Trinitarian *perichoresis*. Such a literal understanding of the social doctrine of the Trinity might run into the Gnostic form of divinization (i.e., the neoplatonic notion of henosis). In the patristic teaching of divinization (*theosis, theopoiesis*),

14. Marion, *God without Being*, 3, 143.

15. Volf, *After Our Likeness*, 4, 202.

16. Ibid., 198–99.

it is not possible for any created being to become God ontologically, or even a necessary part of God (of the three existences of God called hypostasis). Most specifically creatures (created beings) cannot become God in God's transcendent essence (*ousia*). When the social doctrine of the Trinity, in the cases of LaCugna and Volf, eliminates distinction between *perichoresis* and appropriation, *God in self* and *God for us*, God's essence and God's grace, such an understanding tends to head toward the henosis or absorption into God of Greek pagan philosophy.

St. Paul insists that Christ will not sit at the right hand of the Father for all eternity. One day he will return the lordship to the Father and the Father again will be all in all (1 Cor 15:28). Human understanding of God in the mystery of the Trinity remains partial and incomplete until the complete comes. If the doctrine of the Trinity is an interpretation of God in covenant with Israel and the Father of Jesus Christ, it articulates the historical activity of God's mission in God's coming to Israel, highlighted in Jesus Christ in promise, justification, and reconciliation, and finally extended to all through Pentecost. Jesus in his confession of the Shema Israel, affirms the God of Israel in the community of Mark (Mark 12:29–30). In response to one of the scribes, Jesus says that "The first is, 'Hear, O Israel: the Lord our God, the Lord is one.'" The name of Jesus Christ enters into the mystery of the God of Israel who has a Trinitarian-missional history.

The triune God is more than human necessity.[17] The understanding of God in self has an eschatological direction in view of the fact that "God will be what God will be" (YHWH) and "God will be all in all." The name of God finds its locus in Paul's theology of eschatology that "God may be all in all" (1 Cor 15:28). It also relates to the statement of the revelation—"God will dwell with them as their God" (Rev 21:3). The eschatological Immanuel announced as "God will be with them" undergirds God's mission of a promised future and the Lamb of God in the New Jerusalem, which is highlighted in God's comfort of the innocent victims: "God will wipe every tear from their eyes. Death will be no more: mourning and crying and pain will be no more, for the first things have passed away" (Rev 21:4). The gospel narrative identifies its God as the One who sent us Jesus through Israel and raised Israel's Jesus from the dead. Trinitarian language and thought centers on this message of

17. Jüngel, *God as Mystery*, 378.

the gospel.[18] The eschatological Immanuel does not cut loose *Urfaktum* Immanuel (primordial Immanuel) from the life of Israel.

Having considered this, it is pivotal to consider the relationship between the blessing in the Hebrew Bible and the *theologia crucis* in the New Testament. "The only difference between the Old and New Testament in this respect is that in the Old the blessing includes the cross, and in the New the cross includes the blessing."[19] *Theologia crucis* does not nullify God's faithfulness to Israel (Rom 3:3). Rather, *theologia crucis* in a Trinitarian, eschatological perspective affirms Simeon's prophecy: Jesus as "a light for revelation to the Gentiles and for glory to your people Israel" (Luke 2: 32).

Characteristics of the Word-Event Mission

When it comes to the subject matter of divine reality (God's-self disclosure in Jesus Christ), the human witness can be questioned and interpreted anew in different places and times. A theological-hermeneutical question of what makes Christ present brings us to consider our interpretive interaction with text, tradition, and faith community. God's narrative of Christ's *diakonia* in the presence of the Holy Spirit becomes a history of effect in connection to practical reasoning and application (*phronesis*). This (historical) diachronic aspect of human understanding grounded in the text and tradition comes together with a (contemporary-social) synchronic aspect of God's word-event within the life of the faith community located in our social, cultural contexts. The crux of the missiological hermeneutic is connected with the relation between the word, the event, and its meaning through the act of interpretation and practical application in the cultural realm. Interpreting the Scripture amplifies its meaning, by incorporating the remains of secular culture in this understanding.[20]

Such a hermeneutical view relates confessional language to the discursive dimension of practical, public reasoning in terms of dialogue with the public language. This perspective also critically distances itself from the limitations of doctrinal language and engages in improving them by reinterpreting and refurbishing theological language in our

18. Jenson, *Christian Dogmatics*, 1:99.

19. Bonhoeffer, *Letter and Papers*, 374.

20. Ricoeur, *Essays on Biblical Interpretation*, 53.

contemporary context.[21] Interpretation, as seen in light of a history of effect, inheres in human life in social-historical life settings because of the use of language in daily communication. Being "historical" or "interpretive" implies that one's knowledge can never be complete, but is always open-ended and self-renewing for a new horizon of acquired meaning.[22]

In reframing the gospel as the living voice of God in terms of a language event that speaks to us, the subject matter of which language in theological context speaks is promise, forgiveness, reconciliation, and shalom. The interpreter's self-understanding, or pre-understanding, is involved in the hermeneutical process in engaging with the biblical narrative. However, the text as such speaks and interprets and renews the interpreter's self- and pre-understanding. The text is interpreted into a critique of our own self-understanding in terms of the subject matter that the biblical text addresses to us.[23]

The language of *dabar* (Ps 33:9), denoting a speech act, is the meaning of the Word of God, thus a hermeneutical missiology becomes an interpretation of the living Word of God through the faith-experience of God's narrative. *Kerygma*, the proclamation of something as something, functions as an a priori, shaping and influencing human consciousness. Consciousness of translating the text is first translated by the horizon of the subject-matter of the text. The text must translate us before we translate it in a different cultural life setting. When "God comes to expression as event,"[24] this thesis has its ground in the word-event implying a universal human potentiality constitutive of the essence of language. The word-event which takes place in the gospel must be understood in reference to God's speaking to Israel in promise and covenant and God's blessing for all through Jesus Christ. In a linguistic event through which one speaks the gospel to another and opens a future, the Word in the biblical context always refers to the Word of the Speaker, God's saying-in-action. God speaks and uses humanity for God's "speaking," or discursive mission in the sense of announcement of the gospel.

The word-event can be seen in the sense of human correspondence, participation, engagement, and communication. Understanding the Word of God through the language of Jesus Christ becomes the primary

21. Ricoeur, *Hermeneutics and Human Sciences*, 63–100.

22. Gadamer, *Truth and Method*, 302.

23. Robinson and Cobb, *New Hermeneutic*, 54.

24. Ebeling, *Word and Faith*, 325.

phenomenon in the realm of understanding God's mission in the service of Jesus Christ to the world. The word is what opens up and mediates human understanding by bringing something to understanding, so that the word itself has a hermeneutical-missional function.[25]

Missiology, as the science of biblical narrative and mission, can become a hermeneutical theology by actualizing and deepening our understanding of the word of God in conversation with the other through evangelization; witness to the life, death, and resurrection of Jesus Christ; and social commitment in service to those in need. Faith is involved in God's mission through the interpretive imagination of evangelization in the secular, multireligious sphere. In a theological-missional hermeneutic, it is of special significance to heed Luther's perspective on the Scripture (in his preface of the Psalms, 1531): "There [in the Scripture] you see the heart of all saints."[26] The humanity of biblical authors is not covered or hidden, but revealed. This aspect has profound consequences for our theological-missional hermeneutic in a prophetic interpretation of the word-event.

The historical condition in which the biblical writers lived plays a role in shaping their view of the Word of God. A prophetic dimension of biblical interpretation and evangelization penetrates into the word-event in terms of our appropriation of the meaning of biblical narrative. It also entails critical distance from the limitations of the socio-historical environment and political-economic circumstances which shaped and conditioned the world of those biblical writers. Against alien and strange elements which are contrary to the subject matter of the Scripture, a missiological hermeneutic becomes a socio-critical method in communicating the prophetic dimension of the gospel to people in a different location.

The interpretation of expressions of life fixed in written texts (Dilthey) needs to be developed as the interpretation of the subject matter of God's word-event expressed in written texts as well as communicating its meaning in the public realm. Faith, understanding, and acquired meaning in the hermeneutical circle belong to a semantic of missiology, because the idea of announcement, proclamation, and

---

25. Ibid., 93–94.
26. Gollwitzer, *Befreiung zur Solidarität*, 60.

kerygma presupposes "an initiative on the part of meaning, a coming to us of meaning."[27]

God as the chief Speaker promises to make God's self-disclosure and communication in terms of self-giving covenant (in the life of Noah and Abraham), emancipation (Exodus-experience), and justifying and reconciling love (in the life of Jesus Christ). This God in Jesus Christ by the power of the Holy Spirit calls the church to participate in the mission of divine work, weaving God's narrative in the life of the other in the world context. The missiological practice of biblical narrative in dialogue with the other enriches a Christian self, making it amenable to existence for and in solidarity with the other.

In the encounter with the face of the One in the shadow of the cross, we meet the mystery of the One who promises forgiveness and reconciliation in the midst of death and participation in divine life with trust and confidence (Luke 23:46). In the light of the crucified One, all people stand in the grace of God. An encounter with God's mysterious presence becomes meaningful through the face of the other which obliges us to become the existence of *diakonia* for the other. A missiology of word-event engages hermeneutically, encountering identity through the irreducibly other.[28]

---

27. Ricoeur, *Essays on Biblical Interpretation*, 69.

28. Levinas, *Totality and Infinity*, 53; further see Scharlemann, *Being of God*.

6

Church as *Diakonia* and Congregational Mission

In the discussion of the holistic nature of transforming mission, the perspective advocated here calls the community of Jesus Christ to exist in the world and to be active for the world. In the project of the missional church and congregational mission, ecclesiology becomes a central issue, whether in light of Trinitarian missiology, or functional or organizational perspectives. If we were to define the church merely functionally, as a series of ministry functions (worship, education, service, and witness), the church as a unique community of God's people would be undermined. If we were to define the church merely organizationally, the spiritual reality of the church as a moral community would be suppressed. Thus the church would be seen as a patterned set of organizational structures managing and institutionalizing human behavior and religious activity. Rather than a functional or organizational definition, a theological definition of the essence of the church must become a priority issue. A theology of the church (ecclesiology) calls for engagement with social scientific research and methodology.[1]

A New Ecclesiology Missionally, Socially Grounded

In the project of the missional church and congregational mission it is crucial to deal with the relation between service and ecclesiology. Personal being as structurally open has the capacity and necessity to

1. Van Gelder, *Essence of Church*, 18–24.

participate in sociality with others. It also maintains the unity, integrity, and irreducibility of the person, guarding against the dissolution of the personal being into sameness. Genuine sociality presses toward personal unity. From a theological perspective, community does not absorb the individual into itself.[2]

All intellectual acts involved in understanding, self-expression, and being understood are bound up with sociality. In reciprocal interaction with an other, self-conscious thinking, willing, and language became meaningful. Only in the interaction with one another does a hermeneutical experience become effective in the sociality of community. There is no self-consciousness without community because self-consciousness arises with the consciousness of existing in community.[3] This perspective on the social relationship between individual and community remains basic and fundamental to our missional ecclesiology. The missional church and congregational mission are grounded in the present Christ, the principle of vicarious representation. That is "Christ existing as church-community."[4]

Church as *Pro-missio*

In the synoptic context, Jesus is portrayed as the one who promises to build the church upon Peter's confession (Matt 16:13–20). The church is based on Jesus' response to Peter's confession that "You are the Messiah, the Son of the living God" (v. 16). Thus the church is built on the confession of the apostles, while the cornerstone is Jesus Christ (Eph 2:20). The imagery of the church as Christ's *pro-missio* is also connected with the conviction that Jesus Christ as the revelation of God is the historical principle of the church.[5] The image of the temple of God is also found in Paul's writings (1 Cor 3:16–17; Eph 2:21–22). Insofar as the church becomes the body of Christ, the church takes place as the fulfillment of Jesus' promise in response to Peter's confession, accomplished by the Spirit of Pentecost, fulfilled in the preaching and receiving of the gospel and the sacraments of baptism and the Lord's Supper.

---

2. Bonhoeffer, *Sanctorum Communio*, 67. Footnote [19], 75, 80.

3. Ibid., 70.

4. Ibid., 191.

5. Ibid., 153.

The Christian concept of the church is the fulfillment of the Hebrew concept of assembly. The church exists through Christ's action, elected in Christ from eternity (Eph 1:4; 2 Thess 2:13). Insofar as church is defined as the new humanity in the new Adam (1 Cor 15:22, 45; Rom 5:12, 19), Christ as the foundation and cornerstone of the church is a real presence in the church. Christ is in the church and the church is in Christ (1 Cor 1:30, 3:16; 2 Cor 6:16; Col 2:17, 3:11).

Sacramental and Congregational

The term "communion of saints" in the Apostles Creed implies a sacramental-congregational dimension of the church's existence. The body of the risen Lord is a visible body in the formation of the church. Through the preaching of the Word, "They devoted themselves to the apostles' teaching and fellowship, to the breaking of bread and prayers" (Acts 2:42). The teaching spoken of is the teaching of the apostles who witnessed to the physical event of God in Christ and were employed by the Holy Spirit to proclaim the Word. Christ is present in the word of the apostles through the Holy Spirit. This apostolic teaching creates a visible church in the sacraments of baptism and the Lord's Supper. This is characteristic of church as the community of witness through proclamation. The apostolic teaching of the gospel and the apostles' witness to the risen Christ carries out the apostolic proclamation and the missionary charge. The apostolicity of the church is established through the church's faith in salvation and the confessional attitude at home or abroad.[6] The church's foundation and missionary commission continues in apostolic witness to the good news about the kingdom of God and the name of Jesus Christ (Acts 8:12).

The gospel message becomes the reality of the living voice of God, shaping congregational life in worship. It is also acted out through the congregational life in the society. In worship God greets, meets, and renews us in the Word and the sacrament through the Holy Spirit. When the Holy Spirit moves us to set up places of worship, it acts as a conduit for God to reveal God's self to others in the midst of a lost world. In the hopes of showing the lost the way to Christ, worship as public witness becomes a form of engaging in mission. The life of worship is the primary form of mission. Its core refers to God's movement toward the

---

6. Vicedom, *Mission of God*, 71.

world and invitation of us in word and sacrament. By welcoming the stranger, the worship of God practices the hospitality and reconciliation rooted in God's inclusive and open invitation to all humanity.[7]

The sacraments spring from the true humanity of Jesus Christ, making us partakers in the fellowship and communion of the body of Christ. A congregational life of fellowship oscillating between Word and sacrament begins and ends in worship, looking forward in expectation to the final banquet in the kingdom of God.[8] Communion in the sense of assembly or congregation or *ecclesia* is inseparably connected with participation in the sacraments. The church is not a social gathering or moral association of individual Christians, but the fellowship in which the gospel is purely taught and the sacraments are rightly administered according to Christ's institution and in which mutual conversation and comfort of brothers and sisters are present. The teaching of the gospel and the sacraments constitute the basis of the fellowship of the individual congregation with Jesus Christ as the head of the church and with one another.[9]

Fellowship is spiritual and social with Jesus Christ as well as with the people of God. The personal and congregational sense of *communio sanctorum* is linked to a sacramental sense of communion (fellowship) in the saving gifts of Word and sacrament. This sacramental participation is individually and congregationally articulated in Jesus Christ who is truly present in the Word, sacraments, and the people of God. Jesus initiated his fellowship with public sinners, tax collectors, lepers, social outcasts, women, and children by establishing a practice of open table fellowship. In continuity with this practice, the faith community stands in relationship and fellowship with those who are burdened by the reality of the world. It takes place as the fellowship of witness and service in terms of announcing the good news of God to the world by denouncing the structures that generate violence, injustice, and victimization. Special concern is demonstrated for widows and orphans within the faith community (Acts 2:44–45). The community of solidarity cannot be adequately understood and implemented without connection to the

7. Keifert, *Welcoming the Stranger*, 1–13.

8. Bonhoeffer, *Cost of Discipleship*, 254.

9. "Augsburg Confession" (1530), art. V, VII, in BC 41, 43.

vicarious representative action of Jesus Christ, which is the life-principle of the new humanity.[10]

Worshipping Mission

The church-community remains the mother of believers, nourishing the individual, congregational life through Word and sacrament. Through them the Holy Spirit illuminates and inflames human hearts.[11] Gathering for worship is the essence of the church. An office of preaching and administration of the sacraments is established and sustained in the *sanctorum communio*. The relationship between liturgy and mission can be characterized as "inside-out." In the church God's mission is accomplished in forming the congregation into a missional life of fellowship, discipleship, and stewardship. We gather an offering for the poor and God's mission. We hear God's blessing and are sent out in service to the world. This perspective shapes the public character of worship. God's gracious action and presence in worship becomes the driving force for vibrant congregational life and mission.[12] The ongoing breaking-in of the *pro-missio* of God characterizes the missional nature of Christian worship encountering the word of God speaking to us in our daily lives. This missional worship oriented inside-out to the world forms "the Christian's *liturgia* and *diakonia*—their reasonable service."[13]

The fellowship (*koinonia*) is articulated between Word and Sacrament because fellowship springs from the Word and finds its goal and completion in the Lord's Supper. The daily growth of the church is a proof of the power of the Lord who dwells in the empirical community through Word and Sacrament (Acts 2:47). The community is capable of expanding itself and engaging with the world through growth like a seed to a plant. The church's growth includes numerical increase and spiritual formation. The living Lord added daily to the church those who were saved. When the word of God increased, the number of the disciples multiplied greatly and prevailed in the winning of others (Acts 6:7; 19:20). The faith of the churches in Asia Minor was strengthened so that they increased in number daily (16:5). The numerical increase

10. Bonhoeffer, *Sanctorum Communio*, 147.

11. Luther, "Large Catechism," BC 436.

12. Nessan, *Beyond Maintenance*, 10–12; see further Schattauer, *Inside Out*.

13. Keifert, "Biblical Truth and Theological Education," in Keifert and Padgett, eds., *But Is It All True?* 133.

of the community in the Lucan account is the outcome of attesting to the gospel rather than having to do with church business. The church of Jesus Christ should not be a pompous church. As the community grows spiritually, growing in faith and increasing in love, it may also grow extensively and numerically under the guidance of the Holy Spirit.[14] The church's growth cannot be properly understood apart from church renewal under the guidance of the Word and the Spirit.

In the proclamation of the pure teaching of the gospel and proper administration of the sacraments and in service of the people of God, the universal unity of the church across the ages finds its manifestation and validity. The worship of the local congregation is one, holy, catholic, and apostolic, having spiritual fellowship with saints and martyrs in the past and the present. This constitutes the church's ecumenical unity across the centuries while characterizing each local congregation of believers as the church of Christ in its particular time and place.

Body of Christ and World

In this light, the church is the people of God created and called by the Word and Spirit toward the world. Here it is of special significance to consider a diaconal, participatory dimension of the Eucharistic congregation in the world. If God is present in the church through Word and Spirit, the church is a spiritual communion organized within human structures. Church as *sanctorum communio* is social community that consists of people of God coming from the world. It is also characterized by the church's public discipleship and vocation for the world. Christian community is called the body of Christ in which the earthly-historical form of Christ's existence is anchored in the collective person Christ who exists as church-community. The church as the body of Christ is also striking in 1 Cor 10:16–17 (Rom 12:4–5) in reference to the real presence of Jesus Christ. Paul's teaching of the Body of Christ is fulfillment of the Old Testament prophecy about the temple of God (2 Sam 7:5, 11).[15]

Thus the church as the Body of Christ on earth embraces the followers and disciples of Jesus Christ, people of God (1 Pet 2:9) from every tribe and tongue (Matt 28:19; Rev 5:9–10). The people are members of

14. Barth, CD IV.2: 650.
15. Bonhoeffer, *Cost of Discipleship*, 245.

the body of Christ (1 Cor 12:2; Rom 12:4; Eph 1:23, 4:15; Col 1:18) or members of Christ himself (1 Cor 6:15; Rom 6:13, 19) who is the head of the church. "To be in Christ" is to be in the church. The church implies Christ who exists as church-community. The rich imagery of the church in biblical contexts can be seen in the holy temple, the dwelling place of God (1 Cor 3:16; Eph 2:19), living stones built into a spiritual house (1 Pet 2:5), members of the household of God (Eph 2:19), citizens with the saints (Eph 2:19), and strangers and sojourners on earth (Heb 11:13; 13:14; 1 Pet 2:11).

Insofar as the incarnate Christ is the temple of the fulfillment, God finds human being in the Body of Christ as a spiritual temple built out of living stones (1 Pet 2:5). Christ as the sole foundation and cornerstone (Eph 2:20; I Cor 3:11) is, in his Person, the temple (Eph 2:21) in whom the Holy Spirit dwells, justifying, sanctifying, and replenishing the hearts of the faithful (1 Cor 3:10; 6:19). Paul's imagery of the body of Christ, which is the place of atonement, acceptance, and peace between God and humanity, is also of a universal-cosmic dimension coupled with his concept of reconciliation (Eph 1:22–23).

There is an inseparable relationship between the universal church and the local congregation. The faith community dies and suffers with each member. In the empirical life of the church an active sharing of suffering, joy, sin, and grief even unto death must be practiced.[16] Christ is the head of the church and the church is the body of Christ. The life togetherness of the faith community and it, members in the presence of Christ entails the existence of *diakonia* in being-for-each other. The exclusion of the weak and insignificant, the seemingly useless people, from everyday Christian life in community may actually mean the exclusion of Christ. In the poor sister or brother, Christ is knocking at the door.[17]

As long as God and the world are torn apart, in Jesus Christ, the Reconciler of the world, God and the cosmic reality are reconciled. The church's mission lies in witnessing to the reality of the reconciliation of God with the world that transpired in Jesus Christ. In this light, the church has no mission to eliminate the world by making it into the kingdom of God. It does not give support to that pious indolence that gives up the wicked world to its fate.[18]

16. LW 35:55.

17. Bonhoeffer, *Life Together,* 45–46.

18. Bonhoeffer, *Ethics,* 229.

The Sent Community under the Guidance of the Holy Spirit

The church as the sent community is related to vocation in the eschato-logical and missional drama in terms of hope in the expectation of Jesus Christ who is to come. *Communion sanctorum* also as the *communio peccatorum* remains in God's church-community, since "Adam has re-ally been replaced by Christ only eschatologically . . . *in spe* [in hope]."[19] The church originates with the outpouring of the Holy Spirit who is the Spirit of the faith community of Christ. The Holy Spirit is promised to outpour on all flesh (Acts 2:17) in this expectation the dividing wall be-tween Jews and Gentiles has been broken down (Eph 2:14).

As Luther states in the third article of his Small Catechism, "By my own understanding or strength I cannot believe in Jesus Christ . . . but instead the Holy Spirit has called me through the gospel, enlightened me with his gifts, made me holy and kept me in the true faith, just as he calls, gathers, enlightens, and makes holy the whole Christian church."[20] Through the fulfillment of God's promise in the Word of God and sacra-ment the Holy Spirit becomes the foundation for Christian vocation and the community of saints. Congregational mission and diaconal witness become an indispensable duty and task of the Christian community as people of God. The church is catholic, apostolic, ecumenical, and universal in its particular time and place insofar as it is involved in the Reformation theology of *ecclesia semper reformanda*. The confessional statement that we believe in the church does not mean our confession of the church as such, but that we believe in the triune God who creates faith communities through word and sacrament ministry by being pres-ent and working among the people of God.

Jesus Christ exists for the world so the church also exists for the world. The church in the presence of Christ exists only in faith. The Holy Spirit is the awakening power and renews the church as Christ's earthly-historical body, that is the one holy, catholic, and apostolic church. As the church becomes Christ's body, so the congregation in its members fulfills its missional discipleship in witnessing to the death and resurrec-tion of Jesus Christ in terms of justification, reconciliation, and vocation in eschatological hope of the final consummation of the world in light of the new heaven and earth.

---

19. Bonhoeffer, *Sanctorum Communio*, 124.
20. Luther, "Small Catechism" (1529), BC 355.

The very word of Christ is effectively brought to the heart of the hearers by the Spirit. Christ seeks to win the heart by the Spirit, incorporating it into the faith community. Christ participates in building the church, sending his people, and sustaining them through the work of the Holy Spirit. Mission is something done by the Spirit: the free, sovereign, living power of the Spirit of God. In the presence of the Spirit (Acts 1:8; cf. 2 Cor 1:22; Eph 1:14) the promise is given to the disciples about gift, *arrabon*, which is the foretaste, the pledge, the guarantee of the kingdom. The disciples are promised the advance installment, a foretaste of the messianic feast, with eschatological reservation. The prevenient working of the Spirit guides the sent community and its people, bringing the meetings of Philip with the finance minister of Ethiopia, Ananias with Saul, and Peter with Cornelius.[21]

Insofar as the church follows the Word of God under the guidance of the Holy Spirit, Christ's Great Commission (Matt 28:19) characterizes the church as missional and diaconal by nature in its witness to Jesus Christ. This is the community of faith, love, and hope in the expectation of Jesus Christ who is to come. The ministry of the *viva vox evangelii* is charged with the ecclesial task of evangelization. It is the announcement of the message of Jesus Christ which is the word of forgiveness of sin, and reconciliation. This implies the radical alteration of the previous situation between God and humanity. The unity of faith is correlated to the concept of God's reign in the church while the community of love is correlated to the concept of God's realm of mission and *diakonia* in the world.

Missional Church as the Community of Blessing and Inclusion

As we already mentioned with reference to God's *pro-missio* in Trinitarian missiology, the gospel is by nature particularly connected with the history of God's narrative in covenant with Israel, which becomes universally relevant through Jesus Christ. God promises Abraham that he will make him a blessing to others. In the act of the covenant in the Genesis narrative, blessing is a key term testifying to God's work as the creator. Coupled with the blessing, promise is the most basic category, embracing the creation yet moving beyond it. It brings blessing into the sphere of salvation. God makes promises to Hagar and Ishmael (Gen 16:10–11;

---

21. Newbigin, *Open Secret*, 62, 58–59.

17:20; 21:13, 18) by becoming the advocate for them.[22] As Martin Luther provocatively argues, "The descendents of Ishmael also joined the church of Abraham and became heirs of the promise, not by reason of a right but because of irregular grace."[23]

In Abraham's life, furthermore, we are aware that God is pleased to have Abraham blessed by Melchizedek. In contemporary biblical studies Melchizedek is understood to be a non-Jewish leader of the religious community that is outside of the Levitical or Aaronic order. In this event the sacred and the secular are not separated.[24] In our general climate of religious tolerance and indifference, God speaks to us through symbolic figures like Melchizedek on behalf of righteousness and universal peace. God also used Cyrus, a pagan king, to help Israel. God changes Balaam's intended curse by speaking through a donkey. From the mouth of Balaam, God's speech event is not to be neglected regardless of its sinister message (Num 22:22–35). God is the one who accompanies religious outsiders to bless Christian community. This biblical perspective offers a fulcrum for a missiology of word-event.

In the Exodus story (12:37–38) we notice that Israel is an open community. The whole group is referred to as a mixed multitude, "foreigners living among Israel as temporal or long-term sojourners"[25] (*ereb rab; minjung* in Asian irregular theological parlance), not limited to Abraham's descendents. Israel is the starting point of God's salvific drama, while strangers are allowed to enter into the journey of Israel. Israel is the open community inviting strangers to God's salvific drama. Foreigners are expected and allowed to come to the temple to worship (1 Kgs 8:42–43). Concern for the poor and the widow and hospitality for the foreigner are indispensable parts of understanding the prophetic character of God's mission in service to the others. This perspective also remains fundamental in Lev 19:9–18 concerning gleaning laws and the prohibition of unjust dealings with employees or neighbors. God cares for the poor and the alien, commanding Israel to allow them to sustain

---

22. Fretheim, *Abraham*, 10.

23. LW 4: 42–44; further see Luther's affirmative view on the Turkish state, WA 51; 242, 1–8, 15–19. Cf. Ebeling, *Luther*, 187.

24. Westermann, *Genesis 12–36*, 204–5.

25. Propp, *Exodus 1–18*, 414. Moreover, we read of non-Israelites travelling with Israel in the desert (Num 11:4, Deut 29:10; Josh 8:35).

themselves by the owner not visiting their vineyard a second time or picking up the grapes that have fallen (Lev 19:10).

Abraham's faith-righteousness is central to St. Paul and so also to Martin Luther's teaching on justification. What is striking is John's missional framework of integrating Abraham with Jesus Christ (John 8:56). Fulfilling Abraham's faith, the gospel of Jesus Christ entails universality. This position provides an interfaith insight into Jewish-Christian-Islamic dialogue as seen in St. Paul in Rom 4:16–17. "The promise may rest on grace and be guaranteed to all his descendents, not only to the adherents of the law but also to those who share the faith of Abraham." God's grace of justification is linked to the faithfulness of God the creator.[26] The church's mission must be in service to God's mission, following Jesus' role as servant (in Mark 10:45), witnessing to God's *pro-missio* to Israel and accompanying all.

Accordingly, Paul affirms natural knowledge of God in a missional context. According to Rom 1:20–22 and 2:12–16, pagans have natural knowledge of the existence of God without connection to the special revelation of Jesus Christ. Moreover, in the Lucan description Paul recognizes in Athens a religious concern or an awe in the presence of the gods and in the veneration of the unknown God. Perhaps this presentiment is misguided in temple worship and in the cult of images, nevertheless, the pagans are not godless or godforsaken (Acts 17:22–28). Paul's view of people of other cultures is connected with his theology of God's reconciliation in Christ for the world. He does not want people to persist in paganism, but he invites them to faith in the salvific message of Christ. Here we notice that there is a biblical tendency of a particular confession to Jesus Christ (John 14:6) toward the universality of the gospel in light of God's reconciliation in Christ's death and resurrection for all.

Natural knowledge of God can be positively integrated with God's universal lordship through the reconciliation of Jesus Christ with the world. In isolation the claim to exclusiveness leads to fanaticism and to slavery while the claim to totality leads to the secularization and self-abandonment of the church. In light of Christ's reconciliation through which God accepts the whole of humanity, there is a godlessness, full of promise which speaks against pious godlessness vulnerable to the

---

26. Käsemann, *Commentary on Romans*, 103–4.

corruption of the church.[27] The church as the community of reconciliation exists for the world in welcoming, openness, and solidarity with religious outsiders.

27. Bonhoeffer, *Ethics*, 104.

7

Mission as Deaconhood of all Believers

A human being is forgiven and justified as Christ's brother or sister through baptism. In baptism, proclamation, and the Lord's Supper, Christ serves, nourishes, and empowers congregational life and mission. The church becomes the foundation of a new life in God's people, which God creates and sustains through the power of the Holy Spirit. Such ecclesiology puts the ordained ministry and universal priesthood in mutual fellowship and balance. In it, the diaconate, that is, the rendering of service, is based on the equality of all believers and articulates the whole breath and depth of congregational action. Diaconate as a special ministry in the church denotes service, helping those in physical and material distress and need both within and outside the church. For Luther, a social-diaconal dimension of the faith community in the creation of the common chest is an indispensable part in the formation of the church as the community of the saints.[1]

Where the services of listening, active helpfulness, and bearing with others (Gal 6:2) are faithfully performed, the service of the Word of God, that is the ultimate and highest ministry, can also be offered. Genuine spirituality and authority can be found where the service of listening, helping, forbearing, and proclaiming is performed. It exists only in the service of God who alone has authority.[2] Pastoral office, education, support of orphans and dependent children, home relief, community work

1. Luther, "Fraternal Agreement" (1523), LW 45: 176–94. Olson, *One Ministry, Many Roles*, 109–10.

2. Bonhoeffer, *Life Together*, 103, 106–7.

for the common stores, maintenance and construction of buildings, stewardship and care for the poor, aged and infirm are interconnected; in them universal priesthood refers to the Christocentric and pneumatological dimension of the grace of justification. The office is founded on universal priesthood while respecting the office of the ordained ministry instituted by Christ. Jesus is the example of the servant keeling down to wash the dirty feet of the disciples. Jesus on the cross is the embodiment of God's *diakonia* through forgiveness, reconciliation, and eternal life. Feeding the hungry and the needy was performed in the early church by collection and distribution. The designation of deacon as an office in the church is undertaken to promote effective commitment of service to the needy (Acts 6:1–7). Stewardship is a crucial category in understanding the Christian faith.[3] Stewardship is a call from God, informing how we live our lives in terms of learning generosity toward God and neighbor.

Ecclesial Ministry and Vocation

All Christians are equally spiritual priests before God. In the perspective articulated here, there is a dialectical balance in Luther's theology between the universal priesthood and the ministerial office in terms of Word and sacraments. The offices of the church are ministries (1 Cor 12:5) appointed in the church of God (1 Cor 12:28) by Christ and the Holy Spirit (Eph 4:11 and Acts 20:28). The church's ministry comes from the triune God. Ministry is service in obedience to the divine Word and deed accomplished in Jesus Christ in the living present. This is the ministry of the baptized, distinct from the priesthood of the baptized.[5] God has instituted the office of ministry which provides the gospel and the sacraments. Through these external means the Holy Spirit is given by effecting faith "when and where it pleases God in those who hear the gospel."[6]

The ministerial offices exist to serve the church and congregational life. The charismata conferred by the Holy Spirit upon individual members of the church are subject to the discipline of the ministry of the Body of Christ. When everything is done for the well-being of the

---

3. Hall, *Steward.*

4. LW 35,100–1; LW 44, 127.

5. Forde, *Theology Is for Proclamation*, 180–81.

6. "Augsburg Confession" (1530), art. 5. BC 41.

church, the Holy Spirit becomes manifest and visible (1 Cor 12:7). All of those in the offices of the church (1 Cor 12:28; Eph 2:20; 4:11) are ministers of the church and ordained for service to the church and its congregational life.[7] Anyone who is born in baptism by water and the Spirit becomes a priest, while one becomes a minister through vocation or calling. Christ instituted the universal priesthood through faith and baptism in the power of the Holy Spirit. At the same time, he instituted the offices, including the ministerial office, in order to effect his promise of the Word and the sacrament through the Holy Spirit.[8]

The universal priesthood undergirds public witness and service in terms of the doctrine of vocation. We are called to be priests in our worldly tasks for one another. We have the universal priesthood for the mutual comfort and absolution of brothers and sisters as well as for social engagement in rendering service to the needy. "A cobbler, a smith, a peasant—each has the work and office of his trade, and yet they are all alike consecrated priest and bishop."[9] In the *Smalcald Articles* (1537) Luther articulates "the mutual conversation and consolation of brothers and sisters" concerning the content of gospel. This refers to a dimension of the universal priesthood in Luther's interpretation of the gospel. This implies expanding a social-missional implication of God's word as word-event in relation to the ministry of Word and sacrament in public profile.[10]

According to Luther, Christian life and the doctrine of justification are intertwined in missional witness. From the perspective of the biblical message of law and gospel Luther argues that the Word of God is in need of proclamation and everybody should hear it. The gospel is an oral cry, the genuine personal voice of Christ going out to everyone, pure blessing. All grace is established through Christ so that no one is to boast, but everyone is to thank God. Every Christian is bound to give a missionary witness to what God has done in Christ for us. Luther's concept of universal priesthood upholds an idea of universal deaconhood and missionhood because it includes the duty of love looking at the needs of the poor and perishing souls. A Christian life for the sake

---

7. Bonhoeffer, *Cost of Discipleship*, 253.

8. Lohse, *Martin Luther's Theology*, 292, 294.

9. LW 44, 127.

10. Luther, "Smalcald Articles" (1537), BC 319.

of proclamation is "the highest priestly office."[11] This understanding of the initiative of God's word-event has little to do with either the impure motive of colonialism or confessional rivalry.

"Their voice has gone out to all the earth, and their words to the ends of the world" (Rom 10:18) means that this outcome has begun and its goal is set although it is not yet completed and accomplished. It shall be extended through evangelization ever farther until the day of judgment. Evangelization is like throwing a stone into the water. It makes waves and circles around itself, and the waves roll always farther outward. The waves do not rest, but they continue outward. Thus the kingdom of God stands in becoming, not in being.[12] Luther's missionary method is an invitation to the gospel while acknowledging that the non-Christian often leads a morally mature life with respect to the commands of God written upon all human hearts (Rom 1:20–21; 2:12–16).

Jesus Christ as the true High Priest calls all baptized Christians his royal priesthood (1 Pet 2:9; Exod 19:5–6). Jesus as the servant of the circumcised (Rom 15:8) calls the church and congregational mission to be in accompaniment and solidarity with the least of the little ones (*elaxistoi*, Matt 25:40, 45). Congregational mission is engaged in caring for the sick, the mentally confused, and those on the margins—God's *ochlos-minjung*. This perspective characterizes the church as faith community in prophetic-missional witness. The missional church announces the crucified one who was friend of the lost, publicans, and sinners. "The publicans and the harlots go into the kingdom of heaven before you" (Matt 21:31).

In the German Lutheran tradition, evangelization, public diaconate, and foreign mission came together, looking after orphans, helping prisoners, finding new homes for refugees, and conveying the message of evangelization by sending missionaries to America. Examples of diaconal ministry and social engagement in the German Protestant context of the nineteenth century will be discussed in the following section.

11. Luther, *Church Comes from All Nations*, 20.
12. Ibid., 24, 26.

Reformation and Universal Deaconhood in Historical Development

David Bosch argues that the churches shaped by the Reformation have remained as "a place where certain things happen." The marks of the true church exist wherever the gospel is rightly preached, the sacraments rightly administered, and church discipline (an occasional addition) is exercised. These marks narrowed the definition of the church toward an idea of a "place where." Undermining the community as the bearer of missional responsibility, church conceived as the "place where" created an impression of a church where a Christianized civilization gathers for worship and where the Christian character of the society is cultivated. Even the missionary movement throughout the nineteenth century altered in no way this "place where" definition.[13] According to Bosch, the article of justification by faith is the starting point for a Protestant theology of mission. Although there is a positive dimension of the teaching of justification in regard to mission, Bosch argues that it sometimes paralyzed any missionary effort.[14]

Unfortunately, Bosch sidesteps a Lutheran understanding of the church as event. Concerning ministry in the church, the Lutheran Confession articulates that "through the Word and the sacraments as through instruments the Holy Spirit is given, who effects faith *where and when it pleases God in those who hear the gospel*"(italics mine).[15] The church occurs as an event through the Holy Spirit, effecting faith where and when it pleases God, in the recipient of the Gospel. Furthermore, Bosch argues that the Lutheran teaching of the priesthood of all believers was practiced by the Anabaptists. Bosch's reading goes too far, saying that the Lutheran emphasis on justification by faith led to the Calvinist notion of double predestination in which God's sovereignty elects people, so that any "human attempt at saving people would be blasphemy."[16] Bosch fails to see that the Lutheran teaching of single election is built on the grace of justification. This teaching became foundational for implementing universal priesthood in connection with the mission of *diakonia* in the German Protestant context, notably represented by John

13. Guder, ed., *Missional Church*, 80.

14. Bosch, *Transforming Mission*, 244–45.

15. "Augsburg Confession" (1530), V. BC 41.

16. Bosch, *Transforming Mission*, 242.

Wichern (1808–1881) and Wihelm Loehe (1808–1872). The priesthood of all believers was reintroduced by them to emphasize the church's responsibility for society and people; every Christian has a calling and a responsibility to serve God, actively involved in God's ongoing work in the world.

What remains questionable in Bosch's evaluation of Lutheran theology is his misrepresentation of the Lutheran doctrine of *vocatio catholica* as obscuring mission to "pagans." According to Bosch's interpretation, this doctrine affirms that God had revealed God's self to all people through nature and the preaching of the apostles, thus no further mission was necessary. It is true that Johann Gerhard (1582–1637) contended that all nations had long before been reached with the gospel, since the religions of all nations show Christian elements. Bosch interpreted this argument to mean that if the pagans remain in their heedlessness and ingratitude, they should not be given a second chance to be evangelized.[17] In Bosch's specious argument, Gerhard's theology of the universality of the gospel, which implies careful openness to God's inclusive salvation, turns into a Calvinist "in or out" theory of double predestination. It completely neglects the dynamic aspect of the Lutheran teaching of *creatio continua* as related to *vocatio catholica*.

In contrast to Calvinist double predestination, the Lutheran Confession affirms the universal scope of Christological atonement: "For he has preordained this salvation through his eternal intention, which cannot fail or be overthrown, and he has placed it for safekeeping into the almighty hand of our Savior Jesus Christ, from which no one can snatch us away (John 10:28)."[18] The Lutheran doctrine of the universality of the gospel is a counter proposal to the Calvinist notion of double predestination. Furthermore, Lutheran doctrinal theology states that all people stand under the same condemnation. God's call is addressed to all without distinction—thus being universal. This universal call is on account of the purpose of God who earnestly wishes that all people should come to the knowledge of the truth (1 Tim 2:4; 2 Pet 3:9), on account of the command of Christ (Matt 11:28), and on account of the message itself for all people to be called (Mark 16:20; Rom 10:18). The call is extended equally to all people, as much as saving grace is offered to all people through the same means. Opportunity was given to

17. Ibid., 251.

18. "Formula of Concord, Solid Declaration, XI," BC 645.

all then living to hear it. It was possible for them to hand down the glad tidings to all their progeny as seen in the days of Adam, of Noah, and of the Apostles. Although in the course of time some people are found to be entirely ignorant of the Gospel, this does not militate against the universality of the call (*vocatio catholica*).[19]

In this light, Bosch's understanding of Lutheran teaching of *vocatio catholica* remains misleading. Bosch's uninformed reading of the Lutheran orthodox theology of *vocatio catholica* completely contradicts Wilhelm Loehe's (1808–1872) embodiment of confession and foreign mission. Loehe saw the American Indians as those who received God's calling, but this inspired rather than hindered his mission among them. Loehe's approach to mission centered on the grace of justification, the church as communion, and the recognition of non-Christian cultures in light of *vocatio catholica*. Bosch's optimistic view of Puritan mission neglects completely its negative consequences, which are largely responsible for American civil religion, American exceptionalism, and Manifest Destiny.[20] In contrast to this Puritan direction, Lutheran confessional mission implemented by Loehe remains a classic example for mission as *diakonia* to the world. We shall deal further with Loehe's confessional view of mission later.

Having considered this, it is worth repeating that in Luther's missional thought the gospel should be spread like the impact of a stone thrown into the water. Luther was eager to restore the primitive diaconate as a ministry of God's mercy and the helping hand of the pastoral office. He proposed to divide a city into four or five districts and to assign to each district a pastor and several deacons. The pastor supplies preaching and the deacons distribute alms and visit the sick and care for anyone who suffered want.[21] Based on the reading of Acts 6:4—"we, for our part, will devote ourselves to prayer and to serving the word"—Luther assigned the diaconate to the ministry of distributing the church's aid to the poor. It helps relieve the pastors of the burden of temporal matters for the sake of commitment to prayer and the word. Women and men have served in various forms of diaconal ministry and service since the earliest days of the church. At the prophetic beginning of Jesus' ministry

19. Schmid, *Doctrinal Theology*, 443.

20. Bellah, *Beyond Belief*, 168–86.

21. Ohl, *Inner Mission*, 49.

in Galilee (Luke 4:18–19), we read a substantial example of diaconial ministry and mission.[22]

Pietism and Inner Mission

The Pietist movement initiated by Philip Jakob Spener (1635–1705) and August Hermann Francke (1633–1727) retrieved such a tradition in reaction against ossified Lutheran orthodoxy with emphasis on the spiritual renewal of the individual. Spener's book *Pia desideria*[23] can be seen as the actual beginning of the German Pietist movement. The University of Halle (1694) was founded to become a center of Pietistic theology and mission. In Spener's *Pia desideria*, the following pious desires were the program of the movement: 1) a clearer and deeper understanding of Scripture through devout study in small conventicles (or house meetings) that are called *collegia pietatis*; 2) rediscovery of the universal priesthood of believers; 3) actual experience of faith and the practice of Christian life in the whole of life, although accepting doctrinal formulations; 3) all controversies carried out in a spirit of charity; 4) the training of pastors in terms of a profound immersion in devotional literature and practice as well as underlying training and experience in the actual work of shepherding the flock; and 5) regaining of the pupil's original purpose of instructing, inspiring, and feeding the congregation. Within this Pietistic framework, personal experience is more important than ecclesial faith and historical revelation.[24]

Following in the footsteps of Spener, Francke made an institutional contribution by establishing charitable centers, such as a school for the education of poor children and an orphanage. Through Francke the University of Halle was turned into a center for the training of Pietist leaders known for charitable work in Germany and world missions. He emphasized the personal experience of conversion, focusing on the individual, spiritual relationship with God; unfortunately the church as the community of the saints was sidestepped. In Spener and Francke, the Great Commission was given by Christ to all Christians. However, later Pietism went too far, completely marginalizing the sacramental,

---

22. Collins, *Deacons and the Church*, 27.

23. Spener, *Pia Desideria*.

24. González, *History of Christian Thought*, 302–3.

congregational dimension of the church. It became subjective, individualistic, exclusive, and indifferent toward purity of doctrine and sacramental life.

The term "inner mission" was used in a completely different sense than individualist narrowness of Christian mission in an address of Fr. Lücke, Professor of Göttingen, at a mission conference on November 13, 1842. The inner mission movement, a new program of social activism and domestic evangelism, concentrated on establishing churches domestically with focus on social outreach to the poor and marginal of society.

The inner mission movement provided a new form of the diaconate for John Wichern of Hamburg and Theodor Fliedner (1800–1864), the Lutheran pastor in Kaiserwerth. Theodore and his wife Friederike established a new form of diaconal ministry for women. In the Netherlands, he became acquainted with the ancient church office of deacon, spending time among the Mennonites. In England he was influenced by the work of a Quaker, Elizabeth Fry, involved with the nation's impoverished and imprisoned people. Fliedner became interested in prison reform. The Fliedners expanded the scope of their work with the poor by including care of the sick, orphans, neglected children, and the mentally ill. Challenged by the increasing social problems spawned by socio-economic conditions, the Fliedners and others established the Motherhouses of deaconesses to provide services to those in need. Theodor founded the hospital and deaconess training center in Kaiserwerth. Fliedner gave the women the title of deaconess. These institutions spread widely in central and northern Europe, and finally entered North America. Following this example, a multitude of instructions and agencies were established to address the needs of diverse groups in nineteenth-century society.

Independently, however, John Wichern employed the term "inner mission" in connection with his mission work at the *Rauhe Haus*, Hamburg, which began in 1833. Wichern is called the father of the inner mission with focus on domestic evangelization and social reform. Wichern was connected with a Sunday school program in a suburb of Hamburg in which he learned to know the spiritual, moral, and physical wretchedness of children in a thousand families. Wichern delivered his famous address at the Wittenberg *Kirchentag* (September 22, 1848). In it he called for the entire Protestant Church of Germany to undertake the work of inner mission to ameliorate moral disintegration and social maladies in the aftermath of the social revolution of 1848.[25] By virtue of the principle of the universal priesthood of believers, the diffusion of the gospel should extend to all corners of life in society through the ministrations of Christian love and mercy to aid family, church, and state. Christian love, which springs from faith in Christ, seeks to bring about the internal and external renewal of the masses within Christendom through the inner mission and evangelization. The inner mission is the unfolding and active exercise of the faith and vital powers of the entire body of believers in the church, in all forms of social life, and in all the departments of the material and spiritual life of the masses and the nations.

Social improvement is inseparably connected with spiritual and moral renovation. The inner mission as a missionary force was to reach all to whom it ministered and served with the gospel. The congregation of believers was to become a royal people of God that would dispense the blessing of the gospel and the sacraments. They were consecrated to missionary discipleship including the inner mission. Wichern's theology of the congregation was grounded in the inner mission, social *diakonia*, and the doctrine of universal priesthood.

The community of love, bearing the diverse gifts of one sacred Spirit, is central to Wichern's ecclesiology. Such a community becomes a life-filled organism, transforming humanity and filling it with the divine life. This ecclesiology emphasizes the democratic character of a faith community, distinguishing it from the state church. To the extent that the essence of the church is constituted by freedom, truth, and organic community, this principle turns the genuine church into the people's church. The gospel of John (13–17) is the grounding text in Wichern's concept of the church that is spirit-centered and love-filled. Wichern's contribution in the field of inner mission, evangelization, and social *diakonia* can also be seen in his freeing the moribund state church for diaconal discipleship, while promoting the church for the life of people, socially engaging in the public sphere.

Wilhelm Loehe: Confessional Theology and Missional Church

As the contemporary of Wichern, the name of Wilhelm Loehe (1808–1872) is also woven into the history of the Lutheran Church in Bavaria

---

25. Crowner and Christianson, eds., *Spirituality of Awakening*, 233, 305.

and in America through his missional ecclesiology, *diakonia*, and foreign mission. In his writings and public ministrations, Loehe represented Lutheran confessional theology.[26] He is known as a founder of social institutions and the mission department in Neuendettelsau. He was ordained to the pastoral office on July 25, 1831, in St. Gumbretus Church in Ansbach. Since then, the Augsburg Confession, together with the symbolic books of the Evangelical Lutheran Church in Germany, became the guiding norm for his theology and ministry. Finding a pastorate in the tiny farming community of Neuendettelsau in 1837, Loehe made a remarkable contribution toward transforming the insignificant town into a center of Christian mission and *diakonia*. In Loehe's time, America was a chief object of his missional concern and activity.

In 1841 Loehe paid attention to German immigrants by reading a pamphlet of appeals for help from Lutheran pastors who were overworked in ministering to German immigrants in America. Due to the onset of industrialization, there was a large wave of immigration from Germany to America, where immigrants lived in the widely scattered settlement regions without a connection to their church and without the possibility of schooling their children. To relieve the spiritual distress of German immigrants and promote foreign mission to Native Americans Loehe made provision for the training of missionaries and founded the Missionary Institute at Neuendettelsau. Loehe's article in a weekly newspaper (edited by John Frederick Wucherer, Loehe's close friend) called for missionary help for German immigrants in the wilderness of America. On the anniversary of the presentation of the Augsburg Confession (June 25, 1842), Loehe and Wucherer gave their emissaries a set of instructions for their work in America. Their missionaries later became pastors in the Ohio synod.

In Missouri a group of Lutherans were settled, having emigrated from Saxony in 1839. Missouri Lutherans under the leadership of C. F. W. Walther met a group of Loehe's men in September 1845 for the purpose of founding a new synod that would be based on the Lutheran confessions. From this meeting the Missouri Synod was organized in Fort Wayne, Indiana. Loehe was instrumental in the founding of his own seminary in Fort Wayne, and he fostered missionary activity among the Michigan Indians. Colonies of German Lutherans could be established in proximity to Indian settlements. The central part of Michigan

---

26. Loehe, *Three Books*, 1–40.

was chosen as the site for missionary outreach. However, it was not long before the nature of the ministry became a doctrinal dispute between Loehe and Walther. Walther emphasized the office of the ministry and its authority from the congregational transference of power, while Loehe believed that the ministerial office was instituted by Christ within the congregation and for the congregation.[27] Loehe's contribution to American Christianity was the foundation of a new Lutheran body in 1854. The Iowa Synod was formed by missionaries whom Loehe had sent. In this regard Loehe is considered one of the founders founders both branches of the Lutheran church—the Missouri and Iowa Synods.

The year 1848 was the year of revolution in Germany. Loehe understood the terrible restraint of personal freedom, the dishonesty of the administration, and the dysfunction of the bureaucracy as the roots of the revolution. Nevertheless, he was not convinced that revolution was the ultimate instrument for the abolition of social injustice and evil. He was more concerned with the renewal of the life of the church to split off from the state church through the impact of revolution. At the time of writing *Three Books about the Church*, the kneeling controversy (1838–1845) occurred after Ludwig I, the king of Barvaria, ordered his soldiers to kneel at Mass and at *Corpus Christi* procession. A hybrid between throne and altar was an unhappy espousal for Loehe. In the years following the Revolution of 1848, Loehe was involved in protesting against the union of the Lutheran Church with the Reformed Church.

In 1850 Loehe organized the Society for Inner Missions as understood by the Lutheran Church. Because of his creation of the Neuendettelsau deaconess motherhouse and the institutions of mercy (1854), Loehe is remembered as one of the important leaders of the female diaconate in the German Protestant churches. Loehe observed that there were many women in the congregation talented in caring for the sick and meeting the needs of suffering humanity. Serving as the pastor of the deaconesses, Loehe organized a society of deaconesses and personally was in charge of training them and of undergirding their spiritual welfare. The motherhouse in the subsequent year became the center of Christian institutions administered by the deaconesses. The creed Loehe wrote for the deaconesses is expressed: "What do I want? I want to serve. Whom will I serve? The Lord in his suffering and poor. And what is my reward? I serve neither for reward nor thanks but out

27. Ibid., 24.

of thanks and love; my reward is that I may serve . . . Then shall my heart flourish as a palm tree, and the Lord will satisfy me with grace and mercy. I shall depart in peace and be anxious for nothing."[28]

Loehe's view of church and mission in sacramental-liturgical perspective is of special significance to our discussion of congregational mission. For Loehe the Lutheran Church was considered to be the unifying center of the confessions of Christianity.[29] However, his conscious decision for the Lutheran confessions does not mean excluding the contribution of other denominations. Loehe acknowledged the achievements of people in other denominations, paving the way for ecumenical mission. Missional identity is deeply connected with ecumenical relevance and cooperation. As a matter of fact, the universal grace of God in Jesus Christ is the foundation for Loehe's commitment to Lutheran particularity and foreign mission, as well.[30]

For Loehe, Augustine's prayer—"Thou hast formed us for thyself, and our hearts are restless until they find rest in thee"—indicates the human desire for fellowship with God, that is, "fellowship created by God for eternity."[31] Dealing with the church in the one holy catholic and apostolic sense, Loehe sees the church on the pilgrimage toward God's blessed eternity. We are born into fellowship with God and into the church. The church is one in all generations, so mission as the life of one catholic church is the actualization of the one universal, catholic Church. Church and mission are not separable.[32] Liturgy is called the Lord's approach to the Word and the sacrament, indwelling among the songs of praise with the sacraments. The people of God dance in worship around the triune God who guides their steps.[33] The true faith is expressed not only in the sermon but also in the liturgy.[34]

Church springs from the Spirit of Pentecost and the vicarious death of Jesus Christ and is implanted in the bosom of God the almighty. The first congregation became possible based on the oral Word of the apostles. The Word heard at Pentecost is read today as the same Word

28. Ibid., 26–27.

29. Ibid., 152, 156.

30. Ibid., 163.

31. Ibid., 50.

32. Ibid., 59.

33. Ibid., 176–77.

34. Schattauer, "Löhe Alternative," 145–56.

in congregational worship and life. The church is rooted in the fountain of the apostolic Word, based on the apostles' teaching. To the degree that the center of the church is the apostolic word, "apostolic" means "founded on the apostles' teaching."[35] A congregation can be apostolic to the extent that it holds to the Word of the apostles. The principal name of the church is apostolic—built on the apostles' Word. The church is the candlestick while the Word is the light. The church is always bright and beautiful. The sure, prophetic, apostolic Word is its ground.[36] Thus "the Church is the child of God's Word and can never, never stand above the Word."[37] The Word occupied the central place in his understanding of the church that is more than episcopacy and apostolic succession. Doctrine and confession are an internal touchstone for testing all of the external life commanded by God. If people are born into fellowship with God through Word and sacrament, the fellowship is expressed in love among the community of believers, as well as in service toward the world. Confessional integrity is understood in relation to its ecclesial-missional orientation.

The church exists wherever there is a call and people who are called. The church in general has been and will continue to be established, gathered, nourished, and preserved through Word and sacrament. A mark of the church exhibits itself as the most precious treasure, the Word of truth and the sacraments of the Lord. "Its confession is its most precious treasure, its distinguishing sign and mark."[38] The church as a whole leads and directs the congregational life into all good, embraces all good works into congregational mission.

According to Loehe, the Lutheran Reformation is partly complete and partly incomplete. It is complete in doctrine and confessional writings (The *Formula of Concord* and the *Book of Concord*), but incomplete in their missional consequence.[39] Despite Loehe's confessional position ,in which the Lutheran Church in all significant doctrines holds the correct position as compared to the doctrines of the Roman and the Reformed Churches, Loehe was open to an ecumenical dimension of

---

35. Loehe, *Three Books*, 63.

36. Ibid., 74.

37. Ibid., 73.

38. Ibid., 107.

39. Ibid., 152.

mission. This was because the truth other churches proclaim may be blessed with the salvation of the heathen.

Loehe understands living out God's mission as a vocation in light of Luther's teaching on the priesthood of all believers. Everyone serves Jesus Christ in his/her place and every place becomes an altar of praise to God showing forth God's love. For Loehe, "The dwelling of the house-father, the nursery of the housemother, the bench of the mechanic, the field of the farmer, the kitchen and stable where the servants toil, are transfigured through the lovely doctrine of the Call and of the holiness of the works of our calling."[40]

The unchangeable promise of the Word of God is divine assurance, related to all people. The church is asked to convey God's universal call to every nation. The word "catholic" is understood in the sense of God's universal grace. In Loehe's teaching on the church, mission plays a significant role in the characterization of the church as one, holy, catholic, and apostolic. Springing up from the manifestation of the Holy Spirit in Pentecost and the sacrificial death of Jesus Christ, the church, like a beautiful, lovely, and wonderful river, flows throughout all ages until consummated into "the famed sea of eternal blessedness."[41]

In the image of the gathering of the multitude from every nation (Revelation 7) Loehe defines mission as "the one church of God in motion, the actualization of the one universal, catholic church."[42] Loehe's passion for mission is motivated notably by the community model of the early church in Jerusalem: commitment to the apostolic teaching and fellowship, to the breaking of bread and the prayers, and to the *diakonia* to reach out to others (Acts 2:42–47). Mission is the responsibility of Christians and its impulse is born out of Christian vocation grounded in the universal priesthood. Emphasizing a communal-ecclesial dimension of mission, Loehe insists that we are born into fellowship. In the church we experience communal blessing bestowed by the living presence of Jesus Christ in the proclamation of the Word and the celebration of the Eucharist. Foreign mission is an extension of the communal blessing to the "pagans."[43]

40. Ibid., 145.

41. Ibid., 55.

42. Ibid., 59.

43. Ibid., 162.

What transforms the church's mission into God's mission is the peace of God that the Gospel brings, inviting the pagans into fellowship with God. They are one family of God in which the love and brotherliness of humanity should prevail. Loehe takes an encounter between Peter and Cornelius as a model of foreign mission (Acts 10:34). Mission pays attention to God's tolerance and impartiality toward the people outside the walls of the Christian church. The Hindu, the outcast, and the accursed should not be excluded from God's blessing. Loehe was aware that great harm had been done toward the blacks in Africa, as well as in the American colonies and of the plight of widows in Hindu cultures. The peace of God brought by the Gospel should grasp and consecrate every heart. Love should pass from person to person and the thought of brotherliness and humanity should draw into the desolate hearts of the "heathen" as one family of God.[44] In *Die Mission unter den Heiden,* Loehe writes: "We must be driven by compassion for these Indian tribes who are disappearing from the world scene and give them at least this benefit to let the light of the everlasting Gospel shine from them into eternity."[45]

Loehe was in contact with a Pastor Schmidt in Ann Arbor, Michigan, who had a relationship with the Native Americans. The establishment of the mission colonies in Michigan was an important event as a springboard for evangelizing Indians in the American West. A mission colony, Frankenmuth, was established in Michigan under the direction of Pastor August Craemer at the border of the Native American areas and South of the Saginaw Bay. It was unfortunate that the Indian mission came to an end because of the government policy of reservation. On the seventy-fifth anniversary of the Frankenmuth Colony, James Gruest, a seventy-three-year-old Native American, thanked the Frankenmuth pioneers for their help and kindness to the Indians.[46]

Mission in *Diakonia* to God's Word-Event

Loehe's concept of *vocatio catholica* implies that God cannot leave any nation without the necessary call, since God wills that all people be saved (2 Tim 2:4). The dogmatic, confessional claim of a catholic call

---

44. Loehe, *Mission unter Heiden*, 67.

45. Cited in Bickel, *Our Forgotten Founding Father*, 31.

46. Ibid., 32.

can be actualized in the global missional context. An ecclesiology and its mission depend on the doctrine of universal grace, since the gospel has been preached to every creature under heaven (Col 1:23). Loehe observed a confirmation of the teaching of universal grace in these words of Paul. In commenting on Matt 24:14 Loehe contends that the gospel and its call could come to all people and nations in its own age. In light of the doctrine of a *vocatio catholica*, Loehe provocatively argues that the people of America, even before the discovery of Columbus, must have received this universal and irregular call.[47]

As all nations and all people have a calling from God, it is important to encourage and invite the religious outsiders to engage in this call. A Lutheran sense of evangelization can be actualized and deepened in terms of a *vocatio catholica*, recognizing and embracing those outside the walls of the Christian church. As Loehe states, "They (our Christian forefathers) teach a catholic calling of all people on earth. They admit that the form and manner of this call may be different, but they hold that neither before Christ, and much less since Christ, has any nation or generation been without this call."[48]

Paul's concept of natural knowledge of God is redefined in Loehe's confirmation of *vocatio catholica* in the sense of God's word-event in a universal sense. This perspective would become a missional principle in the inclusion of people of other cultures as the children of God. God's universal grace is connected with the freedom of God's Word, the first function of the law. Along this line, Luther affirmed God's irregular grace upon Ishmael and his descendants and God's universal grace in the Turk. As Luther said, "God has subjected and submitted secular rule to reason, because its purpose is not to control the salvation of souls or their eternal good, but only bodily and temporal goods, which God subjects to man . . . That is why the pagans . . . can speak and teach well on this subject . . . They are far more skilled than Christians in such matters . . . For God is a gentle and rich Lord who subjects a great deal of gold, silver, riches, dominions, and kingdoms to the godless . . . [God] also makes lofty reason, wisdom, languages and eloquence subject to them . . ."[49]

47. Ibid., 85. See further Schmid, *Doctrinal Theology*, 443.
48. Ibid., 82.
49. Cited in Ebeling, *Luther*, 186–87.

In this light, Loehe emphasizes the universal dimension of the Spirit in his theology of *vocatio catholica*. God reaches out to everyone and desires them to experience the benefits of salvation. The Ethiopian eunuch (Acts 8:26–40) and the Roman centurion, Cornelius, (Acts 10:1–33) are important examples for Loehe's missional vision of the universal work of the Holy Spirit. The Spirit blows where the Spirit wills, seeking outsiders in every place and every time. Loehe was convinced that there were many "Corneliuses" in the world, and there are some, like the Macedonians, who appear to us as in Paul's dreams at night, calling out, "Come over and help us"(Acts 16:9).[50]

Drawing upon the universal activity of the Holy Spirit and *vocatio catholica*, Loehe understands Peter's confession (Acts 10:34–35) in the way that those who fear God and do what is right are acceptable to God. It is the Holy Spirit who converts people to the gospel of Jesus Christ. As Loehe states, "Remember that the almighty God wills and commends the active participation of the church in the work of heathen conversion. Remember that God converts people through people and will make humans co-workers in the work of God's grace."[51] By affirming God's initiative in the conversion of people, Loehe insists that the universal call of God is extended equally to all. Mission to non-Christians has nothing to do with the colonial mentality of crusade. Rather it undergirds Lutheran mission in *diakonia* to people of other cultures, actualizing our vocation and discipleship by sharing God's universal grace in Christ with those who were already implicitly reached by God in *creatio continua*. The Lutheran confessional teaching of justification affirms Loehe's position, referring to God's initiative as it states that "conversion to God is the work of God the Holy Spirit alone."[52] At the heart of Loehe's missional theology is a dynamic comprehension and actualization of God's universal grace through the Spirit. It underpins discipleship of witnessing to God's particular grace in Jesus Christ for all in the world.

This genuine catholicity can be found in the "Augsburg Confession" (VII). In the characterization of church as one, holy, catholic, and apostolic, the church is planted in God's eternal grace as the true blossom of God's love. Jesus' Great Commission is the revelation of God's mission and *diakonia*. It becomes an eternal place for understanding the life of

50. Loehe, *Three Books*, 163–64.

51. Loehe, *Mission unter Heiden*, 62.

52. "Formula of Concord," Solid Declaration, art. II. BC 561.

the apostles, especially Paul, for Christian mission. Articulating that "mission is nothing but the one church of God in motion,"[53] Loehe in his ecclesial theology envisioned a Catholic church through the ages and claimed that the Lutheran church, with its confessional clarity, became the embodiment of that church for the sake of the mission of *vocatio catholica* in the globe. Mission is the responsibility of the Christian, born out of Christian vocation in terms of the priesthood of all believers. Theory (ecclesiology) and practice (mission) in Loehe's confessional theology can be well articulated by his integration of social service and global mission in light of God's Word in action. This perspective can be expressed further in Loehe's prophetic statement in regard to all living creatures in the web of creation: "The law of mercy does not even find its limit within the boundaries of humankind since it does not forget the animals and the birds in the nests. If we look not to the persons, but rather to the opportunity in which mercy should be manifested, we find God's will to be merciful is expressed."[54]

53. Loehe, *Three Books*, 59.

54. Loehe, "Von der Barmherzigkeit," cited in Ratke, *Confession and Mission*, 188–89.

8

Missional Church as Public Vocation

In our understanding of church as the community of vocation, the Reformation teaching on justification and public discipleship is central. It leads to the development of an integrative model of vocation based on Abraham and Paul in light of the universality of the gospel of Jesus Christ. Sacramental life in the celebration of Word and Eucharist is inseparably connected with church as community of vocation, witness, and stewardship. Here a theology of vocation and congregational mission needs to be developed in regard to stewardship, spiritual formation, and missional leadership.

Theology of Vocation and Mission

Paul claimed that he was called by God for a particular vocation (Gal 1:15–16). His vocation is reminiscent of Jeremiah's confession of calling (Jer 1:5) which is also compared to the prophets (Isa 46:1–6). God revealed God's Son to Paul calling him to be an apostle to the *nations* of the Gentile world (Rom 11:13), not simply to individuals of non-Jewish origin. In terms of his call, Paul's theology assumes a missional character, proclaiming the gospel and establishing congregations as the first fruits of the new creation. Paul proclaimed the gospel to various ethnicities, including those in Syria, Cilicia, central and western Asia Minor, Macedonia, Greece, and perhaps even in Arabia. His ambition was to preach the gospel to the nations in places where it had never been preached before (Rom 15:20; cf. 2 Cor 10:15–16).[1]

In Paul's experience and understanding of Jesus Christ, the God of Israel is seen in light of God in Christ. This God has reconciled the world to God's self and commissioned us to be God's ambassadors of reconciliation (2 Cor 5:18–20). Paul was a child of Abraham, a Benjaminite (Phil 3:5), an heir of the traditions and heritage of Israel. God is living and active in the history of Israel, manifesting God's redemptive work of mission in sending Jesus Christ in the presence of the Holy Spirit. God's righteousness and God's saving deeds become obvious in the deliverance of God's people (Ps 98:2) from their enemies and oppressors (1 Sam 12:7; Dan 9:15–16; Mic 6:5). In the history of Israel, Yahweh was celebrated as the one who bestowed on God's people the all-embracing and saving gift of God's righteousness.[2]

Jesus Christ is sent to us as God's mission in service, conveying and communicating God's grace of righteousness and salvation for all. Given this fact, Paul's theology of justification can be understood in two contexts. All humanity is justified through Christ's act of righteousness (Rom 5:8)—this is known only through the gospel, which entails theocentric and cosmic dimensions. This realized justification becomes possible through believers' faith in the grace of God.[3] The theology of justification by faith is developed in the story of Abraham and in God's promise that all the nations will be blessed in him (Gen 12:3). Paul's theology of justification in two contexts (Abraham and the future promise) is grounded in his missional theology.[4]

Abraham, in Paul's interpretation, was accounted righteous by believing the promise of God (Gen 15:6) while he was still a Gentile. Abraham is to be understood as the father not only of the people of Israel but also of those who believe the promise of God (Rom 4:24; Gal 3:6–9). All believers in Christ form a new community, a new humanity (1 Cor 10:32), in which the distinction between Jew and Gentile is overcome within the body of Christ (Gal 3:28). Nothing in all creation can separate us from the love of God in Christ.

---

1. Hultgren, "Paul as Theologian," 9.

2. Von Rad, *Old Testament Theology*, 1:377.

3. Hultgren, *Paul's Gospel*, 96.

4. Ibid., 145.

Abraham's life of vocation, which is foundational for Paul's theology of justification and mission, provides us with the church as the community of vocation and public service. God promises Abraham to make him a blessing to others. In the act of the covenant in the Genesis narrative, blessing is a key term testifying to God's work as the creator. God's election of Abraham does not exclude God's goodness from "non-chosen" people. Coupled with the blessing, promise is the most basic category, extending blessing into the sphere of salvation.

On the other hand, we see that John's missional framework integrates the story of Abraham with the new reality actualized by Jesus Christ. "Your ancestor Abraham rejoiced that he would see my day; he saw it and was glad" (8:56). Jesus introduces himself as the fulfillment and confirmation of Abraham's faith. The particularity of Jesus Christ seen in light of the universal horizon of the gospel is enmeshed with the centrality of Abraham in the Christian understanding of Jesus Christ. As F. W. Marquardt articulates in regard to the affinity between Jesus Christ and Abraham, "we can hardly in its importance over esteem the fact that in the New Testament, the Jesus proclamation and the understanding of Christian faith is brought into connection with Abraham's faith and history."[5]

Stewardship and Ministry of Taking-Care

Stewardship in the biblical context is grounded in God's act of feeding Israel with manna (Deut 8:3). Thanksgiving in harvest festivals (Deut 14:22–23) and financial care and provision for the widows, the orphans, the resident aliens, the marginalized, and the poor (Deut 14:28–29) are expressions of stewardship based on generosity and hospitality (Lev 19:9–10). In a ceremony of the first fruits of the grain at harvest time we read that a farmer confessed that God's promise of the land, first made to Abraham and Sarah, had come true (Deuteronomy 26). In this confession, the life of the farmer is connected to the ancestors of faith by remembrance of God's protection, deliverance in Egypt, and the promised land. There is the collective confession of Israel to the God of Israel:

> A wandering Aramean was my ancestor; he went down into Egypt and lived there as an alien, few in number, and there he became a great nation, mighty and populous . . . The Lord brought

---

5. Marquardt, *Von Elend und Heimsuchung*, 280.

> us out of Egypt with a mighty hand and an outstretched arm,
> with a terrifying display of power, and with signs and wonders;
> and he brought us into this place and gave us this land, a land
> flowing with milk and honey. So now I bring the first of the fruit
> of the ground that you, O Lord, have given me. (Deut 26:5–10)

The biblical concept of stewardship is a response to God's promise and act of deliverance and generosity. God's gracious generosity and promise create our faith and trust in God. Such faith is expressed in our confession of stewardship, gratitude, and hospitality. This confession of Israel is articulated in Israel's life experience as well as in Jesus' challenge to the Devil. "Human beings do not live by bread alone, but by every word that comes from the mouth of the Lord" (Deut 8:3). In the study of the community of vocation, the biblical idea of stewardship is of special significance for characterizing congregational life and mission. The congregational strategy of stewardship challenges consumerist culture, demonstrating care for creation and the weak.

In the opening chapters of Genesis human responsibility is identified in the care of creation. Human beings as the image of God (Gen 1:26) are assigned a care-taking role and dominion in God's name and stead. This dominion can be a beneficent mandate, because the earth is the Lord's and all that is in it, the world, and those who live in it" (Ps 24:1; Ps 89:11). Creation depends upon God's ongoing activity in sustaining and preserving the earth full of God's creatures (*creatio continua*). The second chapter of Genesis provides us with a picture of the human vocation in terms of "to till (*abad*) it and to keep (*shamar*) it" (Gen 2:15). The first verb is literally translated as "serve it" and the second "to preserve." "Subdue" and "have dominion over" must be understood in the qualified sense in connection with "serve" and "preserve." The mandate of care-taking has little to do with exploitation of the earth, but undergirds ecological stewardship in our endeavor toward transforming mission.[6]

The Noahic covenant (Gen 9:12) expresses God's everlasting covenant between God and every living creature on earth for all future generations. The Torah sustains the life of the people of God in harmony with the well-being of the earth (Exodus 20–24). The land shall be left in rest and lie fallow on the seventh year; the poor may eat and what they leave the wild animals may eat (Exod 23:10). In our stewardship

---

6. Kirk, *What Is Mission?* 177.

and beneficent mandate, ours is a servant role, helping all creatures and resources and the environment survive, thrive, and grow in God's care.

Without this sense of God's miraculous establishment and preservation of creation, we are ungrateful and insensible. Bemoaning the ungratefulness and insensibility of his time, Luther voiced a remarkable aesthetic appreciation of creation: "We do not marvel at the countless other gifts of creation, for we have become deaf toward what Pythagoras aptly terms this wonderful and most lovely music coming from the harmony of the motions that are in the celestial sphere."[7] We are encouraged to listen attentively to the beautiful music coming from the world of creation. The grace of justification would be reduced to blinded anthropocentrism otherwise, for it is connected to God's beautiful voice coming from the creation.

Ecology, which implies living sympathetically with the whole inhibited world, has the same root as economics, that is, the management of material resources. Ecology stands for the symbiosis, interaction, and dialogue of all living creatures. Ecology includes nature, culture, and society. The ecological approach called holism or the holistic approach can be defined as the science and art of interrelationship.[8]

In technological innovation and profit-making, biblical stewardship in care of creation is left behind, resulting in the devastation of the earth. Bringing forth a sustainable globe is founded on respect for nature, economic justice, and a culture of peace. The anthropocentric nature of Christianity has been a target of considerable critique, because it is suspected of causing the environmental crisis. In contrast, a missional ethic of ecological justice is grounded in the Bible and theology of creation. Insofar as the creation belongs to God's salvific drama, missiology should not sidestep an ecological study. Israel's hope looks forward to a total transfiguration of humanity, living creatures, and nature in the universal shalom of God's kingdom. As Isaiah laments, "the earth lies polluted under its inhabitants; for they have transgressed laws, violated the statues, broken the everlasting covenant" (Isa 24:5).

Sustainability implies good stewardship, leading us to solidarity with the earth and all living creatures. When God sends forth God's Spirit, God renews the face of the ground (Ps 104:30). God gives living creatures their food in due season and satisfies the desire of every living

7. LW 1:126.

8. Boff, *Ecology and Liberation*, 11.

thing (Ps 145:15–16). The theology of creation articulates the special vocation of the faith community to promote ecological care in the task of sustaining creation.[9]

Jesus recognized both the essential goodness of creation and God's act of sustaining the life of creation (Matt 5:45; 6:26; 13:7). In the Acts of the Apostles, Jesus Christ as the author of life (Acts 3:15) is portrayed as the one who is related "to the time of universal restoration that God announced long ago through his holy prophets." (Acts 3:20–21). The universe came into being through Jesus Christ (John 1:3) and "for him . . . in whom all things hold together" (Col 1:16–17). God suffers with the whole creation that groans in travail. The creation stands in hope of being free from its bondage to decay (Rom 8:21–22).

Stewardship in mission must raise the issue of carefully planned sustainability and challenge the destruction of the ecosystem. The biblical idea of Sabbath (Exod 20:10; Lev 25:1–7) must be retrieved to promote the stewardship mission of the faith community. This is a day of rest for living creatures that belong to the family community (Exod 20:10). Nature is perceived as God's creation and respected as such. Creation must not be reduced to a backdrop for an anthropocentric Christianity. Human sin must be understood not only in terms of the personal relationship with God and fellow humans, but also in terms of the human-nature relationship. Christian environmental ethics thus occupies an important place in the theology of God's mission. Peace, justice, and the integrity of creation become an indispensable part of the church's mission and stewardship;[10] they call for our participation in God's sustainability and our solidarity with the earth and all living creatures.

Moreover, the eschatological view implies that God's salvation includes the whole creation, thus God's salvation implies a transformation of the social order. In Rom 8:18–23, Paul poetically describes a picture of "the whole creation groaning in labor pains." Here the whole creation is metaphorically depicted as if it were pregnant, straining toward the birth of a new world, free from futility and decay. In Jesus Christ as the firstborn of all creation, all things in heaven and on earth were created through him and for him. Through him as the head of the body, the church, God was pleased to reconcile to God's self all things, whether on

9. Martin-Schramm and Stivers, *Christian Environmental Ethics*, 39.

10. Duchrow and Liedke, *Shalom*.

earth or in heaven, by holding together all things in him (Col 1:15–20). The forgiveness of sin cannot be properly understood apart from God's transformative act of deliverance of the whole creation. In the biblical account, the creation of the animals and the human beings are on the same day. A missional mandate should consider God's activity in the care and protection of the life of all creatures in a universal, all-inclusive life sphere. The church's commitment to the ecological life of all creatures becomes an indispensable part in shaping God's mission in Christ's service in care of the poor and the ecological life of all creatures.

The Grace of Justification: Missional Vocation and Leadership

In light of the missional vocation of Abraham and Paul, it is vital to understand the faith community of Jesus in terms of its calling to be a community of vocation, *diakonia*, and stewardship. The community of vocation is also seen in light of stewardship that is related to generosity and hospitality in service to the world. The generosity and hospitality that Abraham and Sarah showed to three strangers (Gen 18:1–15) may become a model of combining *diakonia* with stewardship and hospitality. The author of Hebrews admonishes: "Do not neglect to show hospitality to strangers, for by doing that some have entertained angels without knowing it" (Heb 13:2).

The congregational vocation, seen in light of union with Christ or of *beneficia Christi* (Melanchthon), presupposes a spiritual formation of *diakonia*, discipleship, and leadership. The grace of justification looks forward to the future event of vocation and missional leadership while vocation and leadership look backward to the grace of justification. Luther's exposition concerning the work of the Holy Spirit underlines a Christology which sharpens a theology of vocation and congregational leadership. The diverse gifts of the Holy Spirit guide missional leadership in undertaking spiritual formation, cultivating people, forming missional environments, and engaging contexts in an interdisciplinary manner. The process of vocation is spiritually and socially engaged as the Holy Spirit has called us through the gospel, enlightened us by the gifts of the Spirit, and sanctified and preserved us in the true faith.

In this regard spiritual formation and leadership cultivation occupy an important place in characterizing congregational vocation and discipleship, fostering faith community and helping God's people live into the world with a sense of Christian vocation and discipleship. In the congregational mission and its leadership individual members need to grow continually with a renewed sense of missional identity, vocation, and mission.

Vocation according to 1 Cor 2:13 is explained as a spiritual reality to which carnal people are blind and deaf. Jesus Christ died and rose again. The risen Christ is also present as the living Christ within our faith. The living reality of Christ is illumination which drives the faith journey of believers in progress, renewal, and formation. The event of vocation must be understood as a sequence of vocation grounded in a once-for-all beginning (the grace of justification). The course of this faith journey includes spiritual cultivation, sanctification, and missional engagement. The whole life of the Christian must be daily repentance (*vocatio continua*). The event of vocation remains effective, continually setting the Christians in fellowship with God (*vocatio efficax*).

In the missional life journey spirituality is grounded in our union with Christ in word and sacrament through the power of the Holy Spirit. Missional leadership as cultivation is the ongoing work grounded in the soil of the congregation, constituting the environment for the people of God to discern what the Spirit is doing among people as a community. This cultivating of leadership in the sense of *vocatio continua* articulates missional leadership in terms of: awareness of what God is doing among the people in the congregation; awareness of how the congregation can envision itself as the center of God's activities; and awareness of what God is already up to in their context. Furthermore, the co-learning networks create an environment in which the missional imagination of a congregation is formed. The scriptural element connects God's people to God's work, emphasizing a hermeneutical process bringing the gospel, church, and the public sphere into dialogue and mutual understanding.[11]

Spiritual Formation and Missional Leadership

For the sake of spiritual formation and missional leadership, we must examine a theology of *unio cum Christo* in the context of vocation. Biblical passages on Christ's union with us—or the metaphor of vine and branches (John 6:56; 15:4; 14:20; 15:4; 17:23, 26), Christ's indwelling in our hearts by faith (Eph 3:17), Christ in all (Col 3:11), Christ living in me (Gal 2:20), the treasure in clay jars (2 Cor 4:7)—do not mean

11. Roxburgh and Romanuk, *Missional Leader*, 31–34.

an extension of the incarnation in relation to the Christian's *unio cum Christo*. Rather Christ has adopted us into unity with his being since we have received a spirit of adoption (Rom 8:15); in virtue of our baptism we have put Christ on like a covering garment (Gal 3:27). A fruitful renewal of baptismal identity, ministry, and spiritual gifts in the church (Eph 4:11–13) is connected with the responsibility to equip the saints for the ministry of reconciliation. Christians, as children of God, promote equality of all in Christ (Gal 3: 28); and they must continually do so, putting on the Lord Jesus Christ (Rom 13:14). This biblical perspective of *unio cum Christo* undergirds the Lutheran notion of deification in an adopted, relational sense based on Luther's notion of the "happy exchange." Nevertheless, it has nothing to do with a mysterious special, ontologically mixed experience of the *perichoresis* of the triune God.

Luther states that the soul and Christ are coupled together in a marriage through the incomparable grace of faith (according to Eph 5:31–32). The soul may possess glory in everything that Christ has (his grace, life, and salvation). Likewise, Christ makes his own everything that belongs to the soul (its sin, death, and damnation). Christ and the soul become one flesh. Faith dwelling in our heart is the source and substance of all our righteousness. In this light Luther states that we are a chosen race, God's own people, and a royal priesthood.[12] In his reflection of Christian freedom Luther argues that a Christian is a perfectly free lord of all, subject to none while he or she is likewise a perfectly dutiful servant of all, subject to all.[13] Thus the rule for the life of Christians means that we should devote all our works to the welfare of others, serving the neighbors by voluntary benevolence and doing good to them.[14] Luther amplifies this view by stating that the Christian must become to fellows a second Christ, since the Christian lives in Christ through faith.[15]

In his exposition of John's Gospel (1528), Luther states that as Father and Son are in divine unity, so Christians with other Christian fellows are one Christian being. Here we see a horizontal expansion in which the unity is grounded in that of Father and Son, of Christ with the Christian, and of Christians with one another. A circle or

12. Luther, "Freedom of a Christian," 398.

13. Ibid., 393.

14. Ibid., 405.

15. Ibid., 408.

crown is made out of the simple sequence of God, Christ, person, and neighbors. Furthermore, in his exposition of Galatians (1535) Luther speaks of the circle as the ring of faith in regard to the relationship between Christ and the Christian. The Christian possesses Christ in faith. Aware that this dimension is a miracle hard to explain with human reason, Luther argues that what is Christ's is actually mine; whatever there is in me of grace, righteousness, life, peace or salvation is Christ's. In this unity the certainty of faith is certainty of salvation, that is unconditional certainty. *Unio cum Christo* is the decisive factor in making the grace of justification through faith related to Christ's indwelling within us (the happy exchange).

According to Simo Peura, the happy exchange between Christ and the believer differs completely from the hypostatic union of the natures of Jesus Christ based on *communicatio idiomatum*. In the model of happy exchange, Christ shares his attributes and grace with the believers. This participation model strengthens our spiritual formation and missional leadership in terms of *theologia crucis* (conformity to Jesus Christ) and *diakonia* of those in need.[16] This perspective strengthens a model of Trinitarian mission of grace and missional leadership.

This integrative perspective on the Trinitarian grace of justification in a forensic and effective sense defends Luther himself against Osiander, according to whom Christ's proper being becomes ours (ontological absorption or deification). In contrast to Luther, Osiander's concept of union with the triune God undermines the human nature of Christ in emphasizing that the believers participate in the divine nature (or Trinitarian *perichoresis*).[17] Here we observe a dangerous tendency toward the pagan notion of henosis, which eliminates the difference between creator and creatures.

In contrast to Osiander, Lutheran confessional theology defends a Christocentric model of *communicatio idiomatum* (the *genus maiestaticum* denotes that divine majesty and power is ascribed to Christ according to the human nature within the unity of person)[18] by distinguishing it from the model of happy exchange. The mystical union as a great mystery (Eph 5:32) is understood in spiritual and supernatural manner, because the Holy Spirit graciously dwells in the regenerate. Within

16. Peura, "Gott und Mensch in der Unio," 44.

17. Ibid., 57.

18. BC 622, 571–72.

a Lutheran confessional framework, Schmidt insists that it is wrong to suppose that in this union the two substances of God and of human being become one or that the one is absorbed in the other. The metaphor of happy exchange has nothing to do with literally conflating the two natures in Christ in the sense of *communicatio idiomatum*[19] which implies the mystery of the triune God.

In contrast to this confessional distinction, Osiander argues that the righteousness of faith is the essential righteousness of God or Christ's divine nature. For Osiander, the triune God dwells in Christians through faith and imparts to them God's own righteousness and nature. Christ's divine nature sanctifies and makes us complete and divinized, so that justification is a result of the indwelling Christ. Becoming more and more Christlike and divine is a basis for justification. Here we observe that the order of salvation is completely reversed. The sins of all are trivialized like a drop of water in comparison with the ocean.

In contrast to Osiander, a model of happy exchange built on the grace of justification must be interpreted in terms of Christ's *diakonia*, cross-formed leadership, and genuine lordship in regard to humility (Phil 2: 6–11). Integrating double justification (God's favor and gift), in other words, forgiveness of sin into the union with Christ, Luther argues that the justified person proceeds to the active life of discipleship for service. Luther's metaphor, happy exchange, in light of an integrative model of justification, implies our union with Christ through faith in the presence of the Holy Spirit yet with eschatological reservation.

Promisio and *Visio Beatifica* for Congregational Mission

The eschatological tension between the already and not yet of salvation is also seen in the *visio beatifica* of Moses and of Jesus. According to 1 John 3:2, "Beloved, we are God's children now: . . . when he is revealed, we will be like him, for we will see him as he is." Knowledge of God in such a vision is a gift of God's grace for the future. An experience of *visio beatifica* is connected with the Hebrew meaning of *yada*. This experience implies knowledge of the personal-holistic event shaping the encounter between God and the human being. Critical thinking and meditation are engaged in eschatological *visio Dei*. This spirituality of *visio Dei* accentuates human participation in God's salvific-missional

---

19. Schmid, *Doctrinal Theology*, 481.

history in the world for the sake of those who suffer on the underside of history. The eschatological vision is promised in faith. Longing for God is expressed in Ps 145:15: The eyes of all look to you, and you give them their food in due season."

In Job's experience of *visio Dei*—"I had heard of you by the hearing of the ear, but now my eye sees you" (Job 42:5)—we perceive that *visio Dei* is the object of hope, thus the promise of God includes *visio Dei*. *Promisio* and *visio* are reconciled in the future. This future unity is the eschaton; what we will be has not yet been revealed. When God is revealed, we will see God as God is. All who have this hope in God purify themselves (1 John 3:2–3). In his experience of the risen Lord Paul implies that his vision of the risen Christ is eschatological. Faith is hope and anticipation in the vision in accordance with the promise. By faith Moses left Egypt as though he saw God who is invisible (Heb 11:27).

In this *visio Dei* God is the provider of place, opening the world to us as the *novum*. Finally, God will become the One who provides us with a new heaven and earth with a new Jerusalem. God's freedom, as seen in eschatological *visio Dei*, defends God over against the human projection of God in terms of pan(en)theism. Cultivating a community in light of the metaphor of happy exchange, I emphasize an eschatological orientation of *visio Dei*. It elaborates a spiritual-communal-holistic dimension of interrelationship in terms of reciprocity, and openness to difference in acknowledgement of the other. Visioning is a communal process in missional context regarding the relation between gospel and culture (Acts 15:6–11) to affirm that we will be saved through the grace of Jesus Christ. It is discussed continually under the prayerful direction of the Holy Spirit. God's vision and calling frequently come from the irregular side of the margins (such as public sinners and tax collectors, Samaritans or Gentiles).

In *visio beatifica*, as seen in biblical perspective, we no longer strive for the knowledge of God for our sake, but only for God's sake and our service to people in need. A spirituality of *visio Dei* and love of God (Deut 6:5) does not lead to an experience of the mystical darkness of God, the desert, or nothingness in a panentheistic manner. Rather it instructs us to love and respect the freedom of God and God's future over and ahead of us by serving people in need.

In our faith journey we receive adoption as children of God and become heirs of eternal life, only because of Christ's presence within us (*in ipsa fide Christus adest*).[20] Our extraordinary power—the treasure in clay jars—belongs to God and does not come from us (2 Cor 4:7). Where the Spirit of the Lord is, there is freedom. "And all of us, with un-veiled faces, seeing the glory of the Lord as though reflected in a mirror, are being transformed into the same image from one degree of glory to another; for this comes from the Lord, the spirit."(2 Cor 3:18). For now we see in a mirror, dimly but the invisible summons us, and we will see "face to face" (1 Cor 13:12) in the eschaton. We become a visible mirror of an invisible gaze and our face becomes the visible mirror of the invis-ible. The invisible converts us and transforms us in its glory shining on our face as its mirror.[21]

This reframing of justification and the happy exchange seen in light of the eschatological *visio Dei* undergirds a spirituality of humility, freedom, hospitality, and *diakonia* in congregational life; welcoming one another comes from Christ's hospitality. This perspective of justification and union shows development of the vitiation of the human in the Spirit through daily repentance. It also undergirds a hermeneutical circle of integrating the confessional dimension of ecclesiology (based on the Trinity or Christology) into the reality of living Christian congregations. This is based on spiritual formation, leadership, generosity, and hospital-ity which are characterized by abounding hope by the power of the Holy Spirit (Rom 15:13).

A Trinitarian model of the missional church would be an abstract, even idle pursuit, if it were dissociated from a living and active con-gregational mission of stewardship, leadership, and spiritual formation which is grounded in fellowship with Christ in the presence of the Holy Spirit. In the event of emancipation in the death and resurrection of Jesus Christ the congregational life stands in freedom from secular power and is driven by God's emancipation to fellowship with God and in solidar-ity with fellow humans. Congregational mission in spiritual formation, leadership, witness, and emancipation drives the church out of solitary life and into fellowship with and service to the world. A model of happy exchange or *unio cum Christo* undergirds congregational mission and leadership leading to the community of vocation.

---

20. Mannermaa, *Christ Present*.

21. Marion, *God without Being*, 22.

Congregational Life in Cruciform Discipleship and Freedom of Gospel

The implications of spiritual theology for leadership call into question solitary, hierarchical, and authoritarian patterns of leadership. The metaphor of the happy exchange gives rise to thought (Paul Ricoeur) and transformation in understanding leadership, as well. God brings Christian life to God's work of creating life-giving relationships between God and human beings, among all human beings, and between human beings and the whole creation. Transformation in Christian life and leadership is embedded with faith journey. Leadership in this regard becomes central as we seek to embody and serve God's mission which aims at establishing life-giving relationships and a life-nourishing lifeworld of shalom and righteousness. Equipping and empowering people to be faithful to their identity as God's people in Jesus Christ, the church's leadership accentuates Christian existence as movement toward God's mission in the world. God's word in action comes to terms with the word-event of evangelization in the world for the sake of our responsibility for and participation in a world under God's universal reign.

The biblical witness to the in-breaking kingdom of God and the way of servant leadership uphold the coexistence of particular leaders and the work of the entire community. The servant of the Word remains culturally readable regarding signs of the times in light of the word-event which may occur in the world of religious outsiders. Word and sacrament (ordained pastor), or Word and service (consecrated diaconal minister) find their integrative and transformative leadership in the dynamism of Gospel (living voice of God). "Your word is a lamp to my feet and a light to my path" (Ps 119:105).[22]

We must also look to the union with Christ in a Trinitarian-salvational sense; this perspective reenvisages the faith community in terms of a spirituality of *diakonia* and missional leadership. Jesus' cruciform leadership in *diakonia* must be discussed through the trinitarian model of mission: *Missio Dei* must not be separated from *diakonia Dei* whose integrative scope embraces God's promise and our *visio beatifica*. The Trinitarian mission of God is known by Jesus Christ *presently* in the grace of justification and reconciliation, and *eschatologically* in the final consummation of the world. God calls and empowers us to be created

22. Everist and Nessan, *Transforming Leadership*, 78.

co-workers in fellowship with Jesus' prophetic mission and to be in communion with Jesus Christ through Word and sacrament.

Leadership is not a function or skill of a single individual, but a mandate of the congregation as a whole. *Koinonia* with Christ points to Christ's ministry, leadership, and mission in company with God's people for the reign of God. This *koinonia* perspective undergirds trusting the called leader, the people, and cultivating a trustworthy environment. Insofar as the church is God's redeemed people, trust of the broader church articulates our understanding of the church as the body of Christ in a collaborative, mutually accountable, culturally open sense.[23] God's mission reaches its penultimate climax in Christ's *diakonia* of reconciliation animated by eschatological hope. The grace of reconciliation is intended to be shared in a mutual life for diversity and recognition of the other. It provides a pivotal insight into today's multicultural world.

Cruciform leadership in the sense of our conformation to Jesus Christ along with reconciliation and the resurrection is central to the biblical narrative of the triune God and God's mission. In Luke 22:24–27 Jesus rejects the benefactors' tradition of leadership, demonstrating a paradigm shift from "lording over" to identification of the disciples as the youngest. Jesus promised his presence and identification among those who serve. This view is sharpened when Jesus identified himself as one of those on the margins—one of the least in the final judgment (Matt 25:40).

Cruciform leadership is shaped in accordance with our leadership in the ministry of reconciliation. This leadership accentuates the congregation as the one with a listening heart for the word of God and the world. The congregation, led in cruciformity is a community in exodus from lordless powers (sin, evil, exclusion, injustice, and domination). This is also a community in liberating leadership for the sake of God's shalom and righteousness in the world. The church's corporate vocation finds its innovative and subversive dimension in the leadership of *diakonia* and reconciliation.

In this light the Lutheran idea of *simul peccator et justus* needs to be actualized for the sake of the marks of the church as the community of vocation, *diakonia* and leadership in eschatological hope. Luther's way of speaking of God retains both an all-embracing and inclusive tendency and a radically exclusive tendency. Luther's so-called particular

---

23. Ibid., 12. See further Gardner, *On Leadership*, 1–10.

exclusive—God alone, Christ alone, Scripture alone, faith alone, grace alone—prohibits speaking of theological issues in an untheological or pseudo-theological manner.[24] Alongside these exclusive *solas* Luther integrates an all-inclusive comprehensiveness into his theological framework of *simul peccator et justus*. The faith community becomes the community of service, witness, hospitality, and stewardship through this particular-inclusive dialectic of law and gospel.

This perspective of the church is connected with Luther's conceptuality of God hidden and revealed through the *theologia crucis* which has a critical, realistic, prophetic basis for the universality of the gospel. A paradoxical concept of revelation penetrates Luther's entire theological program, characterizing Christian theology and church in practical-missional directions. This ecclesial approach has little to do with an abstract distinction between the visible and invisible, or the elect and reprobate. The invisible/visible model tends to add an idealist understanding to God's embodiment in Jesus Christ on which the church is promised and founded.[25] Church order is divine both in origin and character while it is established for ecclesial *diakonia* and congregational mission characterized by spiritual growth, leadership, generosity, and hospitality. All members in the community participate in God's mission rather than dividing the community into the elect and the non-elect, or qualified and unqualified members. *Communio sanctorum* tied with *communion vocatorum* is indispensably associated with *communio diakonae* in prophetic, congregational profile. According to Bonhoeffer, the Augsburg Confession defines the church as the community of those who are persecuted and martyred for the gospel's sake.[26]

Church administration, ecclesial *diakonia*, and congregational mission become matters of service and witness because they are set in the lowliness of Christ's prophetic service through justification, reconciliation, and vocation. Therefore congregational mission as the diaconate, stewardship, and missional leadership describes the church's whole action for, with, in, and through the world. Church as ministry and organization is mandated from Jesus Christ in whom God revealed God's self and God's redemptive announcement through the Spirit. A functional and instrumental approach to faith community can be sharpened and

24. Ebeling, *Luther*, 247.

25. Forde, *Theology Is for Proclamation*, 189.

26. Bonhoeffer, *Cost of Discipleship*, 91.

renewed by a hermeneutical, communal understanding of God's mission in Christ's service to the world.

Under the forces of economic globalization the church's leadership is first involved in the discursive *parrhēsia* (speaking the truth audaciously) of denouncing the reality of mammon, a matter of idolatry in the competing market of gods. Consumerism, technological civilization, and prosperity under the spell of economic globalization are to be seen and judged under the liberating Word of God. Thus a theology of congregational mission and leadership can be deepened by combining an interdisciplinary study of mission (relating to interpretation of the biblical narrative in different contexts: missiology) with a theological-sociological study of church (ecclesiology) and public sphere of economic globalization (world economy as a field of God's mission).

In the context of missiology attention is given to the strategy of evangelization, church planting and organization, and study of the relationship between gospel, law, and culture. In ecclesiology a theological-sociological study of the church, or theology of sociality (Bonhoeffer), examines its apostolic and sacramental nature. This examination includes historical views of different ecclesiologies, church polity, confessional writings, ministry, and organization and structure. A church in miniature (Eph 5: 32) finds its beautiful expression in Gal 3:27: "As many of you as were baptized into Christ have clothed yourselves with Christ. There is no longer Jew or Greek, there is no longer slave or free, there is no longer male and female; for all of you are one in Christ Jesus. And if you belong to Christ, then you are Abraham's offspring, heirs according to the promise."

PART III

Re-envsioning Missional Church and Public Faith

This final section is an attempt to reenvision the missional church and public theology through an analysis of American society and congregational life. In this reenvisioning a missiological hermeneutics of word-event, built on the law-gospel relation, comes into focus in an ecumenical dialogue with Karl Barth. We shall consider Luther's hermeneutics of law and gospel and Bonhoeffer's response to Barth's critique of the Lutheran notion of natural law. An excursus includes a brief reflection about Barth and *theologia naturalis* (chapter 9).

An analysis of American civil religion and millennial culture will be undertaken since this religious mentality has considerably shaped and influenced congregational life in American public spheres. In a sociological analysis of American civil religion, the multicultural reality is displayed in the emerging post-modern condition (chapter 10). I explore the epistemology of public mission in dealing with postmodern theory of paradigm shifts and critical realism. In light of Christ's reconciliation, I am interested in undertaking diverse models in studies of mission to recontextualize a hermeneutical epistemology for God's mission and *theologia crucis* (with a special focus on Dietrich Bonhoeffer, chapter 11). Finally, I engage in an eschatological discussion of American millenarism (or rapturism) in contrast to a biblically grounded eschatology (chapter 12); in it a theology of hope is articulated that undergirds a proper account of the missional church and public mission.

Reclaiming a public mission as theological science, I hermeneutically mediate the practices of the church in correlation with biblical exegesis and other theological disciplines. Public missiology calls for the missional church to adopt an emancipatory ethics in expectation of God's eschatology. This eschatology articulates God as the provider of the place, i.e., a new heaven and new earth. Here a public-missional ethics of *parrhēsia* embodied in *paranesis* endorses mission as a socially engaged interpretation of biblical narrative in solidarity with the other (chapter 13).

9

Public Church and Hermeneutics of Word-Event

Luther's distinctive concept of law (the demand) and gospel (the promise and the gift) remains a basic guiding principle of a theological hermeneutic of word-event in light of God's grace of justification and reconciliation. The proclamation of the Word of God is the process in which the distinction between the law and the gospel becomes manifest. Luther made this distinction in his confrontation with the antinomians as well as with the fanatical group of Thomas Müntzer and his associates. To emphasize law-gospel hermeneutics for the missional church it is important to reinterpret Luther's teaching on the law and gospel relation in regard to the concept of *paranesis*. This clarification undergirds Luther's exposition on the relationship between the first commandment (confession of faith) and the seventh commandment (economic justice) in the *Large Catechism*. This new integration of the grace of justification with justice emphasizes Lutheran public ethics as well as addressing Barth's critique of the Lutheran model of two kingdoms.

Grace of Justification and Law

Paul gives extensive instructions for the Christian life in which his teaching on justification becomes alive and active in public service and ethical exhortation. Faith works through love (Gal 5:6). Along this line, Luther considers the *paranetic* character of the gospel and evangelical delight in doing the law. Luther understands the term gospel in a broader sense, implying the proclamation of Jesus Christ and the apostles. In the narrower sense of the term (forgiveness of sin), Luther finds the law in the proclamation and teaching of Jesus Christ. Luther claims that believers abide by the apostolic imperatives and ethical exhortations in the New Testament. In the New Testament there are promises and exhortations which are different from the law of accusation. Faith alone justifies, without works. However, genuine faith, after justification has occurred, will not go to sleep but is active through love. At issue here is the amelioration of a wrong assumption concerning human work, rather than supporting an antinomian direction.

The admonitions of the gospel walking in newness of life (Rom 6:4–6) do not necessarily mean the third use of the law (or the law as the necessary form of the gospel in a Barthian sense) which "offers little encouragement for its use in a truly evangelical ethic."[2] Luther did not develop a theological view on the third use of the law for the regenerate. This concept was introduced later by Melanchthon and followed by the *Formula of Concord.*

For Luther the gospel includes admonition for God's will of love. *Paranesis* is a significant, indispensable form of the gospel while the justified Christian may have evangelical freedom and delight in doing the law of commandment and exhortation. For Luther the justified Christian may be active in the fruits of the freely given righteousness and of the Spirit, and may exercise love by good works and bravely bear the cross and other tribulations of the world. This is the sum of the whole New Testament.[3]

Luther's integrative model of justification in a threefold sense (*extra nos, pro nos, and cum nobis*) undergirds the grace of justification as both an event and a dynamic eschatological process. In it Christ, justifying us outside of us and for us, becomes the living reality of Christ dwelling in us(*cum nobis*), driving us to public service and discipleship in the sphere of public life. There are a number of apostolic admonitions and exhortations about good morals (*paranesis*) which address Christians. These exhort the Christians to practice the duties of godliness toward one another. According to Luther, as in the New Testament, there are

1. LW 27:30.

2. Forde, *Law-Gospel Debate*, 226.

3. LW 27:47

also certain promises and words of grace in the Old Testament. In them the holy fathers and prophets remain in the faith of Christ.[4]

The Dialogical Principle of Law and Gospel

We observe that there is the gospel in the law of the Old Testament and the law in the gospel of the New Testament: Gospel and law as well as law and gospel are theologically justified and necessary.[5] Luther's hermeneutical principle of "what promotes Christ" in the entire Scripture underlines his heuristic approach to the dialogical relationship between law and gospel. According to Luther, there are three reactions to the law which are established by God for the sake of prevention of wickedness. The first reaction is to hear the law and despise it. The second is to attempt to fulfill the law by one's own power without grace. The third is to learn from the law to recognize sin and to yearn for Christ. This refers to the very nature of the law. Therefore, there are the laws about faith and love by which to measure all other laws. All other laws are kept to the extent that their observance does not come into conflict with the laws about faith and love.[6]

It is certain that Luther distinguished the renewal of natural law from Jewish national, ceremonial law, its obligatory character from the nonobligatory one within the Mosaic law. On the other hand, Luther provocatively argues that Moses bears witness to the sacrament and example of Jesus Christ. Luther beautifully shows on the basis of the Decalogue what it means to be a servant through love. All the admonitions of the prophets in the Old Testament, as well as of Christ and the apostles in the New Testament, concerning a godly life, are excellent sermons on and expositions of the Ten Commandments.[7]

The New Testament flows from a wellspring of wisdom and understanding (Moses) and is grounded in it.[8] This perspective characterizes Luther's way of seeking Christ and the gospel in the Old Testament. Luther's creative reading of Moses as a moral teacher in dialogue with Jesus Christ demonstrates his biblical hermeneutic of evangelically

---

4. Luther, "Preface to the Old Testament," in *Luther's Basic Theological Writings*, 114.

5. Bonhoeffer, *Ethics,* 310.

6. Luther, "Preface to the Old Testament," 116.

7. LW 27:51.

8. Luther, "Preface to the Old Testament," 121.

conceptualizing the moral law. In Moses there are the promise and pledges of God about Christ who was born in the flesh. "In Moses there are the promises of God which sustain faith.[9] "In Moses there is comprehended such a fine order, that it is a joy."[10]

There is a dimension in Luther's complex thought that expresses the law in an evangelical sense or evangelically conceptualized law. "For through Christ sin is forgiven, God is reconciled, and man's heart has begun to feel kindly toward the law."[11] Luther' creative hermeneutic of law and gospel in light of the unity of the Word of God as word-event is more rich and profound than Barth's concept of Jesus Christ as the one Word of God. In the *Smalcald Articles* (1537), Luther understands the content of the gospel in the fivefold sense. For Luther the gospel gives guidance and help against sin in more than one way. The gospel is extravagantly rich in God's grace. Along with the spoken word (the forgiveness of sin), sacraments, and the power of the keys, Luther remarkably includes "the mutual conversation and consolation of brothers and sisters."[12]

This perspective undergirds the *paranesis*-gospel in Luther's hermeneutics of word-event. The *paranesis*-gospel upholds God's communicative involvement as affirmed in the synoptic context: "For where two or three are gathered in my name, I am there among them" (Matt 18:20). In the context of Lev 19:9–18, 34, God is understood as the One who is involved in the life of public sphere. "The Lord is witness between you and me forever . . . The Lord shall be between me and you, and between my descendants and your descendants, forever" (1 Sam 23:42). It speaks of the presence of God in the midst of God's people and the inclusion of the nations, and God will dwell in their midst—Israel and the nations together. ". . . I will come and dwell in your midst, says the Lord. Many nations shall join themselves to the Lord on that day, and shall be my people; and I will dwell in your midst" (Zech 2:10–11; cf. Ezek 43:7; Joel 2:27).

This biblical view of word-event emphasizes the situation of daily human communication while characterizing God's Word as a living

9. Luther, "How Christians Should Regard Moses," in *Luther's Basic Theological Writings*, 129.

10. Ibid., 132.

11. Ibid., 119.

12. Luther, "Smalcald Articles," in BC 319.

event. The Word of God can be received by those who can misuse the Word. God's Word and God's promise of presence are vulnerable. Despite this vulnerability,[13] "the word of the Lord is trustful, and what he promises, he certainly keeps" (Ps 33:4).[14] Deepening the biblical dynamism of word-event, Luther's theology of *verbum Dei* corrects Barth's uninformed critique of the Lutheran theology of law and gospel (discussed below).

The Lutheran understanding of natural law as the unalterable will of God is based on the Decalogue. This natural law is innate in the heart. The gospel presupposes the proclamation of the Decalogue for the establishment of *justitia civilis* in which there is no conflict between the Decalogue and the *lex naturae*.[15] The *primus usus* (the first use of the law) is relative to the gospel, *viva vox Dei* (the living voice of God). Luther's exposition of the Decalogue in the *Large Catechism* provides his ingenious approach to the relationship between the Decalogue and the gospel or theological confession and economic justice. The new world begins with the Word of God which became flesh. The new birth comes out of the Word of God by transforming us into the World of the Scripture. The Word of God is the presence of God (*praesentia Dei*) that is life and forgiveness.[16] God the hidden and revealed, according to Luther, articulates God as the one who is essentially and eternally a glowing oven full of love. The *paranesis*-gospel serves God's will of love for the world, driving the faith community to prophetic witness by inviting the world to God's loving grace of justification, reconciliation, and justice, especially in the economic realm.

A Reflection of Gospel-*Paranesis*

Furthermore, Luther argues that the first commandment is the quintessence of gospel. In contrast to the antinomians, Luther states that Christians receive apostolic *paranesis* (or *paraclesis*) which is the basis for Paul's exposition of the new being in Christ. The uniqueness of apostolic *paranesis* or *paraclesis* can be seen as exposition of the implications

---

13. Fretheim, *Suffering of God*, 99.
14. This is Luther's own translation. See Bayer, "Creation as History," 258.
15. Bonhoeffer, *Ethics*, 305.
16. Iwand, *Luthers Theologie*, 84, 225.

of believers' fellowship with Christ.[17] The ethical directive of the gospel is the corollary of the gospel of justification underlying our spiritual *koinonia* with Christ and fellow humans.

If faith is the root of love, *paranesis* is not a generalized law but a component of the gospel. Luther's theology of freedom undergirds an evangelical and missional ethic of faith in fulfillment of the law. Faith dwells in the heart and is the source and substance of all our righteousness. Once we are justified and forgiven through Jesus Christ we may be active in the fruits of the Spirit and freely given righteousness. We are called to become God's co-workers in the public realm with respect to evangelization, social witness, and the promotion of justice and peace. Through us God preaches, shows mercy to the poor, and comforts the afflicted.[18]

For Luther, the church is the mother that begets and bears every Christian through the Word of God[19] in which the Holy Spirit creates and increases holiness, making the church grow and become strong in the faith and in its fruits. Devoting all our works to the welfare of others, all our life is a surplus. With this in mind, and also by voluntary benevolence, we serve and do good to our neighbor. Luther understands the various walks of life in vocation, callings, and true works as the ethical corollary of the pure Word of God and the right use of the sacraments in the evangelical life. Insofar as the Holy Spirit continues the divine work until the Last Day, the faith community is appointed to the community of God's mission in *diakonia* through evangelization and ethical (*paranetic*) and missional solidarity with those in need through the universal priesthood and public service.

Law-Gospel Dynamism: Confession and Economic Justice

In the discussion of Christian social, ethical responsibility, Lutheran theology often has been caricatured as being submissive to the economic or political status quo, or vulnerable to justifying and sanctioning the reality. Regrettably, we are aware that there are many examples that give credence to this evaluation, most notably in case of the German Church under Nazism and legacies of Lutheranism that were passed on through

17. Pannenberg, *Systematic Theology*, 3. 89.

18. Rupp and Watson, eds., *Luther and Erasmus*, 289.

19. Luther, "Large Catechism," BC 436–68; cf. Lazareth, *Christians in Society*, 224–34.

mission movements around the world, some of which still persist today. The Lutheran idea of general revelation was idolized blindly in favor of the Nazi's racist ideology of blood and soil. Barth's unequivocal witness to the universal lordship of Jesus Christ was the clearest theological "No" to Nazism in the Confessing Church's *Barmen Theological Declaration* (on May 29–31, 1934). Against the Barmen Declaration, the infamous example was represented by Wener Elert and Paul Althaus in the Ansbach Counsel (*Ansbach Ratschlag*, 11 June 1934).

Affirming every authority as a tool of divine preservation, the Ansbach Counsel states that the law as the unchangeable will of God[20] obliges us to the natural orders such as family, nation, and race (i.e. blood ties). "As Christians, therefore, we thank God for every order . . . respecting it as an instrument of the unfolding divine purpose even when it is a distorted instrument." "Recognizing this . . . we thank the Lord God for bestowing on our nation in its time of need the leader, Adolf Hitler, to be 'its pious and faithful governor' and for his desire to grant us a regime of 'discipline and honor' in the form of the National Socialist State."[21]

However, since the 1970s, there have been significant endeavors to correct these misinterpretations or limitations of Lutheran theology in the public sphere, especially with regard to the Lutheran model of "two kingdoms." Ulrich Duchrow did the pioneering work on this doctrine of the two kingdoms[22] on which many other Lutheran theologians have built more on the prophetic side of Luther's insights into the secular realm subsequently. We may also mention that recently the Lutheran World Federation became much more engaged with social, economic, and political realities, including taking a *status confessionis* stance in the case of South African Lutheran churches under apartheid. Accordingly the Lutheran World Federation (LWF) issued "A Call to Participate in Transforming Economic Globalization" (2002) a document which analyzes a dangerous consequence of economic globalization driven by the neo-liberal model.[23]

Luther integrates our confession of God with economic justice by challenging the reality of early capitalism which was characterized by

20. "Formula of Concord," Epitome VI, §6.

21. Duchrow, *Global Economy*, 12.

22. Duchrow, *Christenheit und Weltverantwortung*. See further Duchrow, *Global Economy*, 4–18.

23. Further see Bloomquist, ed., *Being the Church*.

usury and monopoly. Insofar as the details of economics are concerned, Martin Luther wrote three specific texts on economic issues in the context of emerging capitalism, particularly on the problem of interest (usury) and the emerging international, monopolist trading and banking companies (Fugger, Welser, etc.) during the Genoese-Spanish cycle of capital accumulation.[24]

In dealing with "God or Mammon" in the *Large Catechism* Luther integrates God (in the first commandment) with his ethical discussion of economic justice (in the seventh commandment). Speaking of the dynamic relationship between the grace of justification and human discipleship in Luther's thought, Luther's notion of *cooperatio hominis cum Deo* (Human cooperation with God)[25] remains pivotal in his engagement with the economic realm.

Luther's *theological* critique of Roman Catholicism was embedded in his *socioeconomic* critique of its structure and system. Charles V was dependent on the Fuggers. Thus, Luther ironically characterized his Catholic opponent John Eck as a "plutologian" (expert on wealth) rather than a theologian. Luther was keenly aware that there was a "Christian" character to capital accumulation, concentration, and monopoly, which was the basis for Christian colonialism. Luther argued that the big banking and trading companies were only the tip of the iceberg in a system increasingly pervading the whole of society. These were the systems of "devouring" capital: "And it [usury] continues to devour and fetter us; . . . If he has a million, he earns an annual four hundred thousand, which means devouring a great king in one year. In that way a robber can sit comfortably at home and in ten years swallow up the whole world."[26]

⟨In Luther's writings, the grace of justification and economic justice are interwoven, so that economic issues constitute an indispensable part of theological reflection about and confession of God, a *status confessionis*.[27]⟩ This aspect is obvious in his *Admonition to Clergy That They Preach against Usury* (1540): "You let the usurer lie as a pagan in death, and do not bury him/her among other Christians! Because he/she is a usurer and idolater, he/she serves mammon. He/she cannot

---

24. For the detailed analysis of Luther's theology of economic justice, see Chung, *Spirit of God,* 128–32.

25. Rupp and Watson, eds., *Luther and Erasmus,* 289.

26. Cited in Duchrow, *Alternatives,* 219.

27. Marquardt, "Gott oder Mammon," in Marquardt, *Einwürfe,* 194.

have or receive the forgiveness of sins nor the grace of Christ nor the communion of the saints."[28]

A place of prophetic *diakonia* in the mission of God grounded in the light of justification and justice speaks out against the exploitation of the poor and the voiceless and listens to the physical and spiritual suffering of the innocent victims. This perspective characterizes the church as a faith community of God's event through Word and sacrament—just as *The Augsburg Confession* states that the church is where and when God pleases.

The universal priesthood (or the universal deaconhood)[29] indicates a prophetic-diaconal form of engaging the social reality of the poor and the innocent victim. Luther characterizes a sacramental understanding of social discipleship as a prophetic resistance, advocating heartfelt sympathy for those who suffer innocently in the world. In receiving the sacrament of love in the Lord's Supper, we "must feel with sorrow all the dishonor done to Christ in his holy word, all the misery of Christendom, all the unjust suffering of the innocent, with which the world is everywhere filled to overflowing. [We] must [resist], work, pray—if [we] cannot do more—have heartfelt sympathy."[30]

This perspective upholds Lutheran ecclesiology, which is based on anamnesis in remembrance of the suffering of the world. Eucharistic presence upholds our praxis to promote the full humanity of those marginalized in the public sphere. This is already grounded in God's word-event and Scripture, and is rich and multi-dimensional, giving a theological impulse toward a public mission in economic *diakonia*. Such a missional theology is built on the grace of justification and reconciliation and must be undertaken in companionship with other churches by accompanying people of other cultures[31] in a global, intercultural context. This practice of God's mission finds its meaning and actualization in ecclesial discipleship in solidarity with those who are "the outcast, the suspects, the maltreated, the powerless, the oppressed, the reviled, in short . . . those who suffer."[32] This hermeneutical view from below

28. Luther, "An die Pfarrherren," in Fabiunke, *Luther als Nationalökonom*, 207–8.

29. Käsemann, *Jesus Means Freedom*, 53–54.

30. Luther, "Blessed Sacrament of the Holy and True Body," in *Luther's Basic Theological Writings*, 1st ed., 247.

31. *Global Mission in the Twenty-First Century.*

32. Bonhoeffer, *Letters and Papers*, 17.

inspires a public mission that does justice in life-creating and culture-enhancing ways in the web of ecology in the study of world Christianity and economic systems.

For Ecumenical Dialogue: Karl Barth's Dialectic of Gospel and Law

In the debate with the hermeneutic of law and gospel, Barth's essay "Gospel and Law" (1935)[33] marked a controversy with Luther's theology of law and gospel. Barth's claim lies in the reorientation of the law-gospel dialectic by reversing its theological order to gospel-law. This claim retained a political implication in critique of theological positions which used Luther's idea of the two kingdoms to accommodate the concept of law to the German national ethos by dissociating it from the revelation of Jesus Christ. This refers to Barth's dispute with the Lutheran concept of natural theology or general revelation stated by the Ansbach Counsel in collaboration with National Socialism. As Barth argues, the law in the deformation and distortion is exposed to every falsification: natural law, an abstract reason, or history, or the "Volksnomoi" (people's laws).[34]

In this context Barth argued that by distinguishing the law and gospel, we must see them both as God's address to human beings. While the law follows the promise (Gal 3:17), the fulfillment of the promise contains the law's own fulfillment. The gospel is not law and vice versa. However, the law is in the gospel. The unity of law and gospel has its unity in God's address to humanity in which the essential content of God's address is grace. The Word of God in its address to us demonstrates its unity in that the Word of God is always grace, undeserved divine goodness, mercy, and condescension. The Word of God speaking to us is grace under all circumstances.[35]

In Barth's distinction between gospel and law, God's Word remains grace because God's eternal decree of election is the sum of the gospel. This is because God elected everyone in Jesus Christ. The gospel as God's grace includes the content of the law, because Jesus Christ, the eternal Word of God became flesh. Grace as the content of the gospel means that Jesus Christ with his humanity intercedes for us with our humanity. Jesus Christ as the content of the gospel fulfilled the law, in obedience

33. Barth, "Gospel and Law," in *Community, State, and Church*, 71–100.

34. Ibid., 91.

35. Ibid., 72.

to its commands. The law in the Old Testament and New Testament, in every great or small, internal or external command, must be understood from the standpoint of each of them fulfilled in Jesus Christ.[36] In the discussion of the creation and the covenant Barth integrates the Noahide covenant (in Gen 9:1–17) for the whole of humanity before and outside Abraham (including all the living creatures) into the single, universal lordship of Jesus Christ. Jesus Christ is the eschatological realization of the will of God for Israel as well as for the whole human race. Barth's theological approach is undertaken in light of God's particular divine act rather than the universal and general covenant as the grace of God's preservation.[37]

For Barth, Jesus Christ as the firstborn of all creation (Col 1:15) is the one eternal Word of God, as he relates to God's grace of predestination. In light of this Barth tends to sidestep Paul's basic conviction of the Gentiles who do by nature the works of the law and the law is written in their hearts (Rom 2:14). According to Barth, these Gentiles do the works not by nature but by the grace of reconciliation, even though they do not recognize it. In this theological framework the universal lordship of God in creation as well as in redemption is reduced into Christomonistic universal lordship. In it Barth follows Calvin's thought which apprehended the relationship between the Old and the New Testament under the concept of the one covenant.[38]

According to Barth, the law must be seen and understood in light of God's revelation in Jesus Christ. This perspective establishes the validity of the Decalogue along with the Sermon on the Mount and the apostolic instructions. The grace which is promised in the covenant between God and Israel is proclaimed and promulgated in the divine commands. Thus the law is called the necessary form of the gospel, because God's action in Christ moves human discipleship toward the obedience of faith (Rom 1:5). Barth's definition runs: "the law is nothing else than the necessary form of the gospel, whose content is grace."[39] This is because the gospel demands this form of the law. Although the two entities are not identical, the law gives the gospel concrete shape and direction in human life. Here gospel and law are related as the content and form of the one Word

36. Ibid., 75, 77.
37. CD IV/1:34.
38. CD IV/1:55.
39. Barth, "Gospel and Law," 80.

of God which is always grace. Barth's dialectic can be articulated in such a way that the law is in the gospel and the gospel is in the law.

Barth's special concept of law is given in the gospel, the gift of grace, grasped only through faith, so that it requires that we give our free obedience to God's demand.[40] This special concept of the law has nothing to do with natural law which is ontologically inherent to human beings or based on divine preservation of the created order. God's command is a promise, its fulfillment produces fruit. This is because the law is enclosed in the gospel.[41] In Jesus Christ the eternal Word became flesh. He himself is the resolve and the execution of the essential will of God's love. The work of God creates space for the gospel in the human sphere and for humanity in the sphere of the gospel. Jesus Christ has fulfilled the law and kept all the commands so that the law witnesses to the grace of God.[42] There is the claim addressed to us by the gospel, so that the gospel has the form of such claim. Jesus Christ is the basis for the unity between gospel and law. Here Barth agrees with Bonhoeffer's ethical view in which the commands of God are specific directions concerning the behavior, deeds, and omissions of one or many definite people in the historical context.

By integrating the apostolic directions (*paranesis*) into a category of "special ethics," Barth contends that the commands of God in Scripture must be understood in connection with their historical context and reality. Barth appreciates Bonhoeffer's ethical notion of mandates in making reference of the world to Christ, although critical of North German patriarchalism in them.[43]

In contrast to Barth, however, Bonhoeffer accepts the doctrine of the *primus usus legis* according to the Lutheran symbolic writings. Here the law, as the unchangeable will of God, is and remains one and the same law.[44] The first function of the law (the *primus usus*) comprises the whole contents of the law, notably the entirety of the Decalogue. *The Smalcald Articles* (1537) recognize only two functions of the law: the first function for natural and civil office, the second for spiritual office. The second function includes the preaching of the cross of Christ

40. CD II/2:552.

41. CD II/2:556–57.

42. Barth, "Gospel and Law," 81.

43. CD III/4:22.

44. "Formula of Concord," Ep VI, 6, in BC 503; see Bonhoeffer, *Ethics*, 209.

as preaching of the law. However, the cross is always also preaching of the gospel which is contained already in the Decalogue. The law in the Decalogue also runs through the entire New Testament. This is because the *primus usus* should not be preached in detachment from the gospel. The symbolic writings recognize that the law and the gospel are linked together from the Decalogue through the preaching of the cross. Thus God alone distinguishes between the law and the gospel. According to Bonhoeffer, the exposition of the Decalogue in the *Large Catechism* provides the best practical rule and guidance for the teaching and preaching of the *primus usus*.[45]

Relative to the gospel, the *primus usus* brings the worldly order into existence for the sake of preserving the world from disorder and arbitrariness. Secular institutions exist for the sake of life in faith and serve as a prerequisite for salvation through the gospel. It is an integral part of the one unchangeable will of God.[46] The essential purpose of the *primus usus* is to demand and perform the works of the law pertaining to outward discipline and seemliness;[47] its contents are designated as the natural law innate in the human heart which resonates with the law of Moses or the Decalogue. The Decalogue always remains the sole criterion for a *lex naturae*, so that the will of God takes effect in the *primus usus* or the *lex naturae*. The *lex naturae* takes effect through reason which is opposed by the demonic forces (evil lust and devils). Not every human impulse is a result of natural law, but the Decalogue is always the ultimate criterion.[48]

God desires *justitia civilis* of all people including Christians through the purpose of the *primus usus*, therefore proclamation of the Decalogue is essential for the establishment of *justitia civilis*. Thus civil government is placed under God's law and in service of God. The symbolic writings assume that reason does not conflict with the *lex naturae* and the Decalogue. As natural law, reason can be represented as the basis for governmental action. By doing God's will—punishing the wicked and rewarding the good—the government glorifies its divine office and makes its claim to obedience.[49] In the symbolic writings the law-gospel

---

45. Bonhoeffer, *Ethics*, 309.

46. Ibid., 309.

47. Ibid., 303.

48. Ibid., 304.

49. Ibid., 305–6.

order predominates, but the gospel-law order is also theologically justified because "in both cases the gospel is the "actual" kingdom of God."[50]

Bonhoeffer contends that in light of law-gospel-dialectic the universality of the church's mission should not be neglected, even in the case of the congregation in the catacombs. In preaching the law and gospel the church's mission must be professed and kept in view of its responsibility for the world. The word of God does its own function "in the service of the world and of its own universal mission."[51] In Bonhoeffer's view a hermeneutics of word-event maintains that the kingdom of Christ will always be oriented towards its mission toward the world. A missional theology of the law-gospel relationship becomes foundational for congregational mission, because "there is in principle no limit to the mission of the congregation." Thus Bonhoeffer maintains that the congregation must decide how to fulfill the mission in accordance with the signs of the times.[52]

As Bonhoeffer insists on the uniqueness of the *primus usus legis*, "the doctrine of *justitia civils* serves polemically the emancipation and honoring of worldly under the catalogue, in opposition to the Roman doctrine of the perfection of the monastic life."[53] The perverted nature and reason "must be made subject to the law of God by the proclamation of the Church."[54] This perspective is a counter proposal to the Barthian notion of gospel and law as well as to Neo-Lutheran distortions of the symbolic writings of law-gospel hermeneutics.

For Bonhoeffer genuine worldliness and its naturalness stand in obedience to God's word, having nothing to do with the Christianization of worldly institutions.[55] At base, Bonoeffer's notion of ethical mandate cannot be properly understood apart from Bonhoeffer's profound reflection on genuine worldliness. This perspective undergirds Bonhoeffer's theology of the cross and hermeneutics from below as conceptualized in his prison letter. His integration of mandate ethics with the *theologia crucis* sharpens his ethics as corrective to a positivism of revelation from above which functions partially as a paralyzing element in the Barthian

50. Ibid., 310.

51. Ibid., 311.

52. Ibid., 311.

53. Ibid., 306.

54. Ibid.

55. Ibid., 312.

theological-ethical framework. Barth's theology of correspondence tends to assume a hierarchical-analogical framework in a Platonic sense, despite his conceptualization of the *analogia fidei* over against the *analogia entis*.

⟨However, Bonhoeffer perceived that constancy of ethical events must be learned from the Word of God incarnated in our midst.⟩Against the positivism of revelation in Barth, Bonhoeffer paved the way toward renewing what he called "the arcane discipline" of spiritual formation related to the mystery of God as well as retrieving biblical worldliness in which Jesus Christ becomes the Lord even of the religionless world. [56] Bonhoeffer's ethics becomes helpful for Barth to develop a theological concept of the ethical event through the Word of God. Barth, in his letter concerning Eberhard Bethge's biography of Dietrich Bonhoeffer, lamented his own limitation, acknowledging that Bonhoeffer addressed the line and direction coming out the gospel: ethical discipleship, church as *diakonia*, social justice (or social democracy), the peace movement, and political *diakonia* of a church—all in all politics, more than Barth himself did.[57]

According to Iwand, Barth's sharp distinction between God's special law in the gospel and natural law in human life leads to the question of the incarnation of the Word of God. According to Barth, there is the Word of God in itself which stands behind the earthly forms of the Word of God in the dialectic of veiling and unveiling of the Word of God. The veiling is the worldly form (the demand) while the unveiling is the content (the gift). This Barthian dialectic leads to the correspondence or analogy between the earthly form of the Word of God (proclamation, Scripture, and revelation) and the Word of God in itself. This Barthian theory of correspondence in the Platonic and Aristotelian sense of analogy weakens the place of incarnation, threatening the grace of justification and the certainty of faith.

For Barth, God's grace of election in a Trinitarian sense is historically executed and fulfilled in the grace of justification and reconciliation in its salvific-missional context. Against this, I argue that the Word of God for us in the Incarnation is the source of assurance and of a theological hermeneutic which understands God's self in connection with God's mission. The certainty of faith is based on the incarnation as

56. LPP 280.

57. Barth, "Letter to Eberhard Bethge," in *Fragments Grave and Gay*, 119.

the sum of the gospel rather than election.[58] This perspective remains a corrective to Barth's challenge to the Lutheran hermeneutic of law and gospel. Barth's challenge can also be met and overcome by an analysis of Luther's concept of *paranesis* which implies an ethical horizon of the gospel.

Excursus: Barth and *Theologia Naturalis*

It is certain that Barth, characterizing Luther as an irregular theologian, frames the first function of the law in his own way, notably in terms of emphasizing the freedom of God's speech event. In his doctrine of the Word of God, Barth appreciated Luther's hermeneutics of the *viva vox evangelii* and affirmed God's strange voice outside the walls of the Christian church.[59] Later in his so-called doctrine of lights, namely *extra muros ecclesiae* in the Church Dogmatics IV/3:1 §69, Barth affirms a dimension of *theologia naturalis* in light of God's recon-ciliation with the world in Christ. In light of God's free communication, Barth boldly affirms that "dangerous modern expressions like the 'revelation of cre-ation' or 'primal revelation' might be given a clear and unequivocal sense in this respect which they do not usually have in common parlance."[60]

Given Barth's theological development, I am aware that Barth's theol-ogy of reconciliation is connected with Bonhoeffer's ethics of reconciliation. It holds a clue to overcoming the previous infamous Christomonism seen in his confrontation with Emil Brunner. Barth's position later was sharply accused by Bonhoeffer of being a positivism of revelation from above in which the world is left to its own device.

At any rate, before Barth's confrontation with Brunner, Barth's affirmation of the Thomist dictum can be seen in his Amsterdam lecture (1926) "Church and Culture." In it Barth contends that natural theology is included and brought into clear light within the theology of revelation. Thus Barth agrees with Thomas Aquinas's principle that "grace does not destroy nature but perfects it" (*gratia non tollit naturam sed perficit*).[61]

This position is also affirmed in his theological dogmatic development in that there has to be an assumption of the *analogia entis* by the *analogia fi-dei*—*Analogia fidei is sanans et elevens analogiam entis*—namely through Jesus Christ.[62] Barth entered into constructive interaction and dialogue with the Roman Catholic theologian Gottlieb Söhngen. According to Söhngen, the

---

58. For Iwand's critique of Karl Barth, see Forde, *Law-Gospel Debate*, 164.

59. CD I/1:55.

60. CD IV/3.1:140.

61. Barth, "Church and Culture," 342.

62. CD II/1:82.

knowledge of the being of God must be subordinated to the knowledge of the activity of God. Thus, the *analogia entis* is subordinated to the *analogia fidei*. In and through faith, which is the product of God's activity, God's being in act is apprehended and spoken of. In light of theological epistemology *esse sequitur operari* (the knowledge of being follows the knowledge of activity). God can be known only in God's self-disclosure. If the *analogia fidei* takes up and completes the *analogia entis*,the the *analogia entis* in Barth's sense can be a participation of the Word in humanity in which our real participation in the Word of God takes place. According to Söhngen, this participation is not a gracious participation in God by purely human activity or reason, but by a truly human participation in God by the work of divine grace.

Barth is not reluctant to accept a dimension of the Thomist idea when he argues: "One might discern the content of truth in even the so-called *analogia entis*."[63] For Thomas, "the Christian faith instructs humanity about God . . . Hence there occurs in human beings something like a similarity with the divine wisdom."[64] If Christian faith remains central in a Thomist framework, Barth associates himself with Luther's teaching of justification by faith. Barth invokes Luther's formulation of "Christ present in faith" (In *ipsa fide Christus adest*).[65] Interpreting Luther's formulation of union with Christ, Barth accentuates Luther's teaching of justification in a forensic-effective sense. Here Barth remains one of the faithful disciples of Luther.

In agreement with Catholic theologian Söhngen, Barth states that "if this [the relation between *analogia fidei* and *analogia entis* in Söhngen] is the Roman Catholic doctrine of *analogia entis* . . . I must withdraw my earlier statement that I regard the *analogia entis* as the invention of Antichrist."[66]

Critically examining Barth's theological position of the first function of the law and *theologia naturalis*, several prolific scholars in the Lutheran circle such as Prenter, Jüngel, and Marquardt are convinced that Barth's rejection of *theologia naturalis* is to be understood in the context of the urgent political situation during the Hitler regime. It should not be universalized as Christian doctrine. This aspect can also be applied to Barth's complicated doctrine of the sacraments (including infant baptism).

Furthermore, Barth's dilemma can be overcome by hermeneutical refurbishing of the theology of creation. If creation is the external basis of the covenant, human language belonging to the realm of creation may become an analogical servant to God's universal reign. For Barth "all human words can be

63. CD I/1:239.
64. CD I/1:239
65. CD I/2:242.
66. CD II/1:82.

true only as its genuine witness and attestations."[67] So, *theologia naturalis* for Barth becomes a hermeneutical problem, because the gospel can be understood as the event of correspondence. According to Jüngel, the hermeneutical thesis presupposes the event as the subject of the gospel in which the analogy of faith is carried out. He incorporates the ontological notion of *analogia entis* into language event.[68]

However, Barth did not advance a hermeneutical conceptualization of the *theologia naturalis*, thus this issue remains a critical area for us to improve on limitations of Barth's theology of law and gospel. It is safe to say that Barth's christocentric encapsulation of natural law engraved into the human mind shows a tension with the God of Israel in creation. It unfortunately supersedes God's universal lordship based on the gospel and the world—particularly, because of Barth's Christominstic notion of dialectical predestination. Insofar as predestination is defined by Barth as the sum of the gospel, it implies a contradiction with the grace of justification here and now through word and sacrament in the presence of the Holy Spirit. I argue that *theologia crucis* in the incarnational framework rather than predestination must become the theological epistemology for us to know who God is. As human beings we cannot know God's point of view or divine decree of predestination, rather we understand the grace of justification through the communication of the Holy Spirit which comes to us as language-event. God comes to us as word-event through special covenant with Israel and universal covenant with Noah, finally reaching its culmination in the incarnation of Jesus Christ. The Lutheran notion of single election, in contrast to Calvinist speculation of double predestination, is grounded in the word-event and *theologia crucis* which becomes the realistic basis for God's universal reign in the creation.

In this light, Barth's conundrum should be overcome through hermeneutically refurbishing a theology of word-event in which God's universal lordship is specifically affirmed through the grace of justification and also universally respected and instituted in the sense of *creatio continua*. Barth's rejection of *creatio continua* brings a dysfunctional element to his understanding of gospel and law.

Having considered this, hermeneutics of word-event is relevant and even indispensable in today's theological engagement with the others. Beyond Barth's theological metaphysics, hermeneutics of word-event becomes socially and culturally embodied, foundational for elaborating dialectics of socio-critical hermeneutics in the presence of the others. This hermeneutical integration includes appropriation of meaning from the others, critical distance from their oppressive elements, and reconstruction of one's identity in the fusion of

67. CD IV/3.1:122.

68. Jüngel, *God as the Mystery*, 284–86.

horizon. This perspective marks a new terrain in which Lutheran hermeneutics of word-event can be further developed and contextualized in conversation with a hermeneutics of the other in the postcolonial context of World Christianity.

10

Public Church and American Society in Cultural Complexities

The faith community is bound to congregational life shaped by cultural context. In the study of the church and its congregational life in the United States, it is indispensable to analyze social, religious, and cultural factors which have shaped it. For this task I aim at demonstrating the complexity and richness of congregational life by using interdisciplinary analysis of society and culture. Congregational study shows that the congregation has the capacity to influence the wider public world.[1] Recently we have seen a growing interest in the refining of practical theology in dialogue with hermeneutical philosophy. Congregational study is undertaken in light of a fundamental practical theology.[2]

When congregations claim their role as servants of God's mission in the broader context, it is essential to understand the impact American civil religion has had on the church. Denominationalism in American churches is a well known fact, called "an unacknowledged hypocrisy," a compromise between Christianity and the world. The division of the churches follows the division of the people into the caste-systems of human society in terms of national, racial, and economic groups.[3]

1. Dudley's *Building Effective Ministry* utilizes sociological, psychological, ethnographic, church development, theological, and practical theological approaches to the congregational study of the Wiltshire Methodist Church.

2. Browning, *Practical Theology*; Mudge and Poling, *Formation and Reflection*; Schreiter, *Constructing Local Theologies*.

3. Niebuhr, *Social Sources of Denominationalism*, 6.

Characterized by the social, cultural, economic, and ethnic sources of denominationalism, American religiosity is becoming more pluralistic, more individualistic, and more private. Living together among people of many different faiths and cultures is a serious task for the church to address. Together with sociological views on Puritanism in American society, Weber's thesis of the Protestant ethic provides us with a helpful tool by which to examine American civil religion. The sociological study in this chapter configures a new course for the missional church conversation in terms of public theology and the church.

The Calvinistic Ethic and American Religious Life

According to David Bosch, Dutch and Anglo-Saxon Calvinism have succeeded in keeping alive a missionary spirit in the former colonies. Dutch and English missionary endeavors embarked on missionary action on the theological as well as socio-political level.[4] However, Bosch's argument ignores the charge of colonialism tied to the history of Calvinist missionary enterprise. The earliest ideologies of English colonists in the country were embodied by the Protestantism of the Puritan settlers of New England. Many Puritans believed God had made a covenant with their people and had chosen them to lead the other nations of the earth.

As Max Weber and Ernst Troeltsch have demonstrated, the differences in the sociological structure of religious groups are important and even fundamental in the determination of their religious doctrine. According to H. R. Niebuhr, one phase of denominationalism can be explained in terms of a modified economic interpretation of religious history. Economic factors play an important role in the denominational division. Economic stratification is a catalyst in establishing religious divisions.[5]

Weber defines capitalism as the continuous pursuit of profit. This implies rational tempering of the irrational impulse, rather than unlimited greed for gain.[6] The development of the spirit of capitalism could be best understood as part of the development of rationalism as a whole. In the Calvinist framework of predestination, Weber argues, the world exists to serve the glorification of God. God requires social achievement

---

4. Bosch, *Transforming Mission*, 256.

5. Niebuhr, *Social Sources of Denominationalism*, 26.

6. Weber, *Protestant Ethic*, 17.

in order for Christians to fulfill God's commandments and organize social life according to their religious principles. The social activity of the Christian in the world must be to the glory of God (or participation in enhancing *majorem gloriam Dei*).[7] The elected Christians are in a position to demonstrate signs of their state of election for themselves by becoming tools of the divine will. This Calvinistic ethic results in sanctification of one's whole life in order to increase the glory of God through works righteousness or an ascetic methodical way of life. Such external manifestation becomes indispensable, appearing as a sign of election. In effect, God helps those who help themselves. Good works even become a condition for earning God's reward.[8]

In its development, Calvinism went in a considerably different direction than Calvin's own view of economic justice and predestination. Later Calvinists emphasized the necessity of proving and demonstrating one's faith in worldly affairs and activity (practical syllogism). Founding their ethic in the doctrine of predestination and the concept of sanctification, the broader group of religiously inclined people was seen as endowed with positive incentives to a capitalist ethos, asceticism, and divine mission. This conduct of life led to an aristocracy with its *character indelebilis*.[9] The Puritans had undertaken the rationalization of the world as a means to salvation, to the extent that they took seriously the precept of doing everything to the glory of God. The Puritan becomes the embodiment of a rational type of methodical ascetic, because the doctrine of predestination is "the dogmatic background of the puritan morality in the sense of methodically rationalized ethical conduct."[10]

In the early history of the American Colonies, the middle-class outlook of the Puritans favored a rational bourgeois economic life, which became the cradle of the modern economic person.[11] The spirit of modern capitalism was born from the spirit of Christian asceticism, which was central in the Puritan concept of predestination and works righteousness. Benjamin Franklin, under the influence of his strict Calvinistic father, embodies a prototype of the spirit of capitalism which sought

7. Ibid., 108.
8. Ibid., 114–15.
9. Ibid., 121.
10. Ibid., 125.
11. Ibid., 174.

profit rationally and systematically.[12] Richard Baxter, a Presbyterian and an apologist of the Westminster Synod was the representative of the asceticism of Puritanism. Along with Baxter, the devotional books of Bunyan, the Baptist tinker, have nourished the whole of English Pietism and Continental Pietism.[13]

In Weber's analysis of the Western process which he calls the disenchantment of the world, the Protestant ethic, in particular the Puritan ethic, contributed considerably to its culmination; however, its ramifications are unfortunate. The Puritan desired to work for the divine mission in a secular calling. As asceticism was carried out of monastic cells into everyday life, it began to dominate worldly morality. In Baxter's view the care for external goods should only lie on the shoulders of the saint like a light cloak. It should be able to be thrown aside at any moment, but the cloak had instead become "an iron cage."[14]

Weber's sociological evaluation of Puritan culture and iron cage would not satisfy Richard Niebuhr. Niebuhr categorized Calvin along with Augustine under the conversionist's model, "Christ the transformer of culture." Central to this typology is the creative activity of God and of Christ while still emphasizing the nature of the human fall from the created goodness. A dialectical concept of creation and fall leads this conversionist model to a dramatic construal of the interaction between God and humanity. Eternal life is understood as a quality of existence in the here and now with emphasis on the divine possibility of a present renewal.[15] Human culture in this light is a transformed life in and to the glory of God.

According to Niebuhr, Calvin's dynamic concept of vocation as activities may express human faith and love to glory God in their religious-ethical calling. In his emphasis on the actuality of God's sovereignty in Christ, Calvin understood the state as God's minister, as restrainer of evil, and as the promoter of welfare. Calvinism has been marked by the influence of the eschatological hope of transformation by Christ and it was driven by the consequent pressing toward the realization of the promise. Nevertheless, Niebuhr worries that such a religious feature has

---

12. Ibid., 64.

13. Ibid., 162.

14. Ibid., 181.

15. Niebuhr, *Christ and Culture*, 194–96.

invariably been accompanied by a separatist and repressive stance.[16] This expression can be found in American civil religion.

American Civil Religion and the Cultural Ethos of Exceptionalism

The Puritans of New England made important and powerful contributions to American national identity, opening the threshold to American civil religion. Dismayed by the "Elizabethan Compromise" during and following Henry VIII's reign, the Puritans of New England sought to leave and find a separate place to form their congregations and practice their religious convictions. Eventually they founded the Plymouth Colony in 1620. When Charles I (1600–49) came to the throne in 1625, a substantial number of moderate Puritans founded an alternative society based on Puritan principles. This society, the Massachusetts Bay Colony, would be, they believed, "a city upon a hill" as the governor John Winthrop put it in 1630.[17]

The idea of the kingdom of God on earth remained central in Puritanism in its endeavor to attain security in terms of faith in divine sovereignty alone. The evangelizing zeal for setting an example in the virgin place became foundational for their privileged sense of mission as a new Israel that had a transcontinental power assuming America's supposed moral superiority. The second generation of Massachusetts Bay Puritans defended their liberties, strengthened by the belief that they were a divinely chosen people.[18] Although the worldview of the New England Puritans changed dramatically, the Puritans' deep moralistic values remained a significant part of the national identity of the United States for centuries, remaining influential to the present day in American congregational life.

Congregations experience a mixed combination of beliefs and practices incorporating both the Christian faith and American civil religion. Some congregation members bring tenets of American civil religion to congregational life for the embodiment of the American ethos, granting divine sanction for nationalistic and patriotic means and goals. National architecture and shrines became centers for pilgrimages and worship. Loyalty to God goes hand in hand with loyalty to nation.

16. Ibid., 217–18.

17 Marsden, *Religion and American Culture*, 16.

18. Niebuhr, *Kingdom of God*, 8.

Robert Bellah, a sociologist, in his article "Civil Religion in America" demonstrates his sociological analysis of the phenomenon of American civil religion.[19] American civil religion is a term given to a set of certain fundamental beliefs, values, holidays, and rituals shared by those who live in the United States. It affirms "the religious legitimization of the highest political authority."[20] The French thinker Alexis de Tocqueville was an important scholar in unpacking the role of religion in American history. Tocqueville found the role of religion in these societies to be significantly different than the state church in Europe. In *Democracy in America*, Tocqueville described religion in American "as a political institution which powerfully contributes to the maintenance of a democratic republic among the Americans."[21] Most of the American people attributed the peaceful dominion of religion in their country mainly to the separation of church and state. Religious independence was seen as an inspiration for further social freedoms. The basic freedoms such as education, religion, and the press ultimately fostered the spirit of freedom worldwide. In fact, the American people created a form of Christianity in the New World which can be termed "a democratic and republican religion."[22]

Robert Bellah and Martin Marty studied civil religion as a cultural phenomenon, attempting to identify the actual tenets of civil religion in the United States of America and to study civil religion as a phenomenon of cultural anthropology. Marty prefers to use Benjamin Franklin's term "public religion" rather than Rousseau's "civil religion" because it fits the American pluralist pattern.[23]

In contrast to Marty, Bellah's concern, utilizing Rousseau's concept of civil religion,[24] is to clarify that the idea of God played a constitutive role in the thought of the early American founding fathers and political leaders. Civil religion is not simply religion in general, but is specific to the topic of America. Against the critics who refer to American civil religion as American Shinto, Bellah rather contends that American civil religion "is a genuine appreciation of universal and transcendent religious

---

19. Bellah, "Civil Religion in America," in *Beyond Belief*, 168–86.

20. Ibid., 171.

21. De Tocqueville, *Democracy in America*, 1:310.

22. Ibid., 311.

23. Marty, *Public Church*, 16.

24. Bellah, "Civil Religion in America," 172.

reality" that is "revealed through the experience of the American people."[25] There is a sense of common understanding of the will of God as shared in the great majority of American people.[26]

We observe such a pattern in a variety of ceremonial settings such as Independence Day, inaugural presidential addresses, Memorial Day observances, Thanksgiving Day, service club invocations, the American flag in the sanctuaries during times of national crisis, and the insertion of "under God" into the Pledge of Allegiance (1954). The moral teachings of the Bible and Lincoln's Gettysburg Address and his second inaugural address become the sacred texts. According to Reinhold Niebuhr, Abraham Lincoln can be regarded as representative of civil religion; he never joined a church, yet was one of the greatest theologians of America in the sense of viewing the hand of God in the national affairs.[27] In the development of American institutions, civil religion can "provide a religious dimension for the whole fabric of American life, including the political sphere."[28]

Bellah identified the American Revolution, the Civil War, and the Civil Rights Movement as three decisive historical events that impacted the content and imagery of civil religion in the United States. The civil religion was able to build up powerful symbols of national solidarity without getting into struggle with the church. Consequently it can "mobilize deep levels of personal motivation for the attainment of national goals."[29] The idea of American civil religion and the American "Israel" theme are still very much alive in American culture and the national mindset. Several terms within US civil religion are related to biblical categories: "Exodus, Chosen People, Promised Land, New Jerusalem, and Sacrificial Death and Rebirth."[30] The American civil religion is based on the American experience regarding God and its eschatological hope. "It has its own prophets and its own martyrs, its own sacred events and sacred places, its own solemn rituals and symbols."[31]

25. Ibid., 179.
26. Ibid., 171.
27. Ibid., 180.
28. Ibid., 171.
29. Ibid., 181.
30. Ibid., 186.
31. Ibid.

The "gospel" of civil religion is outlined in the phrase "God helps him who helps himself" (Benjamin Franklin). The gospel of self-help is associated with the gospel of wealth in which a theology of glory or prosperity is conceptualized in light of the national sense of calling. It is based on manifest destiny and exceptionalism. American intervention on the world stage is undertaken, claiming a moral purpose of acting altruistically in defense of freedom and democracy. On the other hand, unfortunately, it excludes the religion and culture of its native peoples. Rather, they were consistently treated as heathens to be conquered by God's chosen people in their mission. The Christian missionaries working among American Indians were part of committing cultural genocide.[32] Divine providence had paved the way for Christian Englishmen to engage in the plague-effected slaughter of native Indians and black slavery. Slavery and racism were sanctioned in religious clothing.

According to Bellah, "In considering the continued existence of slavery, Jefferson wrote, 'indeed I tremble for my country when I reflect that God is just; that his justice cannot sleep forever.' The profound contradiction of a people fighting for its freedom while subjecting another to slavery was not lost on Jefferson and gave rise to anxiety for our future if this contradiction were not solved."[33] For H. R. Niebuhr, the kingdom of God in America became the American kingdom of God by the universalization of the particular Puritan ideal. This historical fact shows that the gospel is used and adapted by the new society for its own purpose. The gospel in its genuine sense had little impact upon changing American society. American culture vitiates the gospel.[34]

Cultural Anthropology and Cultural Ethnocentrism

Anthropologists such as Franz Boas argued against a particular form of cultural ethnocentrism. According to him, specific cultural traits (behaviors, beliefs, and symbols) must be examined in their own local context. The activities of individuals are determined to a great extent by their social environment. Their own activities also influence the society in which they live. All cultural forms appear in a constant state of flux. Puritan culture in this perspective is not given its cultural privilege.

32. Tinker, *Missionary Conquest.*
33. Bellah, *Habits of the Heart*, 31.
34. Niebuhr, *Kingdom of God*, 8–9.

Anthropologists have an obligation to speak out on social issues for the sake of cultural particularity in an egalitarian manner. Boas challenged the assumption of any close relation between biological type and form of culture, which might uphold Puritan ethnocentric exceptionalism. The investigation of human life must be based on the study of particular cultural forms and the interrelations between individual's lives and their particular cultures.[35]

Following in the footsteps of Boas, Ruth Benedict's evaluation of the Puritan divines is harsh and unflinching. She examined the Puritan divines of New England and their complete intellectual and emotional dictatorship in the eighteenth century in light of psychopathology. To Benedict, *they* were the psychoneurotics of Puritan New England, not the confused and tormented women they put to death as witches. The Puritan divines portrayed and demanded an extreme sense of guilt in their own conversion experiences. They did not admit salvation without a conviction of sin. Such a conviction prostrated the victim, with remorse and terrible anguish. The minister was under obligation to put the fear of hell into the heart of even the youngest child. If God saw fit to damn the child, it was the duty of the minister to extract from every convert the emotional acceptance of the damnation. In their dealing with "witches" or with unsaved children not yet in their teens, doctrines such as damnation and predestination caused intolerable aberrations.[36]

Although not always carried to this extreme, civil religion continued to be involved in the most pressing moral and political issues of the day, in which God is a central symbol.[37] America has often acted to promote these ideals abroad, most notably in the First and Second World Wars, in the Cold War and today in the Iraq War or in war against terrorism. This view has come under fire due to international condemnation of US global practices in the context of the War on Terror since 2001 and in other cases.

In Transition: Multicultural Reality and Cultural Pluralism

A core argument of exceptionalism is that America is unusually attractive to immigrants from all parts of the world for two reasons. First,

35. Boas, *Race, Language, and Culture*, 12–13.

36. Benedict, *Patterns of Culture*, 266–77.

37. Bellah, *Beyond Belief*, 182ff.

advocates of American exceptionalism say that their economic and political opportunities are unlimited. The United States possesses an unusually high degree of social mobility. The "American Dream" describes the perceived abundance of opportunities in the American social system. Secondly, immigrants can become Americans by accepting American values. Christianity finds itself still as one religious option among many others. This tends to marginalize the reality of multicultural society and religious pluralism within North America.

From Exclusion to Melting Pot Culture

The Puritans of Boston envisioned a society that was decisively shaped by their own version of Christianity. In the period from 1659 to 1661, four Quakers were put to death by the Puritan establishment on the gallows on Boston Common. In the Bill of Rights in 1791, the protection of religious freedom was enshrined. The American model of understanding religious outsiders has undergone a threefold change: from exclusivism to the melting pot of difference to pluralism as the symphony of difference.

Exclusivism demands that difference be destroyed, while the melting pot of difference is summed up in the term *assimilation*. The melting pot opened in 1908 through America's greatest wave of immigration. It provided a foundation for the assimilation of masses of diverse immigrants into the United States. According to Zangwill, "America is God's Crucible, the great Melting-Pot where all the races of Europe are melting and re-forming!"[38] This model of the melting pot that consisted of the Slavic, Anglo-Saxon, and Nordic races of Europe had no place for Asian immigrants, African Americans, or Native Americans. They remained marginalized under the melting pot ideology. The term *pluralism* first appeared in the sociologist Horace Kallen's article titled "Democracy versus the Melting Pot" in *The Nation*, which took issue with the melting pot ideology. In it the ideology of the melting pot is accused of being antidemocratic.[39]

38. Zangwill, *Melting-Pot*, 36.
39. Kallen, "Democracy versus the Melting Pot"; cf. Eck, *New Religious America*, 57.

Multicultural Entanglement

America's plurality and its unity can also be seen in the image of the symphony. It is a symphony orchestra in harmony with all the distinctive uniqueness of our many cultures. This refers to a vision of cultural pluralism grounded in the symphony of civilization. American society has a vision to preserve the inalienable rights of people of different cultures. The rights can be different in religion and creed, while united by participation in the common agreements of American citizenship and ideals.[40]

Allan Bloom in *The Closing of the American Mind* appears to be a leader of an intellectual backlash against cultural diversity and multicultural society by reaffirming the preeminence of Western civilization. By the same token, E. D. Hirsch expresses his worry about American reality becoming "a tower of Babel." The multiplicity of cultures in the American social fabric becomes a threat whose reality causes him to look for a more cohesive culture and a more homogeneous America. According to Hirsch, "If we had to make a choice between the one and the many, most Americans would choose the principle of unity, since we cannot function as a nation without it."[41]

While Bloom and Hirsch react to what they call a vexatious balkanization of America, other scholars respond to our cultural diversity as an opportunity to open American minds with emphasis on the importance of a culturally diverse education. The nation's motto *E pluribus unum* (Out of many, one) becomes a significant project today, inviting us to see American national identities in a different way.[42] This project is a serious endeavor to re-envision American history and identity by listening to peoples of non-white backgrounds who tell and retell their stories to create communities of memory. As Takaki, a Japanese-American sociologist holds, "In the sharing of our stories we create our community of a larger memory."[43]

For instance, Diana Eck argues that the religious landscape of America has changed radically in the past thirty years, beginning with the new immigration driven by the Immigration and Nationality Act

40. Eck, *New Religious America*, 57–58.

41. Cited in Takaki, *Different Mirror*, 3.

42. Ibid., 17.

43. Takaki, *Different Mirror*, 14.

of 1965. The people of the living traditions of faith—Islamic, Hindu, Buddhist, Confucian, Jain, Sikh, Zoroastrian, various African and Afro-Caribbean religions—have moved into American neighborhoods, becoming the architectural signs of a new religious America.[44]

One-third of the American people do not trace their origins back to Europe. Minorities are becoming a majority in several major cities of North America, such, New York, Chicago, Atlanta, Detroit, Philadelphia, San Francisco, and Los Angeles. The United States has become a land of many religions, the most religiously diverse nation in the world. Los Angeles is the center of "American Buddhism." Multiculturalism has become a social reality signaling that every dimension of American culture has become more complex due to immigration and globalization. Anticipations of a clash or a marbling of civilizations and people remain in tension.

A prominent example of this shift was apparent in November of 1998, when President Clinton sent a letter to the Sikh communities of America in the celebration of the 529th birthday of the teacher who initiated the Sikh movement in the sixteenth century. As the President wrote, "We are grateful for the teachings of Guru Nanak, which celebrate the equality of all in the eyes of God, a message that strengthens our efforts to build one America. Religious pluralism in our nation is bringing us together in new and powerful ways."[45]

Interreligious dialogue among people of diverse faith communities has become an indispensable part of understanding American culture for the sake of religious freedom, democratic ideals, justice, and peace. The religious pluralism project is driven toward claiming the principle of religious freedom. It embraces the religious diversity for a new age. In it difference and otherness would become a source of strength in the U.S rather than dividing people. The project of *E pluribus unum* advocates an endeavor to "create a vibrant and hopeful pluralism" in American civil society in favor of "a truly pluralistic, multireligious society."[46] However, it does not mean a principle of syncretism, a religious melting pot that would result something akin to "from many religions, one religion."[47]

44. Eck, *New Religious America*, 1.

45. *The San Diego Union-Tribune*, November 13, 1998. Cited in Eck, *New Religious America*, 7.

46. Eck, *New Religious America*, 25.

47. Ibid., 31.

The Latin motto *E pluribus unum* that has been on the Great Seal of the United States since 1782 suggests that the many colonies, now states, have become one. A trauma in American society stems from a long standing conflict over the way "the one and the many" relate in national life. Two specters of totalists and tribalists have played a role in inducing the trauma of polarization in the United States. Totalism implies the idea that a nation-state is to be organized around a single and easily definable ideology or metanarrative, by sidestepping what happens to minorities and dissenters. Tribalism challenges totalism by beginning with the idea that the nation-state is not to provide ideologies or patterns of life for the varied and multiculturalized peoples within it.[48] Against this conflict the term *pluralism* comes to the scene.

Religious Pluralism and Culture in Tension

In a project toward a new pluralism, the term *pluralism* is understood as the language of engagement, involvement, and participation. It goes, beyond diversity, toward active engagement with the plurality. It transcends tolerance in the active endeavor to understand the other. It goes beyond sheer and valueless relativism in which all cats are gray. Pluralism is engagement with difference and otherness without the eradication of differences and particularities. The process of pluralism is never complete but open-ended, it is in the ongoing work of each subsequent generation, while participating in the idea of America.[49] However, the problem of politics indicates that groups live with an incommensurable difference of discourses and narratives. Many worlds within the nation cannot lay a common basis and foundation for discussion, consensus, or mutual evaluation.[50]

This is because we cannot sidestep a clash of religious culture within North American society. For instance, on August 13, 1993, the temple house of the Cambodian Buddhist community that had recently been founded in Portland, Maine, was vandalized. Pirun Sen, one of the leaders of the Buddhist community rushed to the temple after a call from the

48. Marty, *One and the Many*, 3, 10–11.

49. Eck, *New Religious America*, 70–72.

50. Marty, *One and the Many*, 19.

police department. Inside the Buddha hall, he was shocked to see the words written across the wall: "Dirty Asian, Chink, Go Home."[51]

Exclusivism is still alive in the midst of cultural pluralism. In the post-Cold War, people in American society pursue their own symbols of cultural identity within their different backgrounds of culture and civilization. In multicultural society we still observe cohesion, disintegration, and conflict, since global politics in the post-Cold War world have become multipolar and multicivilizational.[52]

The world's seven or eight major civilizations (Western, Latin American, African, Islamic, Chinese, Hindu, Orthodox, Buddhist, Japanese) are making inroads and increasing in North America, asserting their own cultural voices, values, and identities.[53] The revitalization and resurgence of religions reinvigorates the cultural differences and entities, rejecting Western imposition of civilization and dominion of Western Christianity upon non-Western churches. North American society becomes multipolar and multicivilizational along with globalization. But we also perceive that a civilizational paradigm is entangled with the conflict and tensions among civilizations in a local-pluralist society as well as in the post-Cold War global world. Come what may, it is important to develop a holistic view of this complex society in terms of cultural anthropology.

A Holistic View of Complex Society

We need to examine the society and culture of North America in a holistic way for the sake of enriching the multicultural society in a meaningful way. In his study of the relationship between Christ and culture, Niebuhr defines a culture by combining the work of Malinoswki and Benedict. According to Malinowski, the essential element of culture is the organization of human beings into permanent groups. Culture is based on the idea of an organized system of purposive activities, so that the world of culture is a world of values. Social life is always cultural. Culture and social existence come together. Malinoswki takes a primary interest in the particular by seeking it in the universal. According to him, without some structure for the interpretation of facts, no scientific observation

51. Eck, *New Religious America*, 48.

52. Huntington, *Clash of Civilizations*, 20.

53. Ibid., 45–47.

can possibly be performed. Interpretation sees general laws in the end-
less diversity of facts. Interpretation classifies and orders phenomena
and puts them into mutual relationship.[54] Benedict's view is more holistic. Unlike the individual, particular functionalism of Malinoswki,
Benedict emphasizes the importance of individual and society in relation to culture.[55]

For the anthropological and sociological study of American culture we are more concerned with the underlying hermeneutical side of
cultural life. A concrete, social, historical, and lived experience must be
the starting point for anthropological integration and configuration in
the study of humanity, society, and culture. All experience and thought
arise out of the interaction of human beings with their physical, social,
and cultural environment. We experience life in complex, individual
moments of meaning, of direct experience of life as a socio-cultural
totality. The social-cultural meaning in social life and history cannot
be grasped without reference to the context of the past and the horizon of future expectations. The variegated nature of human life lies at
the foundation of the multitude of diverse cultural worldviews, so that
there is no single universally valid system of metaphysics or cultural
metanarrative. In this regard it is significant for us to remember that
Benedict, in her holism of integration and configuration, has affinity
to the hermeneutical theory of Dilthey. Her anthropological holism
argues against Malinowski's psychological-social functionalism in isolation from cultural whole or totality.[56]

In an understanding of sociocultural life a hermeneutical circle
can be expanded in a historical as well as socialcultural horizon. Lived
experience of cultural life (the lifeworld) in its unity of meaning tends
to reach out and include both the recollection of the past and the anticipation of the future in the total context of cultural meaning. Insofar
as we are imbued with the historicity of human being-in-the-world, we
must understand the present reality of American society in the reference
to horizons of the past and future. The hermeneutical significance of
American civil religion can be investigated through a dialectical interplay of the appropriation of its positive meaning (tied to human rights

54. Malinowski, *Magic, Science, and Religion*, ix.

55. Niebuhr, *Christ and Culture*, 32–34.

56. Benedict, *Patterns of Culture*, 52.

movement and democracy) and critical distance from its rugged individualism and exceptionalism (tied to Manifest Destiny).

Cultural understanding of other people, societies, and their life-expressions are developed on the basis of experience, self-understanding, and the constant interaction between them. The daily existence of socialized individuals in a given society moves in this connection of lived experience, expression, social discourse, and understanding in the comprehensive sense of a hermeneutical circle. Non-Western culture, religious ethos, and ethical values are fully incorporated into the study of the missional church and congregational mission for the sake of public and multicultural configuration. Insofar as meaning and meaningfulness are part of the social historical circle and cultural situation, they are contextual, not fixed or firm but historical, evolving with time in interaction with the others.

Habits of the Heart in the American Lifestyle

In the sociological research on American culture and life, a team headed by Robert Bellah made an in-depth study of what they called the "habits of the heart," the beliefs and values in the dominant American middle classes. Their study went on to become one of the most influential books of the 1980s. According to Bellah, social science as public philosophy advocates for a new relation between sociology and moral philosophy. Social science is embedded within a set of traditions or culture. It brings the traditions and ideals of society into juxtaposition with the present reality.

It is the important task of the public philosopher to take responsibility for understanding the stories and narratives shaping the present. Social science seeks to relate the narratives from the past (our effective history) to the stories current in the society, exposing them to mutual discussion and criticism.[57] In *Habits of the Heart*, Bellah and his associates characterize the active interview as the primary locus for gathering information on their subjects. In terms of dialogue or hermeneutical conversation central to their social scientific research method, they attempt to probe their subjects' thinking, reveal their assumptions, and evoke their subjects' feelings and thoughts which have been shaped by American culture and society.

57. Bellah, *Habits of the Heart*, 301–2.

According to Bellah, the two major definers of American life are the manager and the therapist. The task of the manager is to organize the human and non-human resources which are available to the organization for its improvement in the marketplace. The manager organizes the measures according to criteria of effectiveness set by the expectations of the owner. In this calculation of effectiveness, the manager controls and manipulates the technological aspects of the society which tends to depersonalize life and treats individuals as interchangeable parts. The split between public and private life corresponds to a split between utilitarian individualism and expressive individualism. The first individualism is appropriate in the economic and professional spheres. The second individualism is appropriate in the private sphere. Here religion is avoided as the embodiment of institution, but spirituality is preferred as a way of displaying expressive individualism. Americans are driven by the ideals of utilitarian individualism, making success paramount. Its criterion is greater effectiveness in economic life.[58] Nonetheless, expressive individualism remains in force in attitudes toward religious life.

The therapist assumes the functional organization of the society, like the manager, in order to achieve some combination of occupation and lifestyle, economically possible and psychically tolerable. The focus of the therapist is upon the effectiveness of the means. The social basis of American culture is the world of bureaucratic consumer capitalism. Its center is the autonomous individual, driven according to the criterion of life-effectiveness.[59]

In American society, which is individualistic and privatistic in its modern style, religious beliefs are considered to be private affairs. In both utilitarian individualism and expressive individualism private space is more significant than public space. According to the mindset of the utilitarian individualist, human life is seen as an effort to maximize self-interest relative to one's given ends. Society is seen as emerging from a contract into which individuals enter in order to advance their self-interest. The utilitarian individualist joins public worship to achieve his or her desires.

In contrast to utilitarian individualist, the expressive individualist holds to a unique core of feeling and intuition which should be expressed if individuality can be realized. He or she finds it possible to fuse with

58. Ibid., 46.
59. Ibid., 47.

other people, nature, and the cosmos as a whole through intuitive feeling. Denying the value of impersonal interaction, the expressive individualist seeks intimate relationships in the public space. Such a person joins public worship to experience intuitive fusion with other expressive selves, still seeking to achieve private interests.[60] Modern Americans practice their lifestyle in enclaves. These concern only private life in leisure and consumption in particular. They are socially segmented for they include only those with a common lifestyle. Those with a different lifestyle may be tolerated, but are irrelevant to one's own lifestyle enclave.[61]

American habits of the heart have significant implications for religion. In an interview with Sheila Larson, a young nurse, she said that her religion was "Sheilaism." "I believe in God. I'm not a religious fanatic. I can't remember the last time I went to church. My faith has carried me a long way. It's Sheilaism. Just my own little voice."[62]

Postmodern Condition in American Society

Individualism and commitment in American lifestyles are in transition toward postmodern pragmatism. Postmodern pragmatists see language as a tool to attain a personal identity in terms of one's own private, autonomous language. The Enlightenment elevated the individual self to the center of the world. Descartes laid the philosophical foundation in terms of doubt in which the existence of the thinking self is the first truth that cannot be doubted. Isaac Newton later established the scientific framework for modernity, in which the physical world is pictured as a machine whose laws and regularity could be discovered by the human mind. John Locke contextualized the Enlightenment ideal by influencing the founding fathers of North America. The Puritans conveyed economic rationalism and the Enlightenment project by religiously sanctioning it through Calvinistic economic ethics and their own cultural ethos.

If we view our lives as episodes within a larger historical narrative, the personal sense of identity is shaped in the ebb and flow of our historical context. It is not necessary to seek the absolute beyond the ordinary, concrete life embedded within its historical and social location. According to Rorty, what tradition conveys and mediates is immanent

60. Keifert, *Welcoming the Stranger*, 27–28.

61. Bellah, *Habits of the Heart*, 72.

62. Ibid., 221.

to our society. Our discourse cannot represent the world as it actually is. To cope with reality, we must acquire habits of mind and action instead of "getting reality right." Coherence rather than correspondence is central in understanding the truth. We cannot attain a perspective outside the world in which we live. In the pragmatist tradition of Dewey, beliefs are tools for dealing with reality rather than upholding the assumption that beliefs represent reality. Insofar as statements cohere with the entire system of beliefs, they are true. At issue is making beliefs and desires coherent. There is no such thing as any great metavocabulary under which we could subsume all the various types of human discourse. Pragmatism is the vocabulary of practice with focus on action. What is right is framed by what is useful. Postmodern pragmatism is an advocate of edifying philosophy.[63]

Rorty advocates a quest for cultural pluralism in line with the spirit of tolerance that has made constitutional democracies feasible. He credits the social community with attaining the goal of determining what counts as an appropriate mixture of unforced agreement and tolerant disagreement within the context of cultural pluralism. We attain a renewed sense of community. "Our identification with our community—our society, our political tradition, our intellectual heritage—is heightened when we see this community as ours . . . In the end, the pragmatists tell us, what matters is our loyalty to other human beings clinging together against the dark, not our hope of getting things right."[64]

The postulate of the thinking self, the mechanistic view of the universe, the ideals of civil society (freedom, individualism, moral progress, democracy) become slogans in the quest to unlock and master nature for human benefit while at the same time subjugating and suppressing people of "nonreason" in the colonies. As Habermas summarizes,

> The project of modernity . . . formulated by the philosophers of the Enlightenment in the eighteenth century consists in the relentless development of the objectivating sciences, of the universalistic foundations of morality and law, and of autonomous art, all in accord with their own immanent logic . . . Partisans of the Enlightenment . . . could still entertain the extravagant expectation that the arts and sciences would not merely promote the control of the forces of nature, but also further the understanding

63. Rorty, *Philosophy and the Mirror*, 373.
64. Rorty, *Consequences of Pragmatism*, 166.

of self and world, the progress of morality, justice in social institutions, and even human happiness.[65]

The US version of the modern project was largely formed by the early English Puritan settlers. As we have analyzed a sociological theory of American civil religion and exceptionalism, the US national identity is characterized by world policeman, empire, and exemplar of the democratic idea of individual freedom and economic rights.

In the emerging postmodern condition, the postmodern mind advocates a shift that is to be undertaken from what is known as modernity. In the postmodern condition the late capitalism is labeled as the empire of globalized or consumer capitalism. Neoliberal tenets have turned all of life into commodities that can be marketed. This marks a shift toward a global economy with a worldwide financial structure that is transcending the geographical barriers of the nation-state. The encounter between multiple civilizations has become inevitable. Globalization is leading to multiple ethnic cultures and racial communities living together in the same neighborhood. Technological media such as cable and satellite television, the internet and other electronic technologies contribute to commonly shared experiences, and create a new electronic global community unfettered by the limitation of geographical location.

Such changing reality in everyday life is shaped by new production techniques and an accelerated capacity for mass production in a consumer, electronic society. This new reality generates and multiplies the quantity of sign, configuring the regime of sign-value that forms our everyday life. Sign-value is laden with meaning. Power is accrued through identification with one's new sports car. The sign-value of one's automobile gives prestige in a new modern society. Sign-value produces and proliferates a new world of advertising, fashion, and consumption. The perspective on sign and symbolic exchange, which are produced in information technologies, media, and cybernetics, organizes a principle of postmodern society in terms of the logic of simulation. It postulates a break with the modern society.

We live in a hyperreality of simulation, multiplying images, spectacles, and upholding the interplay of sign in correlation with human consciousness and knowledge. Here, personal identities are constructed and construed by the appropriation of images, codes, signs, and models.

65. Habermas, "Modernity," 45.

Finally, technology, the proliferation of images, information, and signs, dominates in the society of simulation. Our lifeworld is produced, consumed, determined, and colonized by the logic of simulation. Economics, politics, culture, sexuality, and the social—all coalesce into each other, thus leading our postmodern condition to be thought of in terms of "hyperreality." The sphere of the hyperreal—for instance, media simulations of reality, Disneyland, amusement parks, malls and consumer fantasylands, televised sports, and other excursions into ideal worlds—is more real than the real world.[66] Hyperreality, which plays the controlling principle in the organization of society, confronts human life with an overwhelming flux of images, codes, and models. In the postmodern world individuals escape the realm of the real to the ecstasies of hyperreality as they live in the world of computer, media, and technological experience. In fact, we live in a postmodern condition created by simulation, implosion, and hyperreality. How do we reconfigure missional church and congregational life in such a whirl and interdependence?

Missional Church and Congregational Life: Whither?

Every dimension of the church's life is shaped by the individual decisions of the members of the church. In this American voluntaristic cultural system, one chooses one's congregation like joining a club, considering the social activities, professional services related to denominational affiliation, quality of church's program, opportunities for social relationships, economic class, preaching skills and leadership of the pastor.[67]

Individual subjects begin to lose contact with the real and find themselves fragmented and dissolved. In the universe of simulation the masses are baptized into a media message, experiencing the demise of disalienation, emancipation, and revolution. The electronic church has nothing to do with the geographical location of the church. Television viewers become members of a church by experiencing it only through the television ministry or Internet mission. In the acceleration and proliferation of signs, codes, and forms, imposition of the meaning in the media, as it relates to the implosion of the social in the mass, brings the implosion of the mass in a black hole of nihilism and meaninglessness. This is a characteristic of the postmodern condition that is becoming

66. Kellner, ed., *Baudrillard: A Critical Reader*, 5–14.

67. Guder, *Missional Church*, 235.

an "iron cage," bringing a deep crisis to missional church conversation. Although now generally unspoken, the metanarrative of the United States (exceptionalism or Manifest Destiny) has not lost its interplay with political, religious, and institutionalized power.

In what we have analyzed about American society, religion, and culture, a secular age deeply influenced or colonized various forms of Christianity. The steady decline of church membership has been well documented in so-called mainline churches. American secular-religious therapeutic individualism has reduced many important aspects of Christianity into its own hands and interests. In matters pertaining to Christian identity, faith, spiritual life, it is imperative to consider the transformation of American religion.[68] A secular and mature age in modern Western societies also calls for reframing our studies of mission. We must undergo a paradigm shift in the missional church conversation. This task will be taken up in the next chapter.

68. Wolfe, *Transformation of American Religion*, 36.

11

Missional Epistemology and Hermeneutics in Studies of Mission

As we saw concerning American society's cultural complexities in the preceding chapter, a growing awareness of hyperreality, information culture, and difference becomes the key to understanding American society in the emergence of the postmodern condition. The structure of human thoughts arises out of and derives meaning from human experience in interaction with the social-cultural environment. We experience our own self as an other, in our varying life situations.[1] This complex reality implies a challenge at the heart of the missional church conversation. This crisis also provides us with an opportunity to deepen and actualize the church's identity in a post-Christendom world in dialogue with the other.

The emerging postmodern approach to understanding truth is more holistic and relational than its modern forebears. Our understanding of all knowledge is laden with power relations. Understanding the nature of power in relation to our rational knowledge redefines all relationships and all meaning. This interpretive mind "aims at continuing a conversation rather than at discovering truth."[2] The picture of the postmodern condition in American society is also embedded within the American religious way of life as further shaped by cultural factors and interactions from different civilizations. In light of this the question

1. Ricoeur, *Oneself as Another*.
2. Rorty, *Philosophy and Mirror of Nature*, 393.

becomes: To what extent can the theology of the missional church create a missiological epistemology that is more amenable and dialogical
towards secular, postmodern American society?

Paradigm Shift: Continuity in Discontinuity

David Bosch proposes a transformative hermeneutic in his influential
book *Transforming Mission*. Engaging Thomas Kuhn's theory of paradigm in his classic *The Structure of Scientific Revolutions* Bosch attempts
to demonstrate how one theological paradigm is displaced by a new one.
According to Bosch, as one paradigm has become increasingly incapable
of explaining new or newly discovered facts, a new paradigm begins to
be accepted as one that does account for those facts in a more satisfac-
tory fashion. "To be accepted as a paradigm, a theory must seem better
than its competition, but it need not, and in fact never does, explain all
the facts with which it can be confronted."[3]

In Kuhn's view, science does not really grow cumulatively, but by
way of revolutions. Normal science practiced by scientists encounters
anomalies which it is incapable of explaining. A search begins for a new
model or paradigm to replace the old one. The previous problem-ridden
paradigm is abandoned. In fact, a new paradigm grows and ripens
within the context of a network of diverse social and scientific factors.
The old paradigm (for instance, Newtonian physics) is incommensurable with the new one (for instance, Einstein's theory of relativity).
Knowledge is embodied in paradigms and the paradigms are incommensurable with each other. In different paradigms scientists observe
different worlds. They speak different languages and follow different
rules. In the postscript Kuhn defines a paradigm as "the entire constel-
lation of beliefs, values, techniques, and so on shared by the members of
a given community."[4]

In regard to distinctive features of Kuhn's theory, Ian Barbour, a
critical realist, offers a nuanced formulation: 1) all data are paradigm-
dependent and incommensurable, but there are data on which adherents
of rival paradigms can agree; 2) paradigms are resistant to falsification by
data, but data does cumulatively affect the accountability of a paradigm;
3) there are no rules for paradigm choice because criteria for choice are

---

3. Kuhn, *Structure of Scientific Revolutions*, 17–18.

4. Ibid., 175.

paradigm-dependent. However, there are shared criteria for judgment in evaluating paradigms.[5]

In the study of theology and mission, we are aware that old paradigms still live on. They are even influential in inspiring contemporaries to contextualize and reinterpret theological insights from the past. Any specific and simplified paradigm in quest of modernity's project or the postmodern condition could not account for what is going on in missiological study. In Bosch's description of paradigm changes in mission (apocalyptic, Hellenistic, medieval catholic, Protestant, modern Enlightenment, emerging ecumenical) the overlapping is discernable.[6]

What characterizes Christian mission in the midst of non-Western theological challenges is the decline of the dominant position of Western Christian theology and mission. In light of the freedom of religion, which is a basic human right, Christians are forced to reevaluate their understanding of the biblical narrative and attitude toward the wisdom of non-Christian religions in a multicultural society. The new situation of global locality in the contemporary lifeworld challenges us to take into account in a responsible way a new opportunity to be more accessible to the lifeworld in the postmodern and multicultural condition. A clash or engagement between the American religious way of life and non-American religious-cultural communities makes us re-evaluate and re-interpret our complex reality in a more responsible way for the sake of God's mission in Christ's service for all.

Critical Realism and Missiological Epistemology

According to Barbour, there is no direct upward line of logical reasoning from data (observation/data) to theories (concepts/theories), but only the indirect line through the mediation of imagination, analogies, and models. Theories influence observations in many ways. For the epistemological principle of critical realism, Barbour introduces four criteria for assessing theories in normal scientific research: 1) agreement with data; 2) coherence (a theory consistent or interconnected with other accepted theories); 3) scope (theories can be judged by their comprehensiveness or generality); and 4) fertility (a theory is evaluated by its current ability and future promise in providing the framework for an

5. Barbour, *Religion and Science*, 127.

6. Bosch, *Transforming Mission*, 181–82.

ongoing research program). Barbour's critical realist position argues that reality is not fully inaccessible to us, so the criteria of truth must include all four of the criteria mentioned above. This is a *critical realism* because a combination of criteria is used in regard to correspondence with reality.

Barbour seeks to find a consonance of critical realism in belief and experience in religion. Religious experience is always interpreted by a set of concepts and beliefs. These concepts and beliefs result from acts of creative imagination in which, as in the scientific case, analogies and models are prominent. Religious beliefs influence experience and the interpretation of traditional stories and rituals. Six distinctive types of religious experience recur: 1) numinous experience of the Holy; 2) mystical experience of unity; 3) transformative experience of reorientation (followed by the experience of grace or forgiveness, reconciliation or wholeness); 4) courage in facing suffering and death; 5) moral experience of obligation; and 6) awe in response to order and creativity in the world.[7]

According to Barbour, theology also uses four criteria for assessing religious beliefs: 1) agreement with data (the primary data are individual religious experience and communal story and rituals of particular religious communities); 2) coherence (the intersubjective judgment of the community provides protection against individualism and arbitrariness); 3) scope (religious beliefs can be extended to interpret other kinds of human experience beyond the primary data, particularly other aspects of our personal and social lives); and 4) fertility (at the personal level, religious beliefs can be judged by their power to effect personal transformation and the integration of personality).[8]

Following in the footsteps of Barbour, Paul Hiebert maintains that scientific laws are expressions of the processes of human cognition and of the historical and cultural contexts of scientists. Knowledge in critical realism is the correspondence between our mental maps and the real world in an analogical and metaphorical sense. It is objective reality subjectively known, appropriated in human lives. On a higher level, critical realism draws on "community hermeneutics" by engaging in dialogue in which we learn about others and reveal ourselves to them. An anthropological concept of emic (the perspective of the other)

7. Barbour, *Religion and Science*, 111–12.

8. Ibid., 113.

interpretation and etic (one's own perspective) interpretation transcends a literal one-to-one correspondence of photographic description. The information conveyed about reality in an analogical representation in cultural anthropology is limited, but accurate.[9]

An anthropological view of the model or analogy affirms that models are maps of reality, helping us understand the true nature of things. Furthermore, models are maps for action, used to guide our action.[10] A knowledge system in this anthropological framework has three components: 1) a set of beliefs connected with the domain of inquiry made by scientific and cognitive process; 2) a set of questions worth asking; and 3) a set of epistemic and methodological norms in regard to the domain investigated. Within this knowledge system, anthropologists bring both emic and etic analyses and diachronic (historical) and synchronic (cultural-contemporary) models for complementary ways of looking at and understanding reality.[11] Community investigation in this anthropological perspective is an essential part of the hermeneutical process of searching for truth.

However, such a missiological epistemology of critical realism tends to sidestep knowledge or truth embedded within the social constructions of particular cultures and historical periods. In a sense critical realists are careless in using the term "hermeneutics." The term emphasizes human understanding in interaction with historically mediated knowledge and its incomplete character. Furthermore, in religious experience metaphors cannot be fully expressed in concepts. Metaphors will always be valuable in enabling us to re-describe our own experience and in their power to transform our personal lives. Metaphorical symbols are experientially rich and are thus central in ritual and worship. Nevertheless, biblical narratives (stories of creation, the covenant, and especially the life, death, and resurrection of Christ) are not the models, nor the metaphors. Narratives are more personally involving and evocative, foundational for the faith and doctrine than models. This ushers in a hermeneutical issue.

9. Hiebert, *Missiological Implications*, 77.

10. Ibid., 81.

11. Ibid., 85.

Hermeneutical Analogy and Negative Dialectics

For critical realists paradigms can be made commensurable through model and analogy. Missiological epistemology of the critical realm comes to encounter with Tracy's hermeneutical theology of analogy and negative dialectics. For Tracy, analogical and dialectical language can serve as the principal candidates for a systematic theology of analogical imagination. The Christ event is acknowledged as the radical mystery of the self-manifestation of God. In order to honor this mystery, theology needs negations in the interpretation of God-self-world. Similarities must remain "similarities"-*in-difference*. Ricouer's famous dictum remains central to Tracy: "The [linguistic] symbol gives rise to thought, but thought always returns to and is informed by the [linguistic] symbol."[12]

Theological language must rearticulate in the reflective form of a negative dialectics–what the proclaimed word (*kerygma*) reveals to authentic Christian faith. Jesus Christ discloses the reality of the infinite, qualitative distinction between God and the self.[13] Tracy appreciates Tillich's creation of a theological language, maintaining fidelity to both the intensity of negative dialectics and the similarities-in-difference and order in all reality. For the sake of the method of correlation Tillich's theological method ("Protestant principle and Catholic substance")[14] centers on a correlation between concepts denoting the human and those denoting the divine. Finally it is a correlation in the factual sense between human ultimate concern and that about which one is ultimately concerned.[15] "The method of correlation explains the contents of the Christian faith through existential questions and theological answers in mutual interdependence."[16]

However, Tracy's correlational method in a revised and critical sense goes beyond Tillich and further envisions theology as a mutually critical dialogue between interpretations of the Christian message and interpretations of contemporary cultural experiences and practices. For his theological method, the merit of hermeneutics is that it takes the historical context with full seriousness. We are all affected by history and

---

12. Tracy, *Analogical Imagination*, 13, 411.

13. Ibid., 415.

14. Tillich, *Systematic Theology*, 1, 25.

15. Ibid., 60.

16. Ibid.

the influence of the tradition in our language. It is naïve to think that we can be faithful to the tradition to which we belong by merely repeating its *tradita* instead of critically engaging it.[17] The word "hermeneutical" best describes the realized experience of understanding in conversation. All understanding assumes a radically finite and historical character.[18] The ground of real finitude and radical historicity in all hermeneutical understanding sharpens the correspondence theory of critical realism which otherwise sidesteps the sociocultural and historical embeddedness of the interpretation.

That being the case, to what extent does Tracy relate this finitude of hermeneutical understanding to people's life in their sociocultural context? Tracy dovetails with Geertz's careful definition of culture: "An historically transmitted pattern of meanings embodied in symbols, a system of inherited conceptions expressed in symbolic forms by means of which men communicate, perpetuate and develop their knowledge about and attitudes toward life"[19]

However, the controlling principle for Tracy is negative dialectics in the sense of a the *via negativa*. Is this principle of negative dialectics capable of integrating an anthropological analysis of culture (Geertz) into his analogical, dialectical hermeneutics? In a similar fashion to Ricoeur's concept of "the surplus of meaning," Tracy gives the classic text "an excess of meaning."[20] In Tracy's concept of analogy, language of negation in talk about God acts as intensification, challenging any slackening of the sense of radical mystery. The ultimate incomprehensibility of God's event provides the focal meaning for developing analogies-in-difference. Hence, *missio Dei* theology remains theocentric without connection to discursive praxis of evangelization.

In contrast to Tracy's concept of dialectical language, I emphasize that analogy grips us and uses the character of address and discourse found in metaphor and parable. Analogy as a process of speech and discourse becomes a socializing cultural phenomenon, allowing for creative freedom in producing multiple meanings. In the discourse on the kingdom of God, Jesus utilizes cultural parables and narratives standing on the part of *massa perditionis* (public sinners and tax collectors). Jesus'

17. Tracy, *Analogical Imagination,* 100.

18. Ibid., 102.

19. Ibid., 7.

20. Ibid., 102.

gospel narrative is not merely dialectical and negative, but positively grasps and transforms people's lives.

Rather than Jesus' parable about God's kingdom, Aristotle's dictum is more attractive for Tracy: "to spot the similar in the dissimilar is the mark of poetic genius."[21] Thus in Tracy's language of analogical imagination or a critical correlational practical theology, I sense that a reflection of word-event associated with God's Saying is undermined. A language of similarity-in-difference does not fully articulate the interplay between analogy and discourse in a social-cultural location because it does not analyze the power-knowledge nexus in institutional regimes and the socio-material sphere. Tracy's analogical-negative method can be sharpened and renewed by a sociological-cultural analysis of human life grounded in a distinct cultural location. If this perspective is sidestepped, Tracy's project of interpretation or a critical correlational practical theology tends to a principle of negative dialectic by losing sight of the embodiment of God's word-event in solidarity with those who are marginalized and victimized in the world.

A Cultural-Linguistic Epistemology

Tracy's analogical-negative theology is characterized in experiential-expressive manner. Theology is envisioned as mutually critical dialogue between interpretations of the Christian message and interpretations of contemporary cultural experience and practices.[22]

Against Tracy, Lindbeck proposes a cultural-linguistic approach, seeing Christian dogma as having a narrative structure. The linguistic structures of Christian stories and narratives happen without recourse to either external philosophical categories or religious experiences. According to Lindbeck, Tracy's theology, called "experiential-expressive," is vulnerable to the logical possibility that a Buddhist and a Christian might have basically the same faith, although expressed very differently.[23] The various religions are diverse symbolizations of one and the same core experience of the Ultimate. In this light Lindbeck turns Tillich's famous definition upside down: "religion is the substance of culture, and culture is the form of religion." For Lindbeck religion as the ultimate

---

21. Ibid., 409.

22. Browning, *Fundamental Practical Theology*, 46.

23. Lindbeck, *Nature of Doctrine*, 17.

dimension of culture gives shape and intensity to the experiential matrix from which significant cultural achievements flow.[24]

The church has the function of communally authoritative rules of discourse, attitude, and action. Lindbeck's cultural-linguistic approach and his construal of church doctrine are referred to as a regulative or rule theory.[25] He calls a cultural-linguistic approach literally (not metaphorically), intratextual, excluding an extratextual method. A scriptural world is able to absorb the universe. Intratextual theology redescribes reality within the scriptural framework. "It is the text, which absorbs the world, rather than the world the text."[26] In this framework a religion is conceived of as an external word, a *verbum externum*, molding and shaping the self and its world.[27]

For his cultural-linguistic strategy Lindbeck understands that Luther's dictum—*scriptura sui ipsius interpres*—as an emphasis on intratextuality. Scripture was interpreted by its use (proclamation), by the *viva vox evangelii*. Unfortunately, God's word in action (*dabar*) is thus narrowed down to the text for Lindbeck, because God's word functions only intratextually. We are confronted only by the Jesus Christ as depicted "in the narrative"—thereby only the narrated Jesus Christ is the subject-matter of the Scriptures for Lindbeck.[28]

Geertz's term of thick description holds, according to Lindbeck, only within the intratextual-confessional framework. Geertz already warned of the danger of the "hermetic" approach, because it lacks analysis of its proper object and of the informal logic of actual life. For Geertz, culture is a context within which social events, behaviors, institutions or process can be intelligibly—that is, thickly—described. However, Linbeck is not interested in exploring the anthropological concept of thick description in analysis of multiple meanings of the word of God in encounter with those who receive the biblical narrative in non-Christian contexts. His contribution is enriching understanding of biblical narrative and Christian confessions while a missional effort of translation encountering the non-Western world remains underdeveloped.

24. Ibid., 34.

25. Ibid., 18.

26. Ibid., 118.

27. Ibid., 34.

28. Ibid., 120.

Contours of a Socially and Culturally Engaged Mission

In our studies of missiological epistemology in paradigm shift, historical-linguistic tradition (a diachronic hermeneutic) shapes and conditions human existence and understanding; the ever-changing circumstances of life, culture, and history underline our understanding in an incomplete and limited manner. At the same time, human existence influenced by the contemporary public sphere (a synchronic discourse) engages sociopolitical life, offering a critique of a reified and colonized lifeworld.

Postcolonial, liberation, and feminist theologies have clearly demonstrated our problem with history (the tradition) and in history (our present social, economic, political, and ecclesial situation). Their hermeneutics do not merely demonstrate correction, but advocate for the transformation of reality by way of praxis.

For socially and culturally engaged mission, it is vital to integrate the complexities of life into a hermeneutical and cultural-anthropological arc through analysis, reconstruction, appropriation, and distanciation. Cultural history is radically immanent in our contemporary society, normalizing and underlining the discursive practices, institutionalized complexities, and religious worldview of the powerful in the past. A prophetic hermeneutic of discourse moves in search of the time lost to decipher and reveal the life horizon of those who are marginalized and who deviate from the cultural norm and cultural religious texts; thus this socio-critical dimension attempts to reconstruct an emancipation project and praxis by acknowledging the dissimilar discourse of the other in today's public sphere. I call this the irregular side of postcolonial hermeneutics in an archeological rewriting.

According to Gadamer, human existence is thoroughly historical or in the world. We can never escape our historical context, or lifeworld. Behind the Babel of competing interpretation is a shared reality—a world, tradition, and language. Because of this common dimension we can anticipate experiencing a fusion of horizons. Our horizon is expanded in the encounter with the other so that we understand the other's horizon through our own. Nevertheless, this historical/ontological grounding of interpretation in the studies of culture is vulnerable to the underside of religious, cultural history which is in the service of the powerful. Gadamer's theory of history of effect no longer poses a question of what social and cultural factors have shaped and characterized the discursive, ideological, linguistic structure in regard to social-anthropological location. Gadamer's hermeneutical theory needs to be sharpened by socio-critical methods in analyzing language as an ideology of the powerful, and by socio-discursive practices based on the nexus between institutionalized knowledge and political power.

This considered, history as the history of effect is to be reinterpreted as the history of discrepancy because history imposes the domination of the powerful upon those who are weaker. It is essential to review the history of effect in light of its discrepancy and discontinuity; it sharpens a language of similarity-in-dissimilarity and social discourse built on the knowledge-power interconnection in the study of God's mission and *diakonia*. A cultural, anthropological study of culture and religion is a significant arbiter for the church's communication of biblical narrative within the non-Christian context for the sake of thick description of the profound meaning of the gospel as *viva vox evangelii*. In the hermeneutical-anthropological analysis of culture, action for God's mission and evangelization becomes more meaningful and more thickly intelligible to an outsider. This dynamic is central in our discussion of the implication of Bonhoeffer's writings for God's mission.

A Missiological Retrieval of Bonhoeffer: Meaning, Promise, and Compassion

In the task of constructing a theological epistemology of prophetic mission, Bonhoeffer deserves attention. The modern concept of human autonomy and the independence of the world imply a challenge to Christian faith in God, while the postmodern condition brings a crisis to the truth of faith. The autonomy of the world and human reason imply the removal of God as the working hypothesis for the understanding of the world. On the other hand, God as a working hypothesis is dominant in American religious life. Communal responsibility yields to a rampant individualism. The nature of contemporary religion is diagnosed as expressive individualism in which spirituality serves the individual as a therapeutic device to improve the quality of private life. It is also a way of expressing one's idiosyncratic proclivities.

In the American context, the religiosity of culturalized and individualized Christianity invalidates the biblical identity of God. A concept of "Moralistic Therapeutic Deism" occupies a central place among teenagers with a Christian background. According to this religiosity, a God exists and watches over human life. God wants people to be good and nice. The goal of life is happiness and well-being. God does not need to be involved particularly in one's life except when God finds it necessary to solve a problem. A concept of Moralistic Therapeutic Deism operates inherently in American's religious way of life, largely unnoticed in the mainline churches.[29] Religion is a matter of individual, subjective choice and preference. God intervenes in daily life as a problem solver only if a problem arises. God "like a combination Divine Butler and Cosmic Therapist"[30] infuses American religion, undergirding a therapeutic individualism in American culture. Moralistic Therapeutic Deism which is also the predominant faith of American adults has essentially invalidated and colonized Christian faith in the biblical God (including other major religious traditions).[31]

In contrast to Moralistic Therapeutic Deism, Scripture directs human beings to God's solidarity with the life of Israel and the suffering of Jesus in company with those on the margins. The biblical God assumes powerlessness and suffering into God's own life and transforms it. God is not the *deus ex machina* but the one who suffers and helps others through suffering. A false conception of God in human religiosity is dethroned by a way of seeing and understanding the God of the Bible who wins power and space in the world by Christ's reconciliation with the world. A secular or non-religious interpretation of the biblical narrative may pave a new way to a missiological hermeneutic of self-renewal through the gospel narrative and self-exposure to the other in light of Christ's reconciliation. The "world come of age" in its godlessness comes nearer to God who is reconciled to the world. In the situation of the autonomy of the world in which "before God and with God we live without God,"[32] a reflection of God's mission in the life of Christ undergirds an interpretation of God embedded within historical life situations. In the cross where God allows God's self to be pushed out of the world, we can become honest not only with respect to the world but also before God.

---

29. Smith and Denton, *Soul Searching*, 129.

30. Ibid., 165.

31. I appreciate Dwight Zscheile's draft paper, "A Missional Theology of Spiritual Formation," in which he challenges the ethos of American civil religion in the contemporary Christian life.

32. Bonhoeffer, *Letters and Papers*, 360.

In this light one of Bonhoeffer's poems is striking for missiological hermeneutic in recognition of religious outsiders.

> God goes to every man when sore bestead,
> Feeds body and spirit with his bread;
> For Christians, pagans alike he hangs dead,
> And both alike forgiving.[33]

This poem is hermeneutical in character, offering new ways of seeing and thinking about the actual world. The cross is a discursive form of *parrhēsia* (speaking the truth boldly or audaciously). Jesus rejects Peter's understanding of the Messiah, which includes the political restoration of Israel. However, as the "Human One" Jesus inevitably has a political consequence in his discourse of *parrhēsia* (Mark 8:32; openly, frankly or boldly) regarding his vocation for God's sake and *ochlos*-minjung. A *parrhēsia* form of discourse expresses a spirit of resistance, questioning the institutionalized authority in the religious and political sphere. *Parrhēsia*, speaking to each other frankly, finds political-religious meaning and discourse for the sake of promoting the full humanity of the marginalized, the victim, and the voiceless.[34]

Bonhoeffer reflects on the ethical meaning of *parrhēsia*, asking "what is meant by telling the truth?"[35] "Telling the truth," truthful speech of others, means something different in one's relationships at each particular time and according to the particular situation. Trustful speech is indebted to God, since the living God has set us in a life, demanding service of us within this context of life. Our speaking of God refers to the God who entered into the world in Jesus Christ. Trustful speech of God and others contradicts the notion of God as a general principle or a metaphysical idol. Our speech must be trustful concretely, because we owe our language to God in a concrete form in the world. *Parrhēsia* is also hermeneutical, because it is "a matter of correct appreciation of real situations and of serious reflections upon them."[36]

The word of the cross as a discursive form of *parrhēsia* is "as much alive as life itself."[37] It allows us to interpret who God is from the

---

33. Ibid., 362.
34. Cf. Foucault, *Fearless Speech.*
35. Bonhoeffer, *Ethics,* 358.
36. Ibid., 359.
37. Ibid., 360.

standpoint of the subjugated and castigated. The exposed flesh of the crucified one uncovers any secret of the self and dissolves it to God's exposure in the face of Jesus Christ. It is common for people in need to seek and appeal to God. However, the God of Israel in Jesus Christ to whom the Christian appeals, is not a *Deus ex machina*, but the One who stands in grief by the poor and the scorned who lack shelter or bread. "God's truth has become flesh in the world and is alive in the real . . . The concept of living truth is dangerous."[38] The crucified one becomes foundational for understanding God's compassion, which embraces both Christians and non-Christians alike. In the death of Jesus Christ, God is a God who protests against the perpetrators of suffering by co-participating in the life of the victim, Jesus and Israel, under the persecution of National Socialism. Genuine forgiveness comes from the one who is castigated and victimized.

In the *theologia crucis* God is the God of compassion, bringing forgiveness and reconciliation to the world through Jesus—the innocent Jewish victim. God's grace of forgiveness brings the logic of sacrifice and scapegoating to an end. Poetic language is meshed with mimetic praxis in seeking the transformation of the actual world. Poetic reference and corresponding mimetic praxis gain subversive potential in Jesus' parable of the prodigal Son. The parabolic language of the forgiveness of sin turns the conventional orientation upside down while simultaneously changing the life of the prodigal.

God's intensive relationship with the world and God's compassion in its radicality can be seen in God's allowing God's self to be pushed out of the world. This is because the gospel allows the world to exist in its own dimension and reality, in light of God's reconciliation with the world. Bonhoeffer's theology of divine compassion leads us to a missiological hermeneutic of self-exposure to the other in the world come of age. God in the reconciled world speaks to us through the face of the other who is full of God's promise. This perspective leads to protest against bourgeois self-satisfaction built on a convenient reversal of the gospel.[39] The gospel of the living God cannot be domesticated by anything else. *Viva vox evangelii* in Bonhoeffer's sense becomes foundational for a worldly interpretation of the subject matter of the gospel in solidarity with those on the margin. The subject matter concerns us, because the curses of the

38. Ibid., 361.
39. Ibid., 64.

ungodly are more appreciated in a radical gospel of God's reconciliation than a moralistic, therapeutic piety amounting to *deus ex machina*. The hermeneutic of the subject matter implies that the love of God embraces even the most abysmal godlessness of the world in Jesus Christ who contains the whole of humanity and the whole of God.[40] In recognition of a relativity of perspective or self-limitation in regard to the profound meaning of the gospel, the subject matter of the living gospel does not become captive to postmodern relativism.

There is no single universally valid system of metaphysics or worldview into which the subject matter of the biblical narrative can be reduced. There is no transcendental standpoint outside history, no adopting God's point of view. God comes to us as word-event in the embodiment of Jesus. The focus of missiological hermeneutic is an understanding of the biblical narrative through its subject matter, the living voice of God in interaction with the other, constantly deepening our engagement with the gospel in the missional context.

Theologia Crucis: The Aesthetic Dimension of Mission and Discursive Praxis

In this light the *theologia crucis* becomes foundational for our discursive-missional praxis which speaks the truth of the gospel audaciously and fearlessly (*parrhēsia*) in the integrity of life before God and the world. The *theologia crucis* remains a corrective to the *theologia gloraie* built on the American *Deus ex machina* in its civil religious settings. *Theologia crusis* implies the divine self-exposure, so a theological aesthetic can be found in the face of Jesus Christ who was crucified for the mission of *parrhēsia* regarding the kingdom of God.

The new form of the beauty of God discloses the Trinity and its beauty in the life, death and resurrection of Jesus Christ. In Jesus Christ we see the beautiful form of the divine compassion and embrace. Our recognition of God in Jesus Christ accepts *theologia crucis* not only as the source of truth and goodness, but also the source of beauty in recognition of the other. The aesthetical dimension of the *theologia crucis* relates to the beauty of grace which God has and continues to accomplish for the world through Word and the Spirit.

40. Ibid., 72, 74.

Theologia crucis relativizes all worldly measures of beauty and glory and even turns American religiosity of Moralistic Therapeutic Deism upside down. Trinitarian mission in terms of a *parrhēssia* of *theologia crucis* incorporates a postmodern sensitivity to the others, thus ethical responsibility and solidarity with the other comes from God's promise.

In Jesus Christ God has said "Yes" and "Amen" to all. This "Yes" and "Amen" is the sure foundation for the church's discipleship and mission of evangelization. Because of Jesus's life on earth, our life in the midst of turbulent times has a meaning. "The unbiblical idea of 'meaning' is indeed only a translation of what the Bible calls 'promise.'"[41] God's *promissio* finds its place in its life-giving meaning, inviting people to the message of God's reconciliation which recognizes the worldly reality and maturity. A query of life meaning begins with the biblical concept of the *pro-missio* for all, in which God's mission is understood as a *diakonia* of reconciliation.[42] This perspective undergirds an aesthetical dimension of missional theology and evangelization.

A hermeneutic of self-exposure to the other and self-renewal in dialogue with the other strives to seek the meaning of God's narrative in service to the world in terms of the grace of justification (already), justice, and the eschatological coming (not yet). Thus the missiological hermeneutic takes a breathtaking journey between the Scylla of exclusive bigotry and the Charybdis of postmodern perspectivism. A genuine concern about difference and otherness originates in God's act of reconciliation in the life of Christ through justification, forgiveness, justice. This perspective guides the church as the community of vocation and promotes faithful discipleship to Christ's prophetic ministry and mission for the world. "The Church confesses that she has taken in vain the name of Jesus Christ, for she has been ashamed of this name before the world . . . She has stood by while violence and wrong were being committed under cover of this name . . . she has not raised her voice on behalf of the victims and has not found ways to hasten to their aid. She is guilty of the deaths of the weakest and most defenseless brothers of Jesus Christ."[43]

41. Bonhoeffer, *Letters and Papers*, 391.

42. Gollwitzer, *Krummes Holz*, 42.

43. Bonhoeffer, *Ethics*, 113–14.

12

Public Church and Theology of Hope

In the previous chapter we had an opportunity to critically deal with American civil religion and its political ramifications for congregational life. We observed that the millennial view is still influential in American religious life and evangelistic efforts. American civil religion and exceptionalism could be traced to American Puritan roots. The Puritans also had utopian ideals. The Pilgrims had endured a transatlantic exodus and understood their role in creating a millenarian kingdom of God on earth.

In later developments, genuine faith became intertwined with a millennialist view of the role of America in world history. The result is embedded within the idea of manifest destiny. The destiny became manifest in America's success in expansion and conquest. In the development of the American sense of divine mission and providence, we notice that there are two different views of millennialism. Postmillennialists anticipate that the kingdom of God would come more gradually and progressively through evangelism and social reform. They expect Christ to return after ("post-") the kingdom of God had been inaugurated. On this view the vision in Revelation 19 has to do with the missionary outreach of the church. This post-millenarianism (or a historical millenarianism) is also related to utopianism and Jewish messianism. Jewish expectation of the coming Messiah implies the idea that the messiah will one day end the *galuth,* Jewish existence in exile. The thousand year messianic kingdom is the final age of the world prior to God's eternal Sabbath in the new, eternal creation.[1]

⟨ In addition to the postmillennialism, premillennialists expect conditions on earth to worsen through tribulation and cataclysmic change until Christ returns before ("pre-") the kingdom is established on earth.⟩ This apocalyptic view is found in the end-time views that are popular in modern evangelical or fundamentalist circles. An apocalyptic outlook ensnares religious people to take refuge in escapist attitudes.

It is important to critically examine the premillennial notion in the American context. Such a critical examination is helpful for us to understand church as the community of hope and develop the eschatological dimension of Christian mission in a new way. A biblically grounded eschatological view of Jesus Christ and Israel becomes foundational for shaping a missional church as a public church, coming into a critical encounter with eschatological premillenarism. The Reformation teaching of the grace of justification and Christian faith are connected with the church's mission, which will be reinterpreted in an eschatological framework for the sake of cultivating a faith community of hope and mission.

An Apocalyptic Outlook in American Religious Life

The idea of the Rapture was systematized by a British evangelical preacher and founder of a small group known as the Plymouth Brethren, John Nelson Darby (1800–1882). He adopted a young girl's vision of a two-stage return of Jesus Christ.[2] Darby claimed that Christ's first return would be in secret, bringing his church out of the world and up to heaven (the rapture). After seven years of global tribulation, Christ would return to establish a Jerusalem-based kingdom on earth (cf. 1 Thess 4:17). In his mission to America between 1859 and 1877 Darby won many converts to his idea of the rapture. He invented the notion of "dispensations," a scheme which holds that God has divided all of human history into seven distinct dispensations (or ages). The Scofield Reference Bible was published first in 1909 and became an important tool for popularizing Darby's system of dispensationalism. His dispensationalist system of God's end-times plan is based on three verses at the

---

1. Moltmann, *Coming of God*, 149.
2. Rossing, *Rapture Exposed*, 22.

end of chapter 9 of Daniel (Dan 9:25–27). This teaching continues to be influential and popularized in today's American context.

The Rapturist Scenario and Its Implication of Global Politics

More recently the *Left Behind* series (by Tim LaHaye and Jerry Jenkins), a popularization of Hal Lindsey's interpretation of Revelation as expressed in his book, *The Late Great Planet Earth* captured the imaginations of millions of Americans and sold millions of copies between the years 1995 and 2004. Lindsey adored John Darby. A key text for the cataclysmic scenario is Dan 9:20–27. A period of seventy weeks of years—a "week" of years equals seven years—is described as passing before the end time. There is the gap of time of two hundred or more years of church history from the first century to the present. The line between Dan 9:26 and 9:27 is interpreted as predicting that gap. After the Jews rejected Christ, God stopped the clock of prophecy with just one seven-year period remaining. God continued fulfilling prophecies through Dan 9:26, then stopped the clock for over two thousand years without fulfilling 9:27. The foundation of the modern state of Israel in 1948 led many dispensationalists to believe that God was divinely protecting the Jewish nation and to expect that the temple could be rebuilt on the site where the Dome of the Rock now stands.

In contrast, biblical scholars such as Craig Koester claim that seven weeks of years (=forty-nine years) and sixty-two weeks of years (=four hundred and thirty-four years) in Dan 9:25 elapse between the command to rebuild the wall of Jerusalem and the coming of the anointed one. Furthermore, this anointed figure would be Joshua or Zerubbabel (Ezra 3:2; Zech 4:14), or perhaps Cyrus (Isa 45:1). The remaining period of four hundred and thirty-four years is approximately the period from the rebuilding of Jerusalem to the Seleucid persecution in the second century BCE in which Daniel was written.[3]

At any rate, expecting the social historical signals that God's clock was beginning to tick, Lindsey offered a forced interpretation of the events of the end times in the light of the antagonism between the United States and the Soviet Union. It caused an impressive boost in popularity for millennialism in the late twentieth century in North America. According to Lindsey, Armageddon depicts the horrors of war in the

---

3. Koester, *Revelation*, 25; see footnote 25.

day of H-bombs and super weapons. After the antichrist assembles the forces of the rest of the world through communist countries, they will have a conflict with the kings of the East. This war will extend throughout Israel, in the vortex that is centered at the valley of Megiddo. In Rev 14:20 mass slaughtering is predicted. Finally all the cities of the nations will be destroyed (Rev 16:19). It seems to indicate that an all-out attack of ballistic missiles is carried out upon the great metropolitan areas of the world. In the climax of the battle of Armageddon in which all life will be destroyed on earth, Jesus Christ will return and save people from self-extinction.[4]

In the circle of fundamentalist Christians, there is a strong expectation of the great rapture of believers in the image of a countdown of a missile launch before the annihilation of the world in the fire storm of nuclear bombs. The term rapture refers to believers being caught up to meet the Lord in the air (1 Thess 4:16–17). The faithful will be snatched from the earth to spare them from the tribulation transpiring before Christ's second coming. The church will vanish during the tribulation, just as the church is not found from Rev 1:1–3:22 until 22:16. The tribulation is expected to last for seven years, the final week of years in Dan 9:27. Be that as it may, according to 1 Thess 4:16–17 we do not find any hint of tribulation. Rather welcoming Jesus Christ is not done in secret, but "with a cry of command, with the archangel's call and with the sound of God's trumpet."

Armageddon is the name given to the cataclysmic conflicts transpiring at the end of the tribulation. The word Armageddon (Rev 16:16) refers to the mountain of Megiddo located in northern Israel. Old Testament references to Megiddo link it to battles in which the adversaries of Israel are defeated (Deborah's victory over Israel's foes, Judg 5:19) or it is the place where worshippers of a pagan god mourn in light of the coming day of the Lord's victory (Zech 12:11).

According to the rapturist scenario, the word "Armageddon" becomes synonymous with nuclear warfare and the annihilation of civilization featured with missiles, atomic warheads, squadrons of aircraft, and tank brigades in the Middle East. Armageddon is usually extended to various battle scenes depicted in Rev 19:11–21. A composite picture of the ballet is generated by linking Scripture verses from Isa 63:1–6 to other pieces from Joel 3:1–2 and 3:9–17, and to Zech 12:1–9 and

---

4. Lindsey and Carlson, *Late Great Planet Earth*, 152–57.

to additional pieces from Rev 14:14–20; 16:12–16 and 19:11–21. This composite picture is used as a tool to refer to current developments in military technology and global politics. However, the only weapon in John's account of the great battle in 19:11–21 is the word of God.

At any rate, in the rapurist composite picture, Russia is identified as the nation of Gog (Ezek 38–39) and the king of the north (Daniel 11) attacks Israel in order to gain control of the Middle East. When the Russians are joined by the king of the south (assumed to be an Arab confederacy) and by the kings from the east (taken to be a Chinese army of two hundred million soldiers) (Rev 9:13–19; 16:12), the conflict escalates into global war. In the culmination of the battle, Christ returns and defeats his enemies in Jordan (Isa 63:1–6) at Megiddo, called in Hebrew Harmagedon (Rev 16:12–16) in the valley of Jehoshaphat (Joel 3:1–2, 9–17) and at Jerusalem (Zech 12:1–9), leaving carnage on the battlefield (Ezek 39:18). The millennial kingdom begins after Armageddon is over and Satan has been bound for a thousand years (Rev 20:1–6). The Old Testament prophecies then come to their fulfillment (Isa 65:20–21, 25; Isa 2:4; Mic 4:3). After the thousand years have ended, Satan will be released and utterly defeated. The last judgment will occur and eternity will begin. Nevertheless, there is no reference to the rapture in Daniel or Revelation.

The "gospel" of rapturism is escape by glorifying violence and war rather than the incarnation, death, and resurrection. The *parousia* of Jesus Christ is based on the Lamb's self-giving love in the revelation. According to the proponents of the Rapture, Jesus will come to snatch the chosen people up to heaven before unleashing a seven-year period of global tribulation and destruction on earth (Rev 12). Rapture and Armageddon scenarios create a popular, powerful imagery of the biblical eschatology in the American religious soul. James Watt, Reagan-era Secretary of the Interior told US senators that our living at the brink of the end-times justifies removing the nation's forests and reducing other environmental policies.[5] John Hagee, pastor of the Cornerstone megachurch in San Antonio in an interview with BBC stated: "I believe in my mind that the Third World War has begun. I believe it began on 9/11."[6]

However, Revelation was not written for rapturists fleeing from the world, who tell the world goodbye and want to go to heaven. Revelation

5. Rossing, *Rapture Exposed*, 70.

6. Ibid., 15.

does not fictionalize a future seven-year period of tribulation as the ra-
purists do. The rapturist scenario jumps from Daniel 9 to 1 Thessalonians
4 and then to Revelation 6, etc., in a method by which verses of the
Bible are forced together like pieces of a jigsaw puzzle.[7] In contrast to
rapurist expectations, Revelation begins, "John, to the seven churches
that are in Asia" (Rev 1:4), and was written to openly communicate with
seven particular Christian congregations in the first-century Asia Minor
(modern-day Turkey). The message of the Revelation urges Christians
of the first century to resist Roman imperial authority when it comes to
issues of persecution (2:9–11) and eating food sacrificed to idols (2:14,
20) involved in imperial cult and shrines in a number of cities in Asia
Minor. The blood of the saints was shed by the power of Rome, the city
set on seven hills (6:9–11; 17:6, 9; 18:24). As Babylon had destroyed the
first temple, the Romans destroyed the second temple (17:1–18). It is
vital to read the narrative of Revelation *first* in its own historical context,
and only then move to interpret its eschatological meaning for today's
church and congregational life.

Millennialism and Eschatology

The words of Jesus' prayer in Matt 6:10—"Your kingdom come. Your will
be done, on earth as it is in heaven"—are the epitome of Christian hope.
The "eschaton" is the goal of church and history, including two aspects:
end and completion (or fulfillment). God's dwelling with us on earth as
envisioned in Revelation opposes *Left Behind*'s dualism.[8] In such apocalyptic ideas of the destruction of the earthly environment we may see
signs of the end (Mark 13:28–29) which must not be confused with the
end itself. No one knows the time of the end except for God the Father
(Mark 13:32).

Drawing upon the text of Revelation (7; 20), Moltmann proposes
an eschatological millennialism by incorporating a premillennial aspect
into Christian eschatology. The resurrection from the dead leads into
a premillennial reign of Christ before the universal raising of the dead
will begin for the last judgment.[9] Moltmann's project of eschatological
millennialism is at the heart of the resurrection of the crucified Christ. It

---

7. Koester, *Revelation*, 38.

8. Rossing, *Rapture Exposed*, 11.

9. Moltmann, *Coming of God*, 195.

has a very strong political implication. In contrast, Pannenberg's theology of prolepsis draws upon the general resurrection of the dead in the final time of divine judgment. It does not include a millennial reign of Jesus Christ. This has theological advantages, but tends to lose the political dimension of eschatology. [10]

Moltmann conceives of the thousand years' reign of Revelation 20 as the messianic kingdom of Jews and Christians in an earthly, historical context. The thousand year reign of Christ, the kingdom of peace, is the counterpart to the antichrist's destruction of the world.[11] Unlike Moltmann's speculation, however, Revelation 20 cannot be used as the proof text to give credence to a literal thousand year reign of Christ on earth as the messianic community of the Jews and Christians. This is because ". . . with the Lord one day is like a thousand years, and a thousand years are like one day" (2 Pet 3:8).

Moltmann argues that our future resurrection (first resurrection) after the second coming of Jesus Christ leads into a premillennial reign of Christ on earth. In doing so he replaces John's concept of the first resurrection in the heavenly place by his concept of the resurrection from the dead in the historical setting. However, for the Apostle Paul the first resurrection is at the beginning of the Christian life, in baptism: "But if we have died with Christ [in baptism], we believe that we shall also live with him" (Rom 6:8). A "presentative" dimension of the eschatological event of Christ in Word and sacrament (the language of faith) must be seen in connection with an eschatological resurrection from the dead in the context of heavenly worship (language of hope, Rev 7:15). The presentative dimension concerning faith and the sacraments is neglected in Moltmann's theology of premillennial eschatology.

It is certain that John took over the Jewish apocalyptic tradition about the messianic kingdom and the new creation of all things. But he gives it a new outlook and meaning by reframing the Jewish tradition. The millennial kingdom is pictured as the one which fulfills the Old Testament promises (Isa 65:20–21). In this kingdom "the wolf and the lamb shall feed together" and "the lion shall eat straw like the ox" (Isa 65:25). The city of Jerusalem is central to such hopes. People "beat their swords into plowshares and their spears into pruning hooks; nation shall not lift up sword against nation, neither shall they learn war any more"

10. Ibid., 151, 195.

11. Ibid., 198–99, 201.

(Isa 2:2, 4; Mic 4:1, 3). What distinguishes John's perspective from the Jewish one is his emphasis on the Lamb as the center of the throne of God. John also highlights resistance to the godless empire of Rome for the sake of testimony to Jesus and the word of God. It refuses to conform to their idol worship and cults.

It is important to consider that Old Testament passages are extensively used in describing the New Jerusalem in Rev 21:1–22:5. In Rev 20:4–6 the promises of the book of Isaiah will be fulfilled when God creates new heavens and a new earth (Rev 21:1; Isa 65:17), the world of the New Jerusalem (21:24–26). In this context, one is not certain where the vision of the thousand year reign of the saints takes place: on earth or in heaven. The seer John saw [God's] thrones or mentions a throne vision and those seated on them who had been beheaded for their testimony to the gospel of Jesus Christ and for the word of God (20:4) in the heavenly worship setting of God's temple.[12] In this light we can understand the gospel of Jesus Christ as the hope of Israel.

Jesus Christ and the Hope of Israel

Jewish perspective on messianism undergirds apocalypticism, and advocates eschatology of a nationalistic character including the reestablishment of the House of David. As Scholem argues, Jewish messianism is a theory of catastrophe in its origin and by its nature.[13] The days of the Messiah are Israel's, having little to do with days of peace for all nations. Given this fact, it is unfortunate that Moltmann incorporates Jewish messianism into the Christian premillennarian dream of reign with Christ, emphasizing Christ's resurrection from dead.

As the *Augsburg Confession* states, "Likewise rejected are some Jewish teachings, which have also appeared in the present, that before the resurrection of the dead saints and righteous people will possess a secular kingdom and will annihilate all the ungodly."[14] The focus in the Revelation was living and reigning "with Christ" (20:4, 6) rather than establishing a thousand years' reign on earth.[15] Paul's eschatological expectation of liberation of the creation from its bondage to decay and its

12. Whenever thrones are mentioned in the context of Revelation, it is implied that they are always in heaven. See Ford, *Revelation*, 349.

13. Scholem, *Messianic Idea*, 7.

14. "Augsburg Confession" (in the German text), BC 50.

15. Koester, *Revelation*, 184–85.

obtaining of the freedom of the glory of the children of God (Rom 8:21) finds its culmination in John's description of a new creation as the goal of God's purpose. By "destroying those who destroy the earth" (11:18), in the end "the kingdom of the world" can truly become "the kingdom of our Lord and of his Messiah" (11:15).

Within the framework of Revelation we also observe that a new heaven and a new earth are echoed in Isa 65:17. The New Jerusalem appears in splendor like a bride who is adorned for her husband (reminiscent of Isa 52:1; 61:10; 65:18). God's eschatological comfort—God will wipe away every tear from their eyes and death—corresponds to Isa 25:8. The end of mourning, crying, and pain, and the passing away of the former things fulfill Isa 65:17, 19. God makes all things new (Isa 43:19) since God is the beginning and the end (Isa 44:6).

However, from the perspective of Revelation, God's promise given to the prophets is fulfilled, transformed, and completed in the temple which is God and the Lamb whose radiant power and presence are manifested throughout the city. This is a Christian interpretation of eschatology transforming Jewish messianism. It emphasizes the inseparable relationship between God and the Lamb in the presence of the divine Shekinah. John's hope for the healing of the nations (Rev 22:2) stands as a sign of the transformation of the reality of all life and the world. The hope of Revelation is the Lamb of God, the embodiment of God's mission. It represents God's vision for us and for the world, in which the New Jerusalem (Revelation 21–22) becomes an earth-centered vision of our future in contrast to the escapism and rapturist "heavenism." The New Jerusalem comes down out of heaven from God down to earth, and the New Jerusalem announces God's eschatological Immanuel (Rev 21:2–3). Jesus Christ as the root of David (22:16) is also the hope for Israel and he fulfills promises which were made through the prophets and Israel's eschatological vision of the restored Jerusalem. God and Christ as the end of all things (Rev 1:8, 17; 21:6; 22:13) are inseparably connected with "blessed is the one who keeps the words of the prophecy of this book" (22:7; cf.22: 10, 18, 19).

As for Christian eschatology, Christian hope is to clarify and actualize what we have already received as a gift of God through Jesus Christ. It articulates the present reality of the eschatology. God gives a sign of eternal life in our present life through Word and sacrament. "Let anyone who wishes take the water of life as a gift" (Rev 22:17) is foundational for the invitation of all to God's *pro-missio*. This theology of hope, which is interconnected with the *theologia crucis* and the *theologia vitae*, makes us sober and critical concerning millenialist feelings of violence or terror. The biblical witness of the "presentative" eschatology of God in Jesus Christ retains its reality from the eschatological coming of God. As conversely, our language of eschatology can be actualized and embodied in the framework of "presentative" eschatology which has begun in the ministry and mission of Christ. The two forms of biblical eschatology (a presentative horizon and an eschatological coming) are mutually attested in the biblical context. Christian eschatology is the Christian hope which is grounded in God's promise, God's grace of justification through God's reconciliation with the world, by linking the end-time consummation of God's reign to the resurrection of the dead. God's promise proceeds and undergirds the prolepsis, not vice versa.[16]

In understanding Luther's theology of justification (*simul peccator et justus*), the issue is proclamation of the new existence, so that God's grace integrates the human existence into the future of God. Luther's theology of justification should be understood as a theology of God's future in an eschatological sense. A life is not justified by love or by the eschatological expectation of resurrection, but only by faith that sets life upon a new foundation. This foundation is the life, the death, and the resurrection of Jesus Christ who is the certainty of faith. Faith in the true presence of Christ is accompanied by love and hope. The qualitatively final word is the word of forgiveness and the word which justifies by God's forgiveness alone. Justification as the last word is the complete breaking off of the penultimate.[17]

Jesus Christ, Mission, and the Kingdom of Israel

Jesus Christ integrates Israel's existence and hope into his promise of the kingdom of God for all nations in Luke 22:29. In Luke 24:21 the disciples on the road to Emmaus expressed their "political" hope that Jesus was the one to redeem Israel. In this narrative we see the Jewish hope for a Messiah who brings about the liberation of Israel from Roman domination. In this Jewish form of historical messianism, the reign of the Messiah is brought about by a Jewish ruler powerful enough to gather

16. Pannenberg, *Systematic Theology*, 3:585.
17. Bonhoeffer, *Ethics*, 124.

the Jewish exiles back to the land of Israel. There he will reestablish a Torah government, and rebuild the Temple in Jerusalem. It requires maximum Jewish political activity, centered in the land of Israel.

At the beginning of the book of Acts, Luke narrates the Jewish hope as the first form expressed by the disciples. "Lord, is this the time when you will restore the kingdom to Israel?" (Acts 1:6). According to Jesus, God alone has set it in God's power and authority regarding when the times or periods are right to bring the state of Israel into being again. Jewish hope is awakened by God with respect to the death and resurrection of Jesus. However, Jesus' commandment to the disciples to be his witness in Jerusalem, in all Judea and Samaria, and to the ends of the earth is embedded within this context of the restoration of Israel (Acts 1:8).

In Acts 3:21 the verb *apokatastasis* is related to the coming times, *kairoi* and *chronoi*. It speaks of the times of refreshing coming from the presence of the Lord, in the sense of relaxation and relief from the pressures of history. This is the time of universal restoration that God had announced long ago through the prophets. The Bible quotation of Acts 3:22–23 suggests from Deut 18:15 that God will raise up for Israel a prophet like Moses from the people of Israel, and all should listen to him. Peter refers to Jesus—Jesus is the *apokatastasis panton* in person to be awaited in the future, the restorative work of God. In Lev 23:29 "For anyone who does not practice self-denial during that entire day [Yom Kippur, the day of atonement] shall be cut off from the people." However, Luke says: "And it will be that everyone who does not listen to that prophet will be utterly rooted out of the people" (Acts 3:23). Jesus is presented in these verses as the Yom Kippur, the Day of Atonement. The day of liberation from the pressures of history is the day of Jesus, the time of refreshment. "[t]urn to God so that your sins may be wiped out . . ." (Acts 3:19).

In the Hebrew context the aspect of the atoning death of Christ (Heb 9:11–14) can be best comprehended as cleansing from defilement. Christ's exaltation accomplishes what the high priest's action foreshadows (Heb 8:1–2), once for all (9:24–28), that is, a complete and final atonement of Yom Kippur.[18]

In the person of Jesus a new Yom Kippur could be expected in which context *apokatastasis panton* (the time of universal restoration)

18. Koester, *Hebrews*, 412, 427.

is spoken of in an eschatological perspective. The content of the covenant which God made with the ancestors (Acts 3:25) is the blessing of Abraham (Gen 12:3); mission is to be a blessing for the nations. God will bless Israel anew though Jesus who will become a blessing for Israel and the nations. The mission to the Gentiles and God's will for the restoration of the kingdom of Israel belong together. This is because no great difficulties of rigid and strict requirements of the Torah are imposed on the Gentiles (Acts 15:19). The Noahide *mitzvoth* (abstaining from things polluted by idols, from fornication and from whatever has been strangled and from blood) are sufficient for them (Acts 15:20). In the praise of Simeon Jesus is "a light to revelation to the Gentiles and for glory to your people Israel" (Luke 2:32). In Acts 13:23 Jesus is designated as a descendent of David and named a Savior of Israel. The *dabar* allows peace to be preached to the Jews through Jesus Christ the lord of all (Acts 10:36). In this regard, a vision of the thousand year kingdom of peace for Israel would become meaningful in the life of Jesus, a new Yom Kippur who was to bring a time for Israel to breathe more easily.[19] This perspective strengthens the grace of justification (forgiveness of sin in the sense of Yom Kippur) and reframes Jewish hope through the death and resurrection of Jesus Christ. God's covenant with the Jews is unconditional and confirmed through Jesus Christ. "To make disciples of all the nations" (Matt 28:19) is to be seen in light of the gospel of God's shalom in Jesus Christ for Israel and all nations.[20]

In this light it is of special significance to consider Paul's theology of Israel in Romans 9–11. It is unfortunate that Bosch downgrades this biblical text as sufficiently ambiguous because of his preference for transforming mission. He argues that it is a dangerous theological misconception to articulate a direct connection between Israel as a theological entity and the survival of the Jews. It is hardly possible for him to interpret Paul's theology of Israel in Romans 9–11 as proposing a new model of God's mission as a mutual dialogue with respect between the church and Israel.[21] It has been generally claimed that Paul envisions the conversion of the Jewish people through their acceptance of the gospel. However, if the Jewish people will be saved by their acceptance of the

19. Marquardt, *Theological Audacities*, 99.

20. Lindbeck, "Postmodern Hermeneutics," 111–12.

21. Bosch, *Transforming Mission*, 173.

gospel within history, there would be no mystery of God in Paul's consideration of Israel.

In contrast to Bosch, I find it more meaningful and important to involve Paul's theology of Israel for the sake of God's mission as fruitful dialogue between the church and Israel in which mission as constructive theology enriches itself in understanding the gospel in light of God's word of covenant and blessing in a thicker manner. Insofar as Jesus Christ comes to us through Israel, the church's dialogue with the Jewish community remains an indispensable part of the shape of the church's participation in God's mission as it is involved in Israel in both the biblical and post-biblical contexts. Paul's theology of mission must occupy a significant role in the Church's relationship with the Jewish community.

According to Arland Hultgren, in Romans 9 Paul's concern is that Israel might be saved. The only possibility of salvation is a divine act, a miraculous work of God, regardless of Israel's disobedience. He suggests that two possibilities open up: First, the people of Israel will convert at the coming of Christ, confessing him as Lord, thereby being saved by the same confession as Gentile Christians. Second, they will remain in their refusal to confess Jesus as the Christ but be saved at his *parousia* purely by the mercy of God. Hultgren concludes that "Paul envisions the salvation of Israel purely by the mercy of God at the end of history, even though the confession of Jesus as Lord is not made by its people within history itself. All is by grace alone. Israel's salvation will not be based on Torah observance, nor will it depend on their making the Christian confession, but *sola gratia*, by God's grace."[22] Here a Lutheran theology of justification *extra nos* would be projected into deepening the theology of *sola gratia* in the Jewish-Christian relationship.

Paul states that he is bound with a chain for the sake of the hope of Israel in Acts 28:20. In Rev 20, John integrates the Jewish concept of the messianic kingdom (Daniel 7; Ezekiel 37–38; Zech 14:11) with the concept of the thousand years reign with Christ (Rev 20:4); this Jewish hope is transformed, embedded within the setting of heavenly worship (Rev 7:15) in regard to Israel and all nations. As John 17:15 makes clear however, such messianic reality has nothing to do with a premillennialist or rapturist attitude: "I am not asking you to take them out of the world, but I ask you to protect them from the evil one."

22. Hultgren, *Paul's Letter to the Romans*, 423. See also Rom 11:25–32.

Isaiah's prophecy (2:4) implies that the messianic days will become days of peace for Israel. The Jewish idea of messianism can be renewed and reinterpreted as a way of promoting Christian ethics, discipleship, and mission in terms of a reflection of the eternal kingdom of God with peace and justice for all nations. The preparation of the way of God's coming requires that "the penultimate shall be respected and validated for the sake of the approaching ultimate" of God's eschatology.[23] God does not simply destroy this world, but will give it a positive completion. The Christian eschatological hope embraces and transforms the Jewish hope of a messianic kingdom in the universal sense of God's shalom, rather than in a premillennial sense.

The Lamb of God, a new Yom Kippur and universal restorer, is the foundation for the Christian hope for a new heaven and earth and also Israel. The theology of justification whose content is the forgiveness of sin and God's blessing undergirds the church's mission to the Jews and all nations for the sake of God's Shalom.

Eschatology and *Theologia Crucis*

Jesus as the man of the past, the present, and the future, in the presence of the Spirit, will accomplish his *diakonia* eschatologically in company with the people of God. God's arrival in Jesus' mission of solidarity with the poor sharpens our present participation in God's mission in history against the reality of violence and injustice. The gospel narrative discloses Christian understanding of God through the real identity of Jesus Christ in life, death and resurrection. God is the One who disclosed the authentic face of God in liberating Israel in the Exodus and also in raising Jesus of Nazareth from the dead.

In the context of Revelation we observe that there is a parallel between the Lamb of God and the Exodus of Moses (Rev 15:2–3). God heard the outcry of God's people in Egypt. God showed God's self as the liberator by sending Moses to them. The God of Israel also hears the people's distress and predicament under the oppression of Rome, liberating and healing their wounds through the Lamb of God. God's people in the Lamb join in singing the Israelite victory song after crossing the Red Sea in the Exodus story. The fatherly fellow-suffering of God is the basis for God's compassion and solidarity with God's people in the history of

---

23. Bonhoeffer, *Ethics*, 139.

Israel and also in the Son's humiliation and *diakonia* which takes place historically in his life, ministry, and cross. The God of Israel is in deep solidarity with and compassion for human suffering and predicament in the humiliation of Jesus Christ.[24]

The Reformation teaching on justification which is the Word of the gospel and *theologia crucis* is the primary and principal articulation of God's mission as the theology of journey in evangelization, witness, reconciliation, and service. Without the grace of justification there is no calling, no mission, no hope, and no ecclesial responsibility to the world. In justifying faith we uphold discipleship of faith in conformity with Jesus Christ. Congregational mission in solidarity with the public sphere does not mean accommodation or conformity to the status quo of the world, but it is the call to discipleship which follows the costly grace of Jesus Christ.[25]

Theologia Crucis: Parrhēsia and Embrace of the Other

Diaconal service and leadership has nothing to do with service to the ruling powers, rather it is engaged in tackling the cause of structural evil at the social, political, and cultural roots. An emancipating dimension of *diakonia* in congregational mission becomes an indispensable part of the church's participation in God's mission. In the synoptic context, *parrhēsia* is used extensively with reference to Jesus' mission. This discursive form has played a major role in the debate over Jesus' life and his messianic consciousness. Mark's form of *parrhēsia* must be sought primarily in Jesus' ministry and mission in his socio-biographical solidarity with the public sinners and tax collectors. Jesus does speak "plainly" (with *parrhēsia*) about his upcoming rejection, crucifixion, and resurrection in response to Peter's confession (Mark 8:32). Jesus also uses *parrhēsia* in response to the Pharisees (Luke 13:31–32).

A discursive praxis of *parrhēsia* in Christian mission points to the third way: announcing the Good news by caring for the weaker while encouraging the rich to take seriously today's "Lazarus" as the children of God. In the missional context, a Christian discourse of *parrhēsia* can be implemented and promoted for the sake of the testimony to Jesus Christ and the word of God (Rev 20:4).

24. Cf. Fretheim, *Suffering of God*.
25. Bonhoeffer, *Cost of Discipleship*, 1, 57.

The cultural realm is acknowledged in light of God's eschatological-universal reign and its validity finds a place in God's reconciliation with the world. The church of Jesus Christ has nothing to do with racial division, because its congregational mission and witness are grounded in the divine life and communion of the triune God in service, forgiveness, and embrace of the world. "There was a great multitude that no one could count, from every nation, from all tribes and peoples and languages, standing before the throne and before the Lamb" (Rev 7:9). *Theologia crucis*, understood eschatologically, proclaims that the murderers will not ultimately triumph over their victims. This perspective retains the hope that injustice will not be victorious, but that God's justification in wiping away of the tears of the innocent victims will be the last word.

In an eschatological perspective, a formula of Jesus' descent to hell is of special significance to theology of God's mission in the life of Christ. Luther's reflection of this formula is connected with his exposition of 1 Timothy—God desires everyone to be saved—implying that "this is an exclusive proposition expressed in universal terms."[26] It is beyond the theological imagination to rationalize a doctrine of universal salvation in reference to a formula of Jesus' descent to hell, for salvation and final judgment belong to the mystery of God. Such an idea is at most a sigh of theology.

However, the *theologia crucis*, embedded within a formula of Jesus' descent to hell presents itself as the completion of Christ's suffering. Christ "conquered the devil, destroyed the power of hell, and took from the devil all his power."[27] ". . . neither death, nor life, nor angels, nor rulers, nor things present, nor things to come, nor powers, nor height, nor depth, nor anything else in all creation, will be able to separate us from the love of God in Christ Jesus our Lord" (Rom 8:38). The crucified Christ descended to hell preached to the spirits in prison, who formerly did not obey (1 Pet 3:18). Through him gospel was preached even to the dead (1 Pet 4:6).

This biblical perspective implies that a preaching was done before the most dreadful sinners—those spirits that were in prison since their disobedience in the days of Noah (cf. Gen 6:1–4). Jesus' preaching in this regard becomes foundational for Christian evangelization even to the heathen rulers in the midst of suffering and death. The word-event

26. LW 28:260; cf. BC 514.

27. "Formula of Concord," SD. Art. IX. BC 635.

seen in light of Christ's preaching to the spirits in prison is the prototype of Christian evangelization and God's mission in a universal horizon which emphasizes the limitless extent of the gospel of suffering; in other words, the universality of the gospel for all. [28] This perspective contradicts a rapurist elitism which divides the raptured from those left behind through the framework of eschatological double election.

God's Mission and in Eschatological Hope

Christians live between the "already" and the "not yet." This ongoing tension between the "already" and the "not yet" is characteristic of Christian faith and mission in its entirety. The time between the ascension of Christ and his second coming is the "time in between," that is the time of mission. With Christ a new division of time began because the promise of the Old Testament is fulfilled in Christ and salvation is manifested and takes place in Christ.

In this regard we examine the often-quoted dictum of Martin Kähler: "Mission is the mother of theology."[29] This statement leads us to state that theology was formed when church planters and waterers (1 Cor 3:16) reflected upon God's salvific drama in specific cultural and missional contexts. The New Testament writers wrote of a church which, because of its missionary encounter with the world, was forced to theologize. However, I understand this perspective in a qualified sense in regard to eschatology. If mission gives birth to Christian theology, what happened to apocalyptic as the mother of theology (Ernst Käsemann)? Wouldn't it be more correct to say that the in-breaking reality of God in the death and resurrection of Jesus Christ grounded the church and guided the people of God toward God's mission in Christ, pointing to the Kingdom of God? The cross and resurrection is the central apocalyptic moment for mission. The Easter experience in early Christianity recognized Christ's mission and his future in this eschatological light. The church's mission to the world was charged by the risen Christ and continues to be examined and fulfilled in search for the hope of God's mission in regard to renewing and transforming the world.

In other words, the task and mission of the church is shaped and guided by the eschatological hope of the coming kingdom of God which

28. Reicke, *Epistles of James, Peter, and Jude*, 111.

29. Bosch, *Transforming Mission*, 16.

has broken into the world in Jesus Christ, the eschatological Lamb of God. The eschatological hope of Jesus Christ, in whose death and resurrection God's action became a present reality (the grace of justification and forgiveness of sin), was the mother of Christian theology and the ground for God's mission, in which the church is called to participate.

The history of creation must be interpreted in the light of God's *pro-missio* and *missio* in the emancipation of Israel from Egypt and the eschatological event of new creation in Jesus Christ through the grace of justification and reconciliation (2 Cor 5:17). God is the one who causes breath to enter the dry bones and makes them alive (Ezek 37:5–6). In Abraham's life we perceive that faith generates hope in the fulfillment of God's promise (Heb 11:1). Hope springs from faith which is also the basis and presupposition in Christian existence of love through service and congregational life. God in Jesus Christ is God of the future. Hope in diaconal witness characterizes the Christian church as congregational existence in evangelical freedom, action, discipleship, and movement. The Holy Spirit awakens congregational life to life in dynamic hope, making the people of God into God's created co-workers, summoning a new order and orientation toward the life-giving mission of the triune God.

Luther's concept of the "not-yet" *parousia* in understanding a relationship between justification and eschatology underlines the future and is the first installment of the Spirit (2 Cor 1:22). The justified sinner does not live according to the "not fully" known future of God despite its eschatological witness to the new heaven and earth in the context of Revelation. But they live a life of discipleship under God's grace in the mundane world, going toward the new heaven and new earth through evangelization, social service, missional discipleship, and congregational stewardship. Luther is convinced of Revelation as a promise in which if "the word of the gospel remains pure among us, and we love and cherish it, we shall not doubt that Christ is with us, even when things are at their worst. . . . Through and beyond all plagues, beasts, and evil angels, Christ is nonetheless with his saints and wins the final victory."[30] Luther in his exegesis of Rom 3:4 articulates the internal unity between the justification of the ungodly and God proper. Internally, God as well as

---

30. LW 35:409–11.

God's Word are righteous and true. It is essential to give space for God by believing and accepting the Word of God.[31]

The church, as sinner, lives in a sinful reality, but as righteous it lives in hope (Rom 4:7). This eschatological perspective accentuates the faith community as the community of hope and mission. In light of this, I distinguish my position from a pan-eschatological or premillennial illusion of transposing and dissolving everything temporal and particular (even domesticating Jewish expectation) into the principle of hope or future. Exegetically speaking, the resurrection from the dead (Phil 3:11) (indicative of elective resurrection of the believers) and the resurrection of the dead (general resurrection of the unrepentant) does not necessarily presuppose a chronological interval. The resurrection of Christ, the resurrection of the believers at his *parousia*, and Christ's destruction of death at the end corresponds to Revelation's (20:4, 14). Paul does not envisage a temporal period of Christ's reign in a premillenarian way. By thinking in these biblical terms, we are able to avoid the unnecessary puzzles emerging from taking the notion of a premillennial period in a literal sense.[32]

The time of revelation (Christ's mission) as the time of fulfillment is essentially connected with the time of expectation of Christ's *parousia* in our remembrance of Christ's Easter (Heb 13:8). We live in hope and mission because Jesus himself has promised his coming (Rev 22, 7, 20) as the consummator of the church's mission. This shapes aspects of the eschatological hope of new creation. We respond to such promise with maranatha, "Our Lord, come!"(1 Cor 16: 22). Christian hope without faith and love remains vulnerable to the reality of *simul peccator et justus* in human and social life. It is important that we ground Christian eschatology in the *pro-missio Dei* by seeking faith, love, and hope in an integrative way of combining the presentative, social existential horizon of eschatology with the future of the coming of God's kingdom. The "eschaton" as God's coming and arrival (hope) does not make the grace of justification (faith) and reconciliation (love) fragmentary and provisional. The future of God is already occurring in our lives, and is also still to come. [33] Faith and love rejoice in hopeful expectation of what

31. WA 56, 226; Luther's lecture on Romans 1515–16.

32. Bauckham, *Theology of the Book of Revelation*, 108. For the rejoinder of Moltmann's premillennial eschatology see Bauckham, "Millennium," 143–47.

33. Vicedom, *Mission of God*, 31.

is to come, joyously participating in an eschatological-transformative dimension of God's mission in our present history.

Christian mission invites the ungodly to reconciliation with God (2 Cor 5:18ff.) and confirms God's *pro-missio and missio* to Abraham and the prophetic eschatology of Isaiah (Isa 2:1–4; 25:6–8; 45:18–25; 60:1–22). In the end, God in Jesus Christ is the source of all promises, characterizing promise as the Christological structure of eschatology.[34] According to Käsemann, Jesus' prayer "Your kingdom come . . . on earth as it is in heaven" must be interpreted as a petition to God as well as a critical challenge to evil structures. The eschatological coming of God's kingdom must be translated into a prophetic, radical concern for the penultimate.[35]

The missional nature of church is understood and characterized by the metaphor of a pilgrim and wanderer. The church is on a journey like Abraham with God's people. Thus the church lives in the suffering of the people of the world.[36] A hope for the new creation comes from the promise of the Word of God—"See, I am making all things new" (Rev 21:5). God's kingdom is coming in two ways: It comes through the Word and through faith in our present time and, in eternity, it comes through the final revelation of Jesus Christ. Eschatological dynamism in both the "already: and the "not yet" activates God's mission among us through the Word and the power of the Holy Spirit until the final removal of sin and death. As Luther expounds on the third petition of the Lord's Prayer,

> In fact, God's good and gracious will comes about without our prayer, but we ask in this prayer that it may also come about in and among us . . . . Whenever God breaks and hinders every evil scheme and will . . . whenever God strengthens us and keeps us steadfast in his Word and in faith until the end of our lives.[37]

---

34. Marquardt, *Was dürfen wir hoffen*, 1:350–51.

35. Käsemann, "Eschatological Royal Reign of God," 67.

36. Vicedom, *Mission of God*, 136.

37. Luther, "Small Catechism" (1529), in BC 357.

13

Public Church and
Socially Engaged Mission

Martin Marty, in his analysis of Reinhold Niebuhr's work, was interested in studying what distinguishes faith and church in America from that of Europe. Sorting out the several conflicting views about the role of religion in American public life, he used the term such as public religion or the religion of the public. As we already saw, sociologist Robert Bellah published his famous essay on "civil religion," drawing upon Alexis de Tocqueville and also from Emil Durkheim's term of civil religion adopted from Rousseau's *Social Contract*.

For Marty, the term *public theology* is used to speak of biblical and doctrinal sources for public relevance. Interpreting the term public theology as accessible, whether one is a believer or not, Marty integrated the resources and arguments of public theology into an indispensable description of the American common life. Earlier religious figures such as Jonathan Edwards, Horace Bushnell, and Walter Rauschenbusch are appreciated as those who had influenced the American public and used theological language to interpret and guide the basic fabric and structure of the American common life. Furthermore, key political figures such as Benjamin Franklin, Abraham Lincoln, and Woodrow Wilson are regarded as those who drew upon scriptural and doctrinal sources to shape and guide the moral duties of the American nation. In fact, these figures mentioned above differed from civil religion, which is sharply critiqued as a new US form of cultural Protestantism, populist self-worship, or American Shinto.[1]

According to Martin Marty, the public church exists in an interfaith context and exhibits an ecumenical openness to mainline Protestantism, evangelical Protestantism, and Roman Catholicism. When the public church reflexively examines and critiques existing social practices and cultural understandings in light of its deepest religious insights into justice and the good society, it does public theology. In *The Public Church* (1981),[2] Marty included mainline Christianity—Protestantism, evangelicalism, and Catholicism—in a "communion of communions" in order to envision a public church. Marty's notion of the public church as a family of apostolic churches is sensitive to the *res publica*. As "a communion of communions," the public church lives "in response to its separate tradition and partly to the calls for a common Christian vocation."[3]

Public theology is "an effort to interpret the life of a people in the light of a transcendent reference." It is a "specifically Christian polity and witness," extending to the pluralism of peoples with whom the Church was engaged in a larger way."[4] Here the emphasis on pluralism is regarded as a sociological fact as well as a theological challenge. In Marty's view, the Christian contribution to American public theology can be made "as a critical and constructive voice" within public religion which is American public (or civil) religion. This contribution focuses on "ordering faith" by "help[ing] constitute civil, social, and political life from a theological point of view."[5]

Stackhouse further strives to relate the public character of theological discourse in interdisciplinary dialogue with the social sciences. For Stackhouse, Scripture, tradition, reason, and experience remain guides for the reconstruction of public theology in constant interaction with social human sciences in an ecumenical, global, interreligious, and pluralistic age.[6] Subsequently, public theology mobilizes Christian engagement with the major issues of society through intellectual and practical grounding. For instance, if humanity is created in God's image, genetic

1. Stackhouse, *Globalization and Grace*, 88.
2. Marty, *Public Church*.
3. Ibid., 3.
4. Ibid., 16.
5. Ibid., 16–17.
6. Stackhouse, *Public Theology*, 1–15.

research and ecology have implications for a Christian doctrine of creation. The Christian belief system regarding creation needs to be rearticulated and refined in dialogue with the scientific theory of evolution. Public theology views the fruits of modern biological, cosmological, and social sciences in light of the mystery of God's creativity. All the while, it also argues that all human sciences must be conducted in the service of truth and righteousness. This tests the moral and spiritual values of scientific discourse regarding the arrogant exploitations of the earth.[7] It takes issue with the reality of economic globalization.

The Role of Communicative Action in Public Church

Globalized civilization is expanding its international politics and global economy through political power, the extension of capital, and the spread of information through mass media. It has saturated the infrastructure of the world—shaping and generating social, cultural, and religious life according to the image of global capital. As the lifeworld becomes thus colonized (Habermas), we grow of crisis, disorder, and loss of meaning, as well as of the dynamics of protest and the utopian desire for a better life. Challenging the systematic colonization of the lifeworld, a public theology integrating a socio-critical theory of communicative action attempts to invigorate the prophetic vocation of missional congregations as public companions. Congregations are understood as primal and productive centers of theological imagination in which a critical theology of vocation undergirds a model of the church as servant. A critical theology of vocation runs counter to the individualistic notion of vocation and it argues that everyone participates in God's public world, acknowledging social places and institutions as God's companions. Here a concept of civil society is taken as the location for the congregational vocation of public companionship. Communicative moral practice is endorsed as the best ethos which can prophetically nurture the postmodern environment in the direction of sustainable justice, deliberate democracy, and freedom. Critical social theory helps congregations actualize the prophetic imagination in the North American context as well as on the global level. Thus congregations are conceptualized as places of encounter between individual-personal and civil-public life. The congregation as the community of public vocation can be seen and

7. Ibid., 20–21.

developed in light of the communicatively prophetic, public companion and reason. It brings a compassionate commitment and moral contribution to other civil institutions while contesting the systematic colonization of the lifeworld.[8]

Gary Simpson creatively develops Reformation insights into Christian vocation, paving the new terrain in emphasizing a public theology and public church dimension within the missional church conversation. He is right in noticing that the public dimension of the missional church has become a missing part within the missional church conversation as a whole. His public, communicative construction of the missional church conversation attempts to overcome the new Babylonian captivity of vocation which is based on atomistic individualism. It entails a powerful discourse of prophetic speech (in accordance with *parrhēsia*). Simpson's public theology and mission bridges a source for missional church conversation toward postcolonial theology and the World Christianity.[9]

It is essential to consider a communicative understanding and rationality as significant and valuable for the public nature of Christian theology. True public life in a civil society is led and constituted by open conversation, plural discourses, inter-subjective consensus, discursive ethical orientation, and diverse communities. Thus Christian public theology cannot exist independent of the public domain.[10]

Tracy appreciates Habermas's endeavor to develop philosophical discussions of rationality in regard to sociological discussions of modernity. Tracy's proposal clarifies the nature of public theology as fundamental, hermeneutical, systematic, and practical in terms of the revised correlational method.[11] Tracy identifies three publics—society, the academy, and the church—relevant to public theology. A public theology is to: 1) make the structure and logic of the argument explicit; 2) present arguments available to all rational persons, and; 3) demonstrate that the theological position is grounded not in the internal logic of the Christian faith but in some form of general philosophical arguments.

---

8. Simpson, *Critical Social Theory*, 141–44.

9. Simpson, "God in Global Civil Society."

10. Browning and Fiorenza, eds., *Habermas*, 1–5.

11. Tracy, "Theology, Critical Social Theory," in Browning and Fiorenza, eds., *Habermas*, 25–26.

Philosophical arguments generally available to human existence serve as the major warrant and support for all claims.

Sociological research into the social and cultural history and belief systems of American Christianity helps the congregation to become a viable community in engagement with the pubic world. Culture may contextualize the meaning of the gospel as it encounters the dynamic horizon of the living voice of God in the reconciled world. However, the God of the Bible, who provokes *Deus ex machina* in human religiosity, guides public church and missional discipleship to be embodied in a concrete time and place, in critical engagement with cultural bigotry, multicultural complexity, and postmodern suspicion of metalanguage. Here I refine a concept of word-event and its semantic for the public mission, in constructive and critical dialogue with postcolonial theory.

The Semantics of Word-Event and Public Mission

Michel Foucault is hailed by one postcolonial intellectual as "a central figure in the most noteworthy flowering of oppositional intellectual life in the twentieth-century West."[12] According to Foucault, society and human life are dominated in terms of an integrative system of surveillance and disciplinary power. An example of this argument is his analysis of the Panopticon design of Bentham, whose effect was to assure the automatic functioning of power. According to Bentham this architectural apparatus should be a marvelous machine that produces homogeneous effects of power. Foucault defines the Panopticon as a cruel, ingenious apparatus or cage, reminiscent of Weber's "iron cage."[13] The disciplinary power of human life centered, on disciplining, and subjugating bodies and controlling population marks the beginning of bio-power.[14] This bio-power is a strategy of adjusting the human body into economic productivity and sanctioning the institutionalized knowledge system. The exercise of bio-power produces institutionalized knowledge through discursive practices. Special discourse plays a substantial role in underpinning the relationship between political power and social knowledge, thus it becomes socially institutionalized discourse imbued with political support.

12. Said, *Reflections on Exile*, 187.

13. Foucault, *Discipline and Punish*, 205.

14. Foucault, *History of Sexuality*, 1:139.

Following in the footsteps of Foucault, Edward Said made ground-breaking work in his postcolonial critique of colonialism and imperialism. His study of Orientalism[15] attempts to demystify the cultural representation of the Orient propagated by the Western authorities in the colonial period. Said argues that power and knowledge are interconnected, because the knowledge and representations of the Orient are associated with the financial and institutional support of the colonial regimes. According to Said, the Orient was created, or orientalized by the Western discourse which is tied to capitalism and colonialism. Orientalism is a colonial discourse, creating its own object of "non-West" in deploying and disseminating Western colonial discourse itself.[16] The imperialism of European accumulation and expansion has successfully assimilated the non-synchronous experiences of Europe's Other. It brings histories, cultures, and peoples of the non-West into the dialectic of colonialism.[17]

Postcolonial theory of discourse built on interplay of knowledge and power becomes instrumental in reframing a public church and a socially and culturally engaged mission. I find it meaningful that Christ and his Spirit direct and guide people in their own cultural life settings and establish a true *koinonia* in Christ with them.[18] The task of authentic theological re-rooting in Asia and Africa implies a radical transformation as indigenous translation that creates new ways of interpreting and understanding the Word of God. This implies a new task of God's mission as word-event, leading the post-Western church to become a more intercultural form in interpretation of biblical narrative. It supports the emancipation of the World Christianity from Western theological discourse and domination. Multicultural reality in the American public sphere challenges the missional church to be a more publicly relevant church through socially and culturally engaged mission.

The postcolonial strategy is a critical enterprise which aims at revealing the link between ideas and power lying behind Western texts, theories, and learning. It is undertaken in terms of an active interrogation of the hegemonic systems of thought, textual codes, and symbolic practices constructed in the Western domination of colonial subjects.

15. Cf. Said, *Orientalism.*

16. Ibid., 4–5, 104.

17. Said, *Reflections on Exile,* 202, 210.

18. Thomas, ed., *Classic Texts,* 212.

Thus, it implies a discursive resistance to imperialism, imperial ideologies and attitudes, and to their continual re-embodiment in the fields of politics, economics, history, and theological and biblical studies. It promotes an alternative way of perceiving and restructuring society.

However, the postcolonial strategy tends to fix hybridized identity, maximizing the colonizer's standpoint in undermining the resistance of the colonized. Said's colonial discourse of Orientalism replaces other important factors which are instrumental in the anti-colonial movements, for instance, archeological rewriting and re-presentation of the irregular history of the subaltern-minjung. I argue that Said's notion of the [mis]representation of Orientalism must be corrected by an anti-colonial representation of the buried history and discourse of those who are marginalized. Furthermore, a postcolonial critique of Orientalism must be refurbished by further undertaking a critical analysis of the internal, domestic complexities in the field of politics, economics, and the cultural nexus of discursive power and ideological-religious knowledge. Power elites among the colonized carry on their interest and dominion system in cooperation with the colonizing country. They are not a mere mimic people.

It is untenable to dualistically compartmentalize the Western standpoint as a colonizing one, while portraying the non-Western colonized one as a liberating and resisting one. We may find the group within the colonized who has orientation toward colonizing mentality and power. A radical oppositional group within the colonial context returns to create its own discourse of counter hegemony by reviving the traditional story and materials. Additionally, Christian religion in indigenous contexts contributes to human rights movements in protest against military dictatorship, by developing the social, critical mission for the subaltern-minjung. A postcolonial logic of denouncing evangelization as a colonialist hangover remains questionable. A deconstructive passion of binary opposition between colonizer and colonized can be overcome by considering the complicated reality between colonizer, colonized elitist, and the radical oppositional group based on locality. A colonized past cannot be overcome by ahistorical deconstruction of binary opposition. Rather it is critically sublimated by our anamnesis reason in remembrance of mass suffering of the innocent victims and in our archeological rewriting of unearthing the traditional texts and materials.

However, despite this critique, I am convinced of the importance of developing a postcolonial constructive theology concerning God's mission as word-event. A missiological concept of divine discourse and its discursive praxis of *parrhēsia* oppose the rigid vertical hierarchies of a state apparatus supported by power, money, and mass media. It also challenges the quasi-horizontal machine of a colonized and reified lifeworld under the culture of globalized empire. Evangelization in the spirit of *parrhēsia* is central to the missiological reframing of word-event. Here I distinguish my postcolonial-constructive position from the post-colonial-deconstructive attack on missional theology and activity as a colonial discourse and expansion in disguise. I articulate a postcolonial constructive approach to mission as word-event, notably emphasizing the irregularity of God's language-event in connection with the irregular side or underside of the history of those silenced in the past. Thus I con-ceptualize the irregular side of God's act of speech through the face of the others (social discourse) and undertake an archeological rewriting of the irregular side or downside of the history to find more insights, resources, and wisdom from the indigenous past. Unearthing the past of those victimized promotes a postcolonial constructive mission in con-trast to postmodern deconstruction.

In reframing public theology of God's mission and *diakonia*, a theological discourse of *parrhēsia* is decisive as a discursive-subversive praxis of word-event for God's sake and for the oppressed. God's dis-cursive mission as living word-event seeks understanding and dialogue through Christ's reconciliation with people outside the ecclesial walls. This irregular epistemology renews the Western epistemology of "faith seeking understanding" by re-rooting and reinterpreting it in different time and place. So the word of God as language-event seeks understand-ing of and dialogue with people of other cultures which enriches and deepens faith as public faith.[19]

Grounding Public Theology in God, the Place of the World

In the theological realm, John's Prologue expresses the physical embodi-ment of the Word of God. The transcendence of God—"even heaven and the highest heaven cannot contain you, much less this house that I have built!" (1 Kgs 8:27, 2 Chr 2:6; 6:18)—cannot be properly understood

---

19. For this theological epistemology see Chung, *Irregular Theology*, 3.

apart from God's place embodied in the incarnation of Jesus Christ. In John 1:1, "The Word was with God." Jesus Christ as the Son of God was in the most intimate closeness to, or with God. God has the place and grants it to us in our faith relationship with God. Jesus comes to us "in, with, and through" the kingdom of God. The important notion in the Hebrew Bible—that no specific place within the world has the capacity to contain God, not even God's own heavenly abode—means that God works on the world from without.[20]

Grounding public theology in the place of God can be found in a postcolonial approach to God, returning to others who exist in the trace of God the illeity. God is the *topos* of the world. In his concept of a theological utopia,[21] Marquardt hermeneutically retrieves the Jewish category of *topos* (*Makom*), advocating a theology of place-eschatology. God inspires God's people to long for the coming world. The world is contained in God, but not God in the world. From Ps 90:1 ("Lord, Thou hast been our dwelling-place"), it follows that God is the dwelling place of the world, but the world is not God's dwelling place. *Makom* is the term for the divine omnipresence in Psalm 139. God is understood as the Place of the world. A serious question can be raised: whether God is the place of the world or whether the world is God's place. The rabbinic answer is: The Lord is the place of the world, but the world is not God's place. The broad place (Job 36:16) implies the living-space is the safe stronghold enclosed by God.

God's mission in Christ's service to the world invites us to the *topos Dei*, the living-space of the world in a Trinitarian-eschatological perspective. Understanding the Trinitarian life of mutual indwelling within the divine *perichoresis* affirms that God is ahead of us and creates living-space for us in the Word of God. The incarnation of God's Place in Jesus Christ sharpens the discursive dimension of God's mission as word-event in the public sphere. It seeks a space for those who are marginalized and underprivileged in the social place. This perspective of "place-eschatology" helps us to better conceptualize a postcolonial constructive theology in terms of rewriting an irregular side of social discourse of the subaltern-minjung while undertaking a double listening to the word in the ecclesial life as well as God's language-event through the face of the others in the public sphere.

20. Fretheim, *Suffering of God,* 38.
21. Cf., Marquardt, *Eia, wärn wir da.*

Biblical language expressing the closeness between God and human beings is related to the concept of place, articulating an essentially social relation between them. In 1 Sam 20:23, 42, we find an existential-social definition of God's place. When it comes to a biblical concept of God and *topos*, we recall the encounter between God and Moses in Exod 33:21. Here is a *topos* in God's closeness to Moses, in which Moses becomes close to God without risking his life (Exod 33:22–23). From this encounter, we are aware of God as *topos* of the world as the new heaven and earth, while making God's presence in the world. Emancipation and recognition of the other comes from God who provides God's place: "The Lord will wipe away the tears from all faces, and the disgrace of God's people God will take away from all the earth" (Isa 25:8).

God's transcendence drives the transformation of this world toward God's place, while God awakens faith community to uphold an eschatological desire for a better society. A public theology in a postcolonial framework that aims at the place of God becomes foundational for public mission as a challenge to the aftermath of colonialism, socially engaged and embodied in pursuit of communal life in solidarity with those on the margins.

God becomes utopian ("no-place") which implies that God does not find any place in the world. "There was no place for them in the inn" (Luke 2:7). Jesus was the homeless Son of God who was pushed out of our world. The Christian community is built spiritually into a dwelling place for God in the Spirit (Eph 2:22). The church as the body of Christ, who is representative of collective and communal person in solidarity with God's *massa perditionis*, is inseparably connected with the in-breaking of the kingdom of God (God's *topos*). The Eucharist characterizes life in the kingdom of God: forgiveness of sin, reconciling love, shalom, and resistance to the reality of lordless powers (*tikun olam*: the mending of creation). Our confession of the triune God strengthens our acts of service underlying our prophetic *diakonia* in promoting a just, equitable, peaceful social order (family, economy, church, and state). Christ as the head of the body (Eph 1:22–23) makes explicit how the faith community is dependent on Christ and lives as an eschatological sign of God's reign in the world. In the body of Christ, a penultimate-eschatological embodiment of God's *topos*, I maintain that the least, the fragile, and the voiceless are ascribed special concern and honor. God as the *topos* of the world expedites faith community to become the Shalom church. The term "shalom" in Chinese characters connotes the idea of all members of God's creation in harmonious and life-enhancing relationship one with another, especially with emphasis on the fair sharing and distribution of social, material things. Living in shalom with one another in the place of God undergirds fair and harmonious distribution to the needs of the most fragile and vulnerable (Acts 4:35).[22]

Anyone receives a desire for the hope in the *topos* of God. "My eyes fail with watching for your promise" (Ps 119:82). In our desire for hope, we are called to participate in the world-renewing reality of Christian eschatology. A public missiology oriented toward God's place can be seen in light of God the provider of the place renewing and transforming the social reality of the world, and advocates for God's suffering people.

In this regard, God can be construed in a geographical-social-historical relation. As the *topos* of the world, God transforms the reality of the world in the direction of God's shalom and kingdom. The temple-place in the genuine and eschatological sense is the triune God who is revealed as the Lord God the Almighty and the Lamb in the presence of the Holy Spirit (Rev 21:22). Biblical promise and hope are rooted in and oriented toward the kingdom of God as God's *topos*.

A theological deliberation of God as the coming Place embraces not only human cities but also the animal kingdom for an eschatological reign of peace: "The wolf shall live with the lamb, the leopard shall lie down with the kid, the calf and the lion and the fatling together. . ." (Isa 11:6–7). God's holy mountain is the place of eternal peace in which all living beings find reconciliation, rest, and beatific life. In Rom 8:19–23 St. Paul expresses this prophetic vision with emphasis on the solidarity of the children of God with creation. In this light, a public missiology framed within God's *topos* awakens us to long for God's healing, forgiveness, and reconciliation in the public sphere while accompanying all living creatures. All creatures are also blessed to share with humanity the hope for liberation from bondage to decay by obtaining the freedom of the glory of the children of God.

Parrhēsia as Critical Methodology for Public Mission

A public mission for God's *topos* critically engages with political, cultural, and religious institutionalized legitimacy and power structures,

22. Nessan, *Shalom Church*, 7–19.

and develops the discursive activity of *parrhēsia*. Religious discourse emerges in each period of history according to the epistemic structures that make its statements possible. Religious concepts and interpretive exegesis take shape according to the regimes of knowledge available at any given moment in time. It is important to critically examine the condition of religiously institutionalized knowledge system and expose the hidden regimes of power behind religious discourse.

An interpretive strategy in terms of an analysis of the power-knowledge relation in the public sphere is *parrhēsia*, "speaking frankly." *Parrhēsia*, etymologically, is the act of telling all (frankness, open-heartedness, plain speaking, speaking openly, speaking freely) which is generally translated as *libertas* in Latin. At issue in *parrhēsia* are frankness, freedom, and openness: the freedom of the person who speaks.[23] This form of speech is free from rhetoric, and also dismissing flattery. There can only be truth in *parrhēsia*, thus *parrhēsia* is the *kairos*, the occasion in which individuals choose to speak the truth with regard to each other.[24]

A verbal-discursive activity and formation of *parrhēsia* implies a social criticism on behalf of those who are marginalized, silenced, deviated, and suppressed in the public sphere. An ethic of public missiology is grounded in resistance to totalizing metanarratives or totalitarian power, whether it stems from religion, science, or political oppression. The very achievement of global civilization has been built on the backs of women, people of color, and the marginalized. Rationalizing discourses suppress the discourse of marginalized groups and such discourses are sites of resistance.[25] A critical methodology of public mission in discursive-analogical manner is a methodology for the silenced for whom God provides a place. It is important to establish a ground to develop new forms of public theology and missiology and offer new perspectives for rethinking contemporary body theology, a theology of physicality and embodiment.

Foucault sought to rehabilitate *parrhēsia* as a form of speech that is both resistant to the confessional-hierarchical mode and alert to the religious categories, which had come to be employed politically. Fascism cultivated a religious sensibility frequently described as a type of religion

23. Foucault, *Hermeneutics of the Subject*, 366.

24. Ibid., 384.

25. Foucault, *History of Sexuality*, 1:xvii.

of nature, where the sanctification of biological life leads to an adoration of national life. Foucault shows how the National Socialist religious mythology in Germany utilized categories from traditional Christian discourse to make Hitler a messianic figure, construct God as a symbol of vital forces, and articulate doctrines of human nature and redemption. The person who speaks *parrhēsia* articulates "criticism instead of flattery, and moral duty instead of self-interest and moral apathy."[26] This perspective critiques a project of modernity centering on the "divinization" of the "man."

Jesus appears in the Synoptic framework as one who speaks publicly and plainly. God comes to us as expression, speaking through the face of the other. This is always posited as the poor, the stranger, the widow, and the orphan. A Christian form of *parrhēsia* needs to be retrieved against fascist, totalitarian life in the empire of economic globalization. It shapes a postcolonial-missional ethics for the sake of the silenced. [27] Social actual existence and ideological expressions must be considered and undertaken in the interpretation of the text in order to rescind the metanarative of the powerful, and to enhance multiples narratives of the particulars and the different, which have been undermined. A critique of ideology and a deciphering of competing interests and conflicts within society need to be integrated.

Evangelization: *Parrhēsia* and *Paranesis*

In the Synoptic context, *parrhēsia* has played a major role in reference to the mission of Jesus in solidarity with the public sinners and tax collectors. There are considerably more references to *parrhēsia* in the Gospel of John. The disciples beg for Jesus to tell them "plainly" (with *parrhēsia*) whether he is the Messiah (10:24). Jesus' somewhat evasive answer (10:25) is later interpreted for them when he says: "I have said these things to you in figures of speech. The hour is coming when I will no longer speak to you in figures, but will tell you plainly (*parrhēsia*) of the Father (16:25)." Here *parrhēsia* is to be understood as a clarification of the obscure, hidden, or enigmatic statements that Jesus might formerly have taught. The *parrhēsia* is Jesus' language of the cross, socially engaged in the public sphere.

26. Foucault, *Fearless Speech*, 19–20.
27. Bernauer and Carette, *Michel Foucault and Theology*, 77–97.

A related use of *parrhēsia* is found in the writer of Luke's continuation of the story of the church where it means "audacious speech." This refers to the ability of believers to hold their own in discourse before political and religious authorities, as in Acts 4:13: "Now when they saw the boldness [τὴν παρρησίαν] of Peter and John and realized that they were uneducated and ordinary men, they were amazed and recognized them as companions of Jesus." One of the significant things about Luke's portrait of Paul is that he preaches with *parrhēsia*. Paul is arrested in Jerusalem in Acts 21 and spends the rest of the book on trial, speaking in his own defense or under restrictions. In the context of these restrictions the message of *parrhēsia* comes out. First, when Paul is taken to King Agrippa in Acts 26 to defend his preaching of the message of Jesus, he says, "Indeed, the king knows about these things, and to him I speak freely; for I am certain that none of these things has escaped his notice, for this was not done in a corner (26:26)." Here, the Christian gospel has been spoken freely (with *parrhēsia*) in the public sphere.

Moreover, in Acts 28 Paul is ostensibly sent to Rome because he is a Roman citizen and has appealed to the emperor for a hearing of his case. He proclaimed "the kingdom of God and teaching about the Lord Jesus Christ with all boldness (*parrhēsia*) and without hindrance (28:30–31)." Living in perpetual danger, Paul was keenly aware that he needed courage to preach the gospel. In the courageous dimension of *parrhēsia*, a Christian ethic is explicit and obvious, and an ethic of putting oneself on the line in the spirit of *parrhēsia*.

In 2 Cor 3:7–18 we read what Paul undertakes in the rhetorical character of his mission and ministry. In this passage Christian *parrhēsia* amounts to speaking one's mind without fear. In 2 Cor 3:12 Paul grounds his use of free speech in hope (3:7–11) in which Paul focuses on the public dimension of his argument concerning the discursive praxis of free speech. The main point of 2 Cor 3:7–11 is the superiority of the new ministry based upon its source, the Spirit, and its effect, the creation of justice. His confidence in using *parrhēsia* is based on his hope in the life-giving and justice-creating power of the ministry in which he participates. In 2 Cor 3:13–18, where the Spirit is, there is only freedom. Free speech finds its legitimate basis in the freedom granted by a good conscience awakened by the Holy Spirit. Hope is given as a present which makes Paul's confident expression (candid in his speaking) work here. There is a contrast between Paul and Moses in their ways of address and communication, that is a contrast between Paul's *parrhēsia* and Moses' veiledness (3:12–18).[28] *Parrhēsia* is part of the semantic field, involving evangelization as witness to God who brings about justice for those on the margins. In the Greek realm *parrhēsia* was related to the freedom of speech of free citizens in the Attic democracy.

The public sphere referred to in Col 2:15 is provided by the event of the cross. According to John, Jesus' open self-confession is an eschatological possibility (John 16:25). Since Christ's suffering becomes the heart of salvation, proclamation in the post-Easter situation constitutes the distinction between the time of seeing and that of believing. In Acts proclamation plays a role in the sense of fearlessness, candor, and joyous confidence. The Spirit of the exalted Christ authorizes his disciples to preach in boldness and fearlessness. St. Paul has *parrhēsia* in the sense of open and trusting appropriation of apostolic authority (2 Cor 7:4; 6:11). In 1 Thess 2:2 we observe that the statement—"we had the courage in our God to declare to you the gospel of God in spite of great opposition"—refers to the eschatological *parrhēsia* of God's emissaries (2 Cor 3:12ff; 4:1ff.). The gospel is accompanied by its own *parrhēsia*, thus we ask God for the ability to do justice to this power of the gospel in openness and in the public sphere. In Hebrews *parrhēsia* is one of God's salvation gifts. That is "the real identifying feature of Christian existence."[29]

In connection to evangelization in the spirit of *parrhēsia*, it is vital to pay attention to the discursive-ethical dimension of the *paranesis* gospel. Paul's *paranesis* gospel of true freedom based on Christ contains more exhortations, admonitions, and summons to obey the law of Christ (Gal 6:2). Paul's teaching of justification by faith alone comes into sharpened focus in terms of his concept of *paranesis*. Within the framework of the post-Easter witnesses and the apostolic preaching (Epistles, Acts, Revelation), the death and resurrection are the basis and starting point for evangelization in Paul's mission in connection with *parrhēsia*. The real fountainhead in Paul's directions and admonitions was the gospel and the new being in Christ into which God's grace has transposed believers. Paul's *paranesis* originates in God's saving act in Christ as proclaimed in the gospel to which the crucified and risen Christ gives meaning and content. In God's saving action and the new

28. Olson, "Confidence Expressions in Paul," 150–51.

29. Balz, "παρρησία," in Balz and Schneider, *Exegetical Dictionary of New Testament*, 3:47.

being Paul's eschatological statements become a driving force in his *paranesis* (1 Thess 5:1–11; Rom 13:12); it implies strength, confidence even in everyday things that "your labor is not in vain in the Lord" (1 Cor 15:58). In the gospel of liberation in which Christ breaks down the frontiers separating people from people, nation from nation, we gain insights and forces for *paranetic* gospel in terms of *parrhēsia*.

A missional semantic, which articulates the hermeneutic of testimony, integrates a discursive practice of *parrhēsia* with the announcement of the gospel. *Martus* in Greek means witness. The witness is the one who is identified with the just cause, even risking one's life for it. In the Acts of the Apostles all sermons and testimony are guided by the following leitmotif: "This Jesus God raised up, and of that we all are witnesses" (Acts 2:32; 3:15).

God's mission as *viva vox evangelii* underscores the process of human proclamation and interpretation of the word of God, in terms of human words. Christ does not merely abolish the law in the moral way, but also fulfills and confirms God's ethical commandments in terms of *paranesis*. *Parrhēsia* is an indispensable form of *paranesis* for a public theology of God's misison and *diakonia* in Christ.

Missional Self as Ethical Self

God's word-event crosses borders in both a geographical and cultural sense and also boundaries of distinct fields or disciplines, opening up new spaces of knowledge and practice. God's mission in Christ's service to the world effects communication across cultural and geographical boundaries, recognizing the integrity of particularity and the play of diversity. Missiological hermeneutics takes into account God's Saying as social discourse through the Other. Missiology has priority over ethics. In terms of ethical relation with the Other, missional reflection must be put into question in light of the infinite horizon of God's language-event. In the Western tradition, every other is absorbed into the Sameness of individualism and its alterity is neutralized. This philosophical journey is likened to that of Odysseus, "whose adventure in the world was only a return to his native island—a complacency in the Same, an unrecognition of the Other."[30] However, Abraham's journey can be conceived radically "as a movement of the Same toward the Other which never returns

---

30. Levinas, *Basic Philosophical Writings*, 48.

to the Same."[31] This is departure with no return, acting "without entering into the Promised Land."[32]

The missional self is defined not by care for itself, but by the ethical desire for the other. "The understanding of the Other is thus a hermeneutics and an exegesis,"[33] because the other is present in a text by shaping its context. The other comes to us, and the phenomenon of the other's aspiration is a face. Its manifestation is "a surplus over the inevitable paralysis of manifestation."[34] Hermeneutical meaning is situated in the ethical realm of the other. Language can be reenvisioned out of the ethical revelation of the other. The illeity is in the trace of the divine transcendence. Exodus 33 tells us that going toward God means going toward the others who stand in the trace of divine illeity.[35] The relation to the face is straightaway ethical. "Thou shalt not kill." The face is what one must not kill. The human other's infinity reveals itself as a command. Face and discourse are tied in this divine command. The face speaks. At this juncture, Levinas distinguishes between the saying and the said. For him, the said [le dit] does not count as much as the saying [le dire] itself. The otherwise than being is stated in a saying that is unsaid.

Given this fact, Levinas conceives of the language as *Dabar* in a Hebrew manner (Ps 33:9). In Levinas' sense, the saying is basically the eternal meaning of all the said. In the Western tradition, the logos of the saying became the logos-principle of the worldly, that is the said. However, in John 1:2, the Logos was in the beginning *pros tov teon* (in direction toward God or in God's presence). The Word was in the beginning with God the Saying. This Logos marks the other side of Being.[36]

In this light I understand the Reformation principle *semper reformanda* in view of the subject matter of the Scripture (*viva vox evangelii* as Saying) as well as in listening to the voice of God through the face of the other. This aspect is central in my postcolonial construction of God's mission as word-event. In engagement with the others, Abraham is the cardinal example of missiological-anthropological hermeneutics. God's word-event which takes place between Abraham and Melchizedek

31. Ibid.,49.

32. Ibid.,50.

33. Ibid.,52.

34. Ibid.,53.

35. Ibid.,64.

36. Marquardt, *Eia, wärn wir da*, 537–38.

is surprising and provocative to Jews, like Christians and Muslims. Abraham is blessed by Melchizedek, the king of justice. Abraham's journey is different from that of the hero of the Greek myth, Odysseus. Unlike Odysseus who returns to Ithaca, Abraham left his fatherland forever to travel to a still unknown land in wholehearted trust in the *pro-missio* of God. On his return, Odysseus is exactly the same as he was when he left Ithaca. However, Abraham's life journey is rendered in the realism of daily and concrete life, and it becomes a blessing to the other. A missiology is a theology of faith journey with full trust in the promise of God, proceeding into the foreign and different world of other people. This is a world where God waits to bless the church, a people of God.

Mission as Interpretation in the Presence of the Other

Under the terms of the irregular style of God's speech as liberating event, a hermeneutical reflection on God's word-event is grounded in the relationship between creation and reconciliation. Such a reflection is undertaken in an unmethodical and chaotic style. It runs counter to the danger inherent in the theological system of totalizing difference/ otherness into the sameness of Western metaphysics. This irregular side of God's mission, which is based on God's *creatio continua* and reconciliation through Christ, polemically continues, articulates, and promotes the prophetic, diaconal inspiration of the gospel story of Jesus Christ in fellowship and solidarity with the voiceless in the universal history of empire.

An episode in a public cemetery helped my irregular insight into the mission as word-event in a post-western sense. A Caucasian family was visiting the grave of their parents. Placing some flowers on the grave they bowed in silence for a while. Some yards apart from it, a Chinese family prepared rice and fruits for the departed. They knelt down and bowed before the grave. Curiously enough, a Caucasian person approached and asked whether the departed would return to eat rice and fruits in front of the grave. The Chinese person, a little surprised, responded to him by asking: "Do you truly believe your departed would come back to smell the flowers on the grave?" Metaphors of flower and rice imply the significance of different cultural expression of loving memory of the departed or filial piety.

God's discourse in Jesus Christ's reconciliation of the world sharpens God's multiple act of speech throughout all the ages in their plural horizons. "The children of this age are more shrewd in dealing with their own generation than are the children of light" (Luke 16:8). God grants a great deal of goodness, reason, wisdom, languages, wealth and dominion to the godless. "I am with you always, to the end of the age" (Matt 28:20). This promise leads the church not to a laziness but bolsters it to do something by listening anew to the voice of its Lord. Hearing always the testimony of the Word of God in the Holy Scriptures (intratextual narrative) is correlated with listening humbly to the living God in the world who revives the church by the Holy Spirit (extrabiblical narrative). Thus, we give testimony in the highest respect for the freedom of God's grace and also in the respect for people of other cultures who expect everything from God.

The word-event opens up existence in promise, bringing about the recognition of multiple meanings in worldly affairs, as it upholds God's ongoing work in the world. Speaking about God's mission as word-event means speaking about the universal horizon of God's mission as conceived of as past and present and active in history and social location concerning the irregular side of those silenced. The linguistic–transcultural approach to God's mission as word-event reinterprets the essential elements of the Christian narrative by learning from the different cultural languages, symbols, and illustrations meaningful to those who receive the gospel story. Thus evangelization is blessing to the other, and it is a hermeneutic of testimony seen in light of God's mission as Christ's *diakonia*. It remains a joyous and audacious mandate for us to carry on through evangelization in post-Western culture and civilization. "You are a chosen race, a royal priesthood, a holy nation. God's own people, in order that you may proclaim the mighty acts of him who called you out of darkness into his marvelous light" (1 Pet 2:9).

Epilogue

God's Narrative in Congregational Life

We live in a mobile society, and our congregations are filled with mobile people. A reconstruction of the congregation is necessary for us to deal with the reality of mobility and choice which is considerably shaping congregational life and structure in American society. Here I include several challenging factors for the reconstruction of the congregation: the American cultural way of life, multiculturalized narratives of the different peoples brought together by globalization, socio-cultural life setting, and the postmodern condition. These are challenging factors which must be addressed in order to take seriously the project of the *missio* and *diakonia Dei* and the missional church in a wider spectrum.

Reclaiming mission as constructive theology, I maintain that public evangelization should challenge the reality of the world which generates the institutionalized structure of violence, scapegoating, and war. A biblical narrative about God's mission of reconciliation acknowledges and encourages the life of religious outsiders by inviting and weaving their life into the web of the divine discourse of freedom, love, and hospitality. We read a divine narrative of weaving hospitality and love in an encounter between Ruth (a Moabite woman) and Boaz. In this encounter of blessing it is proclaimed by Ruth that the kindness of the Lord has not forsaken the living or the dead (Ruth 2:20). Given the situation of multicultural reality and the individualization of religion it is not enough to stick to one's own cultural religious tradition. Within confessional Christian education and congregational life it is important to develop an awareness of Christian vocation in comparison with other truth claims and convictions. Global consciousness and cross-cultural sensitivity are needed. An intercultural, hermeneutical learning from other religious traditions and competing truth claims becomes indispensable for the envisioning of congregational mission and leadership. This aspect makes the congregational life more amenable to the conviviality and accompaniment between denominations. It also promotes a mature attitude toward the traditions of religious others and the lived reality of public spheres in the multicultural, postmodern world.[1]

I conclude the theological journey of reclaiming mission as constructive theology with a narrative from a multicultural congregation. In a parish in Orinda, California, a pastor met an old lady who had recently joined the congregation. Her daughter-in-law was a faithful member of the congregation. The old lady whom I will call Ms. Grace (not her real name) had an oldest son who was a faithful Buddhist. Because she had to live together with the younger son whose spouse was a church member, she had an opportunity to hear the gospel narrative from her daughter-in-law. Ms. Grace was healthy, intellectual, and peaceful, despite her age of eighty years and became a regular attendant. However, she was reluctant to receive the grace of baptism. The reason was hers, not the church's. She grew up with a Confucian-Buddhist upbringing and education. The Confucian sense of filial piety and respect for ancestors was powerfully impressed upon her soul. Her hesitation about becoming a baptized Christian stemmed from the worry that Christian baptism would sever her cherished relationship and filial piety from the heaven of her ancestors. What she worried about was that she would not be allowed to join the heavenly life of her ancestors, because Christian heaven would exclude them. Her reluctance and agony about the Christian initiation of baptism lay in her expectation of eternal life.

One midnight, the telephone rang. This implies an urgent call to the pastor. Ms. Grace's daughter-in-law sounded sad and depressed, speaking to the pastor that Ms. Grace was dying. In a hurry, the pastor paid a visit to her at the local hospital. In her moment of death she looked so peaceful and calm, as if she was in the presence of the Holy Spirit. Her daughter-in-law asked the pastor about baptism, saying that it was the last word that Ms. Grace left. Struggling with the Christian grace of baptism which would exclude her from the heaven of her ancestors, finally Ms. Grace wanted to live in the Christian heaven if God conferred upon her the grace of eternal life. The reason for her wanting the grace

1. Ammerman, *Growing Up Postmodern*, 77.

of baptism was rather simple, yet profound. In the future her daughter-in-law would join her there. It was partly due to an expression of Ms. Grace's gratitude to her daughter-in-law's filial piety caring for her. It was also partly due to congregational hospitality toward her. Hospitality to the stranger undergirds the intersection of worship and evangelization.

The pastor came to realize that baptism is really a gift of God based on the word of forgiveness and reconciliation. This implies a mystical and powerful dimension of the gospel. The Trinitarian logic and experience of grace in baptism expresses God's self-giving and unconditional love to us. The Christian mission is an integral part of the advent of God to a person in the moment of death. So we will be witness to God's unfailing and compassionate mercy and love to the end of the earth (Acts 1:8).

It is true that experience makes a human being a theologian. A baptismal ceremony with Ms. Grace dying on the bed deepened the pastor's sense of God's mission, pastoral care, and theology of grace in commitment to those with different religious, cultural backgrounds. A few days later, in the funeral service, the pastor came to realize that a Buddhist monk was also invited at the oldest son's request to officiate at his mother's journey to the pure land paradise of Buddhism. It was an exceptional experience for the pastor to officiate at the service together with the Buddhist monk for the burial service on the mountain. The pastor's sermon was about the grace of Christ and Amida Buddha's grace.

It went well. The Buddhist people seemed to take interest in the pastor's funeral homily in embrace of Buddhist hope of the pure land paradise. "The grass withers, the flower fades, but the word of our God will stand for ever" (Isa 40:7–8). The Scripture sees humanity as rooted in nature, returning "to the ground, for out of it you were taken; you are dust, and to dust you shall return" (Gen 3:19). This perspective may appreciate the Buddhist understanding of the human being as Buddha-nature. Christian community is the community of compassion weeping together with those who weep. St. Paul is right because the faith community is that of togetherness in mutual care. Thus the faith community becomes a place for welcoming the stranger.

God's narrative in Christ's reconciliation is woven in a multicultural congregation in terms of hope of eternal life, hospitality, and generosity for people with different religious backgrounds and orientations. Baptismal identity and ritual of filial piety are brought to congregational reality through the working of the Holy Spirit. The dead are in and with Christ who died and was raised for all. *Theologia crucis* in an eschatological contour becomes a realistic basis for God's mission and eternal life in Christ's *diakonia*, shaping a faith community as the community of hope, interpretation, and mission. Central to the *theologia crucis* is God's action, challenging the past and the status quo from a future ruled by God's freedom; resurrection of the dead affirms God's *emunah* (faithfulness) as the reliability of God's *pro-missio*.

This narrative in congregational life includes an encounter between the pastor and a visitor. In a multicultural service on Good Friday, the pastor had a visitation from an anonymous Christian. He had been in agony about the salvation of his parents who passed away without having an opportunity to hear the gospel narrative. His parents sacrificed their whole life in dedication to their son's education and successful life. Their generation underwent Japanese colonialism in Korea, later experiencing the political reality of military dictatorship over many years. They worked very hard to support their son's education, even abroad in the United States. In the United States, the son became a successful businessman and a so-called born-again Christian. When his parents passed away, he was strongly advised not to bow before their dead parents. An expression of filial piety in the Confucian sense of ancestral rites was condemned as an abomination to God. His agony began with a pressing question: Would his parents be granted an opportunity for eternal life? By no means! He was told: "Without faith they will suffer in eternal damnation. You don't need to worry about their future because they were already predestined not to hear the gospel." This word came upon him as the clincher, a thorn to his soul, finally causing him leave the congregation which he had attended over the years.

One day he heard about the Tenebrae service in a multicultural congregation in which all Asian neighbors along with congregation members were invited to bring flowers, photos of their deceased parents, and mementos; they were placed before the cross of Jesus Christ and an icon of Jesus' descent to hell. The Lord's Supper was prepared for church members after the service. If Jesus descended to death, preaching the gospel (*viva vox evangelii*), this Christ who is truly present in the Eucharistic celebration is the Lord of the living and the dead. Jesus Christ is a missional Lord, seeking the dead for his good news of eternal life even in the world of death. After participation in the Tenebrae service, Mr. Anonymous, who struggled over years with the future of his parents came to the pastor, saying with weeping that "Now I can reconcile myself with the crucified God."

What happened to Ms. Grace and Mr. Anonymous in the multicultural congregational life? The common thread in these Asian American Christians comes from filial piety which is a family, interpersonal, and social duty for them. "Honor your father and your mother, so that your days may be long in the land that the Lord your God is giving you." (Exod 20:12). The filial piety is the moral virtue in honoring ancestors, especially parents who brought you into existence. Respect and honor toward teachers and mentors are derived from this filial piety. This ethical filial piety contributes to the social services in caring for the elderly. The core message of filial piety is an indispensable part of shaping the Confucian view of how to become human (*ren*).[2]

What does the gospel narrative mean to those with filial piety who grew up in the non-Western background? If the gospel has already been preached to the dead, shouldn't Christ's descent into hell imply that the dead would receive the message about Christ in order to be judged in the flesh and made alive in the Spirit? Does not this aspect of the gospel refer to the gracious mystery of God's narrative that is woven in the multi-congregation life and mission? God granted the moral law to everybody: "I will put my laws in their hearts and I will write them on their minds" (Heb 10:16).

To the Athenians in front of the Areopagus, Paul bears witness to *solus Christus* in the conviction that all people live, move, and have their being in the universal reign of God (Acts 17:22, 27, 28). In this context Paul is not reluctant to quote poems of pagan writers for his dialogical mission. "For 'In him we live and move and have our being'; as even some of your own poets have said, 'For we too are his offspring'" (Acts 17:28).

We observe the biblical view of reality according to which people live in a world of different cultures and religions, in orientation to integrity of life before God. It is important to define the life horizon of a multireligious society more positively in terms of a missiological study of God's grace of justification and reconciliation with the world, embracing people of other cultures. Evangelization in a non-Western context elaborates the important cultural-religious horizons of those who receive the gospel in their own language, belief system, and life

2. Neville, *Boston Confucianism*, 195.

orientation. The church as the eschatological sign of the kingdom of God is called to attentively and humbly listen to the universal activity of God's reign through the Holy Spirit in the world. This missional project in recognition of and dialogue with religious outsiders implies exposing one's own position to be renewed and enriched by the world in which God continues to speak. The faith community is a hermeneutical community, reading and announcing the biblical narrative in the church and witnessing to the Word of God in the public world. A hermeneutical criterion can be summarized in terms of our interfaith mission: self-exposure to the other, creative appropriation of the meaning of Christian narrative (evangelization/witness), critical distance from the limitation in the past (for instance, espousal between mission and colonialism), self-renewal, and reconstruction of Christian identity in the presence of the other.

God's mission in the grace of justification and reconciliation calls us to serve the faith community and congregational mission for people in a post-Western age. Paul planted the seed, Apollos watered it; but God made it grow (1 Cor 3:6). God can make the community of vocation bear fruit. A sacramental dimension of the faith community as the body of Christ is truly missional, equipping the saints for the ministry of reconciliation, encouraging congregational life to grow toward maturity in Christ, being in the unity of the faith and knowledge of the Son of God. God's gospel narrative as the living voice of God is woven in the rich tapestry of multi-congregational life.

The idea of *apokatastasis* expresses only a hope, not a part of a rationalized theological system. The Holy Spirit is the Spirit guiding the church, and Christ exists as church-community in a communal sense. All are in God, while each remains distinct from God. At issue here is not the ecclesial triumphalism, but the realm of God extending throughout the whole world and creation.[3] God's eschatology is more than the church's rule. "I saw no temple in the city, for its temple is the Lord God the Almighty and the Lamb" (Rev 21:22). This is the hope of the present church for the triune God, who is the God of Israel. This hope awakens the faith community to implement this hope into a present reality through missional discipleship. Christ hands over his faith community to the Father, in order that God may be all in all (1 Cor 15:24). In this eschatological hope the faith community grows strong. The church

---

3. Bonhoeffer, *Sanctorum Communio*, 288–89.

grows in the ministry of reconciliation as it comes spiritually to the maturity of the gospel, namely to the measure of the full stature of Christ. Evangelization and congregational mission are acted out in doxology, in thanksgiving and praise to God. Contextualization or inculturation in a genuine sense lies in acknowledging the free grace of God's mission as word-event. This event transcends the cultural domestication of the gospel in the world.[4]

> There is one body and one Spirit, just as you were called to the one hope of your calling, one Lord and Father of all, who is above all and through all and in all . . . . The gifts he gave were that some would be apostles, some prophets, some evangelists, some pastors and teachers, to equip the saints for the work of ministry, for building up the body of Christ, until all of us come to the unity of the faith and of the knowledge of the Son of God, to maturity, to the measure of the full stature of Christ (Eph 4:11–13).

---

4. Newbigin, *Gospel in a Pluralist Society*, 127, 144.

Glossary and Explanations of Technical Terms and Concepts

Word-Event: For Luther Scripture is a witness to the Word of God. The "canon within the canon" is what urges and promotes Christ. Luther's hermeneutic relates to the *viva vox evangelii* (Gospel as living voice of God). The Word of God refers to a dynamic word-event, because a concept of *viva vox evangelii* implies a priority of the spoken word over the written word (the Scripture).This perspective is developed notably by Gerhard Ebeling and F.-W. Marquardt.

Fusion of Horizons: According to Gadamer, human existence is thoroughly historical, or in the world. Because of the world, tradition, and a language we can anticipate experiencing a fusion of horizon between our horizon and the horizons of others. When one reads the text, the horizon of the text encounters the horizon of the reader. In an encounter between different horizons a new meaning can be acquired. Interpretation is in this regard open-ended and dynamic.

Thick Description: According to Geertz, culture is public, consisting of socially established structures of meaning. Thick description is a descriptive way of involving multiple meanings of the cultural life and experience in intelligible and profound manner.

Missiological Hermeneutic: A missiological hermeneutic is built on the word-event and refines the notion of fusion of horizons by integrating the anthropological concept of thick description. A missiological hermeneutic in dialogue with religious outsiders implies exposing one's own position to be renewed and enriched by God's word-event speaking through the world in the sense of God's ongoing creation. This hermeneutics is characterized by: self-exposure to the other, creative appropriation of meaning of Christian narrative (evangelization/witness), critical distance from the limitations in the past of Christian mission (for instance, espousal between mission and colonialism), self-renewal, and reconstruction of Christian identity in the presence of the other.

For Classification of the Schools of Cultural Anthropology

Franz Boas (1851–1942) is regarded as the father of American anthropology. For him race, language, and culture are independent. In the anthropological study of culture Boas proposed his ideas about culture in direct opposition to racialist hypotheses. Behavorial differences among peoples were not due to differences in racial stock but were attributed to differences in culture.

Ruth Benedict (1887–1948) is affected by the passionate egalitarianism of Boas. In *Patterns of Culture* (1934), Benedict's view of human cultures is "personality writ large." She emphasizes the importance of the study of the whole configuration over against the continued analysis of its parts. Benedict is critical of functionalist approach such as Malinowski.

Bronislaw Malinowski (1884–1948) was the representative of functionalism based on individual needs. Malinowski in his ethnological generalizations was content to emphasize that traits had a living context in the culture of which they were a part. He sidestepped recognition of cultural configuration, each with its characteristic arrangements in the economic, the religious, and the domestic sphere (see *Magic, Science, and Religion, and Other Essays*).

A. R. Radcliffe-Brown (1881–1955) was the representative of social anthropology, using the term function in a different sense from Malinowski. He was influenced by Emile Durkheim and argued that the goal of anthropological research was to find the collective function; a sort of internal logic would cause one level of culture to evolve into the next. For instance, his question centers on what a cultural rule or religious creed about marriage did for the social order as a whole.

Claude Levi-Strauss (1908–2009): In structural linguistics (according to Ferdinand de Saussure), language is seen as a complete and internally coherent system (langue) while linguistic behavior (human speech) is called parole. The bond between the signifier (the linguistic expression) and the signified (what the expression denotes) is arbitrary. Semiology is to explore the nature of signs. Levi-Strauss extended linguistics analysis of sign and signification to other social practices such as kinship, economic relations, food, and myth. Kinship systems, like phonemic systems, are built by the mind on the structure of unconscious thought.

Ethnography (a branch of cultural anthropology): A form of research focusing on the sociology of meaning through close field observation of socio-cultural phenomenon. In the case of congregational study, for instance, emic perspective is to clarify the way the members of the congregation perceive their vision of God's mission and the world. Etic perspective is a research approach to the way non-members (outsiders, including the researcher) perceive and interpret behaviors and phenomena associated with a given congregation. The combined perspective makes a missiological analysis of congregational mission described thickly.

Power-Knowledge Interplay: Foucault makes an attempt at demonstrating the rationality in light of a nexus of power and knowledge. The objective of scientific rationality is to gain mastery over the physical body and the social environment. Power and knowledge directly imply one another built on discourse. Complex differential power relationships extend to every aspect of our social, cultural, and political lives. Foucault calls his alternative interpretation bio-power. Foucault's work provides an opportunity to examine the condition of theological knowledge and expose the hidden regimes of power behind Christian theology. Revealing the unconscious (power) of theological knowledge, Foucault's critical theory underpins a methodology for the silenced. Foucault establishes a ground to develop new forms of negative theology and offers new perspectives for rethinking contemporary body theology.

Infinity and Ethics of the Other: Emmanuel Levinas (1906–1995) presents a critique of the whole of Western civilization, arguing that Western thought and practice are marked by a striving for totalization. For

Levinas, the human and the Divine other cannot be reduced to a totality or sameness. The other is associated with the Infinite. To encounter another is to discover that humans are under ethical obligation. The face of the other is the poor and destitute one. In terms of the ethical relation with the Other, Levinas speaks of God. The God of the Bible signifies the beyond being of transcendence. "Saying" as testimony precedes all that is said. "Saying" therefore leads to a vital activity in the life of ethical responsibility: witnessing.

Bibliography

Ahn, Byung-Mu. "Jesus and Ochlos in the Context of His Galilean Ministry." In *Asian Contextual Theology for the Third Millennium: A Theology of Minjung in Fourth-Eye Formation*, edited by Paul S. Chung et al., 33–50. Eugene, OR: Pickwick, 2007.

Amin, Samir. *Capitalism in the Age of Globalization: The Management of Contemporary Society*. London: Zed, 1997.

Ammerman, Nancy. T., Martin E. Marty, Sharon Daloz Parks, Friedrich Schweitzer, and William Willimon. *Growing Up Postmodern: Imitating Christ in the Age of "Whatever."* Princeton: Princeton Theological Seminary, 1999.

Aquinas, Thomas. *Summa Theologiae*. Ottawa: Commissio Piana, 1953.

Balz, Horst, and Gerhard Schneider, editors. *Exegetical Dictionary of the New Testament*. 3 vols. Grand Rapids: Eerdmans, 1990–93.

Barbour, Ian G. *Religion and Science: Historical and Contemporary Issues*. San Francisco: HarperSanFrancisco, 1997.

Barth, Karl. *Ad Limina Apostolorum: An Appraisal of Vatican II*. Translated by Keith R. Crim. Richmond: John Knox, 1968.

———. *Against the Stream: Shorter Post-War Writings 1946–52*. Translated by E. M. Delacour. Edited by Ronald Gregor Smith. London: SCM, 1954.

———. *Briefe 1961–1968*. Edited by J. Fangmeier and H. Stoevesandt. Zurich: TVZ, 1975.

———. *Die Christliche Dogmatik im Entwurf, erster Band, Die Lehre vom Worte Gottes: Prolegomena zur christlichen Dogmatik, 1927*. Edited by Gerhard Sauter. Zurich: TVZ, 1982.

———. "Church and Culture." In *Theology and Church: Shorter Writings, 1920–1928*, translated by Louise Pettibone Smith, 334–54. New York: Harper & Row, 1962.

———. *Church Dogmatics*. 13 vols. Translated and edited by G. W. Bromiley and T. F. Torrance. First paper ed. London: T. & T. Clark, 2004.

———. *Community, State, and Church*. Garden City: Doubleday, 1960.

———. *Dogmatics in Outline*. Translated and edited by Colin E. Gunton. London: SCM, 2001.

———. *Eine Schweizer Stimme, 1938–1945*. Zurich: TVZ, 1985.

———. *The Epistle to the Romans*. Translated by Edwyn Hoskyns. London: Oxford University Press, 1968.

———. *Fragments Grave and Gay*. Edited by Martin Rumscheidt. Translated by Eric Mosbacher. London: Collins, 1971.

———. *Gespräche 1964–1968*. Edited by Eberhard Busch. Zurich: TVZ, 1997.

———. *The Göttingen Dogmatics: Instruction in the Christian Religion.* Vol. 1. Translated by G. W. Bromiley. Grand Rapids: Eerdmans, 1991.

———. *Letters, 1961–1968.* Edited by J. Fangmeier and H. Stoevesandt. Translated by G. W. Bromiley. Grand Rapids: Eerdmans.

———. "Past and Future: Friedrich Naumann and Christoph Blumhardt." In *The Beginnings of Dialectic Theology,* edited by James M. Robinson, 35–45. Richmond: John Knox, 1968.

———. "Die Theologie und die Mission in der Gegenwart." *Zwischen den Zeiten* 10:3 (1932) 189–215.

———. *Theologische Fragen und Antworten.* Zollikon: Evangelischer, 1957.

———. *The Word of God and the Word of Man.* Translated by Douglas Horton. New York: Harper & Row, 1957.

Bauckham, Richard. "The Millennium." In *God Will Be All in All: The Eschatology of Jürgen Moltmann,* edited by Richard Bauckham, 123–47. Edinburgh: T. & T. Clark, 1999.

———. *The Theology of the Book of Revelation.* Cambridge: Cambridge University Press, 1993.

Bayer, Oswald. "Creation as History." In *The Gift of Grace: The Future of Lutheran Theology,* edited by Niels Henrik Gregersen, 253–63. Minneapolis: Fortress, 2005.

Beaud, Michel. *A History of Capitalism, 1500–1980.* Translated by Tom Dickman and Anny Lefebvre. New York: Monthly Review, 1983.

Bediako, Kwame. *Christianity in Africa: The Renewal of a Non-Western Religion.* Maryknoll, NY: Orbis, 1995.

Bellah, Robert N. *Beyond Belief: Essays on Religion in a Post-Traditional World.* Berkeley: University of California Press, 1991.

Bellah, Robert N., and Phillip E. Hammond. *Varieties of Civil Religion.* San Francisco: Harper & Row, 1980.

Bellah, Robert et al. *Habits of the Heart.* Berkeley: University of California Press, 1985.

Benedict, Ruth. *Patterns of Culture.* 2nd ed. Boston: Houghton Mifflin, 1959.

Berger, Peter L. *The Sacred Canopy: Elements of a Sociological Theory of Religion.* New York: Doubleday, 1967.

Berger, Peter L., and Thomas Luckmann. *The Social Construction of Reality: A Treatise in the Sociology of Knoweldge.* New York: Doubleday, 1966.

Bernauer, James, and Jeremy Carrette, editors. *Michel Foucault and Theology: The Politics of Religious Experience.* Aldershot: Ashgate, 2004.

Bethge, Eberhard. "Dietrich Bonhoeffer und die Juden." In *Die Juden und Martin Luther, Martin Luther und die Juden: Geschichte, Wirkungsgeschichte, Herausforderung.* edited by Heinz Kremers et al., 211–48. Neukirchen-Vluyn: Neukirchener, 1985.

Bevans, Stephen B., and Roger P. Schroeder. *Constants in Context: A Theology of Mission for Today.* Maryknoll, NY: Orbis, 2004.

Bickel, Adolf M. *Our Forgotten Founding Father: A Biography of Pastor William Loehe.* Napoleon, OH: s.n., 1997.

Bliese, Richard H. "Lutheran Missiology: Struggling to Move from Reactive Reform to Innovative Initiative." In *The Gift of Grace: The Future of Lutheran Theology,* edited by Niels Henrik Gregersen et al., 215–28. Minneapolis: Fortress, 2005.

Bliese, Richard H., and Craig Van Gelder, editors. *The Evangelizing Church: A Lutheran Contribution.* Minneapolis: Augsburg Fortress, 1989.

Bloomquist, Karen L, editor. *Being the Church in the Midst of Empire: Trinitarian Reflections*. Geneva: LWF, 2009.

Boas, Franz. *Race, Language, and Culture*. New York: Macmillan, 1959.

Boendermaker, Johannes P. "Martin Luther–ein 'semi-judaeus'? Der Einfluss des Alten Testaments und des jüdischen Glaubens auf Luther und seine Theologie." In *Wendung nach Jerusalem: Friedrich-Wilhelm Marquardts Theologie im Gespräch*, edited by Hanna Lehming et al., 45–58. Gütersloh: Kaiser, Gütersloher, 1999.

Boff, Clodovis. *Theology and Praxis: Epistemological Foundations*. Translated by Robert R. Barr. Maryknoll, NY: Orbis, 1987.

Boff, Leonardo. *Ecology and Liberation: A New Paradigm*. Maryknoll, NY: Orbis, 1995.

Boff, Leonardo, and Clodovis Boff. *Introducing Liberation Theology*. Translated by Paul Burns. Maryknoll, NY: Orbis, 2000.

Bonhoeffer, Dietrich. *The Cost of Discipleship*. New York: Touchstone, 1995.

———. *Ethics*. New York: Touchstone, 1995.

———. *Illegale Theologenausbildung: Finkenwalde 1935–1937*. In *Dietrich Bonhoeffer Werke*, Band 14. Munich: Kaiser, 1996.

———. *Letters and Papers from Prison*. Edited by Eberhard Bethge. New York: Macmillan, 1962.

———. *Life Together*. London: SCM, 1954.

———. *No Rusty Swords: Letters, Lectures, and Notes, 1928–1936*. In *Collected Works of Dietrich Bonhoeffer*, vol. 1. London: Colins, 1965.

———. *Sanctorum Communio: A Theological Study of the Sociology of the Church*. Translated by Reinhard Krauss and Nancy Lukens. Edited by Clifford J. Green. Minneapolis: Fortress, 1998.

Bosch, David J. *Transforming Mission: Paradigm Shifts in Theology of Mission*. Maryknoll, NY: Orbis, 2004.

Brown, Raymond E. *The Gospel According to John*. The Anchor Bible 29–29A. Garden City: Doubleday, 1980.

Brown, Robert M. *Gustavo Gutierrez: An Introduction to Liberation Theology*. Maryknoll, NY: Orbis, 1997.

Browning, Don S. *A Fundamental Practical Theology: Descriptive and Strategic Proposals*. Minneapolis: Fortress, 1991.

———, editor. *Practical Theology*. San Francisco: Harper & Row, 1983.

Browning, Don S., and Francis S. Fiorenza, editors. *Habermas, Modernity, and Public Theology*. New York: Crossroad, 1992.

Buchanan, George W. *To The Hebrews*. The Anchor Bible 36. Garden City: Doubleday, 1972.

Busch, Eberhard. *Karl Barth: His Life from Letters and Autobiographical Texts*. Translated by John Bowden. Grand Rapids: Eerdmans, 1994.

———. *Unter dem Bogen des einen Bundes: Karl Barth und die Juden 1933–1945*. Neukirchen-Vluyn: Neukirchener, 1996.

Cady, Linell E. *Religion, Theology, and American Public Life*. Albany: SUNY Press, 1993.

Calvin, John. *Institutes of the Christian Religion*. The Library of Christian Classics 20–21. Edited by John T. McNeil. Philadelphia: Westminster, 1960.

Carter, Craig A. *Rethinking Christ and Culture: A Post-Christendom Perspective*. Grand Rapids: Brazos, 2006.

Casas, Bartolomé de las. *The Devastation of the Indies: A Brief Account*. Translated by Herma Briffault. Baltimore: Johns Hopkins University Press, 1992.

————. *Indian Freedom: The Cause of Bartolomé de las Casas, 1484–1566: A Reader.* Translated by Francis P. Sullivan, SJ. Kansas City: Sheed & Ward, 1995.

Chan, Wing-tsit, translator. *Reflections on Things at Hand: The Neo-Confucian Anthology.* Compiled by Zhu Xi and Lü Tsu-Ch'ien. New York: Columbia University Press, 1967.

Chang, Carson. *The Development of Neo-Confucian Thought.* London: Vision, 1958.

Ching, Julia. *Chinese Religions.* Maryknoll, NY: Orbis, 1993.

————. *The Religious Thought of Chu Hsi.* Oxford: Oxford University Press, 2000.

Chung, David. *Syncretism: The Religious Context of Christian Beginnings in Korea.* Albany: SUNY Press, 2001.

Chung, Paul S. *Christian Mission and a Diakonia of Reconciliation: A Global Reframing of Justification and Justice.* Minneapolis: Lutheran University Press, 2008.

————. *Constructing Irregular Theology: Bamboo and Minjung in East Asian Perspective.* Leiden: Brill, 2009.

————. *Karl Barth: God's Word in Action.* Eugene, OR: Cascade, 2008.

————. *Martin Luther and Buddhism: Aesthetics of Suffering.* 2nd ed. Eugene, OR: Pickwick, 2008.

————. *Public Theology in an Age of World Christianity: God's Mission as Word-Event.* New York: Palgrave Macmillan, 2010.

————. *The Spirit of God Transforming Life: The Reformation and Theology of the Holy Spirit.* New York: Palgrave Macmillan, 2009.

Chung, Paul S., et al., editors. *Asian Contextual Theology for the Third Millennium: Theology of Minjung in Fourth-Eye Formation.* Eugene, OR: Pickwick, 2007.

Collins, John N. *Deacons and the Church: Making Connections between Old and New.* Leomister: Gracewing, 2002.

Cronin, Vincent. *The Wise Man from the West.* Glasgow: Fontana, 1961.

Crowner, David, and Gerald Christianson, editors. *The Spirituality of the German Awakening.* New York: Paulist, 2003.

Dallmayr, Fred R., and Thomas A. McCarthy, editors. *Understanding Social Inquiry.* Notre Dame: University of Notre Dame Press, 1977.

Deleuze, Gilles. *Proust and Signs.* Translated by Richard Howard. New York: George Braziller, 1972.

Derrrida, Jacques. *Of Grammatology.* Translated by Gayatri Chakravorty Spivak. Baltimore: Johns Hopkins University Press, 1976.

Descartes, René. *Discourse on the Method.* Translated by Laurence J. Lafleur. Indianapolis: Bobbs-Merrill, 1960.

Dillenberger, John, editor. *Martin Luther: Selections from his Writings.* Garden City: Anchor, 1961.

Dobb, Maurice. *Studies in the Development of Capitalism.* Rev. ed. New York: International, 1963.

Driver, Tom. *Christ in a Changing World: Toward an Ethical Christology.* New York: Crossroad, 1981.

Duchrow, Ulrich. *Alternatives to Global Capitalism: Drawn from Biblical History, Designed for Political Action.* Utrecht: International, 1998.

————. *Christenheit und Weltverantwortung: Traditionsgeschichte und Systematische Struktur der Zweireichelehre.* Stuttgart: Ernst Klett, 1970.

————. *Global Economy: A Confessional Issue for the Churches?* Translated by David Lewis. Geneva: WCC, 1987.

————, editor. *Colloquium 2000: Faith Communities and Social Movements Facing Globalization.* Geneva: WARC, 2002.

Duchrow, Ulrich, and Franz J. Hinkelammert. *Property for People, Not for Profit: Alternatives to the Global Tyranny of Capital.* London: Zed, 2004.

Duchrow, Ulrich, and Gerhard Liedke. *Shalom: Biblical Perspectives on Creation, Justice and Peace.* Geneva: WCC, 1989.

Dudley, Carl S., editor. *Building Effective Ministry: Theory and Practice in the Local Church.* San Francisco: Harper & Row, 1983.

Dupuis, Jacques. *Toward a Christian Theology of Religious Pluralism.* Maryknoll, NY: Orbis, 1997.

Durkheim, Emile. *The Elementary Forms of Religious Life.* Translated by Karen E. Fields. New York: Free Press, 1995.

Dussel, Enrique. *History and the Theology of Liberation: A Latin American Perspective.* Translated by John Drury. Maryknoll, NY: Orbis, 1976.

————. *A History of the Church in Latin America: Colonialism to Liberation (1492–1979).* Translated by Alan Neely. Grand Rapids: Eerdmans, 1981.

Eagleson, John, and Philip Scharper, editors. *Puebla and Beyond: Documentation and Commentary.* Translated by John Drury. Maryknoll, NY: Orbis, 1979.

Ebeling, Gerhard. *Dogmaik des christlichen Glaubens, Band 1.* Tubingen: Mohr, 1979.

————. *Luther: An Introduction to His Thought.* Translated by R. A. Wilson. Minneapolis: Fortress, 2007.

————. *Word and Faith.* Translated by James W. Leitch. Philadelphia: Fortress, 1963.

Eck, Diana L. *A New Religious America: How a "Christian Country" Has Become the World's Most Religiously Diverse Nation.* New York: HarperSanFrancisco, 2001.

Endō, Shūsaku. *Silence.* Translated by William Johnston. New York: Taplinger, 1980.

Everist, Norma Cook, and Craig L. Nessan. *Transforming Leadership: New Vision for a Church in Mission.* Minneapolis: Fortress, 2008.

Fabiunke, Günter. *Martin Luther als Nationalökonom.* Berlin: Akademie-Verlag, 1963.

Fiorenza, Elisabeth Schüssler. *In Memory of Her: A Feminist Theological Reconstruction of Christian Origins.* New York: Crossroad, 1984.

Ford, J. Massyngberde. *Revelation.* The Anchor Bible 38. Garden City: Doubleday, 1980.

Forde, Gerhard O. *The Law-Gospel Debate: An Interpretation of Its Historical Development.* Minneapolis: Augsburg, 1969.

————. *Theology Is for Proclamation.* Minneapolis: Fortress, 1990.

Foucault, Michel. *Discipline and Punish: The Birth of the Prison.* Translated by Alan Sheridan. New York: Vintage, 1977.

————. *Fearless Speech.* Los Angles: Semiotexte, 2001.

————. *The Hermeneutics of the Subject: Lectures at the Collège de France, 1981–1982.* Edited by Frédéric Gros. Translated by Graham Burchell. New York: Picador, 2005.

————. *The History of Sexuality.* Vol. 1, *The Will to Knowledge.* Translated by Robert Hurley. New York: Vintage, 1990.

————. *The Order of Things: An Archaeology of the Human Sciences.* New York: Random House-Pantheon, 1970.

Frank, Andre Gunder. *Capitalism and Underdevelopment in Latin America: Historical Studies of Chile and Brazil.* Rev. ed. New York: Monthly Review, 1969.

————. *Dependent Accumulation and Underdevelopment.* New York: Monthly Review, 1979.

Fretheim, Terence E. *Abraham: Trials of Family and Faith*. Columbia: University of South Carolina Press, 2007.

———. *The Suffering of God: An Old Testament Perspective*. Philadelphia: Fortress, 1984.

Freytag, Walter, editor. *Mission zwischen Gestern und Morgen: Vom Festaltwandel der Weltmission der Christenheit im Licht der Konferenz des Internationalen Missionsrats in Willingen*. Stuttgart: Evang. Missionsverlag, 1952.

Frymer-Kensky, Tikva, David Novak, Peter Ochs, David Fox Sandmel, and Michael A. Signer, editors. *Christianity in Jewish Terms*. Boulder, CO: Westview, 2000.

Fung, Yu-lan. *A History of Chinese Philosophy*. 2 vols. Translated by Derk Bodde. Princeton: Princeton University Press, 1983.

Gadamer, H.-G. *Truth and Method*. 2nd ed. Translated and edited by Joel Weinsheimer and Donald G. Marshall. New York: Continuum, 2004.

Gardner, John W. *On Leadership*. New York: Free Press, 1990.

Geertz, Clifford. *The Interpretation of Cultures*. New York: Basic, 1973.

Geis, R. R. *Leiden an der Unerlöstheit der Welt: Briefe, Reden, Aufsätze*. Edited by D. Goldschmidt and I. Übershär. Munich: Kaiser, 1984.

Gerth, H. H., and C. Wright Mills, editors. *From Max Weber: Essays in Sociology*. New York: Oxford University Press, 1958.

Girad, René. *Things Hidden since the Foundation of the World*. Translated by Stephen Bann and Michael Metteer. Standford: Standford University Press, 1987.

Global Mission in the Twenty-First Century: A Vision of Evangelical Faithfulness in God's Mission. Chicago: ELCA, 1999.

Gollwitzer, Helmut. *Befreiung zur Solidarität: Einführung in die Evangelische Theologie*. Munich: Kaiser, 1978.

———. *An Introduction to Protestant Theology*. Translated by David Cairns. Philadelphia: Westminster, 1982.

———. *Die Kapitalistische Revolution*. Munich: Kaiser, 1974.

———. "Kingdom of God and Socialism in the Theology of Karl Barth." In *Karl Barth and Radical Politics*, translated and edited by George Hunsinger, 77–120. Philadelphia: Westminster, 1976.

———. *Krummes Holz-Aufrechter Gang: Zur Frage nach dem Sinn des Lebens*. Munich: Kaiser, 1985.

———. *The Rich Christians and Poor Lazarus*. Translated by David Cairns. New York: Macmillan, 1970.

González, Justo L. *A History of Christian Thought*. Rev. ed. Vol. 3, *From the Protestant Reformation to the Twentieth Century*. Nashville: Abingdon, 1987.

Green, Clifford J. *Bonhoeffer: A Theology of Sociality*. Rev. ed. Grand Rapids: Eerdmans, 1999.

Guder, Darrell L., et al., editors. *Missional Church: A Vision for the Sending of the Church in North America*. Grand Rapids: Eerdmans, 1998.

Gutiérrez, Gustavo. *Las Casas: In Search of the Poor of Jesus Christ*. Translated by Robert R. Barr. Maryknoll, NY: Orbis, 1992.

———. *A Theology of Liberation*. Translated and edited by Sister Caridad Inda and John Eagleson. Maryknoll, NY: Orbis, 1999.

Habermas, Jürgen. *Knowledge and Human Interests*. Translated by Jeremy J. Shapiro. Boston: Beacon, 1971.

———. *Legitimation Crisis*. Translated by Thomas McCarthy. Boston: Beacon, 1973.

———. "Modernity." In *Habermas and the Unfinished Project of Modernity: Critical Essays on "The Philosophical Discourse of Modernity,"* edited by Maurizio Passerin d'Entrèves and Seyla Benhabib, 38–55. Cambridge: MIT Press, 1996.

———. *Moral Consciousness and Communicative Action.* Translated by Christian Lenhardt and Shierry Weber Nicholsen. Cambridge: MIT Press, 1990.

———. *The Theory of Communicative Action.* Vol. 2, *Lifeworld and System: A Critique of Functionalist Reason.* Translated by Thomas McCarthy. Boston: Beacon, 1987.

Hall, Douglas John. *The Steward: A Biblical Symbol Come of Age.* Eugene, OR: Wipf & Stock, 2004.

Hardt, Michael, and Antonio Negri. *Empire.* Cambridge: Harvard University Press, 2000.

Harnack, Adolf von. *Marcion: Das Evangelium vom fremden Gott.* Darmstadt: Wissenschaftliche Buchgesellschaft, 1960.

Haynes, Stephen R. *The Bonhoeffer Phenomenon: Portraits of a Protestant Saint.* Minneapolis: Fortress, 2004.

Heidegger, Martin. *Basic Writings.* Rev. ed. Edited by David Farrell Krell. New York: HarperCollins, 1993.

———. *Being and Time.* Translated by Joan Stambaugh. Albany: SUNY Press, 1996.

Hick, John. *God Has Many Names.* Philadelphia: Westminster, 1980.

Hiebert, Paul G. *Anthropological Reflections on Missiological Issues.* Grand Rapids: Baker, 1994.

———. *Cultural Anthropology.* 2nd ed. Grand Rapids: Baker, 1983.

———. *Missiological Implications of Epistemological Shifts: Affirming Truth in a Modern/Postmodern World.* Harrisburg, PA: Trinity, 1999.

Hinkelammert, Franz J. *The Ideological Weapons of Death: A Theological Critique of Capitalism.* Translated by Phillip Berryman. Maryknoll, NY: Orbis, 1986.

Hoekendijk, J. C. *The Church Inside Out.* Translated by Isaac C. Rottenberg. Edited by L. A. Hoedemaker and Pieter Tijmes. Philadelphia: Westminster, 1966.

Horkheimer, Max. *Die Sehnsucht nach dem ganz Anderen: Ein Interview mit Kommentar von Helmut Gumnior.* Hamburg: Furche-Verlag, 1970.

Huang, Junjie. *Mencian Hermeneutics: A History of Interpretations in China.* New Brunswick: Transaction, 2001.

Hughes, E. R. *The Invasion of China by the Western World.* London: Adam & Charles Black, 1937.

Hultgren, Arland J. "Paul as Theologian: His Vocation and Its Significance for His Theology." Unpublished lecture at Luther Seminary.

———. *Paul's Gospel and Mission: The Outlook from His Letter to the Romans.* Philadelphia: Fortress, 1985.

———. *Paul's Letter to the Romans: A Commentary.* Grand Rapids: Eerdmans, 2011.

Hunsinger, George, editor and translator. *Karl Barth and Radical Politics.* Philadelphia: Westminster, 1976.

Huntington, Samuel. *The Clash of Civilizations and the Making of World Order.* New York: Simon & Schuster, 1996.

Ivanhoe, Philip J. *Ethics in the Confucian Tradition: The Thought of Mengzi and Wang Yangming.* 2nd ed. Indianapolis: Hackett, 2002.

Iwand, Hans Joachim. *Luthers Theologie,* 5 vols. Munich: Kaiser, 1983.

Jencks, Charles, editor. *The Post-Modern Reader.* New York: St. Martin's Press, 1992.

Jenkins, Philip. *The New Faces of Christianity: Believing the Bible in the Global South.* Oxford: Oxford University Press, 2006.

―――. *The Next Christendom: The Coming of Global Christianity*. Oxford: Oxford University Press, 2002.

Jenson, Robert. *Christian Dogmatics*. Vol. 1. Philadelphia: Fortress, 1984.

―――. *The Triune Identity*. Philadelphia: Fortress, 1973.

Jüngel, Eberhard. *God as the Mystery of the World: On the Foundation of the Theology of the Crucified One in the Dispute between Theism and Atheism*. Translated by Darrell L. Gudder. Grand Rapids: Eerdmans, 1983.

―――. *God's Being Is in Becoming: The Trinitarian Being of God in the Theology of Karl Barth*. Translated by John Webster. Grand Rapids: Eerdmans, 2001.

―――. *Karl Barth: A Theological Legacy*. Translated by Garrett E. Paul. Philadelphia: Westminster, 1986.

Kallen, Horace. "Democracy versus the Melting Pot." *The Nation* 100:2590 (February 18–25), 1915.

Kant, Immanuel. *What Is Enlightenment?* New York: Liberal Arts, 1959.

Käsemann, Ernst. *Commentary on Romans*. Translated and edited by G. W. Bromiley. Grand Rapids: Eerdmans, 1980.

―――. "The Eschatological Royal Reign of God." In *Your Kingdom Come: Report on the World Conference on Mission and Evangelism, Melbourne, Australia, 12–25 May 1980*. Geneva: WCC, 1980.

―――. *Jesus Means Freedom*. Philadelphia: Fortress, 1970.

―――. *The Testament of Jesus: A Study of the Gospel of John in the Light of Chapter 17*. Philadelphia: Fortress, 1968.

Kaufmann, Gordon D. *In Face of Mystery: A Constructive Theology*. Cambridge: Harvard University Press, 1993.

Keel, Hee-Sung. *Understanding Shinran: A Dialogical Approach*. Fremont, CA: Nanzan Institiute for Religion and Culture, 1995.

Keifert, Patrick R. *Welcoming the Stranger: A Public Theology of Worship and Evangelism*. Minneapolis: Fortress, 1992.

Keifert, Patrick R., and Alan G. Padgett, editors. *But Is It All True? The Bible and the Question of Truth*. Grand Rapids: Eerdmans, 2006.

Keller, Catherine, Michael Nausner, and Mayra Rivera, editors. *Postcolonial Theologies: Divinity and Empire*. St. Louis: Chalice, 2004.

Kelley, G. B., and F. B. Nelson, editors. *A Testament to Freedom*. San Francisco: HarperCollins, 1990.

Kellner, Douglas, editor. *Baudrillard: A Critical Reader*. Oxford: Blackwell, 1994.

Kelsey, David H. *Between Athens and Berlin: The Theological Education Debate*. Grand Rapids: Eerdmans, 1993.

Kim, Sebastian C. H., editor. *Christian Theology in Asia*. Cambridge: Cambridge University Press, 2008.

Kirk, J. Andrew. *What Is Mission? Theological Explorations*. Minneapolis: Fortress: 2000.

Kittel, Gerhard, and Gerhard Friedrich, editors. *Theological Dictionary of the New Testament*. Vol. 1. Grand Rapids: Eerdmans, 1967.

Klappert, Bertold. *Das Kommen Gottes und der Weg Jesu Christi*. Gütersloh: Kaiser, Gütersloher, 1997.

―――. *Israel und die Kirche: Erwägungen zur Israellehre Karl Barths*. Munich: Kaiser, 1980.

―――. *Miterben der Verheißung. Beiträge zum jüdisch-christlichen Dialog*. Neukirchen: Neukirchener, 2000.

———. *Versöhung und Befreiung: Versuche, Karl Barth kontextuel zu verstehen.* Neukirchen-Vluyn: Neukirchener, 1994.

Knitter, Paul F. *No Other Name? A Critical Survey of Christian Attitude toward World Religions.* Maryknoll, NY: Orbis, 1985.

Koester, Craig R. *Revelation and the End of All Things.* Grand Rapids: Eerdmans, 2001.

———. "Revelation's Visionary Challenge to Ordinary Empire." *Interpretation* 63 (2009) 5–18.

———. "Roman Slave Trade and the Critique of Babylon in Revelation 18." *Catholic Biblical Quarterly* 70:4 (2008) 766–86.

Kolb, Robert and Timothy J. Wengert, translators and editors. *The Book of Concord: The Confessions of the Evangelical Lutheran Church.* Philadelphia: Fortress, 2000.

Konig, Hans. *Columbus: His Enterprise: Exploding the Myth.* New York: Monthly Review, 1991.

Kosik, Karel. *Die Dialektik des Konkreten: Eine Studie zur Problematik des Menschen und der Welt.* Frankfurt am Main: Suhrkamp, 1986.

Kremers, Heinz et al., editors. *Die Juden und Martin Luther, Martin Luther und die Juden: Geschichte, Wirkungsgeschichte, Herausforderung.* Neukirchen-Vluyn: Neukirchener, 1985.

Kuhn, Thomas S. *The Structure of Scientific Revolutions.* Chicago: University of Chicago Press, 1962.

Küng, Hans. *Global Responsibility: In Search of a New World Ethic.* Translated by John Bowden. Eugene, OR: Wipf & Stock, 2004.

———. *Das Judentum: Die religiöse Situation der Zeit.* Munich: Piper, 1991.

Kwok, Pui-Lan, et al., editors. *Off the Menu: Asian and Asian North American Women's Religion and Theology.* Louisville: Westminster John Knox, 2007.

———. *Postcolonial Imagination and Feminist Theology.* Louisville: Westminster John Knox, 2005.

LaCugna, Catherine Mowry. *God for Us: The Trinity and Christian Life.* New York: HarperSanFrancisco, 1991.

Lakeland, Paul. *Postmodernity: Christian Identity in a Fragmented Age.* Minneapolis: Fortress, 1997.

Lapide, Pinchas E. "Stimmen jüdischer Zeitgenossen zu Martin Luther." In *Die Juden und Martin Luther, Martin Luther und die Juden: Geschichte, Wirkungsgeschichte, Herausforderung,* edited by Heinz Kremers et al., 171–85. Neukirchen-Vluyn: Neukirchener, 1985.

Lazareth, William H. *Christians in Society: Luther, the Bible, and Social Ethics.* Minneapolis: Augsburg, 2001.

Lehming, Hanna, et al, editors. *Wendung nach Jerusalem: Friedrich-Wilhelm Marquardts Theologie im Gespräch.* Gütersloh: Kaiser, Gütersloher, 1999.

Levenson, Joseph. *Confucian China and Its Modern Fate.* London: Routledge, 1958.

Lévinas, Emmanuel. *Emmanuel Levinas: Basic Philosophical Writings.* Edited by Adriaan T. Peperzak, Simon Critchley, and Robert Bernasconi. Bloomington: Indiana University Press, 1996.

———. *Otherwise than Being or Beyond Essence.* Translated by Alphonso Lingis. Pittsburgh: Duquesne University Press, 1998.

———. *Totality and Infinity: An Essay on Exteriority.* Pittsburgh: Duquesne University Press, 1969.

Lévi-Strauss, Claude. *Structural Anthropology*. Translated by Claire Jacobson and Brooke G. Schoepf. New York: Basic Books, 1963.

Lindbeck, George. *The Nature of Doctrine: Religion and Theology in a Postliberal Age*. Philadelphia: Westminster, 1984.

———. "Postmodern Hermeneutics and Jewish-Christian Dialogue: A Case Study." In T. Frymer-Kensky et al., *Christianity in Jewish Terms*, 106–13. Boulder, CO: Westview, 2000.

Lindberg, Carter. *Beyond Charity: Reformation Initiatives for the Poor*. Minneapolis: Fortress, 1983.

Lindsey, Hal, and C. C. Carlson. *The Late Great Planet Earth*. Grand Rapids: Zondervan, 1970.

Loehe, Wilhelm. *Die Mission unter den Heiden: Zwei Gespräche*. Värdlingen: E. S. Bed'schen, 1843.

———. *Three Books about the Church*. Edited and translated by James L. Schlaaf. Philadelphia: Fortress, 1969.

Lohse, Bernhard. *Martin Luther's Theology: Its Historical and Systematic Development*. Translated by Roy A. Harrisville. Minneapolis: Fortress, 1999.

Lukács, Georges. *History and Class Consciousness: Studies in Marxist Dialectics*. Translated by Rodney Livingstone. Cambridge: MIT Press, 1971.

———. *The Young Hegel: Studies in the Relations between Dialectics and Economics*. Translated by Rodney Livingstone. Cambridge: MIT Press 1976.

Lull, Timothy F., editor. *Martin Luther's Basic Theological Writings*. 1st and 2nd eds. Minneapolis: Fortress, 1989, 2005.

Luther, Martin. *The Church Comes from All Nations: Luther Texts on Mission*. Selected by Volker Stolle. Translated by Klaus Detlev Schulz and Daniel Thies. St. Louis: Concordia, 2003.

———. *D. Martin Luthers Werke: Kritische Gesamtausgabe*. 61 vols. Weimar: Hermann Böhlaus Nachfolger, 1912–1921.

———. *Luther's Works*. Vols. 1–30. Edited by Jaroslav Pelikan. St. Louis: Concordia, 1955–1967.

———. *Luther's Works*. Vols. 31–55. Edited by Helmut T. Lehmann. Philadelphia: Fortress, 1955–1986.

———. *Martin Luther's Basic Theological Writings*. 2nd ed. Edited by Timothy F. Lull. Minneapolis: Fortress, 2005.

Lyotard, J.-F. *The Postmodern Condition: A Report on Knowledge*. Translated by Geoff Bennington and Brian Massumi. Minneapolis: University of Minnesota Press, 1988.

MacIntyre, Alasdair. *Whose Justice? Which Rationality?* Notre Dame: University of Notre Dame Press, 1988.

Malinowski, Bronislaw. *Magic, Science, and Religion and Other Essays*. Boston: Beacon, 1948.

Mandel, Ernest. *Late Capitalism*. Translated by Joris De Bres. London: Verso, 1975.

Mannermaa, Tuomo. *Christ Present in Faith: Luther's View of Justification*. Minneapolis: Fortress, 2005.

Marion, Jean-Luc. *God without Being*. Translated by Thomas A. Carlson. Chicago: University of Chicago Press, 1991.

Marquardt, F.-W. *Eia, warn wir da: eine theologische Utopie*. Gütersloh: Kaiser, Gütersloher, 1997.

―――. "'Enemies for Our Sake': The Jewish No and Christian Theology." In *Theological Audacities: Selected Essays*, edited by Andreas Pangritz and Paul S. Chung, 3–30. Eugene, OR: Pickwick, 2010.

―――. *Die Entdeckung des Judentums für die christliche Theologie: Israel im Denken Karl Barths*. Munich: Kaiser, 1967.

―――. "Gott oder Mammon aber: Theologie und Ökonomie bei Martin Luther." In *Einwürfe*, edited by F.-W. Marquardt, Dieter Schellong, and Michael Weinrich, 176–213. Munich: Kaiser, 1983.

―――. "Martin Luther und Karl Barth: in tyrannos." *Berliner Theologische Zeitschrift* 1:2 (1984) 275–96.

―――. "Socialism in the Theology of Karl Barth." In *Karl Barth and Radical Politics*. Edited and translated by George Hunsinger, 47–76. Philadelphia: Westminster, 1976.

―――. *Theological Audacities: Selected Essays*. Edited by Paul S. Chung and Andreas Pangritz. Eugene, OR: Pickwick, 2010.

―――. *Theologie und Sozialismus: Das Beispiel Karl Barths*. Munich: Kaiser, 1972.

―――. *Verwegenheiten: Theologischer Stücke aus Berlin*. Munich: Kaiser, 1981.

―――. *Von Elend und Heimsuchung der Theologie: Prolegomena zur Dogmatik*. Munich: Kaiser, 1988.

―――. *Was dürfen wir hoffen, wenn wir hoffen dürften? Eine Eschatologie*. Band I.III. Gütersloh: Kaiser, Gutersloher, 1993, 1996.

Marsden, George M. *Religion and American Culture*. Orlando: Harcourt Brace College Publishers, 1990.

Martin-Schramm, James B., and Robert L. Stivers. *Christian Environmental Ethics: A Case Method Approach*. Maryknoll, NY: Orbis, 1970.

Marty, Martin E. *The One and the Many: America's Struggle for the Common Good*. Cambridge: Harvard University Press, 1997.

―――. *Public Church: Mainline-Evangelical-Catholic*. New York: Crossroad, 1981.

Marx, Karl. *Capital: A Critique of Political Economy*. Vol. 1. New York: J. M. Dent, 1930.

Matthews, Basil Joseph. *John R. Mott, World Citizen*. New York: Harper, 1934.

McCormack, Bruce L. *Karl Barth's Critically Realistic Dialectical Theology: Its Genesis and Development 1909–1936*. Oxford: Oxford University Press, 1997.

Messenger, Jack, editor. *Mission in Context: Transformation, Reconciliation, Empowerment*. Geneva: LWF, 2004.

Moffett, Samuel. *A History of Christianity in Asia, 1500–1900*. Vol. 2. Maryknoll, NY: Orbis, 2005.

Moltmann, Jürgen, editor. *Anfänge der dialektischen Theologie. Teil 1: Karl Barth, Heinrich Barth, Emile Brunner*. Munich: Kaiser, 1962.

―――. *The Coming of God: Christian Eschatology*. Translated by Margaret Kohl. Minneapolis: Fortress, 1996.

―――. *The Crucified God: The Cross of Christ as the Foundation and Criticism of Christian Theology*. Translated by R. A. Wilson and John Bowden. Minneapolis: Fortress, 1993.

―――. *God for a Secular Society: The Public Relevance of Theology*. London: SCM Press, 1999.

Mortensen, Viggo, editor. *The Role of Mission in the Future of Lutheran Theology*. Aarhus: Centre for Multireligious Studies, University of Aarhus, 2003.

Mott, John R. *The Evangelization of the World in This Generation*. 3rd ed. London: Student Volunteer Missionary Union, 1903.

Mudge, Lewis S., and James Poling. *Formation and Reflection*. Philadelphia: Fortress, 1987.

Mueller-Vollmer, Kurt, editor. *The Hermeneutics Reader: Texts of the German Tradition from the Enlightenment to the Present*. New York: Continuum, 1985.

Nessan, Craig L. *Beyond Maintenance to Mission: A Theology of the Congregation*. Minneapolis: Fortress, 1999.

———. *Orthopraxis or Heresy: The Northern American Theological Response to Latin America Liberation Theology*. Altanta: Scholars, 1989.

———. *Shalom Church: The Body of Christ as Ministering Community*. Minneapolis: Fortress, 2010.

Neville, Robert C. *Boston Confucianism: Portable Tradition in the Late-Modern World*. Albany: SUNY Press, 2000.

Newbigin, Lesslie. *The Gospel in a Pluralist Society*. Grand Rapids: Eerdmans, 1989.

———. *The Open Secret: An Introduction to the Theology of Mission*. Rev. ed. Grand Rapids: Eerdmans, 1995.

———. *Sign of the Kingdom*. Grand Rapids: Eerdmans, 1980.

———. *Trinitarian Faith for Today's Mission*. Richmond: John Knox, 1964.

Niebuhr, H. Richard. *Christ and Culture*. New York: Harper, 1951.

———. *The Kingdom of God in America*. New York: Willett, Clark, 1937.

———. *The Social Sources of Denominationalism*. New York: Holt, 1929.

Oberman, Heiko A. "Die Juden in Luthers Sicht." In *Die Juden und Martin Luther, Martin Luther und die Juden: Geschichte, Wirkungsgeschichte, Herausforderung*, edited by Heinz Kremers et al., 136–62. Neukirchen-Vluyn: Neukirchener, 1985.

Ohl, J. F. *The Inner Mission: A Handbook for Christian Workers*. Philadelphia: United Lutheran Publication House, 1911.

Olson, Jeannine E. *One Ministry, Many Roles: Deacons and Deaconesses through the Centuries*. St. Louis: Concordia, 1992.

Olson, Stanley Norris. "Confidence Expressions in Paul: Epistolary Conventions and the Purpose of 2 Corinthians." PhD diss., Yale University, 1976.

Palmer, Richard E. *Hermeneutics: Interpretation Theory in Schleiermacher, Dilthey, Heidegger, and Gadamer*. Evanston: Northwestern University Press, 1969.

Pangritz, Andreas. "Geheimnis und Gebot bei Leo Baeck und Dietrich Bonhoeffer." In *Berliner Theologische Zeitschrift* 15. Jahrgang. Heft 1 (1998) 112–27.

———. *Karl Barth in the Theology of Dietrich Bonhoeffer*. Translated by Barbara Rumscheidt and Martin Rumscheidt. Grand Rapids: Eerdmans, 1989.

———. "Sharing the Destiny of His People." In *Bonhoeffer for a New Day: Theology in a Time of Transition*. Edited by John W. De Gruchy, 258–77. Grand Rapid: Eerdmans, 1997.

———. "Umkehr und Erneuerung. Helmut Gollwitzers Beitrag zur Veränderung des christlich-jüdische Verhältnisses." In *Berliner Theologische Zeitschrift* 12. Jahrgang. Heft 2 (1995) 269–84.

———. *Vom Kleiner-und Unsichtbarwerden der Theologie: Ein Versuch über das Projekt einer "impliziten Theologie" bei Barth, Tillich, Bonhoeffer, Benjamin, Horkheimer und Adorno*. Tubingen: TVT Medienverlag, 1996.

Pannenberg, W. *Systematic Theology*. Vol. 3. Translated by G. W. Bromiley. Grand Rapids: Eerdmans, 1998.

————. *Theology and the Philosophy of Science.* Translated by Francis McDonagh. Philadelphia: Westminster, 1976.

Parish, Helen Rand, editor. *Bartolomé de Las Casas: The Only Way.* Translated by Francis Partrick Sullivan, SJ. New York: Paulist, 1992.

Peters, Ted, editor. *Genetics: Issues of Social Justice.* Cleveland: Pilgrim, 1998.

Peura, Simo. "Gott und Mensch in der Unio: Die Unterschiede im Rechtfertigungsverständnis bei Osiander und Luther." In *Unio: Gott und Mensch in der nachreformatorischen Theologie,* edited by Matti Repo and Rainer Vinke, 33–61. Helsinki: Luther-Agricola-Gesellschaft, 1996.

Phan, Peter C., editor. *Christianity and the Wider Ecumenism.* New York: Paragon House, 1990.

————. *In Our Own Tongues: Perspectives from Asia on Mission and Inculturation.* Maryknoll, NY: Orbis, 2003.

Phillips, James M., and Robert T. Coote, editors. *Toward the Twenty-First Century in Christian Mission.* Grand Rapids: Eerdmans, 1993.

Phillips, Kevin. *The Politics of Rich and Poor: Wealth and the American Electorate in the Reagan Aftermath.* New York: Random House, 1990.

Pieris, Aloysius, SJ. *An Asian Theology of Liberation.* Maryknoll, NY: Orbis, 1988.

Propp, William H. C. *Exodus 1–18.* The Anchor Bible 2. Garden City: Doubleday, 1998.

Rabinow, Paul, and Nikolas Rose, editors. *The Essential Foucault: Selections from Essential Works of Foucault, 1954–1984.* New York: New Press, 1994.

Rad, Gerhard von. *Old Testament Theology.* Vol. 1. New York: Harper & Row, 1962.

Radcliffe-Brown. A. R. *Structure and Function in Primitive Society.* New York: Free Press, 1952.

Rahner, Karl. *The Trinity.* Translated by Joseph Donceel. New York: Crossroad, 1989.

Ratke, David C. *Confession and Mission, Word and Sacrament: The Ecclesial Theology of Wilhelm Löhe.* St. Louis: Concordia, 2001.

Reicke, Bo. *The Epistles of James, Peter, and Jude.* The Anchor Bible 37. Garden City: Doubleday, 1978.

Ricci, Matteo. *China in the Sixteenth Century: The Journals of Mathew Ricci, 1583–1610.* Translated by Louis J. Gallagher, SJ. New York: Random House, 1942.

————. *The True Meaning of the Lord of Heaven = T'ien-chu Shih-i.* Translated by Douglas Lancashire and Peter Hu Kuo-chen. Edited by Edward J. Malatesta. St. Louis: Institute of Jesuit Sources, 1985.

Ricoeur, Paul. *The Conflict of Interpretations.* Edited by Don Ihde. Evanston: Northwestern University Press, 1974.

————. *Essays on Biblical Interpretation.* Edited by Lewis S. Mudge. Philadelphia: Fortress, 1980.

————. *Hermeneutics and the Human Sciences: Essays on Language, Action, and Interpretation.* Translated and edited by John B. Thomson. Cambridge: Cambridge University Press, 1981.

————. *Interpretation Theory: Discourse and the Surplus of Meaning.* Forth Worth: Texas Christian University Press, 1976.

————. *Oneself as Another.* Chicago: University of Chicago Press, 1992.

Rieger, Joerg. *Christ and Empire: From Paul to Postcolonial Times.* Minneapolis: Fortress, 2007.

Rivera, Mayra. *The Touch of Transcendence: A Postcolonial Theology of God.* Louisville: Westminster John Knox, 2007.

Robinson, James M., editor. *The Beginnings of Dialectic Theology*. Richmond: John Knox, 1968.

Robinson, James M., and John B. Cobb Jr., editors. *The New Hermeneutic*. New York: Harper & Row, 1964.

Rorty, Richard. *Consequences of Pragmatism: Essays, 1972–1980*. Minneapolis: University of Minnesota Press, 1982.

———. *Philosophy and the Mirror of Nature*. Princeton: Princeton University Press, 1979.

Rossing, Barbara R. *The Rapture Exposed: The Message of Hope in the Book of Revelation*. Boulder, CO: Westview, 2004.

Roxburgh, Alan, and Fred Romanuk. *The Missional Leader: Equipping Your Church to Reach a Changing World*. San Francisco: Jossey-Bass, 2006.

Ruddat, Günter, and Gerhard K. Schäfer, editors. *Diakonisches Kompendium*. Göttingen: Vandenhoeck & Ruprecht, 2005.

Rupp, E. Gordon, and Philip S. Watson, editors. *Luther and Erasmus: Free Will and Salvation*. Philadelphia: Westminster, 1987.

Saayman, Willem, and Klippies Kritzinger, editors. *Mission in Bold Humility: David Bosch's Work Considered*. Maryknoll, NY: Orbis, 1996.

Said, Edward W. *Orientalism*. New York: Vintage, 1979.

———. *Reflections on Exile and Other Essays*. Cambridge: Harvard University Press, 2000.

Sanneh, Lamin. *Translating the Message: The Missionary Impact on Culture*. Maryknoll, NY: Orbis, 1989.

———. *Whose Religion Is Christianity? The Gospel beyond the West*. Grand Rapids: Eerdmans, 2003.

Scharlemann, Robert. *The Being of God: Theology and the Experience of Truth*. New York: Seabury, 1981.

Schattauer, Thomas H. "The Löhe Alternative for Worship, Then and Now." *Word & World* 24:2 (2004) 145–56.

———. editor. *Inside Out: Worship in an Age of Mission*. Minneapolis: Fortress, 1999.

Schmid, Heinrich. *The Doctrinal Theology of the Evangelical Lutheran Church*. Translated by Charles A. Hay and Henry E. Jacobs. Philadelphia: Lutheran Publication Society, 1899.

Scholem, Gershom. *The Messianic Idea in Judaism and Other Essays on Jewish Spirituality*. New York: Schocken, 1995.

Schreiter, Robert. *Constructing Local Theologies*. Maryknoll, NY: Orbis, 1985.

Segundo, Juan Luis. *Liberation of Theology*. Translated by John Drury. Maryknoll, NY: Orbis, 1976.

Setton, Mark. *Chŏng Yagyong: Korea's Challenge to Orthodox Neo-Confucianism*. Albany: SUNY Press, 1997.

Simpson, Gary M. *Critical Social Theory: Prophetic Reason, Civil Society, and Christian Imagination*. Minneapolis: Fortress, 1989.

———. "God in Global Civil Society: Vocational Imagination, Spiritual Presence, and Ecclesial Discernment." Unpublished paper.

———. "A Reformation Is a Terrible Thing to Waste: A Promising Theology for an Emerging Missional Church." In *The Missional Church in Context: Helping Congregations Develop Contextual Ministry*, edited by Craig Van Gelder, 65–93. Grand Rapids: Eerdmans, 2007.

Smith, Adam. *The Wealth of Nations*. New York: Bantam, 2003.

Smith, Christian, with Melinda Lundquist Denton. *Soul Searching: The Religious and Spiritual Lives of American Teenagers*. Oxford: Oxford University Press, 2005.

Sonderegger, Kristine. *That Jesus Christ Was Born a Jew: Karl Barth's "Doctrine of Israel"*. University Park: Pennsylvania State University Press, 1992.

Soulen, R. Kendall. *The God of Israel and Christian Theology*. Minneapolis: Fortress, 1996.

Spence, Jonathan D. *The Memory Palace of Matteo Ricci*. New York: Viking Penguin, 1984.

Spener, Philipp Jakob. *Pia Desideria*. Translated and edited by Theodore G. Tappert. Philadelphia: Fortress, 1964.

Spradley, James P., and David W. McCurdy. *The Cultural Experience: Ethnography in Complex Society*. 2nd ed. Long Grove, IL: Waveland, 2004.

Stackhouse, Max L. *Globalization and Grace*. New York: Continuum, 2007.

———. *Public Theology and Political Economy: Christian Stewardship in Modern Society*. Grand Rapids: Eerdmans, 1987.

Stevens, R. Paul. *The Other Six Days: Vocation, Work, and Ministry in Biblical Perspective*. Grand Rapids: Eerdmans, 2000.

Sugirtharajah, R. S. *Asian Biblical Hermeneutics and Postcolonialism: Contesting the Interpretations*. Maryknoll, NY: Orbis, 1998.

Sweezy, Paul. *The Theory of Capitalist Development: Principles of Marxian Political Economy*. New York: Monthly Review, 1956.

Takaki, Ronald. *A Different Mirror: A History of Multicultural America*. Boston: Back Bay, 1993.

Tanner, Kathryn. *Theories of Culture: A New Agenda for Theology*. Minneapolis: Fortress, 1997.

Tennent, Timothy C. *Invitation to World Missions: A Trinitarian Missiology for the Twenty-First Century*. Grand Rapids: Kregel, 2010.

Terry, Robert W. *Authentic Leadership: Courage in Action*. San Francisco: Jossey-Bass, 1993.

———. *Seven Zones for Leadership: Acting Authentically in Stability and Chaos*. Palo Alto: Davies-Black, 2001.

Teuffel, Jochen. *Mission als Namenszeugnis: Eine Ideologiekritik in Sachen Religion*. Tübingen: Mohr Siebeck, 2009.

Thiemann Ronald F. *Constructing a Public Theology: The Church in a Pluralistic Culture*. Louisville: Westminster John Knox, 1991.

———. *Revelation and Theology: The Gospel as Narrated Promise*. Notre Dame: University of Notre Dame Press, 1985.

Thomas, Norman E., editor. *Classic Texts in Mission and World Christianity*. Maryknoll, NY: Orbis, 1995.

Tillich, Paul. *Systematic Theology*. Chicago: University of Chicago Press, 1951.

———. *Theology of Culture*. Edited by Robert C. Kimball. Oxford: Oxford University Press, 1959.

Tinker, George E. *Missionary Conquest: The Gospel and Native American Cultural Genocide*. Minneapolis: Fortress, 1993.

Tinsley, E. J., editor. *Modern Theology: Selections from Twentieth-Century Theologians*. London: Epworth, 1973.

Tocqueville, Alexis de. *Democracy in America*. Vol. 1. Garden City: Doubleday, 1954.

Torrens, James S., and Xiaoxin Wu, editors. *Edward J. Malatesta, S.J.: A Friend of China.* St. Louis: Institute of Jesuit Sources, 1985.

Traboulay, David M. *Columbus and Las Casas: The Conquest and Christianization of America, 1492–1566.* Lanham, MD: University Press of America, 1994.

Tracy, David. *The Analogical Imagination: Christian Theology and the Culture of Pluralism.* New York: Crossroad, 1981.

Tracy, David, and John B. Cobb, Jr. *Talking about God.* New York: Seabury, 1983.

Treadgold, Donald W. *The West in Russia and China: Religious and Secular Thought in Modern Times.* 2 vols. Cambridge: Cambridge University Press, 1973.

Tu, Weiming. *Confucian Traditions in East Asian Modernity.* Cambridge: Harvard University Press, 1996.

———. *Neo-Confucian Thought in Action: Wang Yang-ming's Youth (1472–1509).* Berkeley: University of California Press, 1976.

Valentin, Benjamin. *Mapping Public Theology: Beyond Culture, Identity, and Difference.* Harrisburg, PA: Trinity, 2002.

Van Gelder, Craig. *The Essence of the Church: A Community Created by the Spirit.* Grand Rapids: Michigan, 2000.

———. *The Ministry of the Missional Church: A Community Led by the Spirit.* Grand Rapids: Baker, 2007.

———, editor. *The Missional Church and Leadership Formation: Helping Congregations Develop Leadership Capacity.* Grand Rapids: Eerdmans, 2009.

———. *The Missional Church in Context: Helping Congregations Develop Contextual Ministry.* Grand Rapids: Eerdmans, 2007.

Van Gelder, Craig, and Dwight Zscheile. *The Missional Church in Perspective: Mapping and Extending the Conversation.* Forthcoming.

Verkuyl, J. *Contemporary Missiology: An Introduction.* Translated and edited by Dale Cooper. Grand Rapids: Eerdmans, 1978.

Vicedom, Georg F. *Actio Dei: Mission und Reich Gottes.* Munich: Kaiser, 1975.

———. *The Mission of God: An Introduction to a Theology of Mission.* Translated by Gilbert A. Thiele and Dennis Hilgendorf. St. Louis: Concordia, 1965.

———. *Mission im ökumenischen Zeitalter.* Gütersloh: Gütersloher, 1967.

Volf, Miroslav. *After Our Likeness: The Church as the Image of the Trinity.* Grand Rapids: Eerdmans, 1998.

Wallerstein, Immanuel. *The Capitalist World-Economy: Essays.* Cambridge: Cambridge University Press, 1997.

———. *Historical Capitalism with Capitalist Civilization.* New York: Verso, 2003.

———. *The Modern World System.* Vol. 1, *Capitalist Agriculture and the Origins of the European World-Economy in the Sixteenth Century.* New York: Academic Press, 1974.

Walls, Andrew. *The Cross-Cultural Process in Christian History.* Maryknoll, NY: Orbis, 2002.

Weber, Max. *The Protestant Ethic and the Spirit of Capitalism.* Translated by Talcott Parsons. New York: Dover, 1958.

Westermann, Claus. *Genesis 12–36: A Commentary.* Translated by John J. Scullion, SJ. Minneapolis: Augsburg, 1985.

Williams, Eric. *Capitalism and Slavery.* New York: Capricorn, 1966.

Wolfe, Alan. *The Transformation of American Religion: How We Actually Live Our Faith.* New York: Free Press, 2003.

Wolterstorff, Nicholas. *Divine Discourse: Philosophical Reflections on the Claim That God Speaks*. Cambridge: Cambridge University Press, 1995.

Wright, Christopher J. H. *The Mission of God: Unlocking the Bible's Grand Narrative*. Downers Grove: InterVarsity, 2006.

Yangming, Wang. *Instructions for Practical Living, and Other Neo-Confucian Writings*. Translated by Wing-tsit Chan. New York: Columbia University Press, 1963.

Yao, Xinzhong. *An Introduction to Confucianism*. Cambridge: Cambridge University Press, 2000.

Yoder, John Howard. "How H. Richard Niebuhr Reasoned: A Critique of Christ and Culture." In *Authentic Transformation: A New Vision of Christ and Culture*, edited by Glen H. Stassen, 31–89. Nashville: Abingdon, 1996.

Zangwill, Israel. *The Melting-Pot: Drama in Four Acts*. New York: Macmillan, 1919.

Zhu, Xi. *Learning to Be a Sage: Selections from the Conversations of Master Chu, Arranged Topically*. Translated by Daniel K. Gardner. Berkeley: University of California Press, 1990.

Zimmermann, W.-D., editor. *Begegnung mit Dietrich Bonhoeffer: Ein Almanach*. Munich: Kaiser, 1964.

Ziziolas, John D. *Being as Communion: Studies in Personhood and the Church*. Crestwood, NY: St. Vladimir's Seminary Press, 1985.

Index